The Colony

John Tayman

A Lisa Drew Book

SCRIBNER
New York London Toronto Sydney

For my family

A LISA DREW BOOK/SCRIBNER
1230 Avenue of the Americas
New York, NY 10020

For information about special discounts for bulk purchases, please contact Simon & Schuster Special Sales:
1-800-456-6798 or business@simonandschuster.com

DESIGNED BY ERICH HOBBING

Text set in Minion

Manufactured in the United States of America

1 3 5 7 9 10 8 6 4 2

Library of Congress Cataloging-in-Publication Data

Tayman, John.
The Colony/John Tayman.
p. cm.
Includes bibliographical references and index.
1. Leprosy—Hawaii—Molokai—History.
I. Title.

RA644.L3T39 2005
614.5'46'0996924—dc22
2005047767

ISBN-13: 978-0-7432-3300-2
ISBN-10: 0-7432-3300-X

Contents

Part IV

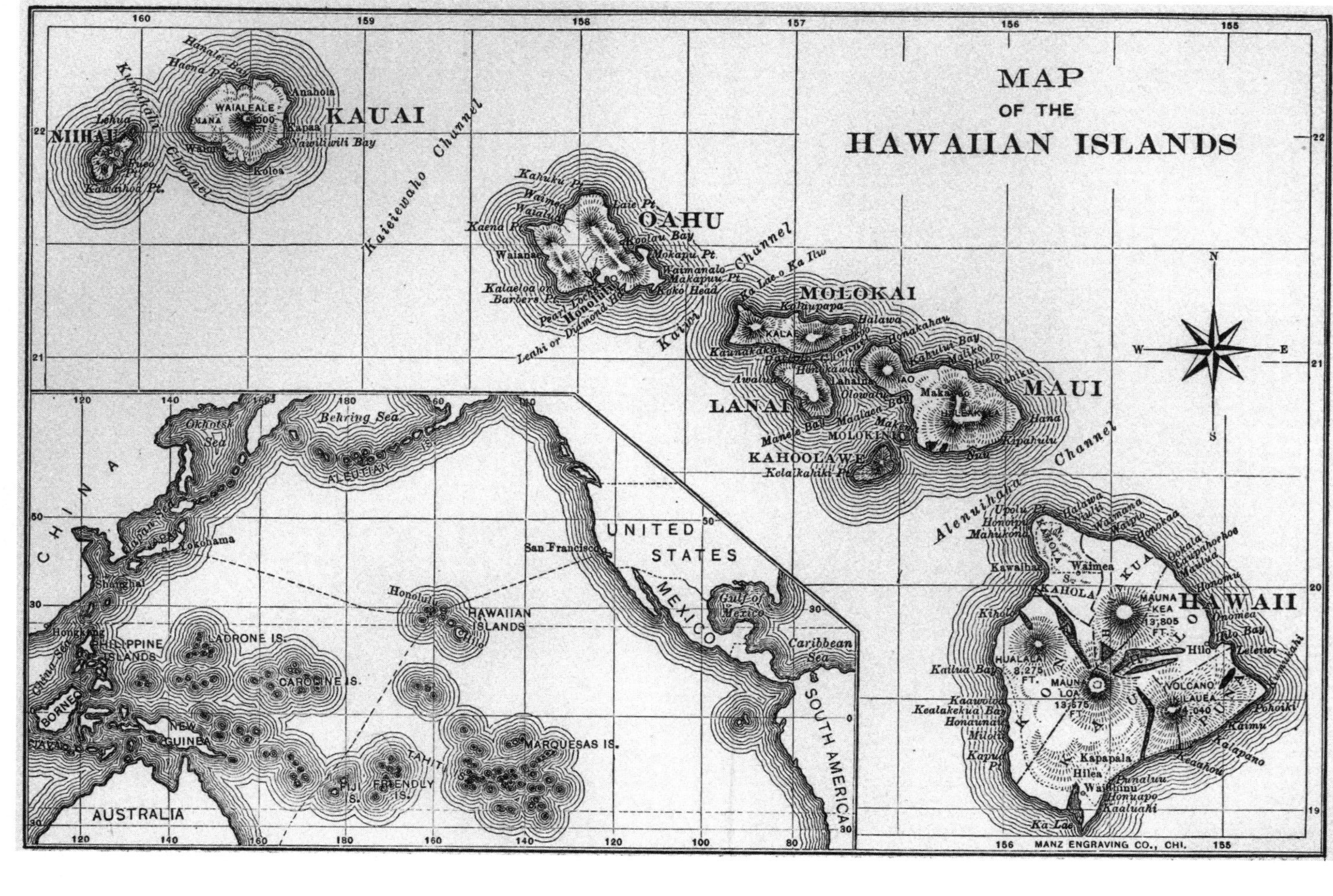
MAP
OF THE
HAWAIIAN ISLANDS
KAUAI
NIIHAU
OAHU
MOLOKAI
LANAI
MAUI
KAHOOLAWE
HAWAII
Kaieiewaho Channel
Kaiwi Channel
Alenuihaha Channel
Hanalei Bay
Haena Pt.
Anahola
WAIALEALE
MANA
Kapaa
Nawiliwili Bay
Koloa
Lehua
Kawaihoa Pt.
Kahuku Pt.
Waimea
Waialua
Laie Pt.
Kaena Pt.
Koolau Bay
Mokapu Pt.
Waianae
Waimanalo
Makapuu Pt.
Koko Head
Kalaeloa or Barbers Pt.
Pearl Lochs
Honolulu
Lenhi or Diamond Hd.
Ka Lae o Ka Ilio
Kalaupapa
Halawa
KALA
Honakahau
Kaunakakai
Kahului Bay
Maliko
Awalua
Lahaina
IAO
Olowalu
Makawao
Hana
Maalaea Bay
Manele Bay
MOLOKINI
Kapahulu
Kolaikahiki Pt.
Upolu Pt.
Halawa
Waimanu
Waipio
Honokaa
Mahukona
Kawaihae
Waimea
KAHOLA
Kailua Bay
HUALALAI
8,275 FT.
MAUNA KEA
13,805 FT.
MAUNA LOA
13,675 FT.
Hilo
Hilo Bay
Onomea
Honomu
Laupahoehoe
Ookala
Leleiwi
Kumukahi
VOLCANO
KILAUEA
4,040
Pohoiki
Kaimu
Kalapano
Kealakekua Bay
Honaunau
Kaawaloa
Milolii
Kapua Pt.
Kapapala
Hilea
Punaluu
Waiohinu
Honuapo
Kaaluahi
Ka Lae
W
E
N
S
Okhotsk Sea
Behring Sea
ALEUTIAN IS.
CHINA
Yokohama
Shanghai
Hongkong
PHILIPPINE ISLANDS
LADRONE IS.
CAROLINE IS.
BORNEO
NEW GUINEA
AUSTRALIA
FIJI IS.
FRIENDLY IS.
TAHITI IS.
MARQUESAS IS.
Honolulu
HAWAIIAN ISLANDS
San Francisco
UNITED STATES
MEXICO
Gulf of Mexico
Caribbean Sea
SOUTH AMERICA
MANZ ENGRAVING CO., CHI.

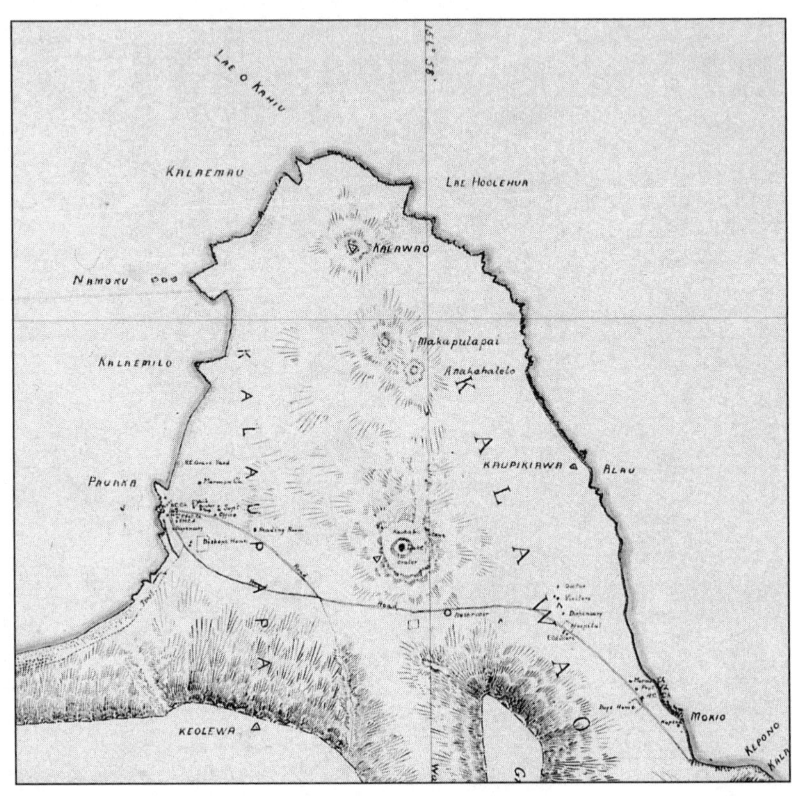

An 1895 map of the Kalaupapa peninsula.

Preface

At 8 A.M. on Friday, September 26, 1947, a thirty-nine-year-old Honolulu physician named Edwin Chung-Hoon began to examine his second patient of the day. Chung-Hoon was a graduate of the Washington University School of Medicine, and his specialty was dermatology. He was currently on active duty with the U.S. Army Medical Corps and had been since the first days following the attack on Pearl Harbor, almost six years earlier. Much of the doctor's time, however, was spent on behalf of the Territory of Hawaii's board of health.

His patient that morning was a sweet-natured twelve-year-old boy. Chung-Hoon noted a slight inflammation of the child's right cheek, and minor thickening of the flesh at several sites on his face and body. Laying his hand on the boy's cool cheek, Chung-Hoon traced his fingertips upward from the jaw, gently searching for the area where the highway of facial nerves flowed together and then branched away. After a moment the doctor took hold of the child's right ear, then his left, and with the corner of a fresh razor blade cut a small incision a few millimeters in length at their base. The boy was silent during the first slice; when the doctor nicked the second lobe, his patient let out a wounded gasp. Chung-Hoon then made a bacteriological examination of the material he had excised. The process took about an hour. He entered the waiting room and told the boy's father the results: leprosy. One week later, the twelve-year-old was exiled.

For 103 years, beginning in 1866, the Hawaiian and then American governments forcibly removed more than eight thousand people to a remote and inaccessible peninsula on the Hawaiian island of Molokai, and into one of the largest leprosy colonies in the world. The governments did so in the earnest belief that leprosy was rampantly contagious, that isolation was the only effective means of controlling the disease, and that every person it banished actually suffered from leprosy and was thus a hopeless case. On all three counts, they were wrong.

With the establishment of the colony on Molokai, officials initiated what would prove to be the longest and deadliest instance of medical segregation in American history, and perhaps the most misguided. In 1865, acting on the counsel of his American and European advisers, Lot Kamehameha, the Hawaiian king, signed into law "An Act to Prevent the Spread of Leprosy," which criminalized the disease. In the first year, 142 men, women, and children were captured. The law in various forms remained in effect through the annexation of Hawaii by America in 1898, the adoption of Hawaii as the fiftieth American state in 1959, and until mid-1969, when it was finally repealed. Under the law, persons suspected of having the disease were chased down, arrested, subjected to a cursory exam, and exiled. Armed guards forced them into the cattle stalls of interisland ships and sailed them fifty-eight nautical miles east of Honolulu, to the brutal northern coast of Molokai. There they were dumped on an inhospitable shelf of land of the approximate size and shape of lower Manhattan, which jutted into the Pacific from the base of the tallest sea cliffs in the world. It was, as Robert Louis Stevenson would write, "a prison fortified by nature." Three sides of the peninsula were ringed by jagged lava rock, making landings impossible, and the fourth rose as a two-thousand-foot wall so sheer that wild goats tumbled from its face. In the early days of the colony, the government provided virtually no medical care, a bare subsistence of food, and only crude shelter. The patients were judged to be civilly dead, their spouses granted summary divorces, and their wills executed as if they were already in the grave. Soon thousands were in exile, and life within this lawless penitentiary came to resemble that aboard a crowded raft in the aftermath of a shipwreck, with epic battles erupting over food, water, blankets, and women. As news of the abject misery spread, others with the disease hid in terror from the government's bounty hunters, or violently resisted exile, murdering doctors, sheriffs, and soldiers who conspired to send them away. Some already banished tried to escape, only to fall from the cliff or get swept out to sea. "The pit of hell," Jack London wrote, as he undertook a tour of the colony, "the most cursed place on earth." The mortality rate for patients in the first five years of exile was a staggering 46 percent.

Leprosy is not a fatal disease. Neither is it highly infectious. It is a chronic illness caused by a bacterium, and communicable only to persons with a genetic susceptibility, less than 5 percent of the population. Transmission takes place much as it does with tuberculosis, through airborne particles expelled by someone with leprosy in an active state. Among untreated patients, only a minority have the disease in its active state; the majority are not contagious. For cases that are active, a multidrug therapy has been developed that quickly renders their leprosy noncommunicable, after which they pose no risk of infection and are, in essence, cured. Every city in America has such cases; in the New York metropolitan area, for instance, more than a thousand people have or have had the disease. There are currently eleven federally funded outpatient clinics in the United States treating approximately seven thousand patients, although health officials believe many sufferers go untreated because of the powerful stigma attached to the disease. Though modern medicine has stripped the illness of its horrors, on a social level leprosy remains among the most feared of all diseases, since untreated leprosy can result in deformity, its precise mode of transmission was until recently unknown, and a cure remained undiscovered for thousands of years. The greatest factor in the stigmatization, however, was the historical intertwining of leprosy with religious notions of divine punishment, which gave rise to the corrosive idea that victims of the disease were sinful, shameful, and unclean. The preferred method of dealing with such people was obvious: banishment.

At its height in 1890, the population in the Molokai colony reached 1,174, and it was arguably the most famous small community in the world. The colony commanded intense scrutiny in the American press, and became the subject of presidential inquiries, heated congressional debate, and irrational public fear. Segregation laws gave the local government the right to arrest and imprison any person suspected of having the disease, regardless of nationality, and the rolls soon included not only Hawaiians and Americans, but also individuals from Britain, France, Germany, Japan, Russia, Spain, Sweden, Portugal, and China. Correspondents came from all over the globe, seeking scenes of thrilling grotesquerie. Physicians and scientists entered, some to offer help, others to indulge their own ambitions, an ethically suspect pursuit that led to one of the nineteenth century's most notorious episodes of human experimentation. Famous authors also secured a visiting pass: Stevenson spent seven days in the colony; London stayed six. "He returns and sits by his lamp and the crowding experiences besiege his memory," Robert Louis Stevenson wrote of the typical visitor, "sights of pain in a land of disease and disfigurement, bright examples of fortitude and kindness, moral beauty, physical horror, intimately knit." As the place grew infamous, celebrity sightseers flocked to it, among them Edward G. Robinson, John Wayne, and Shirley Temple, although she lasted only several hours. Other visitors stayed years, and the stories of their self-sacrifice transformed them into worldwide figures. One was a bullheaded young Belgian priest who fell victim to the disease and in so doing secured sainthood. Another was a fallen Civil War hero, seeking atonement for his dissolute past. Yet another was a modest, well-meaning nun from New York, who arrived to lend aid and quickly found herself the unwilling object of a most unlikely romantic obsession.

The most affecting stories, however, belong to the exiles themselves. Many had been mistakenly diagnosed and spent decades locked away before the error came to light. Thousands were needlessly isolated, their leprosy of a form that did not pose a danger to others. Some exiles were sent away as young children and suffered sixty and even seventy years in isolation before becoming free. Banishment continued well into the modern age. Even as man ventured into space and prepared to walk on the moon, the government kept watch over the colony of exiles, still imprisoned by ancient fears. Their struggle to maintain faith, form a loving community, and help one another stay alive is one of the most extraordinary acts of enduring heroism in American history.

Twenty-eight people remain in the community, passing quiet days in cottages at the base of the cliff. A few hundred yards from their simple homes is the spot where the first twelve exiles straggled to shore, cast away on the morning of January 6, 1866. Within three years all but two were dead. Their swift demise was expected—it was a key component of the segregation plan. But in time the exiles began to defy the policy and accomplished something profoundly stirring and remarkable. They survived.

One final note: This is a work of nonfiction. It is based on more than eight thousand pages of documents, including news accounts, medical records, congressional transcripts, government publications, personal letters, memoirs, interviews, and observations. Anything between quotation marks is taken directly from these sources, and the thoughts and feelings of characters as described in the narrative arise from the same material. No names have been changed.

Today the terms *leper* and even *leprosy* are considered objectionable. As the chronology of the book progresses, all terminology is kept appropriate to its time, and thus when the word *leper* appears I have used it in historical context, or as part of a direct quote. An alternative modern term for the condition is *Hansen's disease,* named after the Norwegian bacteriologist who first identified the germ that causes leprosy. The medical community is split on the adoption of the term, however, and some physicians and patients prefer the older name. For the sake of clarity, I refer to the disease as leprosy throughout the book.

Part One

The account of the first days needs giving in some detail.

Albert Camus, *The Plague*

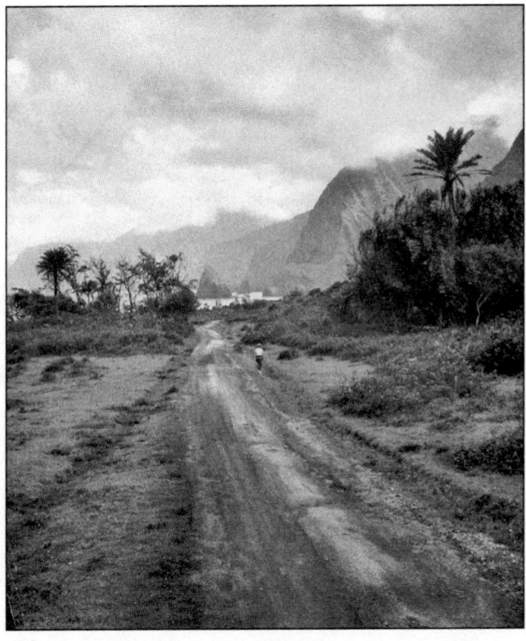

The road leading into Kalawao.

Run

(Population 1,143)

By nine-thirty in the evening on the final Tuesday in June 1893, Deputy Sheriff Louis Stolz had one fugitive in chains. He pulled his prisoner along a twisty shoulder of valley, the path lit by an almost-full moon, until he reached a meadow studded with volcanic rock. At the field's far edge sat a white wooden cottage, with one dark window on each side. Two men hid inside. A young Hawaiian named Kaluaikoolau, known as Koolau, crouched with his wife behind a boulder several yards from the cottage porch.

"I hear something," Koolau whispered to his wife, Piilani. They pressed into the stone, still warm from the sun. Across the meadow floated the sound of dragged links of iron. Koolau nodded toward the path. "There are two of them," he told his wife. "Have courage. We may be going to die."

Just then the cottage door burst open and two forms streaked through the night. One man, a Hawaiian named Kala, sprinted toward Deputy Stolz. "You stand still!" Stolz shouted. He raised a rifle. "You take care! Stop now!"

Piilani felt her husband shift and then stand. Koolau started toward the deputy. A crude triangle formed in the moonlight: Louis Stolz with his weapon trained on the unarmed Kala, and Koolau, standing between the two, covering the officer with a rifle of his own. Stolz began to slide to his right, and as the standoff's geometry shifted, Koolau moved to restore it. Stepping to his left, Koolau's bare foot caught a branch and he stumbled. As he fell, the rifle discharged. "The reverberations of the gun sounded everywhere," Piilani later wrote, "spreading the news of this terrible thing done on this unforgettable night."

The bullet struck Stolz just south of his rib cage, tearing through his stomach. "It hurts," he moaned, collapsing onto his back. In an instant Stolz's prisoner was upon him, cursing and striking the lawman with his iron cuffs. Koolau called for him to stop, and the prisoner retreated.

Piilani clung to the boulder. Koolau turned to her and said, Run to the cliffs. Then another shout broke the quiet. The voice belonged to Paoa, the man whom Louis Stolz had arrested earlier that day.

"He is going to shoot!" Paoa yelled. Peeking over the rock, Piilani saw that

Stolz had partially gained his feet and had his rifle crooked weakly in an elbow's crease. She screamed and Koolau whirled to face the deputy sheriff. One more decision to make. Koolau stepped toward Louis Stolz, pointed his weapon at the center of his chest, and fired.

The disease had struck the Hawaiian cowboy named Koolau four years earlier, in the spring of 1889 when he was twenty-six-years old. Piilani had been the first to notice the bright blemish on Koolau's cheek. It might have been sunburn had it not lingered, then deepened in color to scarlet. "As I observed the appearance of my beloved husband," Piilani wrote years later, "disturbed thoughts began to grow within me."

Hawaiians of the era had several descriptive phrases for leprosy, but perhaps the most apt was "the sickness that is a crime." If board of health agents discovered that Koolau showed signs of the disease, he would be forced onto a steamer bound for the leprosy hospital in Honolulu. From there he would be sent to the colony on the island of Molokai. Law would decree Piilani a widow and their six-year-old son fatherless. Officially, Koolau would be dead.

So Koolau tried to hide his suspect flesh. A photograph from the time shows him in a flat-brimmed hat tugged low on his broad face, with a crisp white shirt buttoned high to the neck. Piilani stands holding the hand of their son, Kaleimanu. Koolau's mother is settled cross-legged on the grass between the young couple. Her son's gaze is distant, as if the box camera were a window revealing an unexpected view.

Leprosy works with a tortuous deliberateness. A person becomes infected and years pass, then he or she wakes one morning lightly marked by disease. Years more can elapse before the sickness deepens. Koolau waited. Then in the early winter of 1892 a government agent appeared at his door. Escorted to the office of the physician for the western half of Kauai, Koolau stripped off his shirt and pants and stood naked. The physician examined the blemishes on Koolau's face and ears, and traced a needle over the surface of the spots, testing for a loss of sensation. The log into which doctors recorded the results of such exams allowed three verdicts: Leper, Suspect, Not a Leper. Board regulations dictated that only the senior physicians at the leprosy hospital could make the final diagnosis, but physicians in the field were skilled enough to anticipate the outcome. Dr. Campbell told Koolau, Say your farewells.

That evening, Piilani and Koolau talked about what would happen next. An agent of the board would hold him for the steamer to Honolulu. He would be taken to Kalihi Hospital, where suspects were processed. Doctors would perform a second exam to confirm his leprosy. And he would be exiled to Molokai and locked in the colony the government had established on a shelf of land that extended from the base of a towering cliff. Awaiting him there, Koolau believed, was a life sentence of unspeakable horror. Nightmarish tales had emerged from the colony. These described an uncivilized community, populated by ghouls with hollowed eyes and limbless frames. Rumors told of patients being starved to death, subjected to bizarre medical experimentation, and conscripted into prostitution and slavery. Even the dead received no mercy: Koolau had heard of corpses scattered to rot or left beneath a thin sheet of earth, to be exhumed by wild pigs. What most disturbed the young couple, however, was that exile would mean the destruction of their family. They chose not to submit to the government. Koolau and Piilani decided to run.

"At sunset on a certain day," Piilani wrote, "in the loneliness and awesomeness of the night," they started for the valley of Kalalau, fifteen miles distant. Over the years other Hawaiians with the disease had sought refuge in the virtually inaccessible valley, part of a rippled landform where the earth heaves up in a series of deep clefts, open to the sea. Carved in the crescent of a horseshoe, the valley's head and flanks drop away as sheer cliffs. Moving by moonlight, Koolau and Piilani followed a thread tramped by wildlife through the lantana brush. The trail reversed and ran upward, cresting at a windblown pass four thousand feet above the valley floor. To the right loomed a blank rock wall, to the left only air. Above them hung a ceiling of pewter cloud, which dropped suddenly and burst forth with biting rain. The storm trapped them in the dark on a ledge the depth of a man's forearm. Piilani clung to the cliff and mouthed prayers into its face, asking "that the Three Heavenly Spirits regard us with love [and] spread their wings in refuge."

Rain curtained off the cliff face, then sluiced along the ledge in a swift current. Feeling their way with their hands, Koolau and Piilani crabbed along the path, the child nestled between them. When they finally reached Kalalau, wrote Piilani, "our first action was to bend our knees and give praise." Creasing the valley was a stream, which tumbled in falls and pools for several miles before spilling into the sea. The flats on either side were patterned with taro fields, tended by the families in the valley. Koolau and his family took shelter in the home of a man named Naoheiki.

Of the 23 households in the Kalalau Valley that winter of 1892–93, only 9 were unaffected by leprosy. The disease had struck 28 of the 120 residents, some severely. No matter their condition, however, the sick found the situation in the valley preferable to the colony on Molokai, which they collectively imagined as a penal hell. To be sent to the colony, they believed, meant to be alone, and then to be abused, and then to be dead. In Kalalau they had created a close-knit community, where the healthy pulled taro and netted fish for the weak, and families helped other families. They were in exile, but at least it was an exile of their own shaping. The board of health, however, considered the lepers outlaws.

Not long after arriving in the valley, Koolau located the home of the leader of the fugitive community, Judge Kapahei Kauai. A revered Hawaiian jurist, Judge Kauai had served in the legislature in Honolulu and had upon retiring become an energetic advocate for Hawaiian rights. Now he was sixty-eight years old, crippled by leprosy, at odds with the government's law.

Propped in a chair in his cottage, with flowers scattered to sweeten the air, the judge and Koolau discussed their situation. The board will come for us, Kauai said. The judge knew who was likely to arrive first: a slender young man with whom the judge had had words one afternoon several years earlier. In anger the man had struck Kauai, drawing blood, and the judge had hauled him into court and won a verdict. Koolau remembered the man: Louis Stolz. When Stolz was named deputy sheriff, he had come to Koolau and asked the Hawaiian to make a celebratory saddle for him, but Koolau did not have the time. Stolz had gone away angry. Later, Koolau heard that it was Stolz who had reported him to the board.

No outsiders appeared in the valley that winter, however. Spring arrived, and Koolau and Piilani began to imagine that they were safe. Then one morning in June of 1893 Piilani heard boots crunching along the path leading to their cottage. Opening the door, she saw Louis Stolz.

Smothering her alarm with exaggerated politeness, Piilani greeted Stolz and invited him inside. The deputy sheriff was thirty-three, a fast-eyed man with a face that narrowed to a neat beard. Stolz scanned the room. Turning to Piilani with what she later described as "a cheerful voice and pleasant expression," Stolz asked, "Piilani, where is Koolau?"

"This morning he went to work in the taro patch," she answered.

"How is that sickness of his?"

"Not much, just a little redness on his cheeks sometimes, sometimes not."

Stolz smiled and stared at Piilani. She said nothing more.

Koolau's flight had caused deep embarrassment for the young deputy. Shortly after he had disappeared, Stolz had written to the board, "As this is the first person who has escaped from the district while I have been deputy sheriff I am anxious to bring him back." Stolz's humiliation also had a personal element. That January, after years of outside pressure, the constitutional monarchy had collapsed. White businessmen now held the levers of power, and Louis Stolz knew many of these men. He was, in fact, related by marriage to the man now heading the new government, a prominent lawyer named Sanford Ballard Dole: Stolz's wife's sister had married George Dole, Sanford's brother.

Stolz craved the attention of men like Dole. To capture a band of renegade lepers—that would demand notice. He had begun to write weekly to the board, advising them of the outlaw situation in Kalalau Valley and insisting action be taken. "The amount and kind of intimacy existing between lepers and nonlepers at Kalalau is simply abominable," he complained. Technically, the deputy had no legal standing in Kalalau Valley, which lay outside his jurisdiction. By invoking Koolau, however, Stolz argued that the problem was his to solve. "I am not hankering for any work in connection with lepers," he wrote, "but the work ought to be done, and *somebody* must do it." Leaving behind his wife and two young children, Stolz had set out for Kalalau. His plan was to use the influence of Judge Kauai, whom Stolz described as the "Archleper," to convince the refugees in the valley to surrender peacefully—rather than risk the government taking them by force. Because of his history with the judge, however, Stolz hesitated to approach him directly. He needed Koolau's assistance.

After the deputy left, Piilani sank to the floor and wept. She wrote, "I was overwhelmed with grief—who would not be—seeing the power of the government come hither to sever the sacred knot of holy marriage, and cutting the golden cord between parents and child. Alas! Alas!" Wailing, she ran to the field and found Koolau. The couple clenched each other, shuddering with sobs, as their son looked on in confusion.

Stolz remained in the valley trying to arrange a meeting with Koolau, but the Hawaiian avoided him. Frustrated, Stolz announced that all lepers in the valley were to gather at the beach, by order of the board of health. The next morning, two dozen men and women milled at the forest's edge. Stolz informed them that a boat would arrive early the next week to collect them. They would be sent to Kalihi Hospital, and then to Molokai. Any person who resisted would be shackled and carried aboard. Stolz asked, Who agrees to go willingly?

Koolau stepped from the trees. "I first ask whether my wife will be allowed to go with me," he yelled.

"No!" Stolz replied. "Your wife cannot at all go with you. You and all those who have the sickness will be taken, no one else."

"Then I will not go," Koolau announced. "I will not be taken by this wrongful law to that place."

The crowd watched to see how the deputy would react. Writing earlier in the week, Stolz had assured the board that, "should the obstinate ones be removed the non-committal ones will undoubtedly go of their own accord."

Now Koolau openly defied him, emboldening the others. Stolz quickly broke the meeting, swallowing his rage.

When he returned to Kalalau a week later, Stolz brought two Hawaiian deputies. They waded ashore, rifles held above their heads to shield them from salt spray. A large group waited on the beach, intending to surrender. Stolz marched through the sand and announced that he intended to arrest Koolau. Using the gruesome imagery of a man disfigured by leprosy to ridicule Koolau, Stolz—whom the Hawaiians called Lui—boasted about what would transpire.

"You will all see," Stolz yelled. "Koolau will run for the mountains and then he will become emaciated and have a big head. Lui will capture him and Koolau will be through in Kalalau. Lui will have the right, Lui will have the power over him. Lui is not mistaken, Koolau is mistaken. He is stubborn and much too proud—afterwards he will cry."

Frightened by his tone, the people who had agreed to leave the valley now fled from the beach. The deputy sent the officers after them. He would find Koolau. Pinning his badge to his vest, Stolz removed his jacket and rolled it into a bundle. He tucked a package of crackers and extra rounds of ammunition into the folds. From the beach to the head of the valley, where he suspected Koolau was hidden, was a muddy scramble of several miles. Before he set out, Stolz scribbled a note to William O. Smith, the president of the board of health. "I will hurry up things as fast as possible," Stolz wrote, "and report progress as it occurs."

Smith received no reports. By midnight the next day Louis Stolz was dead, his body being frisked by a pair of Hawaiians who had found the corpse cooling in the night air. When they departed, the men carried Stolz's rifle, his knife, a packet of papers from the board, and the deputy's polished metal badge.

Details of Stolz's death arrived in Honolulu aboard the steamer *Waialeale,* accompanied by Stolz himself, wrapped in canvas in the ship's hold. After a hurried wake he was buried at 4 P.M. on June 29, 1893. Mourners emerging from the cemetery bought copies of the *Pacific Commercial Advertiser* to fan themselves. In its pages was news of Louis Stolz's bold plan to arrest the fugitive lepers. "Trouble is neither anticipated nor expected," the paper reported. The islands' Hawaiian-language newspaper held a different opinion: the fugitives Stolz sought, reported the *Kuokoa,* "vehemently objected to being taken to [Molokai]." They "did not wish to go and would resist the authorities."

By the next morning the *Advertiser* had updated its reporting and now demanded that Koolau be taken, "DEAD OR ALIVE!" Sanford Dole declared martial law on the western half of Kauai. An invasion force of thirty-five militia and special police boarded the *Waialeale,* and that afternoon it sailed for Kauai, carrying the government posse, four newspaper reporters, a German-made Krupp howitzer cannon, and a crate of long-range artillery shells, ten-pound fists of blunt black iron that would be used to "dislodge the lepers."

In command of the soldiers was Captain William Larsen, a squat man with a shiny face improbably topped by a Mexican sombrero. Larsen was a career soldier, cunning and famously volatile, qualities appreciated more by the men he commanded than those who commanded him. Accompanying Larsen on the expedition was Charles Reynolds, the executive officer of the board of health, and Dr. Charles B. Cooper, an aristocratic twenty-nine-year-old surgeon from Babylon, New York, who counted among his famous relatives the novelist James Fenimore Cooper.

For Larsen and Reynolds, the mission had an unsettling familiarity. Five years earlier the two men had tracked a group of renegade lepers into a similar Kauai valley. Ambushed at the gap of a trail, they managed to escape the initial pepper of gunfire and isolate the leader of the resistance on a stream bank. When they shouted for him to surrender, the man tossed his rifle, tore open his shirt, and slapped his bared chest "to give us a fair mark to shoot at," Reynolds later wrote. Although Larsen and Reynolds had managed to take him alive, they realized that the outlaw was prepared to die rather than face exile in the colony. And he had appeared willing to take others with him.

Immediately after shooting Louis Stolz, at 10 P.M. on June 27, Koolau had raced to a small clutch of cottages near the shore. "Lui is dead," he told the people gathered there. "It was I who shot him with my gun." He spent the night sitting watchfully beside his sleeping wife and child, who had followed after him. When dawn came, Koolau woke Piilani. "Let us go up to the mountain," he said, "to await the result." They began to climb the west flank of the valley, which held denser forest and better cover. Paoa, the prisoner Koolau had helped free, joined them, as did eight other men and women with the disease. The group hiked until they reached an empty cottage partly shielded in a stand of *hau* trees, where they waited. Three days passed with no sign of police or soldiers, but, as Piilani later recalled, the group never once doubted they were coming.

Late on the morning of July 1, Paoa set out toward the beach to gather food and was met by several men jumpy with fright. "Paoa, return upland, as death is coming here!" they yelled. "The *Waialeale* has landed police and soldiers, armed to come fight with Koolau, and there will be shooting until they get him dead or alive, it is not known which." Paoa dropped his basket and raced back to the camp. "Your death is at the shore," he told Koolau, "it has arrived this morning."

Koolau told the others to hide. "For me alone is this death which is swiftly pursuing," he said. As people made ready to leave, Koolau pleaded with Piilani to take their son and go with them, but Piilani refused to leave her husband. They climbed toward the head of the valley until they reached a promontory far up the valley's western face, with a deep overhang and a sheer drop in front. The shelf jutted out five feet and measured five feet wide and was cloaked on both sides by vines and clinging ferns. To reach it required traversing five hundred feet along a spiny ridge eighteen inches wide, balancing between drops of thirty stories or more. Koolau spread bedrolls and laid out his weapons. For food, the family had several small bowls of poi and a six-inch hunk of dried eel. When they grew thirsty, they licked dew from the ground.

The soldiers spilled from the first two skiffs and bunkered in the sand, scanning the cliffs for snipers. Their line broke into wings and angled toward the other's flank, spreading the field of fire. But the nearby cliffs, like the beach, appeared deserted. Tiny honeycreepers made the only movement in the soft air, yellow flits among the laurel trees.

Captain Larsen arrived on the third whaleboat. He had hoped that Koolau would be waiting for his troops with a rifle, and that it would end quickly. Now it seemed they would have to go after him. The men threw up several tents to make a situation camp, which was christened Camp Dole. Larsen sent soldiers to block the trailheads and search the cottages. He told them, Arrest everyone you find.

Judge Kauai was the first to be discovered. The old man had rolled from his chair when he heard soldiers approach, dragged his damaged body across the cottage floor, and scuttled beneath the bed. A soldier plucked him out by his leg, then watched over him until the captain arrived. Other soldiers pushed deeper into the valley, marching from cottage to cottage in the failing light, scattering belongings, and lighting the homes ablaze.

The next morning, Sunday, July 2, Larsen deputized a Hawaiian named Wahinealoha and ordered him to find the fugitives. The deputy returned at midday. He had located nine frightened and hungry runaways in a gulch four miles away. If they are promised they will not be shot, Wahinealoha explained, they will come down.

And Koolau? Larsen asked.

Koolau will never surrender, Wahinealoha answered.

At 9 A.M. the next day troops dragged the howitzer to the top of a hill near camp and aimed it at the east wall of the valley. Larsen gave a signal and the cannon began to cough, five hollow cracks in quick succession. "The noise was terrific and the echoes could be heard rumbling through the valley for some time after the shell struck earth," one reporter wrote. This display, he added, "was made in hope that Koolau would become frightened and give himself up."

When a scouting party returned, however, they reported no sign of Koolau. Larsen decided to send men to search the western side of the valley. Fifteen soldiers left camp on the morning of July 4, led by Sergeant Major J. W. Pratt. Within an hour the company stumbled across fresh footprints in the mud and, near the base of the western ridge, newly spilled poi.

I need volunteers, Pratt announced. Who will climb up and get the bandit? Four men stepped forward, including a Norwegian named John Anderson. The former seaman had arrived in Hawaii only two months earlier, and barely knew his fellow soldiers. The others did not know Anderson at all.

During the night Koolau had made two short forays to collect food, then crept back along the western ridge. His son slept, but Koolau and Piilani sat and ate, watching the distant huts burn. Then the shooting began. Bullets cracked the cliff wall, whistling chips of stone onto the family.

As soldiers lay down cover, the volunteers started up the ridge, Private Anderson in the lead. Koolau motioned for Piilani to move to the rear of the hideout with the child; she was dressed in his clothing and he feared that the soldiers would mistake her for him and fire.

Koolau crawled behind a low breastwork and watched the approaching men through a gap in the stones. Anderson was twenty feet from the hideout—near enough that Piilani could see red underwear peeking out from beneath his shirt—when the private turned and yelled, "Boys, I have got the trail!" Just then Koolau shot him.

Anderson reeled backward onto the second soldier, and the pair tumbled onto a third, Private Johnson, who fell six hundred feet down the mountain. The remaining soldiers quickly retreated. Koolau climbed down to Anderson, who lay gasping. He removed Anderson's tie and uniform blouse. Blood bubbled up from Anderson's pierced lung, and Koolau pushed ferns into the wound to stop the flow. He then dragged Anderson onto the trail so the soldiers would find him when they returned. Before leaving, Koolau dribbled water into Anderson's mouth and placed the peaked soldier cap beneath the dying man's head as a pillow. When Anderson's breathing stuttered to a stop, Koolau folded the private's hands across his chest and made his way back up the cliff.

Captain Larsen led the next assault himself. Larsen, Reynolds, and fifteen soldiers arrived at the base of the western ridge just before dawn on July 5, where they discovered Anderson's body. Larsen ordered the men to draw Koolau's fire. For a quarter hour the soldiers fired continuous volleys, the acrid smoke from their weapons gathering like morning fog. With his binoculars Larsen studied the valley wall. If his men approached from a certain angle, they might take Koolau by surprise. He ordered Reynolds to take some soldiers and climb a seam in the cliff to the side of Koolau's ledge, from which they could shoot directly into the rebel's stronghold.

The soldiers inched up the narrow ridge face, guided by a forty-eight-year-old Irishman named John McCabe, a veteran who had fought for the Union in the Civil War more than thirty years earlier. McCabe moved with an older man's patience. He had climbed just high enough to peek onto the ledge when a shot rang out. Koolau's bullet caught McCabe on the left side of the temple and tore away half of his skull. A moment later another shot echoed. Private John Herschberg, who had yet to reach the cliff, had panicked at the sound of Koolau's weapon and fled into the brush; a branch snared the trigger of his rifle and the twenty-five-year-old Swedish immigrant shot himself fatally in the jaw, the bullet passing upward and then out his right ear. After their bodies were retrieved and brought to Camp Dole, Dr. Cooper performed field autopsies on the three dead men, gently probing their wounds while he cradled the soldiers' shattered skulls. The deaths were a waste, Cooper decided. Koolau's flight endangered no one but himself. They should let him disappear.

One morning, as the soldiers were advancing, Koolau had turned to Piilani and said, "In the midst of this trouble, if I see that nothing remains, then I will shoot you two first and then shoot myself and we shall all die together." Piilani nodded. She had noticed that blemishes from the disease now also marked her son's face. If leprosy was going to take her husband and her son, she wished to die as well. With this decision, Piilani wrote, "We began to lose our doubts and the striking bullets around us seemed as nothing—we lived without fear."

After Private McCabe's shooting, Koolau had told Piilani that they must abandon their hideout: "The soldiers know that we are here and they are preparing for the end." When it grew dark, they crept down the cliff and crossed the valley floor, passing at one point within a hundred feet of where the soldiers sat awake in their camp, puffing cigars and playing cards. Ascending the eastern wall, they arrived at a notch in the cliff, tucked above a waterfall and shaded by a banana tree. They ate its unripe fruit, then lay down to try to sleep.

At first light a howitzer shell exploded, rolling thunder down the valley. Sergeant Major Pratt had wheeled the cannon in range of the hideout that Koolau and his family had vacated just hours earlier. Pratt launched sixteen shells, which tore apart the western cliff and ledge. "The earth and rocks of our little home flew about, and love welled up in us for that nest in which we had sheltered," Piilani later wrote. "But the birds had sprouted wings and flown elsewhere."

At his desk in Honolulu, William O. Smith read the dispatches from Kauai with rising anger. Koolau was making a fool of the board of health and the new government—an affront that Smith, who was also attorney general, felt deeply. Each day the newspapers published sensational stories of Koolau's spectacular flight, and mocking editorials that pondered how such a thing was possible in the face of the largest military action the government had ever undertaken. Surely one rebel could not defeat an army.

"Koolau is a daring and courageous man," the *Advertiser* reported on July 3, quoting one of his neighbors. In subsequent issues the *Advertiser* started to shape the story: "Koolau is not the desperate villain which the Oahu or Honolulu people seem to think.... Stories from the valley are that the shooting of Stolz is partially accidental." The paper related that Koolau "was formerly a most genial and hard working man. He is passionately attached to his wife, and it is the dread of separating from her that keeps him from surrendering."

Smith decided to see for himself why Captain Larsen was taking so long to arrest the fugitive. On the morning of July 10, two weeks after Louis Stolz's death, Smith set sail from Honolulu with ten soldiers, a fresh supply of howitzer shells, thirty pairs of boots, and three zinc-lined coffins. Arriving on Kauai, however, Smith discovered that Larsen had abandoned the search and departed the valley. Smith located Larsen in an adjoining valley and angrily ordered him to return to Kalalau and capture Koolau. Larsen was equally livid—Smith's appearance on Kauai damaged his authority in front of his men. Larsen threatened to resign his command. If you are so certain Koolau is still in the valley, Larsen screamed at Smith, you lead the soldiers in there after him.

Finally, after several hours of arguing, Smith convinced Larsen to make one last assault on Koolau's stronghold. Before dawn on July 13, William O. Smith, Charles Reynolds, and a group of soldiers climbed to Koolau's former hideout. Smith and Larsen eyed the ruined spot, then explored the immediate area. A barely visible trail snaked directly upward from the ledge and threaded over the cliff and into an adjacent valley. Smith decided that Koolau had used the trail to escape. In his notes from the expedition Smith described with wonder the "staggering wilderness" of Kalalau Valley, braided with vegetation so dense it hid the sky. The next valley over was just the same, and the one after that. A man could hide forever in such a place, Smith realized. "It seems useless to keep this force here any longer," Smith wrote. He allowed Captain Larsen to end the pursuit.

Before departing Kalalau, soldiers wrenched the bodies of Anderson, McCabe, and Herschberg from their temporary graves. The dead were wrapped in oiled canvas and laid inside the zinc coffins. Whaleboats shuttled the caskets to the steamer. An afternoon storm had slipped in, and waves lapped at the burdened boats. The crew struggled to keep the coffins from sliding into the sea. By 2:30 P.M. all the bodies were safe on board, and with a single whistle the *Iwalani* heaved toward Honolulu.

Koolau stood on a distant ridge and watched the soldiers depart. When the steamer was a mile from shore, he fed a cartridge into his rifle and fired a farewell salute.

For more than a month Koolau, Piilani, and their son, Kaleimanu, hid in the folds of the cliff, uncertain if the soldiers would return. At night Koolau snuck to a stream to net freshwater shrimp and tiny goby fish, which they roasted and ate whole. By late summer, Koolau believed it was safe to venture into the valley, and the family spent their nights foraging among the taro fields, retreating into the jungle at dawn.

They lived this way for two years, a "wandering life in the wild valleys and rows of steep cliffs, in the midst of awful loneliness," as Piilani described it. At the start of their second year on the run, Kaleimanu, whose condition had remained constant over the months, began to swiftly falter. One afternoon Piilani saw him gesture to her. "When I went to his side," she wrote, "he put his arms about my neck and rubbed his cheek against mine . . . and he whispered: 'Where is Papa? I am going to sleep.'"

Koolau carved a grave on the face of the cliff, at a site with a view of the sea. Piilani layered the bottom with ferns, and Koolau carefully laid him down. For several weeks Koolau and Piilani camped each night beside their son's grave, until, finally, they left him on his own.

Within the year Koolau's health also began to fail. With unsettling speed he grew weak, and complained of pains piercing his stomach. His mind began to cloud, and he no longer recognized his wife. He fell into a coma, and that evening, at midnight, Koolau stopped breathing. Piilani lay down beside him and slept.

In the morning she searched for a place to bury her husband, safe from the hunters who still combed the valley seeking the $1,000 bounty on his body. When she found a site surrounded by ferns and wild ginger, she knelt and started to dig. "I worked with all the strength of my hands and my woman's body to make the grave," Piilani wrote. After a full day of digging, the grave was still too shallow. For a second night, she slept beside Koolau's body.

At dusk the next day Piilani finished. "I lifted him onto some branches and dragged him to his final resting place," she wrote. Placing Koolau's rifle in his arms, she covered her husband with layers of leaves, stones, and dirt. "I planted all around with slips from the forest, kissed the earth, and left him there sleeping the sleep of seasons," she wrote. "Leaving his chilly home I turned away and went weeping with the burden of sorrow upon my shoulders."

Thinking that she might be held responsible for the deaths of the soldiers, Piilani remained hidden for several months. Then she cautiously emerged. Climbing to the head of the valley, Piilani reversed the trip she had made more than three years earlier. She arrived at the whitewashed cottage where Louis Stolz had first surprised her with his appearance in Kalalau. "There I rested awhile, full of sad recollections, and it seemed as though my husband and child were there with me," she recalled. "After some of my weariness disappeared, I resumed my climb, alertly and swiftly, up the steep cliff. Stepping on the high peak of the cliff . . . I rested and drew breath, caressed by the refreshing breeze of the heights, which touched me gently and bathed away the effort made from the base of the cliff to the sheer steeps where every glance reveals death, with no place to escape."

At that moment, more than a thousand men and women and children were imprisoned in the colony on Molokai, penned there by a set of cliffs even more immense than those on Kauai. Among the exiles were those who had been arrested in Kalalau Valley. Piilani sometimes thought about them, her old friends. Were they alive? Were they at peace? There was no way to know. The only thing Piilani ever determined about those who were sent to the colony was this: they never returned.

Scattered Seeds

(Population 0)

No one knows precisely when leprosy entered the Hawaiian Islands. Some said the disease snuck ashore upon the backs of Chinese cooks and laborers, whose foreign bodies contained a teeming riot of unknown ills. Or white men brought it, explorers and whalers and opportunists, who laid it as a blight alongside their gifts of syphilis and rum. Or the Hawaiian chiefs were to blame, having acquired leprosy on tours abroad, then hiding the truth while their own bodies blistered and boiled.

There was no clear villain, however. Suspect cases appeared as early as May 1786, as seen by the crew of the French exploring ship *La Boussole.* Landing on the southwest coast of Maui, the voyagers were welcomed by 120 men, women, and children, many grossly disfigured by disease. In an account he later published as *The Dissertation on the Inhabitants of Easter Island and the Island of Mowee,* M. Rollin, the ship's surgeon, remarked of the island that "the beauty of the climate, and the fertility of the soil, might render the inhabitants extremely happy, if the leprosy and venereal disease prevailed among them less generally, and with less virulence."

Possibly Rollin was mistaken in his beachside diagnosis—leprosy is often confused with simple skin diseases. Yet the illness could easily have been at work among the people by that time, brought by any of the foreign visitors said to have touched land even before Captain James Cook officially discovered the islands in 1778. A Spanish explorer, John Gaetano, was alleged to have encountered the island chain in 1555, blown north on a routine crossing between Acapulco and Manila. Oral histories kept by Hawaiians at the time included multiple tales of shipwrecked sailors from China and Japan, locales already haunted by leprosy.

Opportunities for infection increased as Hawaii was woven into the era's bustling trading routes. The disease might have landed in 1789 with one of the forty-five Chinese immigrants recently arrived from Macao. By 1810 the sixty-person white population on Oahu included twenty Americans and more than eight English convicts newly escaped from the prison colony of New South Wales. Any of these men—or any of the many well-traveled Europeans already living on the other islands—could have introduced the disease.

Almost certainly, leprosy slipped into Hawaii multiple times and in multiple ways, as a concurrent contagion that began in the early 1800s and expanded as the years passed. Whatever its specific origin, the hard effects of the disease began to be noticed with increasing frequency and significant alarm. When the French scientific vessel *Uranie* visited in August 1819, a medical officer aboard recorded much sickness among the population, including "the terrible leprosy." With wonder, he described how "one woman whose nose bones no longer existed was making that kind of whistling noise which is a true symptom of the advanced stage of that disease." In his diary on July 4, 1823, the missionary Reverend Charles Stewart described a stroll through the capital of Honolulu: "We seldom walk out without meeting many whose appearance of misery and disease is appalling, and some so remediless and disgusting that we are compelled to close our eyes against a sight that fills us with horror."

In 1829, the medical missionary Dr. Gerrit P. Judd amputated the badly ulcerated and possibly leprous hand of a fifty-four-year-old local man he knew only as Old Hawaii, and in 1835 a Kauai woman, her sister, and two half brothers were diagnosed with the disease. In 1840 the former postmaster of Honolulu noticed that a well-known bodyguard of King Kamehameha III showed signs of leprosy; about that same time the future queen's father, a minor chief named George Naea, was also found to have the disease. Naea had purportedly contracted the sickness from a low-level royal who had traveled to China and, according to the missionary doctor Reverend Dwight Baldwin, returned infected with leprosy.

By 1840 a thousand Hawaiians had sailed to sea on foreign ships, bound for ports in the Azores, Malaysia, the West Indies, and the southern coasts of India or Africa, all areas where leprosy was endemic. Any one of them might have returned home infected. Just as probably, the disease might have entered aboard a British whaling ship, or on one of the hundreds of American vessels that anchored off the islands' two principal ports in the years following the opening of the Japanese and arctic whaling grounds.

The whaling fleet was a rich source of contagion. Twice each year almost six hundred vessels would call at Honolulu or Lahaina for supplies and leave a million and a half dollars in their wake. Circus performers and acting companies hurried over from San Francisco to harvest the whalers' wages. Businesses sprang up in the harbor towns, including a ten-pin bowling alley in which a young Herman Melville worked, jotting notes about whaler folkways during his idle hours. Women also came to the waterfront to earn, so many that a law was passed to "prevent females from collecting in ports during the times great numbers of ships are at anchor." Each liberty, twelve thousand unclean "blubber heads" stepped ashore to stumble drunkenly from grogshop to brothel and back again, a circuit of propagation that continued until the money vanished or the fleet pulled out. In the annual account they wrote to the American Board of Commissioners for Foreign Missions in Boston, local clergy warned that "the seeds of disease and death are scattered in profusion by the licentious visitants of these islands." By the time the whale oil trade collapsed in the early 1860s, driven down by a war unfolding among the fledgling American states, sightings of the afflicted in Hawaii had become frighteningly common. In rural areas and in the port towns, and from one end of the island chain to the other, people marked by leprosy began to appear in increasing numbers. An epidemic was near.

Dr. Wilhelm Hillebrand had journeyed to Hawaii for his health, but quickly found himself awash in illness. Seeking a palliative for his tubercular lungs, Hillebrand had uprooted his medical practice in Paderborn, Germany, and gone to sea. He arrived in Honolulu on December 28, 1850. It took several seasons for his tuberculosis to ease. The twenty-nine-year-old bachelor passed the time in his garden, watching in amazement as every seed he thumbed into the fertile earth took, and every bud burst into fragrant flower.

Hillebrand was a man of economy, in stature and in movement. Whittled thin from consumption, his eyes myopic from stress and strain, he spent hours carefully cataloging the botany of his backyard. As he strengthened, Hillebrand began to stray from his property, seeking specimens in the surrounding hills and then the neighbor islands. He traveled with small wooden boxes, collecting plants and sparrows and salamanders. In time he also collected a wife, Anna, the stepdaughter of a Honolulu physician.

The newlyweds set up house on a street of crushed coral, near the center of Honolulu. Wilhelm—now answering to William—began to remake its grounds. He introduced strange and fantastic plants into his garden, cultivated from the huge assortment of seeds and cuttings he had acquired during his travels abroad. In his spare moments Hillebrand practiced medicine. Fluent in German, French, English, Latin, Greek, and Hawaiian, he quickly proved indispensable. King Kamehameha IV, the constitutional monarch, took him on as his personal physician. After the king successfully pressured the legislature for $14,000 to build the first hospital for the Hawaiian people, Hillebrand was placed in charge, with a staff of four, drawing a salary of $1,500 a year.

Queen's Hospital sat beneath a scrim of stilled volcano known in Hawaiian as Puu io io, or "tapering hill"—European newcomers called it the Punch Bowl. The modest two-story hospital held deep verandas on which beds could be wheeled, bringing capacity to one hundred patients. Not long after Hillebrand took charge of the facility, a visitor wrote to friends in England that "all was perfectly clean, well ventilated, and orderly, without the machinery by which such institutions are worked in more civilized communities."

The correspondent was an unmarried woman named Sophia Cracroft, niece of famed arctic explorer Sir John Franklin, who perished in pursuit of the Northwest Passage. Miss Cracroft was rambling the islands in genteel Victorian fashion, sightseeing for two months with her aunt, Lady Franklin, and her aunt's maid, Sarah. The trio had met with Queen Emma in the morning and would be guests at a formal dinner in Lady Franklin's honor, there to dine on mock turtle soup and saddle of mutton. But first they were to have a glimpse of the royals' good works.

Hillebrand led the ladies on a brief round of the hospital, which they concluded was "most charming" in spite of the unfortunate presence of forty sickly residents, who reclined behind sheets of mosquito netting. The women then strolled the forty-acre grounds, following after Dr. Hillebrand and admiring the monkeypod trees and royal palms that he proudly informed them he had planted. After an hour the visitors departed, leaving when their host went to tend a group of waiting patients.

What the women did not see on their tour was a small, unpainted wooden cottage behind the hospital, partly hidden at the far edge of the property. This was where patients with leprosy were kept. Dr. Hillebrand believed that leprosy was dangerously infectious, and that the sick should be removed from the well. In his own backyard, Hillebrand, a beekeeper, had watched his bees shove their ill brethren from the colony, ensuring the overall health of their community. Of course, rarely did the banished bee recover. More often it struggled in the grass before expiring, its body curled into a strangely beautiful button of color. But that was the price to be paid.

By the spring of 1861 the house behind Queen's Hospital was growing crowded. Honolulu businessmen, concerned that a plague of leprosy could destroy all trade between Hawaii and the rest of the globe, began to press the government to act. The board of health sent out letters in the winter of 1861 asking island officials to document any encounters with leprosy, theories about the disease, and how many suspect lepers were to be found in their vicinity. The disturbing replies filtered back immediately.

John Brown, sheriff of Oahu, jotted a note on December 2, 1861, identifying six lepers: "No doubt there are others but as yet I have not had the time or opportunity to ascertain who they are." Brown added of the disease, "Its spread seems to be rapid." Four days later Sheriff Brown sent a more complete accounting, having learned of 101 total cases, including 43 on Oahu, 31 on Maui, and 27 on the island of Hawaii. By January 8, 1862, the number of cases on Hawaii was amended to 53.

William Harper Pease, a Brooklyn native who was tax assessor for the city of Honolulu, submitted a list of thirty-two lepers he had encountered, including four in Waikiki and one man who had contracted the disease while living on the northwest coast of America and brought it to the islands in 1853. Pease offered his opinion that a quick canvass of the city would not give a full accounting, since "few cases remain in Honolulu proper, they having been driven away into the suburbs, where they can live more secluded."

The Reverend Dwight Baldwin, a missionary doctor stationed in the port town of Lahaina on Maui, wrote that there had been several deaths from leprosy in the last ten years at Lahaina, and "about the period of 1861 or 1862 there was a great increase of the disease here, both as to the number of its victims, and the severity of its symptoms; and there was a general alarm in regard to it through the place." Baldwin asked the deacons of his church to conduct their own census of suspects; they returned with sixty names.

Another missionary, the Reverend Sereno Bishop, wrote that among the students at his missionary school in 1857 were two or three with "curiously swollen earlobes." He thought little of it until he returned from a year in America and discovered that the boys' symptoms had grotesquely worsened and were now unmistakable. By 1861, Bishop wrote, "the disease [had] spread steadily until lepers were a familiar sight at all times and places."

Of particular interest was a letter from a doctor in Hana, on the southeastern coast of Maui. He had no active cases to report but wished to share a story he had read in a medical journal some years back. It described an epidemic of "leprosy of a very violent character" that erupted on the coast of southern Canada. The doctor explained how the affected men and women were removed to an isolated plot of land, where they were provided with food and the necessities to survive, at least until sickness took them. "In this way the disease was extinguished," the doctor wrote. The letter was passed among the five members of the board of health, which now included Dr. William Hillebrand.

To battle another epidemic was the last thing the board of health desired. Since 1778, when Captain Cook's ships loosed syphilis and gonorrhea on the islands, the inhabitants had suffered one assault after another. New sicknesses broke out with awful regularity, to tear through the fragile brush of a population with little or no natural immunity. Never had Hawaiians encountered even simple "children's diseases" such as measles, mumps, and chicken pox, much less influenza or leprosy. Exposed to the microbes that ignited such maladies, their bodies reddened or whitened or swelled or grew feverish. Then they simply quit.

In the two decades after one of Cook's men, a sailor named Will Bradley, infected his luckless Hawaiian consort with venereal disease, ten thousand persons on Oahu alone perished from the effects of syphilis and gonorrhea. No ship of the era was wholly clean, and no crew untainted. In 1805 an epidemic of what appeared to be typhoid fever broke out, killing more than five thousand and decimating the army of King Kamehameha I, which had been massing for a raid on the neighbor island of Kauai. Influenza arrived in April 1826, lingered as a silent slayer for several decades, then exploded in 1848, killing nearly every child born that year. Epidemics of dysentery and measles and whooping cough burst forth, claimed their victims, and then lay down until the time came to strike again.

As bad as things were, they might have been worse. Isolated in the middle of the Pacific, Hawaii was long protected, by luck of geography, from one of the truly horrific plagues: smallpox. By the time slow-moving ships crossed the length of sea from the nearest port, any smallpox virus aboard would have spread through the crew, killed the unlucky ones, and abated before the islands came into sight.

With each year, however, the ships grew faster. And on February 10, 1853, the merchant vessel *Charles Mallory* had drifted into Honolulu harbor from San Francisco, having made the passage in almost record time. Atop its mast fluttered a yellow flag, a herald of disease aboard. The sick passenger was plucked from the ship and removed to a small hut astride a sanded reef at a spot called Kalihi, just downwind of town. Soon yellow rags fluttered on doors throughout Honolulu, announcing smallpox quarantine. Physicians, including Dwight Baldwin and William Hillebrand, gave hurried vaccinations, but despite their efforts the epidemic leapt from island to island. On Maui, Baldwin raced along the coastline shouting, "Do not let anybody land! Drive them back, drive them back! They bring a terrible sickness!" He managed to keep the island's death toll to 250. The other islands were less fortunate. By July of that year, smallpox had killed almost half the population of Oahu. In Honolulu crews were burying fifty corpses each day. Drivers ferrying bodies to the burial pits grew so inured to death that they routinely stopped at a tavern for refreshment and parked their wagons outside. The epidemic raged until January 1854. Estimates of the dead ranged from ten thousand to fifteen thousand, a fifth of the population. By the time the outbreak had run its course, fewer than seventy thousand Hawaiians remained—and other sicknesses were still at work among the people. Two persons died for every child born in the islands. "They are melting away," wrote the Reverend William P. Alexander. A Hawaiian high chief, Kuakini, put it even more succinctly: "All are dead."

In his address to the legislature of 1855, King Kamehameha IV had brought the woeful topic into the open. Standing before the collected government, which included Hawaiian representatives and naturalized Europeans and Americans, the twenty-one-year-old monarch announced, "The decrease of our population is a subject in comparison with which all others sink into insignificance. Our first and great duty is self-preservation. Our acts are in vain, unless we can stay the wasting hand that is destroying our people." Eight years later death caught him too.

On November 30, 1863, Kamehameha IV died from chronic asthma deepened by alcoholism, and his older brother, Prince Lot, ascended to the throne as Kamehameha V. Intent on succeeding where his brother had failed, the new monarch pledged to preserve the health of his people. Lot gave more sweeping power to the board of health, allowed the licensing of native Hawaiian practitioners of medicine, prioritized education in sanitary practices, and bullied the legislature for funds to be spent on disease prevention. And still the number of patients in the cottage behind Queen's Hospital continued to rise.

Reporting in April 1863 on the first three years and eight months of practice at the hospital, William Hillebrand noted that 6,000 persons had been treated, 16,000 prescriptions filled, and 612 individuals admitted as patients. Of those, 91 had been foreigners and the rest Hawaiian. Commenting on the latter, Hillebrand wrote, "Ignorant and superstitious, accustomed by his ancient kahuna to view only a supernatural agency in disease and remedy, he cannot easily reconcile himself to the sober unpretentious working of a scientific method in curing disease."

Such methods dictated that infectious disease be combated by quarantine and careful observation, procedures Hillebrand already had in place, on a small scale, for the leprous patients at Queen's Hospital. He alluded to this in his report: "Although it may not appear quite in place I will here avail myself of the opportunity to bring to your and the public's attention a subject of great importance. I mean the rapid spread of that new disease, called by the natives *'Mai Pake.'* It is the genuine Oriental leprosy, as has become evident to me from the numerous cases which have presented themselves at the

Hospital." Their numbers were such as to "warrant the application of some radical sanitary measure," he wrote, before explaining that "it will be the duty of the next Legislature to devise and carry out some efficient, and at the same time, humane measure, by which the isolation of those affected with this disease can be accomplished."

A box canyon, Hillebrand imagined, would furnish an ideal place of isolation. Divided with tall, sturdy fences, various classes of the diseased could be kept separate from one another—dire incurables in the far reaches of the canyon, and the lighter cases toward the front, where doctors and nurses could easily gain access. He began to discuss this proposal with his fellow physicians, and eventually with a few newspaper editors.

On May 21, 1864, a letter published in the *Advertiser* asked, "Is it not a shame that no steps have been taken to arrest this scourge [leprosy] in its incipiency, which may yet prove more fatal and far more intolerable than the small-pox? Alas, Government seems to care little for the salvation of its poor dying out population." The letter, and others like it, troubled the king, and he pressured the legislature to act. At its next session, legislators hurriedly passed "An Act to Prevent the Spread of Leprosy," noting that "the disease of Leprosy has spread to considerable extent among the people" and "excited well grounded alarms." The law's critical component was Section 3, which stated that "the Board of Health or its agents are authorized and empowered to cause to be confined, in some place or places for that purpose provided, all leprous patients who shall be deemed capable of spreading the disease of leprosy." The passage went on to assert that every policeman and government agent must "cause to be arrested and delivered to the Board of Health or its agents, any person alleged to be a leper."

For the sake of expediency, the law's authors did not bother to compose an original set of civil codes specific to the disease of leprosy. Rather, they dusted off the hastily written quarantine law from the smallpox epidemic and rushed it through the assembly. At the time, no one paid much attention to a tonal shift that had crept into the new law, or to the omission of a key phrase contained in the old law, which stated that if a person was removed to a place of quarantine, the board would "provide him with nurses and other necessaries." The new law mentioned medical care and treatment, but it took a careful reader to note that such attention would be restricted to patients "in the incipient stages" of the disease. Any person the board decided already had leprosy "shall be considered incurable" and would be sent into isolation—with no mention of any doctors or nurses in this unnamed place.

William Hillebrand introduced his box canyon scenario at the board of health meeting on August 10, 1864. The members of the board quickly adopted the idea. After considering several valleys, the board purchased a piece of property five miles north of Honolulu in a deep-cut ravine called Palolo. A small stream skirted the lot, promising ample water, and although several families were already homesteading the valley, there were "no houses near the spot where the little colony would be established, consequently no reasonable objection could be made to the selection of this place by the people in the valley." But the residents of Palolo had all manner of objections to the scheme and launched a noisy campaign against any colony in their midst. The board renewed its search for a suitably isolated location. In the meantime, it began to assemble the machinery of exile.

Almost-Island

(Population 0)

Moving as swiftly as dignity would allow, Edward Hoffmann raced down the dirt road. He was late. The patients would begin appearing soon, and they could not arrive to find a hospital without a doctor. Hoffmann was fifty-two years old, a violin-playing German-born surgeon who had been one of the original members of the board of health. He had been preparing for this day, Monday, November 13, 1865, ever since notices had gone out from the board to fifty people on Oahu suspected of having leprosy. It asked that they present themselves for inspection at a small hospital that had been hammered together at a spot called Kalihi, on a waterside lot three miles west of Honolulu. Dr. Hoffmann had been named to head Kalihi Hospital. He wondered how many suspects would show up this morning. Not many, he anticipated. Hoffmann and his colleague William Hillebrand often discussed the fear locals still held of modern medicine. It would be better if Hillebrand were at Kalihi today, Hoffmann decided. But Hillebrand was still abroad, sent on a mission by the king to acquire Chinese immigrants to labor in the island's sugar fields, as replacements for the vanishing workforce. Hillebrand had referred to it as his collecting tour.

William Hillebrand was not absent long before his bounty began to land at the Honolulu docks: ten crates from Singapore, nine from Calcutta, one from Ceylon, eight from Java, and two from China. They held camphor, cinnamon, jackfruit and lychee, seeds of mandarin orange and Chinese plum. When dockhands pried apart the screeching cases, they found carrion crows, goldfinches, linnets, and angry mynah birds. Hillebrand sent Chinese quail, Indian sparrows, Mongolian pheasants, and a single pair of rare spotted axis deer, which weaved along the wharf on unsteady legs. Eventually the human cargo arrived: 522 Chinese, including 95 women and 3 children, who were bound by contract to five years' service at a wage of $4 a month. Dr. Hoffmann had read of their arrival in the *Hawaiian Gazette,* which printed a few phrases of Cantonese its readers might find helpful when dealing with the newcomers, including "Don't be lazy," "These two look alike," "The rice is all gone," and, as a final retort, "You can't catch me."

Hillebrand himself would not return for several months—he was touring leper colonies in China as well. So it fell to Dr. Hoffmann to manage the first few official moments of segregation. The horse drew near to Kalihi, and the hospital compound came into view. A little more than a year earlier, his friend had set the government net in motion. Now Edward Hoffmann would see what had been caught.

They began to emerge from the early morning haze. Within an hour sixty-two persons crowded the fenced-in grounds of Kalihi Hospital. A hawk-nosed member of the board of health named Theodore Heuck moved to the edge of the hospital's porch and started to speak. Heuck thanked them for coming, then repeated much of what had been printed on the flyers that had bid them here. A new law was in effect, the purpose of which was "to cure those persons who are afflicted with leprosy." To that end, the board had founded this hospital. Here everything in the power of the board would be done to care for and cure them. "God willing," Heuck announced, "with proper medical aid, comfort, and care, and sufficient and wholesome food, this disease might soon be checked."

J. D. Kahauliko, an educated Hawaiian who sometimes practiced law, stood in the crowd. Like the others assembled around him, Kahauliko had read the board's flyer. As he understood it, the patients would receive attention and medicine until they were well, and then they would be released to return to their families. The suspects had responded to the seemingly benevolent offer in greater numbers than the board or Dr. Hoffmann had anticipated. "It is gratifying indeed to observe the readiness with which the natives come forward," a reporter observed, "the confidence which they feel toward the Board of Health."

That morning, Dr. Hoffmann began to separate the persons with leprosy from those who merely suffered from one of the many skin disorders that mimic the disease. These latter he treated and soon sent home. Each of those he believed had leprosy he settled into one of the hospital's fifty beds for an extended stay. They were bathed and their sores bandaged, salves applied to their skin and compresses pressed to swollen joints. Once a week their families were allowed to visit, although Hoffmann gently discouraged physical contact. "Dr. Hoffmann . . . comes in early and attends very carefully on the patients," Kahauliko wrote shortly after entering Kalihi. "We think he is very earnest and faithful in his endeavors to cure us. There is but one feeling among us all, and that is respect for the Doctor and love to the Government which has thus carefully provided for us unfortunates."

What the patients at Kalihi did not know, however, was that the hospital was merely one component of the segregation system. The board had devised a ruthlessly elegant scheme to rid the islands of leprosy. Agents would comb the islands and compile a list of suspected lepers, who would then be asked to present themselves at Kalihi for exam. If they refused, they would be arrested and brought forcibly to the facility. Once Dr. Hoffmann had confirmed the disease, the person would be banished to an isolated spot, where he or she would remain until dead. In this way the disease would be extinguished. A few months before Kalihi opened, a board member named Ferdinand Hutchison had suggested an exile site. Hutchison explained that the northern coast of Molokai was defined by brutal cliffs, and that midpoint along the shore a shelf of land emerged from the base of these cliffs, which was surrounded on three sides by wave-pounded coast. The board could easily acquire the remote spot and turn it into a prison. After some investigation the board had settled on this plan. An agent of the king, a Molokai resident named Rudolph Meyer, was told to begin buying up the property.

On December 5, 1865, Meyer reported back, "The lands are ready for the lepers to come." He had negotiated the purchase of almost half of the small peninsula, for $1,800. Meyer asked that he be allowed to continue buying land until every acre was government-owned. "It would then make the lepersettlement what it ought to be—that is isolated and no chance of communication with the lepers, as then the lepersettlement would have all natural boundaries and be most inaccessible."

Included with the acreage Meyer bought were several dozen thatched huts, and standing crops of taro, potatoes, and mushrooms; enough harvest to feed three hundred people, he wrote. Meyer advised the board to begin sending patients soon. If the food fell to rot, he wrote, "it may cause want for the lepers when they arrive." The board was also eager to begin—Kalihi Hospital was already dangerously overfull. Writing to the sheriff of Maui, Theodore Heuck explained that the first exiles would be shipped immediately to Molokai. "Their places at the Kalihi Hospital will be taken by other sufferers on Oahu until this island is cleansed; next after that your island," and so on, until Hawaii was free of leprosy. Speed was critical, Heuck wrote. Locked into a series of deadlines made firm by the cycle of crops, by the condition of the seas, and by sheer quotidian logistics, the board recognized that exile had to begin without delay. But there was a problem. They could not find their boat.

The vessel had arrived in Hawaii in July 1850, riding atop the deck of the ship *Eliza Warwick*. She was promptly excised, laid into the sea, and fitted out, her two masts gaff-rigged and finished with the flag of the Hawaiian Kingdom. The *Warwick*, as the schooner was christened, was tiny, capable of accommodating only twenty-six passengers, including captain and crew. The average life of an interisland schooner was twenty years, and by 1865 the *Warwick* was already in disrepair. She belonged to Edwin Jones, a canny trader who advertised himself as a grocer and ship chandler. When Jones had heard that the board needed a ship, he sent word that he had the perfect vessel—but for charter, not for sale.

Earlier, the board had dismissed the idea of chartering a ship. If a greedy owner took healthy passengers on board a contaminated vessel, one board member argued, it "would hardly be right toward the public at large." Time was running out, however, and the segregation plan required a ship. Initially the board offered to lease the *Warwick* for $150 a month. Meyer reported that Jones "thinks this sum is altogether too small and he asks *$250 per month*!" Rudolph Meyer was a frugal, practical man and believed the board was being cheated. He was told to make the deal anyway. After completing the transaction Meyer sent the *Warwick* on its first official business. The captain promptly embarked on a drinking binge, his crew launched a work stoppage, and the ship missed all of its scheduled runs. "As I feared all along so I am afraid now," Meyer warned the board. "The *Warwick* will prove to be a bill of great expenses to the government and little benefit."

On December 14, 1865, more than a week overdue, the *Warwick* finally arrived in Honolulu. Captain Gibson offered no explanation for his tardiness, although a note in the board of health minutes cryptically reports "difficulty with the crew." Theodore Heuck sent a message to Dr. Hoffmann: "The *Warwick* is ready to take the sick to Molokai." Patients were to board by 2 P.M., Heuck advised, and the schooner would depart an hour later. At Kalihi, twelve patients gathered in the yard, clutching small bundles of belongings. Their luggage was transferred to a handcart, and shortly after noon the parade set off for the wharf, half an hour away.

At the head of the group was J. D. Kahauliko, the patient who would soon emerge as the colony's first leader. In the board's logs, Kahauliko was recorded as exile number 1. Eight men followed after Kahauliko, and three women. Although Kahauliko did not know what lay ahead, the attentions of Dr. Hoffmann for the past month and the board's assurance that "all possible care will be extended to them" suggested that what awaited on Molokai was something similar to Kalihi—a place with ample food, shelter, and nursing. From the letters he wrote, it is clear that Kahauliko trusted the government to take care of him and the other patients. He and the others would have been apprehensive about their voyage to Molokai that day, but not panicked.

Even so, there was the emotional matter of separation. At the wharf that afternoon would unfold the first of what would prove to be hundreds of identical scenes of chilling anguish. One was described in a diary kept by a young California woman: "Never, should I live a thousand fair years, shall I forget the memory of that strange, rending, wailing, escaping bestiality by its very deliberateness." Wives, mothers, children, and friends followed after the patients as the group rumbled onto the docks, order kept by a pair of armed sheriffs. Relatives of the exiles clutched fragrant leis of plumeria, which were to be briefly worn by the patients and then thrown in blessing upon the sea. The procession, wrote the Californian, was "a funeral in which the dead themselves walked." By late afternoon Kahauliko and the others were on board. Captain Gibson gave the order and the *Warwick* began to slip away, trailing a wake of blooms.

Under the best circumstances, voyages between the islands were unhappy events. Conditions at sea were almost always rough. Ships were undersized and overcrowded, and the passengers universally beset by seasickness. Lifesaving equipment was rare, captains often drunk or incompetent, and shipwrecks frighteningly common. On most interisland schooners, navigation depended entirely upon sight. If the captain mislaid the next island in the chain, or awoke from night without land in sight, he was lost.

Within minutes of the *Warwick*'s departure, a bank of thunderheads began to slip toward the schooner. The storm traveled low and from the east, stripping away distance until it collapsed atop the little vessel all at once, just as the *Warwick* reached the midpoint of its fifty-eight-mile voyage. In an instant everything rolled to black. Rain flooded the deck from fore to aft, tugging at the trousers of the frantic crew. They were trying to pierce a winter storm, their vessel still under sail in a ninety-knot blow, atop a roiling ocean almost four hundred fathoms deep. Gale winds canted the *Warwick* deep upon its side. The passengers scrambled belowdecks. Bilgewater gathered and mingled with the dung of animals and the leakage from barrels of oil and molasses, forming a vile bath that sloshed high up the staves of the pitching vessel, then washed over the passengers. Rats paddled atop the slop, clambering up the coats of the sick, who were already under siege by scorpions, mice, and roaches, all seeking higher ground.

Captain Gibson decided that the *Warwick* could not safely reach Molokai. He barked an order and the crew turned the ship, broadened her sails, and then held on, while the wind drove her across the channel. Down in the hold, the passengers felt the ship stutter and spin and realized, after a moment's confusion, that they were returning to Honolulu.

Dr. Hoffmann had spent the blustery day deciding which patients would be the next to be exiled. He did not enjoy the duty. It had been wrenching enough to select the first group. After some deliberation, Hoffmann had simply chosen the persons he believed were farthest along in the disease—the ones without much hope.

In his first weeks of practice at Kalihi, the doctor received and examined 165 persons, 104 of whom he admitted as patients. Of these, Hoffmann decided 75 had leprosy and would have to be banished. In none of the cases could he say how the person became infected. Nor could Hoffmann determine the precise methods of the disease: why it lay gently on some and destroyed others, why it sometimes simply vanished from a person. By the winter of 1865–66 the only thing Edward Hoffmann could do with any precision was detail its assault.

A victim first grew depressed, with a general sense of heaviness throughout the body. Fever often swept over him. "The patients are not aware of being sick until spots . . . are visible on the skin," Hoffmann wrote. Livid red marks appeared, first dotting the face and then the ears and nose. "In some instances the whole body more or less is covered with them or a somewhat scaly eruption." Itchiness often ignited the spots, followed by insensibility within their shiny borders. In time, the markings darkened. Those on the face sometimes swelled with both hard and soft tubercles, which grew in sizes ranging from that of a pea to a hen's egg. "The face now becomes much disfigured, the skin rough, full of wrinkles and fissures, similar to the skin of an elephant."

As it advanced, the disease attacked the ears and nose, causing them to enlarge. Cartilage in the nose then collapsed. The eyes became inflamed and began to tear. Eyelids, lips, and chin distended enormously, Hoffmann wrote, "and the whole face has a horrid appearance." The voice grew scratchy and hoarse, and swallowing became so difficult the person often choked to death. Fingernails were levered off by growth beneath their hard surface. The feet and forearms swelled, and "ulcers form on the metatarsal articulations of the fingers and toes, without any pain. The skin becomes gangrenous, leaving the muscles bare. Joints are thus attacked and destroyed in succession by the slow progress of this terrible disease." Through it all, Hoffmann noted, "the pulse is regular, appetite good, and no apparent internal morbid symptoms take place."

On December 16, 1866, Hoffmann wrote down the names of the people who would form the next group sent into exile. He then steeled himself for the most unpleasant part: explaining to each patient that he would have to leave the hospital, leave Honolulu and the cheerful prospect of visits from his family. Some from the first group seemed as if they would never stop sobbing; Hoffmann had watched them march away toward the wharf, clinging to each other. It was a terrible scene, and Hoffmann was grateful that the first exiles were past it. So the doctor was surprised when footsteps sounded on the path, and Kahauliko and the others walked back through the hospital gate.

It grew still, and unseasonably warm, in the islands. Ships floated motionless, while their crews began to bicker and fight. In Honolulu the air turned heavy. Persons hurrying to Christmas services found their clothes dampened with sweat and fanned books of hymns to stir a draft. At the wharf behind Wilson's Store, the *Warwick* rose and fell with the tide, her sails folded and wrapped.

At dusk on New Year's Eve fireworks exploded above Honolulu harbor and traced graceful arcs to the sea, the falling embers unmoved by any breeze. On Molokai, in the colony, the waiting crops began to rot. Yet another week passed. Finally the wind freshened. Theodore Heuck sent a scribbled note by horse to Kalihi Hospital: "It is fine weather, the schooner is ready, let the people get on board as soon as possible!" A month behind schedule, exile was ready to begin once more.

Again the Kahauliko and the others were marched to the docks, tearfully bid farewell, and escorted aboard. In their haste to catch the precious wind, however, none of the officers or crew noticed an addition to the group of twelve, an oversight not reflected in the board of health's official rolls, which recorded that on the afternoon of January 5, 1866, three women and nine men departed for the colony on Molokai, as its first inmates. But there was one other. A small boy, the healthy child of one of the patients, had crept onto the *Warwick* as a stowaway.

Rudolph Meyer lingered at the lip of the cliff, gazing down at the empty brown tongue of land. The board had alerted him to expect the first inmates weeks ago, but their boat had never arrived. Meyer knew the *Warwick* had set off a second time with a load of patients, but he could spot no sign of it on the western horizon.

Meyer reined his horse away from the cliff. The trail to his farmhouse threaded past a meadow of sheep and a reedy pond, and with each step the colony fell away into the distance. Rudolph Meyer was thirty-nine years old, with thin red hair and a wiry scruff on his chin, which his eight children repeatedly tugged. He was a native of Hamburg, an exacting man with an engineering degree and intolerance for idleness. Meyer's discipline was one reason the board had asked him to oversee the colony's creation. Another was purely practical—he and his family lived at the top of the cliff, and their homestead overlooked the site. For more than a year, Rudolph Meyer had managed every detail associated with the prison's founding: purchasing the land, leasing the *Warwick,* and hiring the resident superintendent who was to live down there, a quick-tempered Frenchman named Louis Lepart. Meyer anticipated that his own obligation to the asylum would soon be fulfilled. What he did not know was that the colony had already ensnared him.

It was, one observer remarked, an "almost-island," defined by a soaring curtain of stone that ran the length of the northern coast of Molokai. At the foot of this impassable wall—the tallest sea cliff in the world—emerged a two-mile-wide triangle of earth, "sunburnt and dust-covered," as a visitor reported that year, "blackened at the edges, where the rough lava rocks were uncovered, and frothed from end to end with tumbling breakers."

The peninsula was known, variously, as Kalawao or Kalaupapa, after the two tiny villages that sat upon its barren plain. Kalawao lay on the eastern shore, a few thatched huts tucked tightly to the cliff—"pali" in Hawaiian—whose shadow swung out and removed the sun for much of the day. In winter, evenings arrived in Kalawao at 3 P.M., and wet, easterly winds raked the village almost year-round. Kalaupapa occupied the plain's opposite edge, farther out from the looming cliff and thus washed longer by the sun. Underfoot the land was brown and dry, but the breeze didn't bite as hard as at Kalawao, and at the border of the village patches of morning glory and nightshade grew.

Rudolph Meyer had succeeded in purchasing for the board almost all of the land in Kalawao, and much of the property down the center of the plain. But a handful of Kalaupapa's residents refused to sell. Meyer tried upping the price and dangled prime land off the peninsula in exchange—the residents stayed firm. The board decided to allow the holdouts to remain, at least temporarily. It fell to Louis Lepart to keep the sick away from the healthy residents of Kalaupapa.

A month earlier, Lepart had torn open a letter that said he was hired as resident superintendent of the government's new enterprise and would be expected "to live among the lepers." Salary would be $400 a year, a fair wage. "The board trusts you will try to do your best for the good of the suffering lepers," Theodore Heuck wrote. At each appearance of the schooner *Warwick,* Lepart was to greet the newcomers, escort them to Kalawao, and make certain no one left. To Lepart, it sounded as if he were being made warden of a prison.

While Rudolph Meyer acted as general supervisor of the colony, making bimonthly inspection visits, Lepart would manage things day to day. Meyer had sent him onto the peninsula several weeks earlier, so he could begin to learn the place. For his home Lepart chose a cottage near the broken cone of an extinct volcano that stood midway between the two shores. Within this crater shone a lake of brackish tidal water, eight hundred feet deep, into which the dead of the two villages had historically been sunk. The practice supplied the crater with a name: the Given Grave. Seen from atop the cliffs, the ancient volcano and its winding tail of collapsed lava cone looked like a sea creature now crawled to land. Lepart's home lay at its head.

A life in such a frontier was something Lepart had always sought, although his role was not exactly as he had once imagined. Years ago, Lepart had joined the Society of the Sacred Hearts of Jesus and Mary, a Catholic missionary order commonly known as the Sacred Hearts. Lepart had abandoned the order, however, and he no longer dwelled much on the divine. What he was concentrating on these days was how to shoot a gun.

With no landing site anywhere along the peninsula's rocky shore, vessels arriving at the colony had two choices. If the sea was calm, a captain could anchor a half mile offshore of Kalawao, and using a whaleboat, oarsmen would try to ferry cargo to a narrow beach of rock at the mouth of a valley east of the peninsula. Surf was treacherous along this stretch, and whaleboats were often upended or swamped. Cast adrift, passengers might be hoisted on waves to the stony beach. But they could just as easily get sucked backward by the current and drowned at sea, or be launched toward land and killed upon the lava rocks.

Landing on the Kalaupapa side offered only slightly better prospects. An attempt required settled seas and high tides, infrequent conditions that occurred only from May to September. The remainder of the year storms complicated the procedure. Although the peninsula itself blocked the swells generated by the easterly trade winds, the village's northwest-facing shore lay exposed to breakers thrown off by the North Pacific's winter storms, which sent fifteen-foot waves rushing toward land every ten seconds. A captain might send off a loaded whaleboat, then watch helplessly as a massive breaker leapt to life, snatched the craft, knocked its steersman from his berth, and splintered her on the rocks. To try to make land at either shore carried the looming possibility of loss. Often a captain would simply refuse an attempt. If he was impatient or corrupt, he might pitch his cargo overboard and mark it as delivered. One island skipper named William Sumner was notorious for encouraging his passengers to leap over the rails and swim for it. In time, he would come to serve the Molokai route.

According to a letter Louis Lepart wrote on January 8, 1866, the *Warwick* brought the first group of patients around to the Kalaupapa side on Saturday morning, January 6, then anchored a quarter mile out while the crew readied a whaleboat. Boarding the small craft required descending a loosely strung contraption of rope and wood. Even for a nimble sailor, such a climb was risky. To a person made weak and clumsy by disease, it was terrifying.

After the patients had boarded the little boat, several crew members climbed in, took up a set of long oars, and attempted to pilot her to shore. In the last day the warm weather had broken, and now driving rain swelled the sea. An audience of Kalaupapa residents watched with interest as the whaleboat was flicked to shore and spilled forth the first exiles. Lepart met the patients onshore. To each he handed the items the board of health had purchased for the settlers. Men received a shovel or an ax, and a single gray wool blanket. Women got only the blanket.

The Frenchman spoke little Hawaiian and poor English. Struggling to make himself understood, Lepart assembled the small party and began to march them toward Kalawao. He rode horseback. The patients followed on foot. One of them asked, Where are the doctors? Where is the hospital? Lepart did not answer the question.

It took an hour to reach their destination. With each step, the air grew bitter. A dirt path ran between the two villages, crowded with rocks that had tumbled from the cliffs. After several hundred yards the trail began to rise, and brambles closed in from the sides, squeezing the group into single file. A mile along in the hike they reached the near edge of the Given Grave. Wind blew across the empty mouth of the dead volcano, a low and constant moan.

On the far side of the crater the carpet of brush vanished in waist-high grass, and the path curved toward the immense cliff on the right. Soon the trail topped a low bluff. Before them lay an abandoned village and behind it blue ocean. A twenty-foot-high wall of black lava divided the two. Every few seconds the sea rushed the rock with startling violence, then exploded into glittering foam.

This was Kalawao. The patients looked around. Six months had passed since Rudolph Meyer had fixed the departure of the village's original residents, and storms had peeled roofs from the cottages and burst once-snug brown grass huts. The village appeared haunted.

Still midday, it was already becoming dark. Lepart tried to explain about the angle of the cliff and the long shadow now creeping toward them. The patients would need to get quickly settled, find wood, and put their fires in place. By this time, however, the exiles had gone without sleep for more than twenty-four hours. In the last day they had eaten only a few scraps of bread and had walked on damaged feet for more than two miles. Their clothing and bandages were soaked from the sea voyage, then made filthy from the overland hike. Bone-tired, sore, and disoriented, they sank to the ground and slept. Lepart climbed onto his horse and rode away.

"A Kind of Colony"

(Population 13)

The world into which they awoke was terrifying. Lepart had left a few bags of salt beef and bread, but these made for meager rations. The two educated exiles, Kahauliko and a part-time attorney named J. W. Lae, took command. Scouting the abandoned crops, Kahauliko was able to salvage a few sweet potatoes and bulbs of taro root. Moving from one empty dwelling to the next, Lae found a pair of habitable cottages and helped settle the others inside. Several desperate patients tried to sneak across the plain and seek shelter in Kalaupapa. Lepart dragged them back.

Survival required immense effort. Most critical were water, firewood, and food, and the exiles spent their hours in search of all three. The nearest source of good water was Kalawao Creek, a hard trek of more than a mile. Because they did not have barrels for storage, as soon as one water detail ended, another was required, and the bearers sent back out with an armful of makeshift buckets.

While several patients scoured the land for food, others spent the day combing the shore for driftwood and the foot of the cliff for fallen branches. Fires had to be kept alive throughout the day, as much for heat as for cooking. Yet even a feeble flame consumed wood too quickly. Within the first few days the land around Kalawao was stripped bare of timber. To locate more required venturing farther and farther from camp, then stumbling back with a heavy load.

Complicating matters was the collapsing health of many of the settlers. Dr. Edward Hoffmann had chosen the most advanced cases to be the pioneers of Kalawao, a decision that made rational sense when viewed in the context of the board's overall plan to eradicate the disease. Since the physicians on the board believed that advanced cases were likely more contagious than incipient ones, and that spending money on care and treatment was foolhardy given their almost certain mortality, the most efficient first step in the program of exile was to speed the terminal cases to Kalawao and allow them to quickly expire.

Such an approach, however, was at odds with the other budgetary principle of the exile program—self-sufficiency. Immediately after arriving in Kalawao, five patients became incapacitated. Several of the stronger colonists thus had to spend their days in an effort to try to keep the very sick alive; they were lost as workers in the jobs of gathering water, firewood, and food.

During the first days of the segregation policy, the board had decided to sometimes allow a family member to join a relative in exile. Such persons, called *kokuas*—"helpers" in Hawaiian—were usually a parent or a spouse of an inmate. Kokuas were bound by the same strictures that applied to the patients. They were not to mingle with any healthy persons on the peninsula, nor were they to leave Kalawao. In theory, kokuas would act as nurses and laborers in the colony, and as an unpaid workforce. Or so the board believed.

Three helpers, including Kahauliko's sixty-six-year-old father, sailed with the first group of twelve exiles, along with the stowaway boy. Five of these sixteen people were soon too sick to work. The boy could not contribute much, and two persons were required to nurse the very sick. That left eight workers to see to the daily needs of sixteen. Of those eight, four were primarily occupied with water and firewood detail. The four who remained were in charge of food.

The board of health had envisioned that the exiles' rations would be harvested from the plots that Rudolph Meyer had purchased months earlier. But these crops had failed. Confronted with their hunger, Lepart gave the exiles the rest of the small supply of bread and meat that the board had sent, and he arranged for emergency taro to be purchased from farmers living in a nearby valley. Each time he appeared in Kalawao to deliver the rations, however, he warned that this food supply was temporary. The patients should be planting taro for the future, Lepart said, and making poi for their present needs.

Poi, the primary product of taro, was a staple in the local diet—a starchy, bland gruel so fattening and easily digested that physicians prescribed it to consumptives. The board imagined it the perfect foodstuff for a colony of the ill. They expected that the patients would subsist on an essentially all-poi diet, leavened with fish or the meat of a slaughtered hog or sheep or steer. But to create poi from the taro root proved beyond the capability of the patients. The taro plants in the colony were aquatic, grown in swampy plots similar to rice paddies. Forty square feet of well-planted patch could feed a man for a year, but the work was tiring, wet, and dangerous, fraught with the possibility of a misstep and the risk of drowning in a foot or two of yielding brown muck. Once harvested, the tubers had to be baked in underground ovens and then mashed to flour on planks of wood. A single bowl could require an hour of effort, and more calories might be spent making the meal than were gained by eating it. Even if the kokuas did nothing else all day but hunt down ripe plants and pound them into poi, they could never make enough to feed everyone.

Because kokuas were not patients, the board did not consider them to be their responsibility. When the board had arranged for food and blankets, they did not include the helpers. Yet the patients willingly shared with those who had accompanied them into exile. As Kahauliko wrote, they felt an obligation to the kokuas, "for all of these persons have come with us and will die for us." The result of their compassion was a colony that tumbled into crisis even faster than it might have otherwise. There were simply too many mouths and not enough healthy bodies. Far from being an able workforce, kokuas were soon as weak and frail as the sick.

Life in Kalawao became an exercise in conservation. At night the settlers crowded together on the dirt floors of their huts, sharing blankets and body heat. Water could not be wasted on bathing or washing wounds, no matter how foul they became. Bread and meat went into a porridge, which could be stretched, and poi was thinned to a liquid, so that all sixteen people had a taste. The rationing extended down the chain of indispensability. Kahauliko and Lae would have commanded full shares. The kokuas, whose work kindled their appetites, ate full shares too. Those who were slowed but able to work received a bit less. The two worst off, a woman named Lakupu and one named Nauhina, were given just enough to still their moans. They were the first to die, expiring within hours of each other on August 5, 1866.

Lepart visited irregularly. When the exiles begged him for food or blankets, or any of the promised medical attention, the Frenchman replied that he had nothing more to dispense. Although the board repeatedly had told Lepart to "make these poor people as comfortable as possible," it failed to provide the resident superintendent with the materials to do so. And Lepart showed slim interest in serving as caregiver. The inmates had shelter, and if they worked, they would have food. Lepart felt anything else was beyond his purview. The exiles quickly recognized his disinterest. A few weeks after landing, Lae managed to get a letter to the board explaining that they desperately needed supplies and assistance. Lae asked if Lepart's duties included helping the patients. "It is not so, is it?" he wrote. Lae feared if the government's man in the colony would not aid them, no one would.

Misunderstanding clouded every aspect of exile. Some residents of Kalaupapa believed that they had been hired to care for the patients, but when they lent shelter or pressed food upon the newcomers, Lepart would threaten them with fines and arrest. The Frenchman was enforcing what he understood to be the board's command for total segregation—the Hawaiians simply considered him cruel. One afternoon Kahauliko went to Lepart and asked for medicine, and Lepart explained he could not give any without orders from the board. Another time Kahauliko asked that someone who knew the cliffs be allowed to guide them to the sweet potatoes rooting there. Lepart refused, explaining that the sick and the healthy were not to have contact with one another. When Kahauliko found a volunteer himself, Lepart chased the guide back to Kalaupapa. The potatoes remained untouched.

Writing for the board, Theodore Heuck stressed to Lepart the need to show compassion, since "they are strangers there." The board was anxious for the exiles to settle as contentedly as possible in their new home. Then, Heuck assured Lepart, "they will give a good account of their position on Molokai. This will best help to endorse others to follow them." Thus far the board's agents were encountering scant resistance to segregation. "It had been anticipated that no little difficulty and opposition would be experienced in attempting to carry out the provisions of the Act," the board president reported to the king, "but the reverse of this was the case." If the colony gained a negative reputation, however, suspects would begin to resist exile, and the disease would move underground.

By the third week in January, the settlers appeared to be making progress. They had planted taro and sweet potato, and discovered banana, orange, and grapefruit trees hidden in the forest near Kalawao Creek. Fresh fronds patched the holes in their two huts, and twists of firewood lay stacked against them, enough fuel to last through several days of rain. If they took care with their rations, they had enough food to sustain them until the taro grew plump enough to eat. Their situation seemed almost manageable. Then, on January 21, Lepart appeared on the rise above the village and led eleven more people into Kalawao.

Crops that Kahauliko and Lae had rescued were quickly overrun. The board sent three barrels of beef and two bags of bread via the *Warwick*, but when Lepart took an inventory, he discovered that the crew had pilfered much of it. The board had hoped that each new group of inmates would enjoy the fruits of the labors of the exiles who had come before. This proved to be a gross misjudgment of human nature. When the second boatload of patients arrived, they began to eat the produce the first group had saved—Lepart had told them that the food was for the community. Kahauliko thought otherwise and came to blows with some of the newcomers. Having struggled to scratch out a few rows of healthy sweet potatoes, Kahauliko and the other original exiles were loath to share them with strangers who had contributed nothing.

Within the month the number of sick in the colony stood at fifty, along with a dozen kokuas. Patients quickly split into factions. Fights erupted over the ownership of huts or a water cask or bowl. Feuds from Kalihi Hospital spilled over to Kalawao, and rivalries from home villages renewed themselves. Battles over women occurred daily. Kokuas fought with each other, and with the patients. Set on edge by the feeling that they had been tricked into exile, the settlers seized on any excuse to explode into violence. They soon focused their anger on Lepart, the only available official. He began to display his gun on his hip.

By early March, Lepart was writing daily to Theodore Heuck and the board, warning of a revolt. He asked Heuck to send several pairs of handcuffs and grant him the authority to arrest and imprison patients. Instead, the board asked that the Frenchman, who feared that at any moment he would be overrun by a swarm of lepers, "organize a kind of Colony or municipal sort of government for the people." Lepart protested to the board that its scheme would never work because of a "want of harmony" among the settlers. The board insisted he make the effort: "Be kind, considerate, just, but firm and decisive on all matters."

On the morning of Monday, March 26, Lepart called a meeting of patients and kokuas. A day earlier the *Warwick* had delivered the fifth shipment of exiles, bringing the patient population to sixty-three. The ship was also to have delivered thirty-five boards of lumber, to patch houses for the new arrivals. By now, however, the crew was stealing anything possible from cargo, and lumber, which had to be imported from the Pacific Northwest, was extremely valuable. The *Warwick* landed only two dozen planks, and many cottages could not be repaired. Lepart moved the newcomers into them anyway.

The latest arrivals joined the throng outside Louis Lepart's house. A patient translated Lepart's words into Hawaiian. Lepart began by announcing that the mingling he had seen between the healthy villagers of Kalaupapa and the people of Kalawao had to end. Contact was forbidden without written permission from the board. This rule applied to kokuas as well. The reminder, Lepart later wrote, was met with "much grumbling."

Next, Lepart outlined a system of social order for the settlers. He had devised something based on food and labor, the two most contentious issues in Kalawao. His plan was to divide the exiles into work parties of ten to twelve people and give each crew several plots to oversee. A crew could eat only from its plot. Each crew would also be responsible for producing an extra amount of food, to feed patients too infirm to work. Thus "the idle ones will have no alternative but to work for their own needs, and the comfort of each individual might be proportionate to their work," Lepart explained to Theodore Heuck. "Moreover, I do think that it might create a kind of competitive spirit among the lepers."

Someone asked Lepart, Why did the government not simply feed them until they were released? Surely farming was senseless, since they would soon be returning home. Lepart answered, You are never going home. There was a moment of stunned silence as his words sunk in, followed by an explosion of voices. The patients screamed that Lepart was lying, that he was trying to dupe them into working so that the government might profit. Several men rushed forward, menacing Lepart, and the superintendent pulled his gun. The men froze, and after several tense minutes they began to file away.

When the mob had dispersed, Lepart went inside his cottage and wrote to Theodore Heuck. He asked Heuck to post a letter directly to the exiles, clarifying the board's policy. "There is a basic point I ask you to mention in your letter, the lepers being sent to Molokai by the Board of Health are there not for one month or one year, but for all their lives. Several think they have to return to Kalihi in two or three months and because of this they care little about planting taro. I did all one can to convince them that they were mistaken, but several cannot agree."

As the weeks passed, the weather at Kalawao worsened. Storms chased each other across the peninsula, and the sun went missing for days. Seas grew violent, and for almost a month the *Warwick* could not land new patients. For those already in the colony, life grew even more harrowing. Fires blinked out in the rain, and cold drove many patients deeper into illness. Lepart reported, "Five or six of the patients are worse than when they arrived at Molokai." He predicted they would soon be dead.

Several patients, including Kahauliko and Lae, wrote pleading letters to relatives describing the horrible conditions at Kalawao, which were snuck to Kalaupapa, then carried up the cliff path and mailed. "We are receiving great many difficulties continually," lamented one letter. "We are in difficulty on account of our diseases, and also for poi and fish, and clothing. We are in difficulty in not having any medical aid. You must not think that we are getting any better, no! Not at all!"

Soon dozens of families had received the news from Kalawao. Alarmed, the relatives wrote en masse and asked the board what it intended to do about the situation in the colony. "We . . . thought that the government would care for these persons who are on Molokai in the same manner as they are cared for at Kalihi, but alas, no." The families sent copies to the newspapers serving the Hawaiian community. "We think the members of the Board of Health are ignorant of the improper care taken of these patients, and the manner in which they are treated by the sub-agent [Lepart] while the truth is that they are not well taken of." The letters asked that readers send clothing and money to the exiles, because the government was shirking its responsibility to them. Thus emerged the first public sketch of the colony: an appalling place with a cruel and armed overseer, cold and ruined huts, and a starving, unkempt, and dying population.

Theodore Heuck never got around to writing directly to the exiles. In many ways the board itself was still confused about its segregation plan—it pursued a policy of treatment and care, as evidenced by Edward Hoffmann and his hospital at Kalihi, but also supported a massive program of arrest and imprisonment. This uncertainty trickled down even to semantics. In formal and informal reports, board members shifted among a bewildering array of terms to describe the exiles at Kalawao: "patients," "prisoners," "settlers," "colonists," "the sick," "lepers," and "inmates." Often they chose as neutral a phrase as possible and simply referred to the men and women and children in the colony as "the poor unfortunates."

Similarly, the place itself gathered multiple names, at least in the neat penmanship of Heuck, the board's recording secretary. Kalawao was usually called a colony, or a settlement. Yet it also was written of as a prison, asylum, hospital, pesthouse, and leprosarium. For a brief time the board and its correspondents tested an original coinage: *lepersettlement.*

If leprosy were the only matter of concern to the board of health, they might have been able to resolve some of the confusion. But it was one problem among many. The overall health of the Hawaiian population had continued to decline. In a typical account, Dr. G. W. Smith of Kauai reported to the board a list of ailments that had taken hold among 240 of his patients, including 39 cases of cutaneous diseases, 30 ulcers of various kinds, 20 cases of rheumatism, 14 of syphilis or venereal disease, 13 incidents of dropsy, 4 of pleurisy, several of elephantiasis, more than 40 cases of colic, gastric disorder, diarrhea, and constipation, and a smattering of cases of asthma, menorrhagia, ophthalmia, and scrofula. He also found 7 cases of leprosy, and 22 instances where he could not identify the ailment at all. All of these required sending medicines from Honolulu, at the expense of the government.

With each meeting of the board, the issue of funding grew more critical. For the two-year period ending March 31, 1866, the board had spent $7,231 on medicines and vaccinations made available, at no cost, to island residents and administered by volunteer medical officers. "It is believed that many lives have been saved and much misery relieved by those philanthropic persons," the president of the board, Ferdinand Hutchison, wrote in his report to the government. In ordinary times, such an outlay would not have been a reason for worry. But over the same period the board had spent more than $16,000 in its battle against leprosy. And each week Lepart asked that additional food and supplies be purchased by the board and sent to the colony. By all previous reckoning, the settlement was supposed to be declining in maintenance costs, not increasing.

The board decided to accelerate the system of exile. Once all the sick were confined at Kalawao, there would be a sizable enough workforce to make the colony self-sufficient—and the enormous costs of rounding up and shipping the patients could be put behind them. The board instructed sheriffs to make the identification and arrest of lepers their highest priority. "We will try to keep the ball in motion and examine all affected or reported to be in the islands," Theodore Heuck wrote to one sheriff. Many of the sick still arrived voluntarily at Kalihi Hospital, lured by the promise of treatment. But an increasing number were vanishing into the forest at the first sight of an agent of the board of health. Thinking that doctors would arouse less suspicion, the board assembled teams of medical men to comb the isles. Heuck wrote to a sheriff on the island of Maui, "If the sick won't come to us, we'll go to the sick."

By the end of March, the board thought that they had identified every leper remaining on the island of Oahu, about fifty individuals. Many of these suspects were already under observation at Kalihi Hospital, although, the board cautioned, "there is reason to believe that a few still remain concealed by their friends." Even so, they thought the hard work of segregation was nearly complete on Oahu and would be finished on the other islands within a matter of months. By summer, the board assumed, the population in the colony would have stabilized. As for those already at Kalawao, Hutchison wrote, "We are informed that those sent to Molokai have settled contentedly on the place, and those able to work have commenced to erect new houses and cultivate the land, feeling that they are permanent settlers there." To tide them over, Hutchison instructed the board to purchase "a few beef cattle, sheep, goats, &c . . . in order that it may, as far as possible, become self-supporting in the future."

The board relied on two sources for information about the colony: Rudolph Meyer, who had not set foot in Kalawao since mid-December, and Louis Lepart, who knew that he would be blamed for any problems that arose in the place. Neither man filed entirely accurate accounts. For the public, Dr. Hutchison put an additional rosy sheen on the conditions at Kalawao. But it is also unlikely that he or the board knew just how dire things had become.

By late April, every habitable cottage in Kalawao was filled to overflowing. Some held as many as eight people, who struggled for space inside a single open room, twelve feet square. Few of the homes were watertight, and when the clouds burst, the dirt floors softened into mud. Some patients lived outdoors, slotting themselves into gullies between rocks, then pulling palms or mats over their heads as roofs. Others climbed into the Given Grave and found shelter in caves that pocked the interior walls of the dead volcano.

During the last week of April, the *Warwick* arrived at Kalaupapa with yet another group of patients. Lepart had been told to expect thirteen exiles, but only a dozen landed. He asked where the missing man was. The captain shrugged. Lepart suspected that the man had been thrown overboard or allowed to escape after paying a bribe, and neither outcome would have surprised him. Of late, the captain's actions had become increasingly erratic. Patients tumbled from the *Warwick* with cracked lips and vacant eyes, pleading for water, complaining that the captain had refused to let them drink during the voyage. Earlier in the month the schooner had picked up a load of patients from Honolulu and bypassed Molokai altogether, landing instead at Lahaina, on Maui, where the captain kept the exiles locked in the ship's hold for a day while his men drank beer in town. Eventually, Sheriff Peter Treadway managed to roust the crew back into service. On another occasion, the captain charged kokuas $1 each for passage to the colony, and he seized their belongings as ransom until they handed over the fare. Two weeks after that incident, on April 13, the captain arrived on the Kalawao side of the peninsula in a fury. Unwilling to wait while whaleboats ferried seven new exiles to shore, he forced them to leap overboard. The crew tossed the patients' belongings into the ocean, pulled anchor, and the *Warwick* was gone again, less than twenty minutes after she had appeared.

Fed up with such episodes, the board decided to purchase the *Warwick* and install a new captain. Edwin Jones, the *Warwick*'s owner, set a price of $975. Having already paid $1,000 to charter the ship, the board considered Jones's price absurdly high. But no other ship owner was willing to accept lepers aboard his vessel. Jones was paid, and the *Warwick* was given over to a new captain. When the schooner next reached Honolulu, an inspector discovered that the *Warwick*'s hull was peeling free and that she was rotting from the inside out—it would cost an additional $800 to keep her seaworthy. As Rudolph Meyer had once warned, the *Warwick* was proving to be a colossal blunder.

The population of Kalawao now exceeded one hundred patients and several dozen kokuas. All clamored for food and supplies. Hoping to appease the most vocal of the exiles, Lepart slaughtered some of the animals the board had sent as breeding stock. Carving up an ox, several goats, and two horses, he portioned out the meat. But, he wrote anxiously, "they are not satisfied." Lepart reported that the population was now "almost unmanageable" and "always ready to mutiny." Some of the patients seemed to delight in terrorizing Lepart, rushing toward him with arms outstretched, threatening to wrap him in an embrace and smear their faces against his. Lepart began to spend his days hidden in his cottage, with his gun loaded and ready.

On the afternoon of June 11 a gang of thirty-six patients and kokuas advanced on Lepart's home. They shouted for him to come out. Lepart crept onto his porch. The mob demanded that Lepart hand over all the food and supplies in his possession. If he did not, they would beat him, bite him, and then drive him from Kalawao. Lepart responded by threatening to shoot any person who challenged him. The standoff lasted several hours. Eventually several settlers loyal to the resident superintendent convinced the others to back down. But Lepart knew the peace would not last. "Alone as I am among about 100 of these individuals it is very difficult to bring them back again to order," he wrote. Because no punishment could exceed the awfulness of exile, the patients feared nothing. Lepart believed the only effective threat was to send troublemakers to a tiny uninhabitable island south of Maui called Kahoolawe. He asked the board, Can we exile the exiles?

The path of sacrifice and piety that Louis Lepart once sought was lost to him now, vanished in a thicket of wounded souls. Fear hardened his actions. Assembling the exiles, he announced that he had been made magistrate for the district, with the power to arrest and imprison them. At Lepart's request, the board had a cage of steel and wood built in Honolulu and shipped to the colony to use as a jail. Its arrival, he noted, "produced a good impression on the lepers; they are now convinced that they are not out of the law's reach. Moreover the sight of the handcuffs you sent me and which I did not fail to show them, convinced them of the truth." Selecting eight of "the most quiet and laborious lepers," Lepart formed a constabulary. He assigned them to nightly patrols of Kalawao, with three of the lawmen stationed among the struggling crops to prevent looting.

Indulging the exiles had become irksome to Lepart. He asked that the board no longer purchase poi and beef and bread to cover the food shortages. "I have no doubt that one or two months on short allowance will do much good," he wrote. "If they refuse to work cultivating taro, etc., etc., they must feel the consequences; hunger and hardship must teach them to do their duty." If the board kept sending food, Lepart announced, it would only "help them in their laziness."

Six boatloads of exiles landed on the peninsula during the month of July, increasing the patient population to 127. Soon the first foreign lepers arrived, two Chinese men. A popular theory held by the Hawaiians was that the Chinese—known as *Pake* in Hawaiian—had brought leprosy to the islands, and the disease was often referred to as *mai Pake,* the Chinese sickness. Patients promptly chased the two foreigners from Kalawao. Lepart wrote, "Circumstances force me to build a house apart from the natives, who are afraid of the Chinese ones without reason, but I am not able to put them right."

As the community swelled, it continued to stratify. At Kalihi Hospital, the first patients to present themselves to Dr. Edward Hoffmann for treatment were mostly destitute, villagers who sought a free cure for their disease. Within a few months, however, the sweeps began to trap suspects from other classes, including the wealthy. Hawaiians with sufficient money or influence could forestall exile for a time, and the rich were allowed to indulge in home remedies or private physicians. But eventually even these maneuvers failed, and agents arrived to escort the sick person to Kalihi. Political influence could buy a longer stay at the hospital than that afforded a poor villager, but even that reprieve eventually came to an end. For white foreigners, the wheels turned most slowly. Dr. Charles Guillou diagnosed John Boehle, a German who had been examined three times previously for leprosy, with the disease on May 14, 1866. The board released him.

Among those already at Kalawao, status was conferred in several ways. Wealth was the most powerful badge, and by early summer a number of well-to-do patients moved among the population. Their money made life incrementally more manageable. They could purchase extra food, either from their fellow exiles or on the sly from merchants in Kalaupapa, and affluent relatives sent blankets, lamps, oil, sugar, and tea—things that the strapped board did not adequately supply. The rich could hire kokuas to build or repair their cottages, tend crops, cut and carry firewood. Not long after they arrived, the two Chinese patients were employed as cooks, a situation that proved satisfactory as long as the foreigners left the village by nightfall.

For patients without money, it was better to be a longtime exile than a recent one. Survival bestowed status, and men such as Kahauliko and Lae carried authority that the others lacked. The downside was the rising mortality rate among the longtimers. Just when the community grew large enough to merit a pecking order, the early patients began to die. Of the original twelve patients, four would not live out the first year. Lae passed away that summer, on July 24, 1866.

Yet another emblem of rank was the possession of a woman or a child. Both were still rare in the colony. The stowaway boy had been discovered by Lepart and placed aboard the *Warwick,* bound for Honolulu. Later, Lepart remarked that such mishaps "might be avoided if the Board was to list the number and names of the leprous sent to Molokai, in order to avoid errors in the future shipping of patients." The women and children who remained in Kalawao often found protection among exiles who were blood relatives or members of the informal extended clans that many Hawaiians claimed. If they were truly alone, however, they were fair game. Children were valuable commodities, as servants and sexual objects. Women could also be taken for personal use, raped, or sold to another for food or a draw of liquor. Patients were not the only players in this harsh game. Kokuas took chattel or enforced the aggressions of their patient relative. As in a prison yard, power soon gravitated to those brutal enough to wield it.

On July 30, 1866, Lepart scribbled a note to Theodore Heuck about conditions in the colony. "The lepers begin to feel the consequences of their folly for not having planted taro in the last 7 months. . . . I believe that before two weeks more there will be no taro left." Heuck took his pen and slashed a line beneath "two weeks" and "no taro left." He was stunned. These people were wards of the government. If they starved to death, the board would be blamed.

Over several animated meetings, the board debated the emergency. "Do you mean we will have to feed them?" one member asked. "They must fully understand that they must work to maintain themselves." Dr. Ferdinand Hutchison, a forty-seven-year-old from Edinburgh, Scotland, believed responsibility for the crisis should shift to the exiles themselves. Hutchison declared that an ethical rot accompanied leprosy's signature physical rot. Describing the first months of exile, he later wrote, "The terrible disease which afflicts the Lepers seems to cause among them as great a change in their moral and mental organization as in their physical constitution: so far from aiding and assisting their weaker brethren, the strong took possession of everything, devoured and destroyed the large quantity of food on the lands, and altogether refused to replant anything." Hutchison added, "In fact, most of those in whom the disease had progressed considerably showed the greatest thoughtlessness and heartlessness."

It had been Hutchison who had first proposed the Kalaupapa peninsula as the site for the colony, having spied the plain while canvassing the island as a circuit judge. Professional men in Hawaii at the time often assumed multiple roles, and Hutchison was no exception. After sixteen years in the islands, his résumé included stints as a surgeon, a magistrate, the founder of a sugar mill, and president of the board of health. He was primarily a politician, however. Hutchison currently served as minister of the interior, and was known for his garbled public pronouncements. Reacting to one mangled declaration, the *Hawaiian Gazette* published the advice that Hutchison abandon his office, retreat to a public school, and learn to "write passable grammar when he entertains the public with letters." After sitting in on a legislative session in 1866, Mark Twain—who was sketching a Hawaii primer for the *Sacramento Union*—reduced the bland and haughty Hutchison to a caricature. "He has sandy hair, sandy mustache, sandy complexion—is altogether one of the sandiest men I ever saw, so to speak: is a tall, stoop-shouldered, middle-aged, lowering-browed, intense-eyed, irascible man, and looks like he might have his little prejudices and partialities."

Dr. Hutchison's theory on leper amorality was one such bias. When a board member raised the possibility that bad behavior was the result of the misery of exile, the president silenced him. Hutchison returned the dialogue to the immediate dilemma. Costs were already out of control, and now it seemed that the government would be required to, as Hutchison wrote, "supply absolutely for the future all the wants of these people." The budget did not allow for that. The board's biennial funding "was already heavily drained upon," with the greatest single expense being the troublesome *Warwick.* Of the original appropriation, with which the board was to maintain the hospital at Kalihi, the colony on Molokai, and pay for the apprehension and examination of all suspects, only $700 remained.

As the money slipped away, each board meeting dissolved into argument. Most often, the debate split between members such as Hutchison, who were attuned to the politics of public health, and those members for whom medicine remained the highest ideal, such as William Hillebrand. When Hutchison suggested that they find a way to cut costs, Dr. Hillebrand exploded, "Insufficiency of means can never be a just reason for half-measures, the work is urgent and must be done!"

Hutchison was determined to save money, however. He suggested Kalihi Hospital be closed, and all suspects sent immediately to Kalawao. A few healthy people falling through the cracks was an acceptable risk. Hutchison also thought that kokuas were a drain on resources and should no longer be admitted to the colony. Although Hillebrand managed to talk down most of these suggestions, Hutchison's politics and economizing continued to define segregation policy and made life in the colony more crippling than it already was. Hutchison might have been more sensitive to the exiles' plight had he become aware of one distressing fact: his son Ambrose was already infected with leprosy.

Order

(Population 106)

Exile began as a list. "I forward you six lepers (or such as are supposed to be such) and I have enclosed a bill of charges for services rendered," wrote a deputy sheriff to the board of health, before closing with the postscript, "I think I shall send another as soon as I can get him, the police are after him." Another sheriff wrote to Theodore Heuck, "I send this day . . . 16 supposed lepers, i.e. 6 women and 10 men." Dr. David Lee reported with a long list of suspects, adding, "It is a fearful thing that the number is so great." The marshal of the islands, William Cooper Parke, wrote, "I beg to enclose herewith a list of the names and places of residence of persons on the islands of Hawaii, Maui, Molokai, Lanai & Oahu reported to me by my several deputies as having the disease known as Mai Pake or Leprosy."

Rosters of suspects ricocheted around the islands, followed by the suspects themselves, bound for Kalihi Hospital. Teachers reported students, neighbors volunteered neighbors, and, in rare cases, family turned in family. Jealousy, envy, fear, and ignorance contributed to the list. Businessmen whispered to the sheriff that a rival had leprosy, and spurned lovers betrayed the object of their unreturned desire. Anything abnormal drew suspicion. The victims of venereal disease, whose skin erupted and grew discolored with the effects of the malady, filled the lists, as did the deranged. A bout with psoriasis or eczema could land a person on the list, or the bite from a poisonous insect. Indulgers in the home-brew narcotic known as *awa* expanded the lists, since the habitual awa drinker "becomes emaciated, and the skin is covered, as in leprosy, with large scales, which fall off, and leave lasting white spots, which often become ulcers," the writer Charles Nordhoff noted. Physical oddity could also result in being mistakenly hustled off to Kalihi Hospital. One day Dr. David Lee spotted a forty-year-old Hawaiian named Kepapu limping along the road, the large toe on his right foot missing and the surrounding area inflamed. Lee scratched Kepapu's name on the list, launching him on the path to Molokai. But Kepapu did not have the disease—a hog had bit off the toe.

Once a person appeared on the list, the gears of bureaucracy took hold.

The board of health tracked the name to an address and mailed a notice, instructing the suspect to appear at Kalihi Hospital for an exam. Each recipient was to travel from his home to the principal seaport on his island, and there the local sheriff would arrange transport to Honolulu and Kalihi Hospital. If the disease was proved, the person would be banished. The system was imperfect. Several times each month suspects slipped into the harbor towns and camped on the docks. When the sheriff moved among them, he often discovered the majority showed no trace of ill health. "I fear very much that the list has not been made out judiciously," Sheriff Peter Treadway wrote to Theodore Heuck. "I have seen two persons today who are on the list and who no more have the leprosy or any other cutaneous disease than you or I have." He was required by law to ship them anyway. Of eighteen suspects sent from Lahaina on one occasion, fourteen were returned as healthy, a common occurrence that mocked the board's effort to protect the well from the sick. "How these people came to be reported as infected puzzles me," Treadway wrote. "It shows that the assessors did not look closely into the matters, to make such reports. For the idea of sending a man or a woman who showed no symptoms in a vessel with bad cases of Leprosy appeared to me worse than useless for it gives them double chance to get the disease."

As the season deepened, bringing rain and cold to Kalawao, a lawyer named J. H. Hao found himself on the list, and a man named Muolo, and an educated half-white Hawaiian named William Humphreys. All three men soon arrived on Molokai. There the exile population continued to expand. Those who were able applied themselves to the routines of the colony: turning soil for planting, tending the animal stock, throwing hand-stitched nets into the surf with a prayer that the net return wiggling with silvery moi. The strongest workers cleared land of blackened rock and created one hundred acres of field. They lay down seed, but it would take months before any crop was edible. In the interim the settlers scavenged fern root for food and slid seaweed into their pots. Still, they starved. "Had the present number of lepers come immediately after the place was left by the former people there would probably not have been any scarcity of food now," Rudolph Meyer explained to the board, in response to Ferdinand Hutchison's angry letter demanding answers as to why the place was not yet self-sufficient. Meyer assured the board that it would only have to feed the settlers for six more months until the harvest was ripe. Then, he insisted, things would proceed according to plan.

At present, however, only two cases of hard flour biscuits remained for food in the colony. Lepart continued to slaughter the male goats and oxen, but spared the females to grow the herd. The meat lasted only a few days. At night the bolder exiles snuck into the homes of others and stole their rations. Plots of sweet potatoes, still not ripe, were rooted free and carried off by those uninterested in labor. The aggrieved gathered a petition, asking that a pair of patients be expelled for thievery. Another petition followed, accusing two patients of stealing food and threatening to kill and eat the colony's breeding stock. The letter named the men: Hao and Muolo. Lepart's constables arrested the pair and clamped them with cuffs. After several days had passed, Lepart reported that the prisoners "beseech forgiveness" and "it brings back the undeniable conclusion that irons make them very humble." Lepart intended for the men to remain shackled for a month, but "in light of the acute sufferings, swellings and grazes on the wrists and the legs, will not be able to keep them there more than 2 weeks." Even so, he wrote, "order has been restored in Kalawao."

As Louis Lepart and his constables attempted to impose discipline on the colony, a criminal class arose in opposition, composed of thieves, gamblers, rapists, and men who made moonshine from the waxy leaves of the ti plant. Other castes also formed. In Kalawao, people identified themselves by their specific skill, as farmers, fishermen, or herdsmen. Although no one had medical training, several settlers presented themselves as nurses, and others toiled as gravediggers when the nursing had failed. Those with education penned letters for the illiterate, and several patients with legal training adjudicated disputes. Faith overlay order on the exiles too. By the end of 1866 the colony held thirty-five persons who considered themselves Protestant Congregational, and who had been active church members prior to banishment. They asked for permission to assemble as a new body, and at the annual meeting of Congregational churches in Honolulu, the group was "released to form a church by themselves at Kalawao." The Reverend Anderson O. Forbes, an American missionary who served a station on topside Molokai, was named as pastor. On December 23 he made his way down the cliff and called the fledgling church to order.

Lepart had offered the largest building in the settlement for their worship house, a battered thatched-roof structure whose dirt floor was littered with rubbish and weeds and brambles. To clear the brush, congregation members lit a small fire and promptly burned down their chapel. When the Reverend Forbes arrived, they gathered instead around a patient's hut with a small veranda. Forbes led the Lord's Prayer and then christened the makeshift church Siloama, after the Bible's healing spring. The congregation then elected nine deacons, including Muolo and Hao. Both men still showed bruises from Louis Lepart's shackles.

The Reverend Forbes brought two men with him to Kalawao, an Austrian physician named Bechtinger and a photographer named King. Although visitors required the board's permission to enter the colony, King and Bechtinger had slipped past Lepart with the assurance that they were men of science come to lend aid. Only afterward did it occur to Lepart that Dr. Bechtinger's request—that Lepart race ahead and instruct the exiles not to touch him under any circumstances—was odd behavior for a man of medicine. Lepart also noticed that Bechtinger's main concern was composing tableaux for King's camera, featuring himself in thoughtful concentration alongside the grateful grotesques. Lepart realized: this will end badly.

After Bechtinger departed, the doctor promptly supplied the *Pacific Commercial Advertiser* with a sensational firsthand account of life in Kalawao. "There they are," Bechtinger reported, "thrown together, in all stages of disease, with no medicines, no physician, no comforts—furnished only with the absolute necessities for keeping soul and body together—AND PUT ON STARVATION RATIONS AT THAT—a mass of seething, festering corruption, rolling to death." The Reverend Forbes also published his own mordant observations of the colony, writing of "human infamy, and of official neglect!" and of hearing the cries of "the emaciated and ghastly inhabitants of this place, like the wailing of damned souls in hopeless hate, in the hell of the divine poet Dante."

The dispatches touched off a firestorm in the Honolulu press. "Here is a clear impartial statement of the Molokai leper hospital, reflecting sadly on the Hawaiian government," the *Advertiser* stated in an editorial. Editors knew exactly who was at fault: Ferdinand Hutchison. The president of the board of health, the *Advertiser* announced, "is responsible for the condition of these lepers . . . the whole plan of isolating the lepers in such an out-of-the-way place on Molokai was a great mistake." Hoping to refute the criticism, Rudolph Meyer sent a letter to the paper explaining that conditions were not as poor as the visitors had reported. "There is no doubt that many of the lepers are far more comfortable in the settlement than they were in their former homes," Meyer wrote. But in a second heated editorial, the *Advertiser* pointed out that Hutchison "has been to the spot, has witnessed [the patients'] misery and heard their cries. Let him now come forward, state the facts, correct the abuses, and collect these doomed and dying wretches into some asylum where they themselves may enjoy at least the hope of recovery."

Hutchison quickly arranged for the board to hire a former British army officer named Donald Walsh, along with his wife, Caroline, to build and staff a hospital at Kalawao. Mr. Walsh was also to form a small school, "to keep the children occupied" until they die, as Walsh later wrote. They would be paid $75 a month. It was more money than the impoverished couple had seen in years. When they packed to leave for Kalawao, Donald and Caroline Walsh discovered that all their belongings fit into one small chest, with room left for their copy of *All for Jesus,* by Father William Faber. The book of homilies was well used. By 1867 the couple had lost seven children to a variety of deaths, and only a son still survived. William Walsh was an excitable young man, emotionally fragile and prone to sudden violence. He came along to the colony too.

Their home in Kalawao was a two-room cottage. The living room served as a dining room, kitchen, dispensary, and even a guest room. One visitor later recalled the mood in the hardscrabble home. "I remember the charity, the loving kindness, and the deep poverty of these gracious people," he wrote. "I remember their efforts at merriment: how they tried to make light of their sorrowful strait; but their very mirth was pathetic." At the time, the physicians on the board of health could not state with certainty how a person became infected with leprosy. Walsh was told that if he and his family kept clean, disinfected their hands, prepared their own food, and avoided using any item handled by a patient, they should be safe. Louis Lepart followed such measures without fail, as did Rudolph Meyer on his visits. Neither man had become infected.

Immediately upon arriving in Kalawao, Donald Walsh began to utilize his army training. He reconnoitered, inventorying huts, blankets, tools, and rations. Walsh then surveyed the colonists themselves. His reports were not optimistic. "There are some desperate characters here among these people," Walsh wrote on February 27, 1867. His first order of business was construction of a proper camp. Walsh envisioned an orderly assemblage of buildings kept separate from the surrounding chaos by picket fence and rock wall. Its boundaries would be one hundred yards on each side. Within this square would sit the school, the hospital, barracks for boy and girl exiles, a food warehouse, and paddocks for animal stock, such as calves and kids.

Walsh's scheme launched with such militaristic vigor that the settlers assumed he was the new *luna,* or overseer, come to replace Lepart. Walsh encouraged the misunderstanding. He began to issue orders to Lepart as if the Frenchman were his subordinate, as Lepart soon complained to Hutchison. "I do not want to be working like a slave under Mr. Walsh's commands," Lepart wrote. After the board admonished Walsh, he insisted that he would try to "cultivate a good feeling" with Lepart. But friction between the men continued, and Lepart grew frustrated by the increasing labor the booming colony demanded. "My situation is quite different from my assumptions at the beginning," he wrote to Hutchison. "I have hardly time to take some necessary rest, being occupied from morning to evening for the settlement." Lepart demanded a raise. When the board refused, Lepart resigned. Hutchison named Donald Walsh as resident superintendent. Before departing Kalawao, Lepart happily handed his replacement the materials of his office: seven law books and nine pairs of iron handcuffs.

Crime grew more frequent, the lawlessness fueled by moonshine and the certitude that the days were never changing. More than two thousand miles southeast of Molokai, the painter Paul Gauguin later exiled himself to an empty forest in Tahiti and felt seized by wildness, even as his eczema and syphilis transformed him into something the locals took for a leper. He wrote, "Civilization leaves me bit by bit and I begin to think simply. . . . I function in an animal way, freely—with the certainty of the morrow [being] like today." Physical escape from the daily repetition of Kalawao was almost impossible, although several patients attempted it nonetheless, only to drown at sea or fall from the height of the cliff. Emotional escape, however, came more easily.

Patients brewed alcohol from ti root and sugarcane, or boiled it from molasses. From roots of the awa plant, which grew abundantly along the cliff, settlers prepared batches of narcotic, gathering root in the mouth, chewing vigorously, then spitting the pulp into a bowl to be strained through coconut husk. "The taste is very nauseous, disagreeable to the last degree," wrote Charles Nordhoff in 1874. "But its effects are particularly pleasant." Sleep overtook the user, and "delicious dreams charm this long torpor." Repeated use reversed the effect, however, producing a "strong desire to skip about," Nordhoff observed, "although one can not for a moment balance himself on his legs." As he made his daily rounds, Donald Walsh saw troubling evidence of awa abuse, which he reported to the board. "I am sorry to acquaint you that for some time past there has been much drunkenness among the lepers and that the people from the outside visit the settlement and come out frequently drunk and noisy." Even more distressing than the drinking was the prostitution that Walsh feared was occurring. One morning he discovered a healthy woman hidden in a patient's house; the man was apparently keeping her as a concubine for his teenaged son. Such an arrangement shocked the pious Walsh. Gathering a dozen children from the school, Walsh armed them with "tins, kettles, and saucepans" and the party proceeded to "drum her out of the settlement." She snuck back the next day.

Often William Walsh, the troubled son of Donald Walsh, trailed after his father on his administrative rounds. Believing that William required some responsibility, Donald appointed him as a constable. Yet William's changeable moods frightened the patients. Rudolph Meyer warned the board that William was dangerous, and Dr. Hutchison instructed Walsh to dismiss his son as constable and confiscate the pistol he carried. Walsh replied that William was merely passing through a difficult phase.

At night the family soaked biscuits in goat's milk, ate the simple meal, and then brought out their rosaries and the battered book of prayers. Donald Walsh's eyesight was failing, and so Caroline read aloud by oil lamp, her husband's eyes closed behind glasses of double green. Afterward she took dictation while Donald composed letters to the board, describing adultery, alchoholism, and whoring in Kalawao, and other acts of immorality too "fearful to contemplate." Walsh lamented how sad it was that no clergyman was available to prepare the exiles for "that eternity to which they are all so rapidly hurrying along."

Every week Donald Walsh logged deaths among the settlers. In his first weeks in Kalawao he reported that eight had died: "a fearful mortality which I hope I shall never again have to record." Since lumber was precious, the deceased were buried in the older tradition, roped with knees to chest, then dropped into a circular hole. Long in disuse, the Given Grave began to again swallow bodies. Walsh soon found that the sick in the colony were perishing with remarkable ease: of the 179 persons exiled in the first twenty-four months of segregation, 47 were dead. Yet the disease was not wholly to blame. During the same period at Kalihi Hospital, where Dr. Hoffmann kept the ill warm and well-fed, 326 persons had been admitted, and only 16 passed away.

At Kalihi, Edward Hoffmann had discovered that several minor factors greatly influenced the condition of a person with leprosy. Foremost among these were nutrition, cleanliness, and climate. Supplied with a "generous diet" and good water and settled in clement surroundings, they "greatly improved in appearance . . . and the usual apparent despondency observable in the countenance seemed to have given place to a happier feature," Hoffmann wrote. "But 24 hours of cool, rainy, and blustering weather would soon make the symptoms reappear more prominent than ever." For people with leprosy to have any chance at survival, Hoffmann realized, they needed ample food, good shelter, ready water, and a locale that was warm and dry. In Kalawao the sick had none of these things.

When Donald Walsh performed a hut-to-hut census that spring, assessing the health and living situation of every outcast, he discovered a population perched on the razor's edge between life and loss. "This house is cold," he remarked of one hovel with three occupants, "filthy and wretched." At another cottage he found a man and a child "advanced in leprosy," each with a single pair of pants and one "old blanket" to clutch for warmth. He itemized their possessions: a pot, knife, oil lamp, and two spoons.

In hut number 17, where J. D. Kahauliko lived, Walsh saw that the original exile had managed to accumulate "a good deal of necessaries" during his time in the colony. But even Kahauliko, who had seniority over every other resident, could not secure a home free of abundant "leaks." Neither could the church elders Hao or Muolo, although in possessions each seemed better equipped than most. Some settlers, in fact, appeared awash in luxuries. "By what means I know not, but the men in Houses No 14 & 15 seem to want for nothing from the soft slippers to hair-oil." Walsh eventually discovered the source of the bounty: Louis Lepart. The Frenchman had taken up residence near Kalaupapa and was sneaking into Kalawao to broker the sale of rations for the exiles. Lepart would collect food and supplies from the patients, then sell them in Kalaupapa, pocketing a commission. Often the goods were stolen, and the money ended up in the hands of the thieves. The black market further drained the colony's dwindling resources.

Long-simmering animosities between Walsh and Lepart now erupted daily, and Walsh wrote furious letters blaming his predecessor for his inability to achieve order in Kalawao. "It appears to have been his wish to leave everything in as bad a state as possible for his successors," Walsh complained to Hutchison. The feud fed odd alliances. When mobs formed to challenge Walsh over food distribution or the division of labor, Walsh would peer into the crowd and see Lepart. Onetime adversaries, the exiles and Lepart had become comrades, united in the war against Donald Walsh.

On October 15, 1867, a schooner approached Kalawao, and the shore filled with spectators. Boat day, which occurred once a week on average, was eagerly anticipated. When storms accompanied the ship, boat day offered sport, as newcomers fought the surf to land; in fair weather it granted a reprieve from boredom. Boats brought the possibility of new lovers or friends, fresh meat, bags of bread, bolts of calico, and damp copies of the island press. At the end of August the board had furnished stamps to the exiles for the first time, sanctioning correspondence. Settlers often sent letters home via Rudolph Meyer, who collected the mail packet from a kokua who climbed to the top of the cliff; Meyer then sent the correspondence to Honolulu on one of the regular interisland ships that serviced topside Molokai. Mail for the colony sometimes returned the same way, although usually it arrived aboard the *Warwick*, and on boat day the rocks teemed with settlers awaiting word from home.

The crowd studied every incoming rowboat with interest. Colonists governed by compassion looked to see if any newcomer was a friend or family member, or a stranger who needed aid. But the audience also included the criminally inclined, who scanned for casks of molasses, which could be stolen and used to brew beer, or for an orphan girl with a comely face, to take as a sexual slave. The cruelest delighted in terrifying the frightened arrivals. As a child or woman approached the shore by whaleboat, men with faces terribly damaged by disease would aim a gnarled hand toward them and shout, "You are mine." If the schooner arrived at night, the scene unfolded by torchlight, amplifying the horror. Often someone would seek to terrorize the newcomers further and greeted them with a whispered warning: "In this place there is no law."

But the arrival of October 15 was disappointing by boat day standards. Only a single man disembarked, the German merchant John Boehle. At first the people onshore mistook him for a tourist, or a government official. As he drew nearer, they recognized him as one of their own. Boehle moved into Lepart's former home, and Donald Walsh soon named him assistant superintendent, having found Boehle "a man with whom I think I could get on well." Continuing the effort to salvage the colony's reputation, Ferdinand Hutchison had decided to allow Boehle, the first white man to be exiled, to operate a small general store in Kalawao. The board was taking significant labors to silence its critics. A hospital and schoolhouse had been built in the settlement, slates sent for the students, bundles of tea and rice and flour provided, and a case of medicine shipped over, mostly Epsom salts and citrine ointment and a patent remedy called Doctor Wright's Pills—ineffective remedies, but Hutchison knew such things were symbolic anyway.

Boehle was to stock some of these goods in his store, and the rest was for distribution. Livestock also received reinforcement, but logistics bedeviled the operation. Often when Rudolph Meyer arranged for sheep or cattle to be driven down from topside Molokai, a confused or clumsy beast would leap from the cliff and lead the others over the side. Shipping the animals offered no better solution. In June a schooner had arrived with 306 sheep, but 63 had expired during the hard voyage, 50 died shortly after landing, and eight escaped altogether. When the schooner brought replacement animals, the captain refused to risk his whaleboats shuttling the sheep in the heavy surf. His crew began tipping the animals over the side. Frantic, Donald Walsh begged every man within earshot to swim out and tow the floundering beasts to land. Almost the entire shipment drowned—or arrived so traumatized that they were butchered on the spot. The meat was quickly lost to seabirds and crabs and the underfed dogs that many patients kept as pets. After an agent of the board visited to assess the situation, his main recommendation was that all dogs in the colony be killed, and each household given a lamb instead—later to be slaughtered for mutton. "If they must have pets," he wrote, "let them be useful ones."

With the reinforcement of Boehle, Donald Walsh believed he could finally create a functioning community. "Mr. Boehle and myself will do our utmost to bring things to what we think they should be," he wrote to Hutchison. Although Boehle was already weak from the disease and often bedridden, the two men slowly began to roust predators and adulterers, shame the drunkards, and pressure the idle to work. When Walsh discovered that several boys had sabotaged the colony's only oxcart to escape the chore of gathering firewood, he knotted lengths of rope and whipped the young men. After finding a female patient in bed with one of the schoolboys, he thrashed both and sent the woman fleeing, screaming Bible passages after her. Still, many of the healthier young men refused to work, and Walsh reported that he felt powerless to force the issue: "If I were to handcuff and tie the boys the place would be stormed and the parties released."

Leaving the moral rescue of these youth to his wife, Walsh turned his focus to the licentious adults. He began to identify the wicked and pen a blotter of their sins. Of a man named Kameo and his wife Walsh wrote, "They are probably the most depraved married people living here—their house is the rendezvous of the vicious from within and formerly from without." If Walsh found a man abusing a child, he removed the child; if he saw a woman selling herself, he humiliated her with scripture; if he noticed someone drunk in the full warmth of day, Walsh dragged him or her to the fields to burn away the alcohol in work. Every few days a dispatch from Donald Walsh landed on Dr. Hutchison's desk, describing one sinner after another wrenched from immorality and put to constructive labor. In truth, however, only a small percentage of the settlers were lawbreakers or laggards—most spent their days simply trying to survive. And although Walsh believed himself to be the lone instrument of the Lord in Kalawao, the colony had practicing Catholics, Mormons, and Congregationalists, these last attended by the Reverend Forbes, who continued to make regular visits. To Walsh, however, the souls of the exiles depended solely on him.

Such self-prescribed salvation was exhausting. The Walsh family labored, according to one visitor, from "dawn to dusk" and "a hundred times a day were these gentle people called to the door to minister to the wants of some pitiful creature." In time, however, their effort brought some success. "The health of the settlement is in general good and I am happy to observe a better disposition among our people than has hitherto existed," Walsh wrote on December 10. Contributing to the calm was the temporary absence of new arrivals. In September the *Warwick* had wrecked on the rocks of Kauai, and the board was finding it difficult to contract a replacement vessel while the schooner underwent repairs. Shipments of patients stalled after the twenty-second load, which had carried the 179th exile to Molokai. Eight months passed before they resumed.

In the lull, Kalihi Hospital filled to capacity, straining Dr. Hoffmann's facility. Though Ferdinand Hutchison had intended to close Kalihi once Walsh erected a hospital at Kalawao, the board tabled the action because "of fresh armies of lepers now emerging." Suspects no longer came so willingly to Kalihi, however. Stories from the colony had spread, a sheriff on Kauai complained in April 1868, and people "seem to have a holy horror of it." This fear complicated Dr. Hoffmann's job as well. At Kalihi Hospital, patients desperate to avoid a boat trip to Molokai began to burrow beneath the fence that ringed the grounds.

Now edited by a man even less sympathetic to the board than his predecessor, the *Pacific Commercial Advertiser* warned of "several lepers at large among us" having fled from "that farce at Kalihi." Again, Hutchison caught the blame: "It would seem that the whole system employed to prevent the spread of this king of terrors (for it is worse than death) is little better than useless," the editorial declared. "From all quarters . . . we hear the repeated echo that the leprosy is spreading at a fearful rate, and the groans of the poor creatures, hid away in huts and caves, are heard night and day praying for relief. Something must be done, or five years hence will see a thousand lepers where now there are a hundred, and ten years later the island of Molokai will become the grave yard of the Hawaiian people."

As pressure on the board increased, Hutchison struggled to focus on the positive. He incorporated Walsh's brightening dispatches into his biennial report to the king, relying on Walsh's letters for color: "As may easily be imagined, one of the most serious troubles . . . had been the difficulty of maintaining order. Drunkenness, pilferings, immorality, and general insubordination were very prevalent . . . and great orgies took place. But the Board is happy to report for the last few months a very different state of things has existed." The change, Hutchison wrote, was entirely the work of Mr. Walsh.

When the report was printed in the newspapers and found its way to Kalawao, the settlers were livid. Hutchison had infantilized them, made them out as misbehaving children who required the stern hand of a moral father. "Their poor weak heads are quite turned by the notice taken of them," Walsh wrote to Hutchison. Almost immediately, the exiles began to rebel. All work stopped, and patients spent the days in clandestine meetings, debating their fate and their reputation. In one aspect, Hutchison's report had succeeded where Walsh had failed: it united the community. The small clique of lawbreakers so vividly described in Walsh's bulletins were now embraced by the remainder of the population, as the entire community turned its wrath toward Walsh. The settlers massed and demanded better rations, warmer clothing, decent shelter. When Walsh waved away their ultimatum, the mob was commandeered by several of the most ruthless patients and ambushed Walsh near Kalawao Creek.

"Don't let him away!" the gang yelled, according to Walsh's account. "Keep him fast!" Four exiles, including Hao, "talked of killing me." The men threatened to cripple Walsh as they were crippled, snapping his arms and legs and leaving him to die in the rocks. Walsh managed to flee. That evening, another mob surrounded Walsh's house, trapping his family inside. Walsh stood on the porch and defiantly screamed, "I know your evil intentions and I am not afraid!"

To prevent the resident superintendent from being murdered, Ferdinand Hutchison was forced to board a fast ship to Kalawao. There he outfitted the colony's eight constables with fresh firearms and had them assemble the settlers. As he later reported, Dr. Hutchison announced that "henceforth their revolts would be severely punished." Before departing, Hutchison made a quick tour of the colony and discovered four misdiagnosed children living among the exiles, and arranged for them to return to Honolulu. Midway in the crossing, the captain brought the children on deck and ordered them to strip. He threw their tainted clothes into the sea.

In the aftermath of the rebellion Donald Walsh's health declined, and he began to lose his eyesight. When the exiles realized that Walsh's vision was failing, several of them became bolder in their defiance. The patient Hao, in particular, maintained a running battle with Walsh. Hao had many colleagues in his harassment of Walsh, however, including the half-Hawaiian William Humphreys, the son of a New Hampshire man who had settled on Maui. On arriving in the colony, Humphreys had joined the faithful of Siloama and even wrote to the press on behalf of the congregation, soliciting funds so that they could construct a proper church. "You must not think that all of us here are living in sin and degradation," Humphreys wrote. "That is not so. Our greatest longing is to make a memorial to God here . . . we are minded to put up this church and to call it by the name of Siloam's healing pool." Humphreys explained that "Deacon Muolo" had collected only $125.50 for the effort, and the job required more. "Is there not somewhere among you a good Samaritan?—one who will not look at us . . . and pass by on the other side?"

William Humphreys appeared to be a natural leader, a quality that initially impressed Donald Walsh. He wrote that soon after arriving in Kalawao, the newcomer had a large party of settlers working for him. Shrewd and well educated, Humphreys was, as Hao himself later wrote, "skilled at flattery and defense" and a man of "schemes." With his eyes milky and his strength ebbing, Walsh was no longer alert to what patients did behind the doors of their thatched cottages. But Caroline Walsh saw things her husband missed. She wrote that Humphreys engaged in gambling, bootlegging, assaults, and worse. His dwelling was a hothouse of sin, with all occupants participating. "Last night Humphries [*sic*] woman got drunk and abused a little half white girl shamefully," she wrote. "This is the second offense on the same girl." By the time Caroline Walsh reported this behavior to the board, however, Humphreys had become one of its regular correspondents, filing accounts of his aid to the exiles, and dropping hints that the ailing Mr. Walsh was no longer similarly able. Humphreys had also befriended John Boehle, taking a chair in Boehle's small store and watching with interest as the German grew increasingly weak. On October 4, 1868, one year after he arrived in Kalawao, Boehle passed away. Humphreys took over the store.

During the last twelve months of his life, Boehle had served as Donald Walsh's assistant. Now the position was vacant. Walsh had hoped that his son William could become assistant superintendent, and ultimately resident superintendent. He had tried to assign William tasks of increasing importance, to grow him into the role. But the younger Walsh's instability had only deepened during his time in Kalawao. Where once the patients had been bemused by William's strange antics, now they regarded him with dread. Several times he exploded in violence, attacking patients and destroying their cottages. Rudolph Meyer warned the board that William "has been quite deranged in mind since some time past, at times he is violent and dangerous at other times he is tranquil, and it may become necessary to confine him in an asylum to effect a cure."

Donald and Caroline Walsh decided to send William to Honolulu to be examined by Dr. William Hillebrand. "With what tenderness they spoke of their . . . boy and his infirmities," wrote one of Donald Walsh's acquaintances. "With what fearful hope they pictured his future." Their worries were well-founded. When Hillebrand completed his psychological report, it confirmed that William Walsh was mentally ill. In an anguished letter to Ferdinand Hutchison, Donald Walsh—who knew that he was dying—

asked that his wife not be burdened with the costs of his son's upkeep, "in the event of his being detained at an asylum."

As Donald Walsh's health grew critical, his son was allowed to return to the colony. On November 9, 1869, William Humphreys updated Ferdinand Hutchison on Donald Walsh's condition: "I am very sorry to have to report of Mr. Walsh's illness and I think he cannot live long." Humphreys suggested he be named superintendent. "It is the peoples wish," Humphreys declared, then boasted that because of his efforts the settlers were again planting crops and building houses and were always orderly: "Your Excellency would hardly know the place now." A few days later Donald Walsh, now fully blind, was led aboard a schooner to seek emergency medical care. William Walsh accompanied his father. As the ship neared Honolulu, Donald Walsh convulsed, locked stiff, and died, and the final fragment of his son's sanity tore free. The crew had to tie the berserk young man to the mast to keep him from harming himself.

The board of health did not name William Humphreys superintendent. They placed power instead with the widow Caroline Walsh, and appointed Humphreys as one of her assistants. The colony rapidly fell into chaos. That season, storms plowed across the peninsula, flattening the crops that had been planted for summer. Schooners could not land in the unsettled seas, and weeklong spells of bitter cold took hold, "causing a great deal of sickness amongst the people," Caroline Walsh wrote on February 25, 1870. Walsh was a delicate and insecure woman, unexpectedly marooned among almost two hundred unwell and angry people. After a lifetime of struggle she had only a dead husband, seven dead children, and an institutionalized son to show for her days on earth. Now fate had handed her another hard task, one for which she was woefully unprepared. "I am very sorry to inform you that the lepers in the settlement have this day broken out in a state of mutiny," she scribbled to Ferdinand Hutchison several weeks after taking command. Two patients had stormed the government store and stolen bags of rice, scattering it among a mob of forty agitated settlers. Later another mob formed, wielding torches and clubs, and screaming that they meant to kill "that white woman." William Humphreys, Walsh's chief of constables, was suspiciously absent during both melees.

Abetted by Humphreys, the crueler patients began to ceaselessly taunt Caroline Walsh, piercing her with words, she reported, "not fit to write." Humphreys's main proxy seemed to be a young Hawaiian named Kahoomiha. Caroline Walsh would awake at a noise and find he had slaughtered one of the settlement's milk cows or was standing in silent threat at the edge of her porch, just visible in the moonlight. She turned to the constables for help, but they were useless. Walsh complained that Kahoomiha brewed liquor "stronger than brandy" that sparked rebellions almost weekly. When she asked Humphreys to destroy the still, he refused. She wrote, "They are all jolly companions over the bottle."

Kahoomiha was thirty years old and only mildly touched by the disease. According to a letter Dr. David Lee sent to the board in August 1868, Kahoomiha's wife had died as a young woman, leaving him in charge of their seven-year-old daughter. After Kahoomiha was apprehended and taken to Kalihi Hospital, he pleaded to be allowed to remain and find some way of providing for the girl, who had no other means of support. If he was sent to Molokai, she would be orphaned and forced to the streets. Kahoomiha was shipped to Kalawao anyway. After he had arrived, Humphreys apparently took note of the young man's smoldering rage and decided to tap it for his own purposes. Just now, that meant aiming it at Caroline Walsh.

Several patients reported to the board that Humphreys paid Kahoomiha and a few others to create trouble. Humphreys would take his keys, unlock the government store, and then steal meat to bribe his partners. Walsh wrote of Humphreys "committing adultery with women, using force," and "committing rape on little girls, with fearless hands." Even men who had once been accomplices were wary of Humphreys now, alarmed at the brutal power he was amassing. "Oh dismiss him! Oh dismiss him!!" wrote Hao. "That he may not rule the lepra people and the Board of Health with a hard iron hand." Hao begged Hutchison not to reveal the author of the letter, apparently believing that Humphreys, who once sat alongside him during sermons, would slit his throat as he slept. In his entreaty for church funds, Humphreys had written, "Most of us were born in the Christian era . . . and we know that a village without a church is destitute, godless, pagan." Two years after he wrote those words, Siloama Chapel was completed, and its cast-iron bell rung in consecration. Yet even as the peals sounded, William Humphreys continued his unholy ways.

Ready to Believe

(Population 214)

"We were dropping, slipping, shambling down a sharp flank of the cliff, that cut the air like a flying buttress. By a series of irregular steps we descended, leaping from rock to rock when practicable, but often putting off our packs, sliding into the little ledge below, and then dragging the packs after us." So wrote one outsider, after braving the narrow switchback track that Rudolph Meyer had hacked into the cliff face several years earlier. "On each side of us was a dense growth of brush, a kind of natural parapet, over which we could hurl a stone a thousand feet into the sheer depths, but could not hear it strike. Sea-birds soared above us and below us; sometimes they hovered just over our heads, and eyed us curiously; then with a stroke of their powerful wings they would soar away, with a cry that was half fearful, half defiant." The initial step of the journey, the visitor wrote, was "like plunging into space."

In July 1870, Dr. William Hillebrand leaned over the precipice edge, peering down at the red-dirt calligraphy of Kalawao. He was determined to visit, for the first time, the place he had willed into being. Time was growing short. Hillebrand planned to leave Hawaii within the year, to return home to Europe.

Before Hillebrand departed, however, he wanted to do some "botanizing" on topside Molokai and visit his countryman Rudolph Meyer. When he arrived on the rugged, sparsely populated island, Hillebrand felt as if he had entered a distant world. "Molokai is a more isolated place than I imagined," Hillebrand wrote in wonder to Ferdinand Hutchison, a few days after landing on topside Molokai. Almost immediately he had fallen ill and convalesced at the Meyer homestead, self-medicating for five days until his color returned. Once the illness passed, Rudolph Meyer guided Hillebrand and his collecting partner, a Honolulu schoolboy named Lydgate, to the lip of the zigzag trail. Watch out for falling rocks, Meyer warned. Never solid, the path had become dangerously eroded; Meyer had already begun to survey spots where a safer trail into the colony might be cut. At present, however, there was only one route down.

Exertion from the descent quickly fogged Hillebrand's glasses, blinding him. He cried out to Lydgate, and the boy took the doctor's hand. They shuffled hesitantly downward. Midpoint along the trail, the pair came on a grisly discovery: a bloodied body. Lydgate later wrote that the man had apparently been "struck by a falling stone, started by someone higher on the trail, which came crashing down through the undergrowth, and hit him in the head, fracturing his skull badly and leaving him pretty badly mangled." It seemed probable that either Lydgate or Hillebrand had loosed the rock that struck the climber, and now Hillebrand rushed to attend the injured man. With some "simple instruments" he carried in his bag, the doctor trepanned the victim, opening a hole in the skull to relieve pressure from the swelling brain. Lydgate watched Hillebrand dress the wound and make the victim comfortable until help arrived. It was afternoon before Hillebrand and Lydgate continued. An hour later they reached the base of the cliff, paused to collect their breath, and began the final hike into the colony.

As Hillebrand and Lydgate approached Kalawao, a group of men galloped toward them on horseback. The exiles swung from their saddles and stepped forward, pausing to see if the visitors would offer their hands in greeting. Most did not. Lydgate watched the doctor, who moved forward smiling, shaking each outstretched palm. To Lydgate, these men seemed to be in fine health, although several had grips that had frozen closed, or a weakened arm that dangled uselessly. A few also moved with a curious, exaggerated stride, as if they were climbing phantom stairs. Although Hillebrand could not fully explain it to the boy, all these debilities were the consequence of nerve damage, a signature feature of leprosy.

During the previous few days, Hillebrand had attempted to describe to Lydgate what it meant to have leprosy. The boy should be prepared for the scenes that waited in the colony. But although Hillebrand was perhaps the most learned physician in the islands, he recognized that he knew alarmingly little about the precise workings of the disease. In time, physicians would begin to fathom the true nature of leprosy, but much of that understanding was still a hundred years distant. Had the knowledge been available to Hillebrand and the board of health, a tremendous amount of suffering would have been avoided. Leprosy, research would later reveal, was a chronic infectious disease caused by a specific germ. Contrary to the level of panic the disease elicited, it would prove to be among the least contagious of all communicable diseases. For someone to become infected, a number of uncommon circumstances had to exist, foremost being intimate contact with a person who had an active, or infectious, case of the disease in a form later to become known as lepromatous leprosy.

Despite common fears, skin-to-skin transmission of the germ was virtually impossible. Most often leprosy bacilli entered a body the way almost all germs did, through the nose or mouth, having exited an infected person during a cough or sneeze. Simple hygiene, such as hand washing, hugely reduced the risk of transmission—a precaution Hillebrand understood and stressed to Lydgate. If the leprosy bacilli did gain access to a fresh host, however, in most cases nothing at all occurred. An overwhelming majority of people, about 95 percent, had a natural immunity to leprosy. With these people the bacilli entered the body, floundered, and died, their host blissfully unaware.

If active bacilli did manage to locate a susceptible target, what happened next depended on the person's immune response. All germs have a primary task: to swiftly multiply. Leprosy bacilli, however, can remain dormant for as long as three decades, although incubation usually lasted between three and seven years. Until the germ became active, the person had no idea that he or she had caught the disease.

Once roused, leprosy attacked skin and nerves. Since the germ multiplied more easily at low temperature, about 93 degrees, it swarmed first to cool areas of the human body: earlobes, nasal passages, and eyes were favorite targets, as was the skin of the cheeks, shoulders, arms, and legs. When the germ struck at nerves, it concentrated at joints such as the knee, ankle, elbow, and wrist, where the nerve typically lay atop bone and near the surface. In four cases out of five, the infected person's immune system was strong enough to blunt the attack, and these people developed a lesser form of the disease that would become known as tuberculoid leprosy. One day the person would notice a single or perhaps several flat blemishes on his or her skin, as small as a penny or as large as ten inches, vaguely resembling scar tissue or a birthmark. These spots might be light in color, or as dark as copper. Devoid of sensation, they were smooth and dry to the touch, and without sweat even on the hottest day. In many instances these spots vanished as the body's defenses counterattacked, and the person would likely believe—wrongly—that the danger had passed.

When attacked by a capable immune system, leprosy germs sought refuge inside the nerves themselves, where they were more difficult to kill. As the furious battle shifted to these spots, the nerves became inflamed, pressing against the protective sheaths of protein that surround them, like insulation on a copper wire. Eventually, as one physician detailed years later, "the swollen nerve squeezes shut its own blood supply and dies. A dead nerve will no longer carry the electrical signals for sensation and movement." Such nerve damage was not terribly disfiguring, although it was often crippling.

Typically, anesthesia caused by compromised nerves appeared first on the little finger and lower half of the ring finger, and also on the toes and outer sole of the foot. It often spread from these points until the entire arm and leg and even part of the person's torso was insensitive. The loss of feeling usually had an orderly progression: "First, the ability to distinguish heat from cold disappears," a physician later wrote. "Next in order come loss of light touch, pain, and deep touch perceptions." Despite this handicap, tuberculoid leprosy was never fatal and, because bacilli were held in check within the nerve, it was impossible for someone with this form of the disease to infect another person. Often with tuberculoid leprosy the germ quieted spontaneously, and though the damage already wrought remained, in these cases the disease was finished.

In one of every five people who became infected with the leprosy germ, however, their immune system offered no resistance: faced with an assault of bacilli it simply collapsed. These people developed lepromatous leprosy, the most severe form of the disease. Once active, the leprosy germs in the victim's body ran riot, multiplying until they numbered in the trillions. With almost any other germ such an explosion of bacilli would be fatal, but with lepromatous leprosy the person sometimes did not even feel ill until long after the first symptoms developed—most often small blemishes on the forehead, nostrils, and ears. Unlike the flat, unfeeling lesions of tuberculoid leprosy, these spots remained sensitive and were markedly raised. With the body surrendering to the germ, such blemishes increased in number, hardened and ulcerated, and often merged into terrible growths that crept along a brow or jaw until the person was virtually unrecognizable. Germs swarmed the nerves, but because they were not hounded there by a working immune system, as in tuberculoid leprosy, the assault was more methodical: persons with lepromatous leprosy sometimes did not experience sensory loss until the late stages of the disease and often never lost muscle control. Even so, in these cases the leprosy germ gradually destroyed its victim. Hands and feet swelled hugely. Lips and ears distended, at times enlarging until they flapped atop the victim's shoulders and chest—in Kalawao, ears that had bloated in this manner were called bells. Billions of bacilli inflamed the nasal passages, collapsing the nose and choking the airway, which then had to be opened with a tracheotomy. Germs infiltrated the eyes and lids, stealing the ability to blink and creating a brutally appropriate condition in which the sufferer seemed to be continuously weeping.

Accompanying Hillebrand around the colony, Lydgate was confronted with such cases—victims of the disease in its most merciless, often-imagined form. Dr. Hutchison had referred to them as "loathsome and disgusting looking object[s]." Most of these severe cases were male: lepromatous leprosy occurred more frequently among men than women, and the disease in general struck males twice as often as females. Although the immune system of someone with tuberculoid leprosy could falter, and their disease downgrade to the more harsh lepromatous form, the reverse never occurred. Occasionally the germ went abruptly dormant, but this happened far less frequently than with tuberculoid leprosy. Usually a person with lepromatous leprosy died, typically within a dozen years and often much earlier, killed not by leprosy but by some condition enabled by the disease.

Caroline Walsh hurried to greet Hillebrand and Lydgate. Unkempt tangles of auburn hair sprung from beneath her scarf, and her dress was creased and grimy. Her pale hands fluttered nervously around her face as she spoke, frantically describing another "little rebellion" that had erupted that morning, which had further roiled the settlement. Desperately pleased to see the doctor, Walsh launched a fusillade of questions at him: about her son William, and her salary, and the board's expectations of her. Hillebrand realized that she had reached her limit. The widow's "private interests are of greater importance to her than those of her office," he later wrote, and recommended that she be replaced as resident superintendent. After following Walsh to her cottage, Hillebrand and Lydgate dropped their knapsacks and accepted a cup of coffee. Then Dr. Hillebrand creased open a page of his notebook, marked the date, and began his official tour.

The crops were wormy and most of the cottages were a fright, but Hillebrand found that if he glazed his eyes to hide the rot, the place was actually rather pretty. As Ferdinand Hutchison wrote after a similar visit, "The view is generally picturesque; vegetation is luxuriant, the scenery is beautiful, and its whole appearance, apart from the lepers themselves, pleasant and agreeable." Copse of papaya and banana tree had taken hold in the volcanic soil, throwing fingers of shade on the cottages, some of which had tiny lawns fenced in by stone walls. Wiry dogs raced by, and laughing children, and Hillebrand and Lydgate passed men whose backs bristled with fishing poles, on the way to catch their dinner. In front of a few of the cottages russet-colored chickens were leashed with twine to sticks, scratching circles in the dirt until they ended up as a meal.

The scattering of cottages surrounded a neat quadrangle, formed with white fence and dark stone. Walsh's home sat within its boundary, as did the schoolroom in which she gave lessons to about twenty students in "the ordinary school instruction of the islands—reading, writing, arithmetic, geography and singing." The children, Hutchison had written after a recent visit, "do not seem to feel their misfortune . . . when they leave school they act as others of the same age, running or playing their way home, apparently unconscious of the fate that awaits them."

A small hospital compound, consisting of two buildings, stood opposite the school. Hillebrand went to the door of one ward and swung it wide, releasing a cloud of foul air. "To get an idea of the smell," one resident later wrote, "imagine the stench of a coffin just opened." Hillebrand found the facility "dirty and neglected," with insufficient bandages and clean water to wash wounds. Infections among the patients were rampant. Each ward could hold twenty-four patients, but when Hillebrand toured them he found one grossly overcrowded, while the other held only a single patient—a white man who reclined on a mat in a dusty corner. When Hillebrand asked why he was alone, the patient replied that the Hawaiians preferred to die among their own kind. Hillebrand told Caroline Walsh to redistribute the patients and, in his notebook, expressed doubts that it would ever be done.

As he left the hospital, Hillebrand was stopped by a kokua—the father of J. D. Kahauliko, the first exile. The elderly man explained that his son was nearing death and no longer required a kokua. Now the father wanted to go home. He had begged Donald Walsh to send him to Kalihi Hospital so that Dr. Hoffmann could declare him healthy. But Walsh had refused. Hillebrand said he would see to the transfer and made a note to also arrange the release of four others who had mistakenly been exiled, including a boy about Lydgate's age.

The doctor's impressions of Kalawao and the settlers continued, written down in a neat, flowing hand. Most distressing to him was the overall health of the colony. Many people were in horrible straits, and not simply from leprosy. The cold and wet weather, lack of water, poor nutrition—all of these had, as Dr. Edward Hoffmann once warned, aggravated disease among the exiles. Made weak by the conditions, they now suffered from pneumonia, tuberculosis, liver and kidney problems, and more. Simple cuts became ulcerous, and deeper wounds turned gangrenous. With medicine and care, the exiles might be cured of ancillary ailments, but the board had not succeeded at providing regular medical attention. In July 1868 it had hired Dr. David Lee to make calls at Kalawao, an assignment Lee referred to as his monthly "pleasure trip." But the following August it let him go, when the money ran out. Lee did not protest, reporting, "This leper business is frightful." Hillebrand recognized that the board had to hire another physician, whatever the cost.

At the time when Hillebrand and Lydgate visited the colony, the most efficient killer of exiles was infection. Few patients had the materials or skill required to cleanse wounds and sores. Lacking a pain reflex, the person repeatedly injured his hands and feet, inviting additional infection. It was this chronic trauma, and not the disease itself, that caused the loss of fingers and toes. Yet the public assumed leprous body parts littered the ground in Kalawao, a scene Lydgate had imagined seeing until Hillebrand put him straight.

Of the numerous misconceptions about the disease, that sensational notion was relatively benign. Others were not. Many newspaper reporters, editors, politicians, clergymen, and a sizable percentage of the islands' population believed that every person in the colony was grossly disfigured and highly infectious. Of almost three hundred patients in the colony, however, fewer than half had the severe lepromatous form of the disease. Among those people, only the ones in whom the germ was currently active posed any threat of contagion—typically about a third of such cases. Less than one healthy person out of twenty was susceptible to this narrow risk, and taking basic precautions could greatly safeguard their health. For most people trapped in the colony, their exile was pointless.

Death became an opportunity, a release from the prison in which the exiles were double-bolted, by landscape and disease. One Saturday in July, at seven in the morning, a young woman named Heanu awoke to the smell of breakfast cooking. She thought her sixty-year-old grandfather, Kuaaina, was "roasting fish or meat" for the meal, she later said. The odor was delicious, and Heanu climbed down from her sleeping loft. Instead of breakfast, however, Heanu found "the room afire." Then she caught a blur of her grandfather, racing through the open door.

Heanu's grandmother was already awake, busy with chores in the yard outside the home. When she looked up she saw her naked husband, charred black by fire, hair scorched off, running from the house. "He did not speak, neither groaned nor showed any expression of pain," she later testified. He ran until he reached a neighbor's yard, then stood there smoldering, the skin dripping from his frame. The neighbor, a man named Levi, explained that he "took hold of him and tried to lead him back." But Kuaaina had screamed, "Let me go!" He wanted to remain there, in the cool open air, among the birdsong, and die.

When Rudolph Meyer arrived to investigate the suicide, he found a broken bottle of kerosene and what remained of the old man's shirt. Kuaaina had poured the fuel over himself, lit the cuff of his sleeve, then let fire wick across his body, burning away the disease. "He had often described himself as tired of living," Levi said. The dead man's wife testified that he had remarked that life in the colony was not worth surviving. "But, I never thought anything of it," she added. As horrible as the morning was, it might have been worse. The man's son-in-law remembered that Kuaaina had talked of taking a hatchet and killing his family before killing himself—in that way, all would be free. Meyer told them to bury the body, then rode home.

News of additional suicides passed among the exiles with disturbing regularity. One patient hanged himself from a tree, but the branch bowed down and released the tension, so he dropped to his knees to tighten the noose, then toppled to his side to complete the task. He died lying on the grass, as though he were napping. Several exiles chose the handiest path to death, wading into the surf to swim until they drowned or were taken by sharks. After the first power plant sparked necklaces of electric streetlamps across Honolulu, it was possible to just glimpse the glow of the island from the far north tip of the peninsula, and swimmers set off from that point, knowing they would never reach the light. Usually their bodies returned to Molokai, carried back by the wind and tide. Others merely stepped from the cliff or drove a knife into their body. One man took a butcher's blade to himself, and hacked away at the damaged flesh until there was hardly anything of him left.

Sometimes desperation alchemized into daring, and people tried to escape. At Kalihi Hospital flight was easily managed; just burrow beneath the fence or, after guards were stationed, arrange for a bribe or the distraction of a pretty girl. In the colony the simplest exit route was up and over the cliff, a deliverance that existed only for the strong and hardy, and only until Rudolph Meyer decided, after one year with twenty-two such escapes, to seal the path with a gate and armed guard.

In the weeks after Hillebrand departed Molokai, the matter of who would assume the mantle of power in the colony remained a preoccupation of the board. Caroline Walsh was told to begin packing. To replace her, the board preferred to name a white overseer, but after the anarchic Caroline Walsh regime, the settlers had begun to demand a manager with Hawaiian blood. William Humphreys, with his abundant political skill and ability to lead, was suggested for the position, promoted in part by Rudolph Meyer. But the complaints against him troubled the board, as did his past violent behavior—after one episode, the board had even ordered Humphreys removed from the colony and briefly locked in Oahu Prison. What the government required was a leader beyond reproach.

As it happened, Ferdinand Hutchison knew such a man: a burly former captain in the king's corps of guards, named W. H. Kahoohuli. Hutchison remembered him from 1865, when Kahoohuli mustered a posse and took off in pursuit of a retired British naval officer named Thomas Hanham. The Englishman had reached Honolulu aboard his private yacht, *Themis,* out of the Royal Thames Yacht Club. Invited to the palace by the king, Hanham spotted a Hawaiian girl in the hallway and, smitten, decided to take her to England as his mistress—a decision undeterred by the presence of his wife on the cruise. After grabbing the girl, Hanham "rode hastily to the wharf, jumped into his boat . . . and set sail," as the marshal of the islands reported. Hutchison had ordered Kahoohuli to take a schooner and twenty soldiers and go rescue the kidnapped youth. Kahoohuli proceeded to chase the *Themis* eastward over the Pacific for several days, until Hanham grew weary of being pursued and released his captive.

When Dr. Hutchison learned the news that Kahoohuli had been diagnosed with leprosy, it seemed like a tragic blessing. Hutchison quickly named him resident supervisor, and Kahoohuli arrived in the colony on April 12, 1871. Although weakened by disease, the king's former guard remained an impressive figure—a plainspoken, honest man who commanded others with natural ease. Hutchison anticipated a period of calm in the colony.

What the doctor had overlooked, however, was that Kahoohuli's abilities had become compromised by his belief in the supernatural: he imagined himself the victim of a curse. At the time, the specter of otherworldliness was still deeply embedded in Hawaiian culture. For generations, the islanders' religious faith had been organized around the worship of a collection of gods who were considered the personification of natural objects or elements of nature such as wind, storms, and fire. Intertwined with this worship was a system of religious laws, known as the *kapu* system. These were an intricate series of proscriptions and penalties intended to keep the sacred and the common separate from one another. In practice, this meant that the king, who was considered divine, could mark anything as kapu, or forbidden: a stretch of beach or land, a species of fish, a house, a bird. Implicit in this system was the idea that certain things, including some people, embodied a potent supernatural energy, known as *mana.* Strict observance of kapus helped to control this awesome force, and the policy sought to regulate almost all behavior, affecting what a person could eat, where he could travel, whom he could marry, and a thousand other things. To violate any kapu was to offend the gods and possibly unleash their terrible strength. Transgressors were clubbed or burned or strangled to death.

Although the king was himself sacred, only priests, called *kahunas,* could interpret and enforce the will of the gods and thus administer the kapu system. For many Hawaiians in the latter half of the nineteenth century, to be touched by disease meant that you had angered a god or angered someone powerful enough to route a god's supernatural rage toward you. By this same logic, only a kahuna could rid a person of disease. William Hillebrand had struggled at Queen's Hospital to convince his patients that Western remedies would ease their discomfort more quickly than the cures applied by their local kahuna, but they usually refused to believe him. At Kalihi Hospital, Dr. Edward Hoffmann often saw the consequences of such conviction, as occurred in May 1871, when a twelve-year-old boy was brought to the hospital in a horrific state. His mother had hired two kahunas to treat the boy's leprosy. With shards of broken glass they had sliced tracks in the child's afflicted hand, then plunged it into a pot filled with a boiling mash of banana and coconut. They held it there "until the skin came off and the flesh was a pulp," the *Pacific Commercial Advertiser* reported. "He was made also to hold his head over the mouth of the steaming calabash, until the skin of his face was like rags. At this stage . . . the boy was much worse." During the subsequent trial of the kahunas, "the principal witness was the boy himself, and he was a most repulsive looking object—his face swollen and distorted, lips protruding, eyes that were unnaturally bright, with a deprecatory expression of portending ill—it was fearful to look at him." Dr. Hoffmann managed to save the boy's hand, then, when he was well enough, sent him to Kalawao. The kahunas were found guilty of practicing medicine without a license, fined $75, and released.

Such medicine men were known as *kahuna lapaau,* and although their herbal cures sometimes brought needless pain and even death, they were essentially well meaning. Equally well-intended were the class of kahuna who foretold the future or predicted weather or acted as mediums to channel the dead. But there were also more destructive kahunas. Most terrifying of these were the sorcerers, *kahuna anaana,* who were said to be able to kill a person through prayer. One such assassin, named Wailiilii, lived on topside Molokai. He was not the most feared sorcerer on the island, however. A notorious female kahuna, named Paniku Hua, had contracted leprosy and been banished to Kalawao. Rather than negating her reputation, the disease deepened the mystery surrounding Hua. Many settlers alleged that she too could kill with words.

Captain Kahoohuli was especially susceptible to such supernatural suggestion, the consequence of a bizarre episode from his past. Several years earlier, a self-proclaimed prophet named J. Kaona had assembled a cult of white-robed followers on the island of Hawaii, preaching the end of days and a coming reign of fire. When he trespassed on private land, pitched a miniature village of grass huts for his brethren, and called for the "utter extermination of any who should oppose him," Kaona was arrested. In March 1868 he was locked inside the insane asylum on Oahu, under the care of Dr. Edward Hoffmann, who also oversaw the island's lone facility for "lunatics." From his cell, Kaona shrieked of the approaching apocalypse, of rivers of flowing flame, ashen skies, the earth split open like a plum. The prophecies continued nonstop for several weeks. Then one morning they began to come true.

On March 27 a column of smoke one mile high belched from the crater of Mauna Loa, one of two active volcanoes on the island of Hawaii. The next day a series of temblors rumbled the ground, accelerating in violence and frequency, until, by the warm afternoon of April 2, some three hundred earthquakes had rattled Hawaii. One convulsed the entire Hawaiian chain, five hundred miles across. According to Charles de Varigny, a French-born diplomat who served as cabinet minister to the king, the effect was instantaneous: "Pedestrians and riders were flung upon the ground, all stone structures tumbled down, trees rocked in all directions, fiercely shaking their branches and striking against one another as if beaten by a wild wind; yet there was not even at the time the slightest stirring of a breeze." People on land grew seasick from the motion of the ground, and it felt, residents later marveled, as if the island itself were "the lid of a boiling pot." The volcanoes were erupting. In Honolulu, above the insane asylum, the sky "slowly darkened and the sun turned a dusky red."

A deep crevasse rent the southern part of the island of Hawaii, and a stream of boiling mud, water, and stone shot thirty stories into the air, then "rolled along the earth without stopping, at a speed greater than that of a bullet," de Varigny wrote. This wave of molten earth, one mile wide and thirty feet deep, consumed humans and animals in its path, and "along the banks . . . the carcasses of beef cattle and goats were still visible where they had been seized by the moving flood and now lay embedded within its thick mass of solidified mud." Loosed by seismic upheavals, a huge wall of cliff broke free from the island's northern coast and collapsed into the sea. The ocean withdrew almost a mile from the normal coastline, a phenomenon repeated on every island in the chain. On Molokai the water retreated, paused with a gurgle, and came barreling back, to the horror of fleeing residents. At Kalawao the resulting tsunami leapt the rocks and rushed over the plain, sweeping homes from its path. Tide gauges monitoring the California coast clocked the wave at four hundred miles an hour, and it reached San Francisco, two thousand miles away, in just five hours. Charles de Varigny reported that on Hawaii "men, women, children, canoes, dinghies, houses—all disappeared within the wink of an eye . . . everywhere one saw only waste, desolation, ruin." The toll of dead reached the hundreds. Aftershocks continued for days, thousands of them, and traumatized islanders began to attribute the catastrophe to an angry Pele, goddess of the volcano. De Varigny wrote, "Their terror had risen to such a pitch that they were ready to believe anything."

In the weeks following the disaster, Kaona won release from the asylum and made his way back to Hawaii. There he reassembled his disciples. As the New Hampshire–born marshal of the Hawaiian Islands, William Cooper Parke, later commented, "Kaona, understanding the superstitious character of the natives, made the most of the events." Soon he had a gang of two hundred followers. When the local sheriff, R. B. Neville, went to confront them, he was met "by a shower of stones, and surrounded by a large force of the fanatics, armed with clubs, stones, and lassos." The mob pulled Neville from his horse and beat and decapitated him. As a warning to others, Kaona stuck the sheriff's head on a pole.

Dr. Hutchison ordered Marshal Parke to gather a company to arrest the murderers. Kahoohuli was named co-commander of the expedition. When he arrived on Hawaii, however, Kahoohuli discovered that a posse headed by another local sheriff had already captured the fanatics. All that remained was for Kahoohuli to take possession of the prisoners and bring them to Honolulu for trial. Kahoohuli went to collect J. Kaona, who was locked in handcuffs, spitting curses at the government's men. The prophet screamed that he would have vengeance on them. Not long after that day, Kahoohuli noticed blemishes forming on his skin.

By the time he landed in the colony, Captain Kahoohuli had concluded that his leprosy was supernatural retribution. According to the other settlers, he also believed that he was slowly being prayed to death, possibly by some of Kaona's followers. Both beliefs affected his abilities. Although he fulfilled his superintendent duties capably and brought to the settlement a rare season of harmony, Kahoohuli grew increasingly anxious about conspiratorial dark forces—he became "frozen," as one patient recalled, by his fears.

The enchantments took their toll on Captain Kahoohuli. Fourteen months after Ferdinand Hutchison named him supervisor, Kahoohuli was dead. With no ideal candidate to replace him, the board did the only thing it could think to do. It chose a person who, as a visitor to the colony remarked, "must either rule or rebel." William Humphreys was to be the boss. The man had risen, one observer wrote, "from the prison to the throne."

A Far Different Position

(Population 385)

A truism held that Hawaii was a place to be fled to, to escape a debt or a crime or an unloved spouse. Communication with the world, as everything beyond the islands was called, remained random and exceedingly slow. Dispatches were routinely waylaid for months, having traveled two oceans or ridden the rails from one coast to the next. Letters hot with gossip from America or Europe landed long after the scandal had settled and cooled. By the time correspondence was unbundled with the ship's mail packet, the whispers within the letters might well have turned on themselves already, the romance healed or broken and in either case moot.

A man's transgressions were also subject to this communication gap. Each newcomer arrived with a clean slate, deserved or not. His place in island society was most often determined by the weight of his family name, or the confidence with which he declared his past accomplishments. Men and women disembarked from the ships, were presumed respectable, and were welcomed into island life.

When Georges Trousseau reached Honolulu harbor on May 8, 1872, aboard the *Nevada,* no one suspected that he was on the run. Trousseau was the son of a celebrated Paris physician, Armand Trousseau, author of a masterpiece on clinical medicine, *Cliniques médicales de l'Hôtel-Dieu.* The younger Trousseau had earned distinction as well—a graduate of the École de Médecine, battlefield medic in Algiers and Italy, and, as the *Advertiser* informed its readers upon his arrival, "a Knight of the Imperial Order of the Legion of Honor." Three weeks after landing, Trousseau was appointed port physician for Honolulu. He was soon also named to the board of health.

A skirt of beard split Trousseau's face, shading his turned-down mouth. With his expensive wardrobe and his European manners, the doctor came across as refined and distinctly unapproachable. His medical talent rapidly became obvious. Only three months after arriving, Trousseau performed the first skin graft in the islands' history, slicing a patch from his own arm and stitching it onto the leg of a man whose limb had been shattered in a buggy collision.

Within island society, Dr. Trousseau quickly became a desirable guest and escort. He cut a mysterious figure. It was said that he had married once, but the woman was in France and the romantic ties legally severed. His current personal life was a subject of eager speculation. Not long after landing in Hawaii, Trousseau entered into a communal relationship with a Hawaiian woman named Makanoe and her husband, Kaaepa. Such liaisons, in which two women, often sisters, shared one husband, or two men a wife, were not unknown among Hawaiians. But for a white man, a sophisticate, to engage in plural marriage was shocking and a little offensive to Honolulu society.

One day a fellow physician, George Fitch, tore open the packet of mail just arrived by ship and found a copy of a book, *The Story of My Life,* by J. Marion Sims. The author was the former president of the American Medical Association and a friend of Armand Trousseau's. In the book, Fitch read the following about Armand Trousseau: "He had an only son, who was a scapegrace. He was a gambler and everything that was bad. His father was worried to death with his dissoluteness and foolish extravagance, and had to pay enormous sums of money to extricate him from his disgraceful orgies and gambling complications." Georges Trousseau had been married to a "fine woman" but "he neglected and made her miserable." He had become estranged from his loving father. At one Paris "gambling hell" Georges lost his bankroll and "more than he could pay besides." He determined to kill himself and wrote parting notes to his mother and wife. He then disappeared, and his father assumed he had committed suicide. The news, Sims suggested, pushed Armand Trousseau into the grave. The book told how Georges Trousseau had read of his father's death and slunk back to Paris to say his good-bye. "I saw the tall, handsome, wretched man bending heart-broken over his great father's coffin," wrote Sims. The fantastic tale rattled the island grapevine.

Alert to the gossip, Trousseau scribbled a note to Dr. Fitch: "Sir, I hear from various sources . . . you mentioned what Marion Sims says about myself in his posthumous book. One thing I always have had a horror of has been to sail under false colors, there fore I own that I am the person mentioned in the book, and that most of his accusations although written in a sensational way are true." Trousseau explained that he had made no attempt to hide his past sins—he had simply never been asked. He wrote that "had I not, as well as many in this underworld, a skeleton in my closet, I would not be in Honolulu." Rather, "if I had been wiser, I might by this day have in Paris a far different position from the one I have in this little corner of the earth." As for his father's death, it was from stomach cancer, "not of grief by my account (I know by personal experience that nobody dies of grief)."

When Georges Trousseau joined the board of health, he became one of its few members to wholly subscribe to an emerging hypothesis known as germ theory, which assigned blame for disease on microorganisms known as bacteria and viruses. The crude outlines of the theory had existed for centuries, but experimentalists in Europe and America were using the improved microscope and advances in culturing to push it toward scientific fact. Doctors in a position to influence policy, such as Edward Hoffmann and Ferdinand Hutchison and the now-absent William Hillebrand, all inclined toward germ theory, but each had different ideas as to how it affected the transmission of leprosy. This lack of consensus, along with the political nature of the segregation policy, had allowed the exile program to escape absolute enforcement in its first seven years. Trousseau felt that the situation should be corrected. When the king died in December 1872, leaving no successor, a royal by the name of William Charles Lunalilo was elected to the throne. The new king was a solitary, hard-drinking man known to his subjects as Whiskey Bill. His personal physician was Georges Trousseau.

Dr. Trousseau's control over the exile policy increased almost immediately. At a board of health meeting soon after Lunalilo came to power, Trousseau announced that the government would henceforth pursue "the immediate, energetic, and to a certain extent, unsympathetic isolation of all who were afflicted with the disease." Endorsed by Trousseau, the unforgiving concept of germ theory spread from the board to the editorial pages. The leper, one paper announced, "carries with him the seeds of death, he must not be allowed to destroy his brothers and sisters." The author wrote, "Some people consider this enforced isolation as a violence to personal rights. It is so, no doubt, but a violence in behalf of human welfare." A week later a Honolulu broadsheet screamed, "LEAVE NOT A LEPER . . . Whoever has this dread disease, be he chief or commoner, be he white or brown, must be separated from the healthy, and removed to Molokai." At about the same time, Ferdinand Hutchison had written, "Let us think for a moment and imagine what a state we should be in, if all these lepers, instead of living together [on Molokai], were running free. We could not go anywhere without meeting a leper; there would be hardly a valley on the islands without having lepers among its population. Strangers not used to such sights would receive evil impressions [and] the island would be shunned on all occasions, and no vessel would enter our ports unless forced by sheer necessity, and would make their escape as quickly as possible."

The board of health relaunched its crusade. Dispatching fresh teams of bounty hunters to scour the islands, it hounded agents until they followed suspects deep into hollows and caves, then dragged the unlucky person out and off to Kalihi. Suspects only fled farther into the wilderness, as the *Advertiser* reported: "The infected ones are getting more cautious in showing themselves."

In the chaotic first six months of William Lunalilo's reign, almost twelve hundred men, women, and children were arrested and brought to Kalihi for exam—as many as had been examined in the entire seven years of segregation thus far. Of these 1,200 potential cases, 487 were deemed lepers and swiftly exiled, almost doubling the colony's population in only a matter of weeks. The operation's scope and swiftness were staggering, and soon the board and Dr. Trousseau became, as one paper reported, the subject of "prayers, threats and worse."

On a leaden-skied Wednesday in April, Dr. Trousseau and Dr. Edward Hoffmann arrived at Kalihi Hospital to begin a day of examinations. By now, Hoffmann's hospital was little more than a processing center. Streams of people channeled through its doors, were shorn of clothing, pinched and photographed, and assigned a number. Suspects wailed as they were cut from line and escorted to a holding room. Among those anticipating a final voyage that morning was a shipping agent named Jim Kamai, pronounced by Trousseau a leper. The young man did not agree with the diagnosis.

Removing a pistol from his coat, he leveled it at Trousseau's head and announced that he was going to kill the doctor. Trousseau ducked behind a pillar, and the bullet whistled into the ceiling. Rushing Kamai, Hoffmann and Trousseau wrestled him to the floor. By the time Marshal William Cooper Parke arrived, Kamai had wormed free. "As Mr. Parke, with a revolver pointed, advanced," the *New York Times* reported, "[Kamai] fired point blank at that officer, both barrels going off simultaneously, but fortunately again without effect, his nervousness and excitement probably preventing accuracy of aim." Parke arrested Kamai and tossed him in a cell until trial. A jury subsequently found Kamai not guilty due to "emotional insanity," the first such verdict in Hawaiian history. "The deprivation of his liberty and the prospect of a lingering death from leprosy may have depraved his reason," one news account noted. At the conclusion of the trial the judge ordered Kamai released. Trousseau was waiting. Agents seized Kamai and threw him on a ship bound for the colony.

* * *

In Kalawao, cottages sprang up to accommodate the expanding population, single-room affairs that quickly overflowed with newcomers. Lean-tos lined the dirt road between the villages, inching nearer each day to the peninsula's western shore and the healthy residents of Kalaupapa. Rudolph Meyer had continued to try to negotiate the purchase of the holdouts' homes in the village, but without success. So Meyer ordered the new resident superintendent, William Humphreys, to begin evicting kokuas to make room for patients. Humphreys took to the task energetically. Soon kokuas were hiding in caves, to prevent their exile from Molokai.

After years of scheming, Humphreys finally held the power he craved. Yet the kingdom he now claimed was rapidly changing. The relative calm of Captain Kahoohuli's administration had given way to hardship and disorder, of a sort that Humphreys found difficult to manage or exploit. Shortages struck constantly, of food and blankets and firewood and medicine. Strange new faces appeared each week, and some were as morally flawed as Humphreys had once been. They paid scant attention to the old-timer. Adversity and disease had mellowed Humphreys, and his days as a rebel were over. Now he mostly sought to keep the peace, but without much success.

As word leaked from Molokai of mounting lawlessness, the local newspapers shrugged in resignation. Such behavior was to be expected, given the situation. Wrote one politician, "Alas, we dare not think what we might be or do, if we were a confirmed leper, sure to rot daily unto death." An *Advertiser* editorial offered, "There might be written over the landing at Molokai, 'Let him abandon hope who enters here.'" A puckish reporter scratched the same phrase above the *Advertiser*'s door.

In March, William Humphreys fell suddenly ill. He believed it to be dropsy and asked Trousseau to send a remedy. When the vial arrived, Humphreys swallowed a single dose and professed to be improved. Then he took a second dose and abruptly died. The exiles decided Trousseau had murdered Humphreys, and that his potions would poison them too. "They smashed the Bottles of Medicine on the rocks," one patient wrote to a relative in Honolulu. The next time the doctor visited the colony, an enraged settler shot at him. Again Trousseau escaped unscathed.

With Humphreys dead, Rudolph Meyer and the board, lacking any better option, asked Louis Lepart to return as resident superintendent. Incredibly, Lepart agreed. Less than two weeks into his second tour, a mob of settlers encircled him and threatened to beat him bloody. Lepart fled up the cliff, never to set foot in the colony again. To fill the vacancy the board named Jonathan Napela, the sixty-year-old husband of one of the patients. But neither the board nor Rudolph Meyer held much confidence in Napela's ability to manage a troubled asylum growing at such a furious pace. In effect, they had decided that the settlement would have to smolder untended for a time, until a better leadership solution revealed itself. When it finally did, the events to follow would explode Molokai into an unrivaled notoriety. The colony was about to become the most infamous spot in the world.

Part Two

I do not believe in special providences. I believe that the universe is governed by strict and immutable laws. If one man's family is swept away by a pestilence and another man's spared it is only the law working: God is not interfering in that small matter, either against one man or in favor of the other.

Mark Twain, from his notebooks

Kalawao circa 1880. Damien stands at left.

Rush Slowly

(Population 749)

The eight missionary priests knelt before the vicar apostolic of the islands, Bishop Louis Desire Maigret. They had gathered to consecrate a new chapel in the town of Wailuku, which sits on the neck of a wide valley dividing the island of Maui into halves. The church had taken six years to build. Bishop Maigret, who oversaw the Hawaiian mission of the Paris-based order known as the Society of the Sacred Hearts of Jesus and Mary, had called in his priests from their districts to celebrate the event, and to discuss mission matters. Among other things, Maigret hoped to resolve a dilemma the order faced in Kalawao.

In the colony's first few years, the mission had dispatched a priest once or twice each year, to briefly deliver sacraments to the small number of Catholic exiles. As the population grew, however, so did adherents to the Roman Church. To meet their needs the mission had a small chapel built and shipped to the colony in pieces, and in early 1872 a missionary worker named Victorin Bertrand visited Kalawao for six weeks to hammer the structure whole. When it was standing, a priest arrived to bless the chapel, called St. Philomena; he performed twelve baptisms, then he and Brother Bertrand departed Kalawao.

By early 1873 the congregation of St. Philomena numbered more than two hundred, and they had recently sent Bishop Maigret a petition. "They ask me for a priest who can remain habitually with them," he recorded in his journal, "but where to find one?" Maigret felt he could not risk sending any of his missionary priests to live permanently in Kalawao. Yet Maigret believed the lack of a Catholic leader in the colony reflected badly on the mission. Protestants had a minister in the settlement, an exiled Hawaiian clergyman who had the disease, and Latter-Day Saints had the husband of an exiled woman, a healthy Mormon priest who had gone as her kokua. Bishop Maigret raised the topic sometime after the activities of the consecration, which took place May 4, 1873. According to one account, Maigret told the eight priests of "his anxiety over the sufferers at the Settlement who were becoming more numerous every day. No one on the islands needed a pastor more than these poor, sick, and dying outcasts."

"Bishop, say the word and any one of us will go to the Settlement," one of the priests answered. Maigret, however, feared that if a priest spent appreciable time in the colony, he would be infected. "Couldn't you set up a sort of rotating system?" Maigret asked. "Then you could take turns replacing each other." They settled on an arrangement whereby four priests would alternate, each spending three months in the colony. Bishop Maigret chose the first to serve: a thirty-three-year-old priest named Joseph de Veuster. By coincidence, the steamer *Kilauea,* which the board occasionally used as a transport ship, was scheduled to arrive that day at Maui to pick up fifty new exiles and a load of cattle for the colony. Maigret told de Veuster, We must hurry.

Even in a family that produced two nuns and two priests, Joseph de Veuster's attitude toward religion was unusually intense. As a boy he practiced self-mortification, slipping a wooden plank beneath his back at night to make sleep difficult. From an early age he expressed an unshakable certainty that he had been given talents specifically designed for the priesthood, and when his father had attempted to steer the teenager toward the family grain business, Joseph responded with an aggrieved letter: "Are you not afraid of making an irreparable mistake if I lose a vocation for which God has destined me since my childhood, which would make me unhappy forever?" De Veuster's parents relented. Shortly thereafter Joseph entered the Society of the Sacred Hearts of Jesus and Mary, known simply as the Sacred Hearts.

On the day that he took his vows as a member of the order, Joseph de Veuster was nineteen years old, a strong-willed and naive young man from the Flemish countryside. In a formal portrait taken to commemorate his new life, Joseph stares at the camera sternly, clutching a blindingly white crucifix with both of his large hands, as if the cross might get away. As was customary, Joseph adopted a religious name on entering the order—he chose Damien.

The Sacred Hearts was a missionary order, and in 1863 the motherhouse in Paris had received a request for more workers from its Hawaiian mission. Damien's brother Auguste, a Sacred Hearts priest known as Father Pamphile, was selected to make the journey. Before Auguste could sail, however, an epidemic of typhus broke out. While attending the ill, Pamphile caught fever. Damien nursed his brother for twelve days, until the sickness subsided. By then it was obvious that Pamphile would not survive a sea voyage. Although he had not yet been ordained, Damien asked to take his brother's place in Hawaii. When the decision arrived, he had burst into Pamphile's room. "Yes," Damien cried. "I am to go instead of you!" Shortly before his ship sailed from Bremerhaven, Damien composed a letter to his father and mother: "Farewell, dear parents, farewell. Be careful always to lead a good Christian life, and never let the slightest willful sin stain your soul. Walk in the right way. This is the last thing I ask of you; promise it to me, and I shall be without fear on your behalf."

At the time, the Catholic mission in Hawaii was in a perpetual hurry, and Bishop Maigret drove his priests hard. Having come late to the islands, seven years after the first company of Protestant missionaries arrived in 1820, the Catholics had fallen behind in the harvest and needed to catch up. Although outwardly tolerant, the various faiths were heated rivals—the moment a missionary departed a village, his sectarian counterpart arrived to dispute everything he had proclaimed. Locals absorbed it all with aplomb. As Charles de Varigny wrote in 1873, "The Kanaka believes the Catholic priest when he describes the Protestant missionary as a wolf in sheep's clothing; but he also believes the Protestant minister who speaks of the Catholic priest as an idolator, and of his ritual tainted with paganism."

Within a few weeks of venturing into the Hawaiian field, Damien remarked, "I find sheep everywhere, but many of them are outside the fold. Calvinism has drawn many into its nets." His missionary district was a vast, sparsely populated territory of one thousand square miles on the island of Hawaii, which he covered on foot and horseback and sometimes by canoe. It took six weeks to complete a circuit. Entering a village, Damien would climb from beneath the pack he carried, drive four stakes in the ground, and assemble his portable altar. "Here I am a priest, dear parents," the twenty-four-year-old had written. "Here I am a missionary in a corrupt, heretical, idolatrous country. How great my obligations are!"

Damien quickly discovered that leprosy was prevalent within his district. "There are many men covered with it," he wrote. "The disease is very dangerous, because it is highly contagious." Nonetheless, and despite the fears, he administered sacraments and medical care to persons marked by the disease—people he knew were destined for the "government prison," as he described the colony. Damien claimed to have felt an unseen hand moving him toward Molokai as well. "Many of our Christians here at Kohala also had to go," he wrote in April 1873, a few weeks before the church consecration on Maui. "I can only attribute to God an undeniable feeling that soon I shall join them." When Damien mentioned the premonition to his parishioners, they had reacted with horror: "Even just joking about my going to Molokai upsets them."

* * *

On Saturday, May 10, 1873, Bishop Louis Maigret and Father Damien landed at Kalaupapa, along with the fifty patients. A hundred settlers watched from shore. Climbing onto a pair of borrowed horses, the priests traveled the two miles to Kalawao, where Bishop Maigret said a hurried mass at St. Philomena. Then, according to an account he later wrote, Maigret announced to the congregation, "Here is Father Damien, who wishes to sacrifice himself for the salvation of your souls. He has not yet a house; we shall get him one as soon as possible." The bishop bid the exiles farewell, rode back across the peninsula, and sailed from Molokai.

Tradition dictated that Sacred Hearts priests rely on the Lord to provide, and in this way Father Damien arrived in the colony very much as had the first exile, J. D. Kahauliko, seven years earlier. In his pack Damien had only a few necessities, and one luxury: a clay pipe and a pouch of sweet tobacco. It would help with the smell, he had been told.

The colony that the priest looked out on that day had changed in many ways from Kahauliko's time, and in others not at all. Inhabitants took refuge in every type of shelter imaginable, from unfinished huts made of fallen branches to neat wooden cottages, erected either by the board of health or privately, by those exiles who had money. Kalawao still lacked a water supply, and the small government store, William Humphreys's old haunt, remained meagerly stocked. The hospital that Donald Walsh had built held about eighty patients on the day Damien landed, and the mortality rate among the entire population was a sobering 40 percent. A makeshift post office occupied one corner of the dispensary, through which two hundred pieces of mail passed each week. The resident superintendent was Jonathan Napela, who also happened to be the Mormon priest. The board did not regard him as an especially competent manager. Napela struggled to keep order in the settlement, with only partial success. As Damien later wrote, the exiles "passed their time with playing cards, hula (native dances), drinking fermented ki-root beer, home-made alcohol, and with the sequels of all this."

During his first hours in the colony Damien sought out any patient nearing death, to perform last rites. Then he went among the others. Later, he recalled the scenes that awaited him. "Nearly all the lepers were prostrated on their beds," he wrote, "in damp grass huts, their constitutions badly broken down. The smell of their filth, mixed with the exhalation of their sores, was simply disgusting—unbearable for a newcomer. Many times in fulfilling my priestly duties in their huts I have had to close my nostrils and run outside for fresh air."

A missionary doctor on the island of Hawaii had provided Damien with some basic medical instruction. He knew to give quinine for a fever, and pills made from the powdered leaves of purple foxglove, known as digitalis, to ease a failing heart. Opium in small doses could calm the stomach, and a pinch of arsenic could clear a blocked colon. But Damien had few of those things in Kalawao. On his first long day in the settlement, the priest spent most of his time simply comforting people, moving from hut to hut until all of Kalawao was asleep. Bishop Maigret had warned Damien against resting in the cottage of any person with the disease, and so he spread his sleeping blanket beneath a spiky tree that shadowed St. Philomena. Two days after arriving, on May 12, Damien wrote the bishop: "From now on there ought to be a permanent priest in this place. Boat loads of the sick are arriving, and many are dying." He added, "The harvest appears to be ripe here. Pray, and ask others to pray both for me and for all here." Damien also asked Maigret for supplies. "Send me some wine," he wrote, "hosts, religious books and some for study, rosaries, shirts, pants, shoes, a sack of flour, a bell and razor."

On May 13 the news of Damien's arrival in the colony broke in Honolulu. Newspapers excitedly detailed the self-exile of a healthy white priest, who "was left ashore among the lepers without a home or a change of clothing except such as the lepers offer." The article suggested that martyrdom was certain for the priest. "We care not what this man's theology may be, he is surely a Christian Hero." When the news rebounded to Molokai, Damien paused long enough in his activities to write a letter to his brother Pamphile. "They are talking about me in the papers," he reported. "It would be better if they kept quiet. Things here are much more serious than any esteem they might give me."

Damien's superior in Honolulu, Father Modeste Favens, was initially confused by the publicity, and a little perturbed. Then, as the *Advertiser* later described, a group of Protestant businessmen spontaneously started "a subscription for the benefit of [Damien]." They collected $130, which they handed to a startled Bishop Maigret. The following Sunday ten Protestants attended Catholic mass to honor the young priest's sacrifice. Damien, mission officials realized, was proving to be a public relations boon. Writing to the motherhouse in Paris, Father Modeste remarked that in Honolulu "one could only hear of the devotion of Father Damien. Of the danger he ran of contracting this incurable disease. They admire him, they exalt his sacrifice."

The tributes to Damien presented a problem for the mission, however. According to plan, the priest was to be rotated out of the settlement in a little more than two months. Now, however, the press would treat Damien's departure as a retreat, even if another priest took his place. Father Modeste concluded, "Considering the circumstances that led him there [and] the good effect his appearance has had on the public, we are so to speak forced to leave him there."

Damien had decided that he would visit each exile at least once a week. The circuit required five days. He usually began at the hospital. Inside the lamplit ward, patients lay on woven grass mats and rusted cots, sporadically attended by untrained kokuas. Some weeks after Damien arrived, the board exiled William Williamson, a brick mason from England who had been studying nursing with Edward Hoffmann. Joining Williamson in exile was his twenty-two-year-old wife, Hannah, and their son; all three had the disease. "Mr. Williamson," wrote the president of the board, "has been appointed by the Board as overseer of the hospital and in charge of the medicines." The board maintained low expectations. Williamson was simply to see to patients' "ordinary ailments and to the relief of their miserable condition." This meant changing bandages. Williamson had learned the art from Dr. Hoffmann: fill a metal basin with medicinal water, soak the cotton bandages, then wrap them tight over the cleaned wound. After several hours, use shears to slice away the poultice, pat dry the wound, and cover the open sores with fresh clean cloth. The next day, do it all again.

When Dr. Trousseau came to Kalawao for a routine inspection, along with several other official visitors, he noted that the hospital had improved, a change he attributed to Williamson and also Damien. One of the visitors later wrote of the wards, "I expected to be sickened . . . but these are so well kept, and are so easily ventilated by the help of the constantly blowing trade-wind, that the odor was scarcely perceptible in them." The visitor noted the "astonishing tenacity of life" exhibited by the patients—although he also reported that forty-two had recently expired.

That spring, Damien's first season in the colony, someone died every twenty-four hours on average. Both William Williamson and Damien helped make coffins for the dead, which Williamson presold to the faltering patients. The fee covered the wood, with a tiny profit besides. If lumber was scarce, the deceased was buried in his sleeping mat. Animals dug at fresh graves, and so Damien split pickets and strung a fence around the main cemetery, a bit of enterprise that was not wholly appreciated. When the Protestant minister in the colony noticed the enclosure, he fired a complaint to the board: the fence was the priest's net, he charged. Damien was catching souls.

The assertiveness with which Father Damien took to his perceived duties rankled some in the colony. Several men in the community considered themselves leaders, including the settlement sheriff and the other clergymen. Officially, Jonathan Napela, the Mormon priest, was resident superintendent, and thus the settlement's administrative head. Yet Damien swiftly became the primary force in the colony, a development that worried his superiors. One Sacred Hearts official wrote that Damien "acts as though he were director, doctor, fac-totum, and gravedigger of the Settlement . . . and he's none of them." Damien suggested otherwise in a letter to Pamphile: "Picture to yourself a collection of huts with eight hundred lepers. No doctor . . . A white man, who is a leper, and your humble servant do all the doctoring work." He then described to his brother how he lent spiritual aid to all the exiles. "Consequently," Damien wrote, "everyone, with the exception of a very few bigoted heretics, look on me as a father." Damien implied that he was also the community's lone civic force: "You may judge by the following fact what a power the missioner has. Last Saturday some of the younger people, discontented with their lot, and thinking themselves ill-treated by the government, determined on an attempt to revolt. All, except two, were Calvinists or Mormons. Well, I only had to present myself and say a word or two, and all heads were bowed, and all was over!"

By the end of Damien's second month in the settlement his ministry was booming. St. Philomena now overflowed at mass. He could hear the faithful following along from outside the chapel, the men peeking in the windows on one side, women watching from the other. Damien typically preached without a script, although he carried a small book in which to record ideas for the sermons, scratched down with a carpenter's pencil stub. Themes came to Damien as he worked. "The earth is only a place of temporary exile," Damien wrote on one page of the notebook, and on another declared, "We shall be transfigured, happy and beautiful in proportion to our patience in bearing our trials here below."

On boat days Damien would hurry from his tasks and travel to the waterfront, to see what the ships had brought. Exiles landed every week, arriving onshore damp and often in shock. Damien attempted to greet each newcomer personally. He made notes on which of the banished seemed willing to embrace his lessons, and which seemed poised to fall astray and possibly founder in drink and vice. These received unannounced visits from the priest. "Almost from one house to the next I have to change my tone," Damien wrote, describing his outreach methods. "Here I give words of sweetness and consolation; there I mix in a little bitterness, because it is necessary to open the eyes of a sinner; finally the thunder sometimes rumbles, and I threaten an impenitent with terrible punishments, which often produces a good effect."

His days began before dawn, when he woke, said prayers, and ate a breakfast of boiled rice, dried biscuits, and strong coffee. Then he stepped out into the colony. If someone was dying he anointed them with the oil of last rites, and if someone had already passed he slipped on a clean cassock and performed the burial service. During a good week he might bury as few as three people; during the bad stretches, amidst rain and cold, several died every day. When he had a spare moment, Damien would hurry to the hospital to work alongside William Williamson, spinning bandages, dressing sores, and passing out medicine: protiodide of mercury, half-grains of opium, potassium arsenite, and swigs of watered laudanum. He took the settlers' confessions, scolded them, and gave them praise. He performed baptisms, played games with the children, and conducted lessons in carpentry. He gave detailed advice, often unwanted, about gardens and crops and the state of an exile's home. He knelt with people in prayer, so frequently that the fabric at his knees turned to tissue. By the time his rounds were finished, Damien had circled on foot for ten miles. The cliff overshadowed the colony, and the early moon had risen. In the chalky light Damien would find his way to the small white rectory he was building and light a candle, and then begin to write. He penned dutiful reports to the mission house, lists of the supplies he needed, snippets of sermons, and many letters home. He expended the last of the guttering candlelight writing messages to himself in the margins of the notebook: things he wanted to accomplish, things he must remember to do. One evening not long after he landed in the colony Damien scribbled, *Festina lente.* Rush slowly.

Toward the close of the nineteenth century a physician named George Thin repeated, in his widely read treatise *Leprosy,* a belief that was commonly held in the 1870s: that those described in the Bible as lepers suffered from "modern nerve leprosy." As a means to control the disease, Thin endorsed the edict set down in Leviticus 13:44–46: "Whosoever shall be defiled with the leprosy and is separated by the judgment of the priest . . . shall dwell alone without the camp." In Leviticus, Moses communicates this policy to the Israelites, explaining it is heaven-sent. With that message of unsympathetic ostracism, Moses is considered by medical historians to have laid the foundation of lepraphobia. More than three thousand years later, Dr. Thin argued, the Bible remained the most useful authority on how to combat leprosy. This approach contained a significant flaw, however: The lepers in the Bible did not have leprosy.

The earliest accurate account of true leprosy was set down in the first century AD by an Alexandrian physician named Areataeus of Cappadocia. "There is no disease which is graver and more violent," he wrote. "Its power is indeed formidable, for of all diseases it is the one which possesses the most murderous energy.... Also it is filthy and dreadful to behold, in all respects like the wild animal, the elephant. Lurking among the bowels, like a concealed fire, it smolders there ... [then] blazes forth.... The respiration is fetid ... tumors predominate.... The hairs on the whole body die prematurely.... The skin of the head [becomes] deeply cracked ... nose elongated ... ears red, black, contracted, resembling the elephant.... Sometimes, too, certain of the members will die, so as to drop off, such as the nose, the fingers, the feet, the privy parts, and the whole hands; for the ailment does not prove fatal, so as to relieve the patient from a foul life and dreadful sufferings."

Areataeus' summary is remarkable for the precision with which it illuminates leprosy's symptoms, in contrast to the vague diagnostic method related in Leviticus. Biblical lepers are identified simply by skin appearance: "And the Lord spake unto Moses and Aaron, saying, When a man shall have in the skin of his flesh a rising, a scab, or a bright spot ... he is a leprous man, he is unclean: the priest shall pronounce him utterly unclean." True leprosy is characterized by alopecia, fevers, insensitivity, and partial paralysis, none of which is mentioned in the Bible in connection with lepers. In the Bible, depigmented skin and scaly flesh are the principal evidence of a leper. Yet neither symptom is a reliable hallmark of leprosy, and both are more likely an indication of boils, scabies, psoriasis, or some other defacing disease.

Whatever the cause, in biblical times the instant a mark appeared on a person's skin the priest pronounced him unclean. The sufferer could not remain among the camp nor approach God in worship until they were again "pure." Thus the prescriptive chapters in Leviticus are devoted not to treatment, but to how a leper could ritually be cleansed. In fact, a biblical leper might not actually be sick, but merely a sinner in the opinion of the priest—someone who required penitential purification. Although Leviticus contains no explicit moral diagnosis, scholars have determined that priests likely viewed any skin disorder as a sign that someone had offended God, and had been punished with a sinful mark. In the context of the Bible, this blurring of boundaries between medical and ethical diagnoses had one critical consequence: almost all skin conditions became stigmatized.

None of this might ultimately have mattered, however, if not for an editing error. In the third century, Jewish scholars created a Greek translation of the Old Testament. The Hebrew word *zara'at,* which means "ritually impure" and had been used generally in the Bible to refer to unclean flesh, was translated by these scholars into the Greek word *lepra,* which had the specific meaning "rough and scaly." The moral associations of "impure" now became linked to *lepra,* a term that this and subsequent translations misapplied to myriad skin diseases.

Not every physician observed skin disease from the perspective found in Leviticus. Some, like the Alexandrian physician Areataeus, took a more medically informed, ethically neutral view, which did not connect sickness with moral behavior. During the next several centuries other Arabic scholars continued in this vein, creating a medically precise description of true leprosy, a disease they called *judham.* Thus two distinct terms emerged: *lepra,* a priestly definition for the biblical, sin-soaked, multiform skin diseases that created "lepers"; and *judham,* a specific chronic illness that was unfortunate, but not the result of divine punishment or a curse.

These conflicting terms—one describing a disease of the soul and the other a disease of the body—existed apart from each other until the eleventh century. About that time, an Italian monk began to translate existing medical texts into a consolidated Latin text, which eventually became the standard literature for physicians in the West. When the Christian monk encountered the clinically correct description for the disease *judham,* he consulted his Bible, pondered a moment, and affixed the word *lepra* to the description. With a few short strokes of ink two thousand years of biblical stigma was permanently transferred onto the disease.

On June 10, 1873, one month after Damien's arrival on Molokai, the Hawaiian Evangelical Association released its official statement on "this loathsome, incurable and deadly disease [that] has fastened upon the vitals of the nation." The evangelists looked to the Bible for the solution. "He has given a remedy, which the experience of wise men and wise nations has made certain. Nay He has laid the rule down in the law given to Israel by His servant Moses. It is this; Strict, thorough isolation from us, of all infected persons, not merely of established lepers but also all who are reasonably suspected. If we obey God's leadings, and follow this rule [we] will be saved. If we do not, we are doomed to an early and shameful death." In future sermons the ministers decided that they must preach heavily to their Hawaiian congregations on "the duty of isolating their lepers, especially as illustrated by the Mosaic law in the thirteenth chapter of Leviticus." They set July 18 as a day of fasting and repentance, "especially for those sins which promote the spread of this disease." When the day arrived in the colony, parishioners filled Siloama Chapel. The faithful begged forgiveness for the sins that they had committed, and for relief from their punishment of leprosy.

At St. Philomena, Father Damien also led a group of penitents in prayer. He looked out over his flock. They dressed as finely as they could in their circumstances, the men in white shirts and the women in flowing holokus, wrapped around the waist with folds of colorful cloth. Garlands of flowers encircled their necks or were worn as bands on broad-brimmed hats. The bouquets served double duty. As the disease attacks the nose, it fouls the person's breath, clogging the throat and nasal passages, which then have to be cleared by hacking and spitting. Damien had carved holes in the chapel floor between the pews, and worshipers aimed for these. Skin eruptions also gave off an odor even beneath fresh bandages. At times the air inside the church grew so thick that Damien struggled to continue. "I have had great difficulty in getting accustomed to such an atmosphere," he confessed to Pamphile. "One day . . . I found myself so stifled that I thought I must leave the altar to breathe a little of the outer air." He had weighed his moment of suffering against his congregation's and forced himself to remain.

In his sermons Father Damien often stressed that leprosy offered an opportunity for grace. Although their disease was divinely inflicted, the exiles' torment was "helping them to get out of sin and to return to God," as one Sacred Hearts priest wrote. Father Damien had long ago embraced the Christian notion that leprosy was a type of curse; most people in Kalawao who were religious believed the same. Yet something about this idea began to trouble Damien. After several months in the colony he began to voice suspicions that the concept was faulty, or theologically incomplete. Certainly the afflicted children in the settlement were innocent of sin; already Damien had charge of a half dozen orphans, and if a divine plan existed for their leprosy he did not yet see it. He began to wonder if the disease might also perform a worthy function. Eventually Father Damien arrived at his conclusion. If a person had been selected by Providence to serve a noble purpose, then their infection could not possibly be interpreted as punishment. In such rare circumstances, leprosy would arrive as a blessing—as a gift from God.

"Be Ambitious and Bold"

(Population 742)

On a Wednesday morning in early 1873, the interisland steamer *Kilauea* completed its weekly run from Honolulu to Hilo, by way of Molokai and Maui. Isabella Bird, of Yorkshire, England, was among the passengers, a genial forty-two-year-old with chronic back pain and a tendency toward depression. Her doctor had recommended travel as a cure for both complaints. Twenty years later, Bird was still at sea, keeping a journal of all she observed.

As the steamer entered Hilo Bay, young men shoved canoes from the beach, followed by swimmers and boys hugging nine-foot-long surfboards. A welcome party stood onshore, and "brilliantly-dressed riders galloped along the sands," Bird wrote, "till a many-coloured tropical crowd had assembled at the landing." She saw a whaleboat launch, rowed by eight singing men in white linen suits. Carrying garlands of flowers and bouncing with glee, the men scrambled aboard the ship and rushed past her to embrace a slender figure dressed in suit and hat and light kid gloves, with a silk scarf twirled around his neck. She had met him a day earlier: this "very handsome half white gentleman, a lawyer of ability" whose speech was "eloquent and poetic." During the two-day voyage he had changed his outfit three times and kept the passengers entertained with his theatrical manner and a "combination of patois, invective, and sarcasm." The man was returning home, he had explained, and his name was William Ragsdale.

Isabella Bird was not the first writer to capture the dandified Ragsdale in a journal. Seven years earlier, Mark Twain had stood in the gallery of the Hawaiian Supreme Court, where the legislature met, observing the lawmakers. "The mental caliber of the Legislative Assembly is up to the average of such bodies the world over," he wrote. "And I wish it were a compliment to say it, but it is hardly so." At the time the legislature included a dozen white men among the forty or so Hawaiian representatives. Dr. Ferdinand Hutchison was present, and the future king, David Kalakaua, and also the government's official interpreter, the lawyer William Ragsdale, whose role it was to translate every speech. This he accomplished "with a readiness and facility of language that are remarkable," wrote Twain. "Without departing from the spirit of a member's remarks, he will, with apparent unconsciousness, drop in a little voluntary contribution occasionally in the way of a word or two that will make the gravest speech utterly ridiculous." Ragsdale was the son of an American lawyer and plantation owner who had migrated to Hawaii from Virginia and wed a Hawaiian chiefess. The couple had three children, who were raised, as Twain imagined, "in the midst of the ancient idolatrous system." Twain began to jot an outline for a novel, with William Ragsdale as its protagonist.

In Hilo, while Isabella Bird watched, Ragsdale climbed from the whaleboat and was lofted delicately ashore, clasped, and kissed. When the greetings subsided, he straightened his suit and ambled off, stepping gingerly over the puddles in the path so he would not soil his spats. Bird collected her bags and went to find the home of Hilo's sheriff, Luther Severance, with whom she had arranged to stay. The village did not have a hotel.

On a lane set back from shore was the cottage that served as Ragsdale's law offices. He often worked late. One evening that spring, Ragsdale lit an oil lamp against the gloom, then returned to his law book. The case he studied was complicated, and Ragsdale later explained that he became distracted and accidentally tipped the lamp. Just as quickly, he snatched it back up, grasping the hot chimney. A strange sound started, followed by a sharp odor, but Ragsdale did not feel anything. He pressed his palm against the glass again and watched the skin blister. It occurred to Ragsdale that he had leprosy.

During the next few months Ragsdale prepared himself for exile. Later there was talk of a fiancée, a beautiful half-white girl whose touch he now forbade, but much of that was myth. What was fact was that he seems never to have considered running, or hiding the disease, which barely marked him. Instead, he made a show of his surrender, hoping to encourage others. When he sent a letter to Sheriff Severance's home to report himself, he had already booked passage for the colony, by way of Honolulu. "I therefore surrender myself to you so that I may be disposed of as by law directed," he wrote the sheriff. At Kalihi Hospital the doctor ran a needle across the unfeeling hand and marked William Ragsdale on the list, as patient 1008.

Two days before his disease was confirmed, Ragsdale had sailed from Hilo for the final time. He spent the morning riding the village's shaded lanes, saying his farewells. At the pier, ten persons with leprosy were being rowed to the ship, to join thirty other exiles aboard. "The relations of those who have been taken from Hilo are still howling on the beach," wrote Isabella Bird. By chance she was in Hilo again, for a second visit. Just as the ship weighed anchor, Ragsdale appeared on the waterfront, "carefully dressed as usual, decorated with leis and ohia and gardenia, and escorted by nearly the whole native population," Bird wrote. "Tears and sobs accompanied him, and his countrymen and women all clung to him, kissing him to the last moment, whilst all the foreigners shook hands as they offered him their good wishes." His belongings had been sent ahead to the colony: law books, a Bible, his linen suits, and a horse. Ragsdale turned to face his audience. Speaking in Hawaiian, he praised the government's segregation policy as a sad yet necessary measure. He announced that he expected life to be livable in the colony, despite rumors of the place, and hoped his example of "quiet submission" would inspire others to come forward. He told the crowd that he loved them and would remember them in prayer. "Aloha," he said, "may God bless you, my brothers." Then he repeated the speech, this time in English.

Ragsdale arrived at the colony on June 29, 1873, aboard the schooner *Kinau,* which rounded the point and anchored on the Kalaupapa side. Damien was not in the village that morning. Several hundred exiles hooted and waved from shore. Ragsdale may briefly have imagined that the festive welcome was in his honor, but the celebration existed entirely for its own sake—it was boat day. Studying the spectators who stood along the shore, he spotted a lost friend. Ragsdale raised his gloved hand in greeting, and then burst into tears.

Landing with Ragsdale that day was a thirty-seven-year-old Hawaiian of noble rank named Peter Young Kaeo. Although Kaeo had served in the legislature and thus knew Ragsdale, the two men occupied different social strata, and were not friends. Kaeo was royalty, the cousin and favorite relative of the dowager Queen Emma. He had contracted the disease sometime during the previous decade and managed through considerable influence to avoid being exiled, although as early as January 1868 his condition had been so obvious that the king had gently suggested to Emma that "Peter Kaeo ought to be put in Kalihi Hospital." Yet Kaeo had remained free until the death of Emma's husband, after which the new monarch began to tighten segregation.

With his royal rank, Kaeo immediately became the most prominent citizen in the colony. In letters, Queen Emma urged her cousin to develop his influence, to "be ambitious and bold," and "speak and act with weight or authority" appropriate to his status. Kaeo was a chubby, self-indulgent, preening young man, with a moon-shaped face and pursed mouth; he did not cut a confident figure. Emma hoped that exile, terrible though it was, might sharpen her cousin's character and forge him as a leader.

A day after landing, Kaeo reported to Emma, "I have arrived safe." One of his pet doves had expired on the voyage over, he explained, and his mirror was broken. Some of his possessions had also gone missing among the ship's crew: his saddle, the headboard to his bed, a teapot. But otherwise he was fine. He had purchased a wooden cottage in the colony, set a comfortable distance from the other huts, but not too far from the hospital compound. Wealth, and the resource of Queen Emma, made Kaeo's situation more livable than most. Emma shipped weekly packages of bread, potatoes, pumpkins, beef, and seeds for his garden, which Kaeo hired workers to till. The supplies spared him from having to eat the board's rations, on which the others depended for survival. "My share of Poi I dare not touch," he informed Emma, "so it goes to my fowl."

On July 16 Kaeo wrote, "I have had a call from the Catholic Priest." Father Damien had stopped on his rounds to introduce himself, as he usually did with newcomers. Having apparently been told by William Ragsdale that Kaeo, like Queen Emma, belonged to the Anglican Church, Damien kept the visit brief. "He has not spoken a word about Religion to me," Peter Kaeo wrote, then added, "He is a very nice man." The queen quickly responded with a long letter on the history of the Roman and Anglican branches of Catholicism, the corruption of the pope, the Reformation, and the "numerous wicked things" that the Roman Catholic Church had done. "If you were to tell a Roman priest that," Emma cautioned, "they will deny such events occurred." She then asked if Kaeo was maintaining his journal. "It keeps one in the habit of writing and you know practice makes perfect." Kaeo's spelling was awful, Emma had noticed.

The letters of Peter Kaeo in his first weeks of exile are narratives of want and melancholy. "I must humbly bow my head to the maker of all things and say, Thy Will be done," he wrote. Letters passed between the relatives every few days, often addressed "Dear Coz." Kaeo asked Emma to send pickets for his fence, tinned sardines and halibut, white canvas shoes with soles of India rubber, his "little dogey" named Spring, and yet another snow dove, because the bird widowed on the voyage had "pined right away" and joined its mate in heaven. One day Emma unfolded a letter and read Kaeo's description of his prison walls: "I have sat on my Horse watching the wild waves comeing with all its fury and dashing itself against the Pali, which towers Majesticly up quite perpendicular, and I have immagened this Mountain looking down and mocking its efforts." A few days later, her cousin confessed that he had become immobilized by his own misery. "I felt so sad that I sat watching from my Verandah the Island you are on—Home."

* * *

Ragsdale's correspondence served a far less elegiac agenda. Within weeks of landing he was actively campaigning for the job of resident superintendent, the leadership position that Jonathan Napela held. "I will carefully post you on everything that occurs here, either to yourself or through Mr. Meyer," he wrote to the board. "There seems to be no head or tail to the institution just now because the luna does not preserve his dignity, or at least the dignities of his office." Aware that the board faced a constant budget crisis, Ragsdale played to their desire that the colony be cost-efficient. He offered to undertake a "study of economy" and promised that he would "try to the *best of my ability* to carry out the wishes of the Hon. Board in *every particular.*" Ragsdale's lobbying succeeded—by autumn Jonathan Napela had been removed from office, and Ragsdale named in his place.

Shortly thereafter, Ragsdale announced in a letter, "I mean to make the balance of my days here, useful to my friends in affliction . . . as well as to the public at large." After years as a mere functionary to more powerful men, Ragsdale relished his new authority. "Governor Ragsdale," as he asked to be called, quickly assembled a miniature legislature of twenty exiles, "by whom ordinary controversies and disagreements are settled," one visitor later described. There was no question who had final say, however. "The superior mind of Ragsdale guides and regulates his little principality in most matters of government," the visitor wrote, "quite as absolutely and undisputedly as the captain of a ship whose word is law." Even Queen Emma recognized Ragsdale's abundant skills and advised her cousin Peter Kaeo to make a study of him, "for he is a superior mind, and [while] you are away improve yourself without his suspecting you, using him for your means."

Ragsdale's methods, however, appeared inscrutable to the young Hawaiian. When Kaeo ventured out his cottage door and into the settlement, he saw only suffering. The meat that the board provided was poor, the poi often inedible. "Some have no cooking utensils to cook with," Kaeo reported, and the hospital overflowed with untended patients. "The poor natives are beginning to die almost daily," he wrote. To Emma he described how one infirm exile had lain forgotten for a week, living "on what he could find in his Hut, anything Chewable." Another time Kaeo stumbled across seven people living in a damp cave within the Given Grave's dead lava tube: "Oh you cannot form any Idea how they looked." He told Emma the story of a patient who had buried his deceased father, but too shallowly, and the corpse "was eat by the Hogs." Constables tossed the man in jail for six days, as a lesson to the others to be more thorough.

All of these scenes appalled the fragile Kaeo and offered a clear indictment of the board's management. Yet the newspapers Kaeo received from Emma were filled with quotes from Ragsdale about how satisfactory things were in the settlement. Ragsdale had written Sheriff Luther Severance "a few short lines from this place, where my responsibilities are so heavy." He remarked, "I have found that the lepers living here have been very well fed and clothed, better cared for than they were in their own homes." The sheriff passed Ragsdale's politic account along to a Hawaiian-language newspaper, which Kaeo later read. "I cannot see how Ragsdale [could] say in his letter that the people here are better provided for then at their own homes," Kaeo complained. Ragsdale might be better off, Kaeo told Emma, but most people in the colony were suffering.

The board nonetheless continued to try to find ways "of reducing the expenses of the asylum." After some debate it resolved to "entrust Mr. Meyer to report to the Board . . . the best means of carrying on the asylum—that is to say—the cheapest and most feasible method." One scheme called for Ragsdale to acquire "all the horses he could" from the patients, then "kill them for beef, serving the meat out on the regular days of supplying meat." Another decision involved the more than one hundred kokuas who lived in the settlement. Although the board had over the years begun to allow these volunteers to draw rations, it now decided to rescind that costly decision. Ragsdale was told to drop all but "real lepers" from the ration book. Kaeo soon reported, "Ragsdale is actually starving the poor Natives. Since he has been Luna he has made more Enemyes and less friends." When a group of residents massed in protest of the board's decisions, Ragsdale arrested the leaders and threw them in jail.

One day in the midst of the unrest Kaeo wrote Emma, "The sick persons are moveing to the Beach for fear of the comeing Winter." What he described was the seasonal migration of the exiles who lived in the creases of the cliff. Fierce winter gales, known as kona winds, whistled rain directly into these small valleys, battering the residents. "And being weak they generally die," Kaeo wrote. Kona winds could rival those of a hurricane and could howl for days, as Father Damien recounted: "A heavy south wind blew . . . and many a weak leper laid there in the wind and rain, with his blanket and clothes damp and wet." The storm Damien described destroyed twenty-two homes, and half of the buildings in the settlement required fixing. Rudolph Meyer arranged for emergency lumber, and teams of kokuas made most of the repairs—Damien later alerted the board that he also "did the work of erecting a good many small houses." In a letter home Damien was more obviously pleased with his effort: "I lend them my arms for several days, and lo! They are housed."

* * *

During September 1873 the king, Whiskey Bill, embarked on a weeklong drunk. It culminated with his collapse on the lawn of his beach house in Waikiki, where he slumbered through the night. Already weak from tuberculosis and alcoholism, he "took cold in his injured lungs," Queen Emma informed Peter Kaeo. After examining the king, Dr. Georges Trousseau reported that the monarch "cannot live very much longer, unless he abstains from the use of intoxicating drink." He did not. A few months later, after a reign of one year and twenty-five days, William Lunalilo died. The government budget was further broken by the elaborate royal funeral.

Lunalilo died without naming a successor. In the weeks before his death two candidates had emerged: a Hawaiian politician with royal bloodlines named David Kalakaua, and Peter Kaeo's cousin, the dowager Queen Emma. Kaeo was desperate for Emma to rule, as were many exiles. In the past year more than four hundred men, women, and children had arrived at the colony, and the majority blamed the monarchy for endorsing the policy that had ensnared them. If elected, Emma might ease the segregation laws to benefit her cousin—perhaps she would end exile altogether. Seeking insight into the upcoming vote, Kaeo went to visit Paniku Hua, the colony's infamous kahuna.

Hua proclaimed that Emma would be victorious. But when the legislature met, Kalakaua received thirty-nine votes and Emma only six. Her supporters in Honolulu, known as Queenites, stormed the courthouse and confronted the lawmakers, then smashed the chamber's furniture, tore apart books, and shredded public records. Their riot accomplished little, however. David Kalakaua took the throne.

The new monarch arrived to inspect the colony one Tuesday morning soon after his election. Anticipating the visit, Peter Kaeo feared he would be forced to host his enemy. "I am sure that if they come on shore the only Place fit to enter, without being afraid of catching the disease if Contagious, will be mine," he remarked to Emma. He would be "pleasant" toward the king, he wrote, but his heart would "be burning for Satisfaction." Kalakaua, however, stepped ashore only long enough to utter a few words about sacrifice. After he had gone, several exiles upbraided themselves for their inaction, Kaeo reported, since the king "could have been easily dispatched before any assistance could have come."

When David Kalakaua had retreated to the *Kilauea,* several reporters and what remained of the landing party started for Kalawao, led by Georges Trousseau. William Ragsdale rode up to greet them. "Mr. Ragsdale is well known all over the islands," a reporter wrote, and "his authority among his fellow-exiles . . . is almost autocratic." Proceeding to the hospital, the party encountered William Williamson, the brick mason turned nurse. A reporter asked Williamson how he was feeling. "Smart as a cricket," Williamson replied, though by this date the disease had badly damaged him. Then the reporter turned and saw "a sight that will ever remain fixed on the tablets of memory. A little blue-eyed, flaxen-haired child, apparently three or four years old . . . that looked up at us with an expression of timorous longing to be caressed and loved; but alas, in its glassy eyes and transparent cheeks were the unmistakable signs of the curse—the sin of the parents visited upon the child!" The reporter ran from the hospital and had soon reboarded the ship.

Having "spent fully three hours" in the colony, the reporter attested that "nothing short of actual duty will tempt us to make another visit." However, he concluded, Trousseau and the board were to be praised for their efforts. "Every impartial mind must admit that in the isolation and management of the unfortunate few among its population who have contracted this dreadful disease [the] Board of Health, has acted with a promptness, efficiency and humanity that entitles it to the utmost credit; and which in this particular places it in the foremost rank among civilized nations."

Peter Kaeo held a different opinion. His dispatches from the colony, however, failed to appear in the newspapers. "So whatever is now printed must pass for true," he complained to Emma, "and the Public at large take it for granted that all is true, and believe it as such. And not for a Moment dream of Men's Cruelty to Human being."

A few weeks after the king's visit, a second group of outsiders arrived for an inspection tour. Among them was a legislator named Kapahei Kauai, an old friend of both Peter Kaeo's and Queen Emma's. Kauai carried a letter from Emma to her cousin. And after he delivered it, he remained with Kaeo for several hours, talking about politics and Honolulu society. Soon, the discussion progressed to more somber things. Kauai lamented the board's treatment of leprosy victims. He felt certain, however, that public opinion would force the board to find a more humane approach. The suffering was bound to end. Kaeo need only hang on a short while longer.

Nineteen years later, Kapahei Kauai, now known as Judge Kauai, would have a similar conversation with another sick and angry young man. By then the judge would also have leprosy. And as his friend, Koolau, fled into the sheltering cliffs of Kalalau Valley with his wife and child and a loaded rifle, government soldiers would burst through the door of Judge Kauai's cottage and drag the Archleper screaming from his hiding place beneath his bed.

Escape

(Population 673)

Since the first days of exile, 750 people had died in the colony. The board had banished 1,509 men, women, and children. Those who still survived formed the fitful community overseen by William Ragsdale. The government now believed the work of segregation was mostly complete. Although "[we] are not prepared to advance any new ideas or theories as to the cure of leprosy," the board reported, "at the same time [we] feel assured that the disease is under control; and that another two years of active action like the past will have isolated the afflicted and checked the disease." All issues concerning rations and shelter had been resolved, the board boasted.

The settlement store held a thousand dollars of board-supplied inventory, including clothing and food. Exiles with funds, such as Peter Kaeo, could buy the things they needed. Most others were destitute, however. Often the board had seized their property and savings to underwrite their exile. As compensation, the board granted each patient a yearly $5.75 allowance, though that was barely enough to cover the cost of a single pair of pants and shoes. As another budgetary action, the board instructed Ragsdale to substitute rice and tinned salmon for the costlier beef and poi, an economizing that the settlers quickly decided was deliberately cruel.

Residents began to look to Kaeo to lead a revolt against Ragsdale. "A man just said to me that they were only waiting for order from me," Kaeo wrote. The discontented exiles "were willing to do anything I said in the way of disturbance, as they were sent here to die by the Government, and as they were willing to die now as any other time." When Ragsdale confronted several patients on a road crew and accused them of shirking, they threatened to crush his skull with rocks. Afterward Kaeo cautioned Ragsdale to remain wary—several of the men had announced, "We're dead people," and thus felt they could murder with impunity. The next argument, Kaeo told Ragsdale, "might end with something that you . . . might not anticipate."

Certain that Ragsdale held the board's interests above theirs, two hundred residents signed a petition calling for his dismissal, and for Kaeo to replace him. Although Kaeo insisted to Emma that he was not orchestrating the unrest, Ragsdale told the board that he believed Kaeo and his accomplices "are trying to do all they can to make mischief among the ignorant portion of the lepers under my charge." He assigned a man to spy on Kaeo, and to watch for a gathering mutiny. Ragsdale then heard whispers that Kaeo was assembling an armed militia and meant to torch the hospital and seize control of the colony. Imagining that Kaeo would strike one particular Saturday night, Ragsdale stationed men near his cottage, "armed with Knife and Axes," as Kaeo later wrote.

That evening, Ragsdale waited in the dark for Kaeo. He had placed constables along the path leading into the main compound, with instructions to attack when the rebels approached. During the night, patients friendly to Kaeo had also gathered, aware that trouble was brewing. "Knowing Ragsdale to be armed [they] had armed themselves with Stones and Sticks," Kaeo wrote. "The Cook house being near, [some] were also ready to set fire to the building, while others pelted Ragsdale and his backers with Stone, thus keeping them in the House." Just past dawn, Kaeo rode into the compound. He stopped his horse several yards away from the hospital. One of the exiles ran to him.

"Ragsdale is armed with a pistol and a knife," the man announced.

Kaeo glanced at the cottage and replied, "I am going to see if there is any shooting in him."

Climbing onto Ragsdale's porch, Kaeo started for the door. A constable kicked a bench across the doorway, blocking the way. "I stepped over it and stood in front of Ragsdale," Kaeo wrote. "I stood so near to him that he turned pale. He stood with one hand in his Coat brest, but could not move."

With his fingers resting on his pistol, Ragsdale demanded to know Kaeo's business. Kaeo replied he had come to discuss an upcoming holiday feast—at the previous feast several patients felt they had not received a fair share of roasted pork and had asked Kaeo to raise the issue with Ragsdale.

Ragsdale stared at Kaeo in disbelief. Then he let out a long breath and suggested Kaeo write to the board about the pork. Kaeo thanked him and left. As he walked across the compound to the settlement store, the crowd set down their weapons and began to disperse. "On Account of the . . . affair the Store [was] closed," Kaeo later complained to Emma. "I should like to have [had] a fiew bars of Soap."

Rudolph Meyer rode down the cliff a short time later, having heard of the near mutiny. "He, Ragsdale, and I talked the subject over," Kaeo wrote, "and Ragsdale said that he was misled by the different rhumours, and was glad to apologize to me." Meyer lifted a bottle of claret from his coat pocket and asked the two men to drink and shake hands, which they did willingly. What they now had in common, Kaeo and Ragsdale decided, outweighed past differences.

Neither man was yet terribly disfigured by the disease. In Ragsdale's case, one visitor reported, "leprosy had only developed to the extent of affecting his nasal bones, with some flattening of the nose as a consequence, and deformity of the fingers." Leprosy had crippled both men's hands, however, and they commonly wore gloves—Kaeo shoved wooden splints into the fingers to straighten his frozen grip. Later the disease began to damage their feet, and they discovered that their shoes no longer fit. Kaeo asked Emma to send him a new pair, and gave his size elevens to the smaller Ragsdale. Ragsdale tugged them on, twirled a silk scarf around his neck, and set forth on his administrative rounds. Lack of feeling in his soles tipped him into an awkward, rolling gait, which observers likened to that of a wandering drunk. The stuttered stride supplied Ragsdale's nickname in the colony: Vagabond Bill.

As they awaited the onset of leprosy's more serious symptoms, Ragsdale and Kaeo searched for salvation. When two visiting physicians came to the colony offering a cure, they both volunteered for trials. One of the doctors, a black physician from New York City named William Powell, quickly exited the colony. A Chinese physician named Sing Kee Akana persevered. Akana's alleged remedy, Kaeo informed Emma, consisted of "Centipede, a black Skin from a Snake or Eel, Cocaroach, and other nasty things. Now if these are the medecins which he thinks will Cure the Leper all right, but for my part I put very little faith in him." Kaeo added, "Ragsdale . . . told me that he does not feel the slightest change, but he takes the Medicine according to his humor, and not by directions." After six months Akana announced that he had cured one of his six subjects. The patient was sent to Honolulu and determined to still be sick. Reported the board, "This ended Dr. Akana's attempt to cure leprosy."

Though the exiles repeatedly begged for a resident physician, the board continued to try to service the settlement with visiting doctors and untrained nurses. When William Williamson died in September 1875, the board put a patient named David Ostrom in charge of the hospital. Ostrom was a fifty-five-year-old former New Yorker who had acquired some simple medical skills, and who harbored a grudging, slightly academic respect for medicine. "He feels satisfied that his case is incurable," a physician reported of Ostrom. "Would be willing to surrender his body to be vivisected, if necessary for the benefit of medical science."

Though Ostrom was the only full-time medical practitioner in the colony, Damien also gave out medicines and tended the sick, but the board did not endorse his practice. Together, the two men managed to better the condition of many patients. As Damien later reported, "The people perceiving that by the use of such simple medicines as we had to dispose of, their troubles were greatly ameliorated, and therefore they began to call more and more for the simple remedies, and thus gradually a perceptible improvement took place." He added, "As we had no doctor . . . we tried to do the best we could."

The board, however, had abandoned any pretense of treating the disease. It closed Kalihi Hospital and replaced it with a spartan, heavily guarded building next to the police station in Honolulu. There, the board president wrote, "the sick are retained until the physicians decide they are lepers or not." He offered a rationale for the move: "This arrangement reduced considerable the expenses of the board." Suspects would now simply be arrested, given cursory examination at the Leper Detention Station, and then either released or sent to Molokai to die. Kalihi Hospital was disassembled and the lumber shipped to the colony, where some of it was used to construct coffins. Soon thereafter the exiles coined a new name for their overseers: the Board of Death.

As Ostrom and Damien labored to aid the sick, Peter Kaeo and William Ragsdale settled into their respective routines. Ragsdale concentrated on his duties as resident superintendent. Kaeo, meanwhile, fixated on becoming free. He had grown convinced that if he could return to Honolulu, he might reclaim his legislative seat and remove the king. Then Emma would rule. The two cousins were soon plotting his escape. Using an English lawyer to manage the details, Emma arranged for boatmen to attempt a channel crossing in a canoe. They were to land in the colony, creep to Kaeo's cottage, retrieve him, and make haste for Oahu. While the daring scheme took shape, Emma continued to send Kaeo his weekly care packages, "in order to carry on the pretense that I [know] nothing of the plans for your rescue." But the plot soon came apart. One of the boatmen, an exasperated Emma wrote, "had been so indiscreet as to tell many people of the object of his trip. Everyone had it on the tip of their tongues."

Just weeks later, however, the board announced a sudden decision to release Kaeo, with the stipulation "that he should remain under the surveillance of the Board, [and] that he refrain from mingling in public life." Exactly how Emma achieved this was never determined. The details mattered little to Kaeo—he was free. Bidding an emotional farewell to Ragsdale, Kaeo boarded a steamer and sailed for Honolulu.

A few weeks after Kaeo's return, the *Advertiser* printed a letter to the editor, signed "Righteous Indignation." The author complained about several "well-authenticated cases" of leprosy loose in the city. Righteous Indignation asserted that the board "know[s] all about these cases, but it is not policy to notice them. Cool, is it not?" Despite the protest, the board never again bothered Kaeo, and at the next legislative session, he reclaimed his seat in the House of Nobles. His bitter opposition to the king proved futile, however. David Kalakaua was still monarch when, as the *Hawaiian Gazette* reported, "the Hon. P.Y. Kaeo died at his residence on Emma Street," on November 26, 1880. The funeral took place two days later, and Peter Young Kaeo was buried with "appropriate honors." The obituaries never mentioned leprosy.

In July 1876 the United States Bureau of Medicine and Surgery sent a prominent naval surgeon named George Woods to Molokai, to undertake a weeklong investigation of the colony. He debarked from a warship anchored off Kalaupapa and was plucked from a lighter as it approached the settlement in heavy seas. Men hoisted Woods aloft and, he later wrote, "passed me from hand to hand, over the slippery rocks and up the bluff." William Ragsdale and Father Damien were there to greet the doctor. Ragsdale offered Woods "his contracted claw-like gloved hand," Woods reported, and "announced himself as Governor Ragsdale." Introducing Damien, Ragsdale exclaimed that here was the "the true 'Father' of the settlement and his 'right-hand coadjutor.'"

Dr. Woods took the now-standard tour: past "churches, the hospital, the store, the numerous comfortable whitewashed houses surrounded by gardens." When evening arrived, Ragsdale led the doctor to "a simple roughly built bungalow of 3 rooms, opening upon a verandah." This was Ragsdale's cottage. At one end was a small room, set apart for use by visitors. After dining on the boiled chicken and tomato salad that had been laid out for him, the doctor joined Ragsdale on the veranda. The two men smoked cigars and talked. Ragsdale, Woods later wrote, could recite "pages of Scott and Byron, and Tennyson, often manifesting great dramatic emotion." One of Ragsdale's favorites was Sir Walter Scott's minstrel tale of honor and sacrifice, which he acted out for Woods on the porch of the cottage. In a deep, melodic voice, Ragsdale declaimed: "Here, where the end of earthly things / Lays heroes, patriots, bards, and kings; / Where stiff the hand, and still the tongue / Of those who fought, and spoke, and sung."

Afterward the men were silently admiring the view when Woods heard "distant music, strange and shrill." What on earth is that? Woods asked.

"That is Father Damien and his boys," Ragsdale explained, "coming to serenade you."

Woods saw a dozen children marching across the lawn, playing makeshift flutes. A dozen more hurried along behind the band, swinging lamps in the dusk. Two boys flanked the procession, hoisting Hawaiian and American flags. When the parade reached the cottage, Damien stepped forward.

"Permit me, monsieur le doctor, to present my boys," Father Damien announced. "They have come to welcome you and to thank you for coming so far to inquire after them, and see if anything can be done to cure them."

Damien handed Woods one of the instruments to inspect. It was "made of old oil cans," Woods wrote, "fashioned by himself, on which he had patiently taught the boys to play by ear. The harmony and musical character was perfect, though very strange and peculiar."

As Woods sat enrapt, Damien began to lead the band through a haunting rendition of "The Star-Spangled Banner." Just then, the doctor saw something flare across his vision. A moment later another shower of sparks arced through the night. Again Woods asked, What on earth is that? Ragsdale explained: Rudolph Meyer and his sons were hurling chunks of burning wood from atop the cliff, in a display of homemade fireworks. It was Independence Day.

By the following year Ragsdale's declining health had reached a crisis point. "Our beloved Bill Ragsdale is nearly at the term of his days," Damien wrote. Meyer advised the board that they would need to decide on Ragsdale's replacement. At its next meeting, the board voted to send an official notice of thanks to Ragsdale "for the very efficient and faithful manner in which he had discharged the duties of Superintendent." They offered their "deep sympathy" for his affliction. Ragsdale listened as someone read the letter aloud, but he could not reply. Leprosy had finally taken his most valued possession: his voice. Ragsdale died several days later, on November 24, 1877.

"DEATH OF THE KING OF THE LEPERS," the *New York Times* reported. A brief sketch of Ragsdale's life followed, and the opinion that "by his tact and kindheartedness Ragsdale made the most extraordinary and saddest community on the face of the earth as cheerful and happy as . . . could be." The local press was more animated in its grief. "Who will supply his place?" asked the *Advertiser*. "Who among the unfortunates there has the ability, the industry, the energy, the intelligence, and love of country displayed by William P. Ragsdale?"

When Mark Twain read the news of Ragsdale's demise, he recalled his idea of a novel, which he had let languish. Now that Ragsdale had succumbed to, as Twain described it, "the loathsome and lingering death that all lepers die," he decided to return to the tale. In time he had enough completed to alert his friend William Dean Howells of the project, which followed Ragsdale as he grew from a willful half-native boy into a "highly civilized" and educated man. Then, Twain explained to Howells, he jumped the narrative to "do Ragsdale's leper business." This meant having Ragsdale exiled to the colony, where he fell into a world of paganism and lawlessness—thus illustrating, Twain wrote, "a but-little considered fact in human nature: that the religious folly you are born in you will die in." Later, Twain informed another acquaintance that he had finished his novel and was about to give it a "most painstaking revision."

The book never appeared, however. No trace has ever been found, except for seventeen typewritten pages of a partial manuscript. In 1958 a Twain scholar realized what had apparently become of the novel. Stalled with revisions and needing to stanch the financial losses of an ill-fated business venture, Twain had reworked his story of a modern man transported to a place of ancient hardship. He shifted the setting from Hawaii to Camelot, and the court of King Arthur. William Ragsdale had become Hank Morgan, a Connecticut Yankee.

The Likes of Us

(Population 824)

The death of William Ragsdale had, once again, left the settlement without a resident superintendent. During Ragsdale's final days, Father Damien had written a letter in which he warned the president of the board that he "will grumble him—if he appoints a bad man for this place." The board tried several different leadership arrangements, but none of them proved satisfactory. Then, to the surprise of all, it named Damien as resident superintendent.

With characteristic zeal, Damien tried to immediately resolve more than a decade of strife in the settlement. He considered no matter too minor for his attention. An acquaintance later wrote of Damien that "he was easily excited, easily peeved, supersensitive, and difficult to get along with at times." The man greatly admired the priest, but thought him hardheaded: "He had very fixed views and brooked no interference with his will." Less than a month after Damien assumed his new role, Rudolph Meyer sent some advice down the cliff: "I would caution you to make as little change as possible for the present, and put up with little irregularities for now, or else in case of need you will find that there is nobody to rely upon." Damien charged ahead anyway. Several tumultuous months later, however, he resigned from the position, by mutual agreement with Meyer and the board. Apparently in relief, Damien exclaimed to Father Modeste, "And now I'm free again!"

At Meyer's suggestion, the board then attempted to spread the responsibilities of the resident superintendent among several patients. The effort only created chaos. Soon the settlement jail overflowed, and constables began detaining lawbreakers with a ball and chain. The "order and quiet which [Ragsdale] established," as the board had written, had vanished.

What the colony required, one legislator announced, was a person "with first rate executive ability," someone who was "an enthusiast in the cause of humanity." Such a man was more easily described than found. Every week, as the documents of exile crossed the desk of the board president, he scanned the sheets for names, to see who might be approaching on the horizon. The president would notice a name creep once onto the suspect list, then see the same name more frequently as the person passed through the system, was arrested, examined, declared a leper, and exiled. If the name was that of a white man, the board made a note to investigate, to see if they might use him. In time, the board found the new resident superintendent in this way. His name was Clayton Strawn.

Strawn was the child of Pennsylvania Quakers, proprietors of a Bucks County establishment called the Court Inn. One family member later wrote that Clayton "never cared for this kind of life. He yearned for the life on the waters." While still in his teens Strawn made his way to New Bedford to join a whaling ship. He returned to Pennsylvania only once, in 1875, to secure his small inheritance. While home, Strawn entertained his relatives with tales of his life at sea. He told of jumping ship in Tahiti, doing battle with cannibals, and living on Easter Island, "the isle of nameless gods and forgotten deities," as one of Strawn's acquaintances later recounted. "[He] led in all way the career of the south-sea adventurer." Most of Strawn's stories were false, however, enlarged by whiskey and imagination. The one that was apparently most true was one he rarely shared—Strawn had been a slave trader in the South Pacific.

One morning in 1876 the schooner on which Strawn crewed was sailing Hawaiian waters. Strawn rose from his bunk, stropped the blade of a straight razor, and brushed his face with lather. Just as he began to shave, the ship's captain appeared, and Strawn quickly turned. The razor sliced through something solid. Strawn felt only a tug.

"Good God, Strawn!" the captain cried. "You have cut off a piece of your ear."

"He had indeed, and did not know it," the man to whom Strawn later told the story wrote. "The plague, long latent in his blood, was now declared."

Clayton Strawn reached the colony on August 23, 1878. He was thirty-nine years old. After a few weeks he reported to the board, "This place can be made very comfortable by a little forethought and industry." One of his first acts was to distribute small zinc tags, each scratched with a number. Every exile was assigned a tag, and Strawn used the numbers to monitor ration taking and other administrative matters. By design, the system also allowed Strawn to track his adversaries. His enemies list soon filled. "As things are at present I have very few friends," he wrote to the board that autumn. He asked to be alerted if someone filed a grievance with the board—not to exact revenge, he insisted, but to smooth away the trouble. "I want to know what is going on they do not like me at all," he wrote, "nevertheless I shall continue to do my duty faithfully."

Strawn's suspicions about his unpopularity were well-founded. Almost immediately after his arrival, patients began to send letters to the board accusing Strawn of cruelty and incompetence. Then residents started a petition to have him removed as luna. Unaware of Strawn's slave-trading past, the board had no reason to believe that the criticism was anything more than the usual sour reaction to a strong leader. When Father Damien also began to denounce Strawn, and complain about his drunkenness and his endorsement of patient-run speakeasies, the board assumed Damien was merely being a moralist. Frustrated, Damien confronted the profane Strawn, but the seaman mocked his message of temperance. "I wanted to put some life in the thing," Strawn later said of the settlement. Very quickly Strawn became one of "Father Damien's bitter slanderers," one resident wrote. In his reports to the board, however, Strawn downplayed the tensions. "The Priest," he wrote, was harmless—a meddlesome fool.

Strawn lived in a cottage with what he proudly described as "a multitude" of mistresses, some of whom were married. The arrangement scandalized Damien, as did most aspects of Strawn's behavior: allowing an illicit trade in liquor and sex; selling patients' rations to outsiders; demanding protection money. In the words of one resident, Strawn was "a degenerate, and immoral man," who soon found himself locked in a tense battle of wills with the priest. But Damien was as physically imposing as the stocky Strawn and far more stubborn. He had the habit of standing close to a person when he spoke, bending forward as the argument built. "Damien was a good fighter [and] held his ground," a board physician later wrote, "he bided his times and returned to attack as defiant and undaunted as ever." Describing the growing animus between Damien and Strawn, a resident observed, "The good Father Damien was not the kind of man to give away to despair."

Embracing Strawn as his personal cause, Damien began to pray intensely for, as Damien described it, Strawn's "leprous soul." In the notebook that he maintained, Damien remarked, "To do good to souls I must lead a hard and mortified life not getting discouraged over anything. There are sinners that can be converted only by doing penance for them." Strawn's other adversaries sought quicker resolution. One afternoon a mob of fifty patients confronted Strawn as he rode from Kalawao. Most men in the colony carried knives, and although the board forbade firearms, many patients also owned guns. The exiles surrounded Strawn and threatened to kill him. Strawn laughed.

"Why don't you do it?" he yelled. "I'll be the sooner through with this leprosy."

* * *

On a single day in September one hundred patients landed in the colony, including forty-eight women and two eight-year-olds, a boy and a girl. Clayton Strawn was waiting. To each newcomer he handed a zinc tag, and then sent them away to find shelter. Even after a dozen years, living conditions in the settlement were often atrocious. A party of legislators had recently visited and reported the news that Kalawao was cold, wet, and horribly overcrowded. Cottages were "entirely too small, badly constructed, and in unfavorable situations." People curled at night beneath crude lean-tos, "roof[s] without walls . . . covered with a thatch of partly ferns and sugar cane blades." Many residents lacked lamp oil, soap, salt, bowls, buckets, and utensils. Bandages were scarce, and since the board did not provide caskets, Damien and a few others organized "coffin feasts for the indigent." The price of a casket in the colony was now two dollars.

When he had returned from the inspection, one prominent legislator wrote that the colony was "a spectacle of terrible human woe made more miserable by mismanagement." If the government did not correct matters, "it will sink us in disgrace." After publication of the blistering report, the board agreed to finally station a doctor in the settlement. Nathaniel Bright Emerson, a thirty-nine-year-old who had previously practiced at Manhattan's Bellevue Hospital, reluctantly agreed to go—with the condition that his tenure last only twelve months. Dr. Emerson had cresting black hair and a neat mustache, and a brooding gaze that made him resemble Edgar Allan Poe. He was mortally afraid of leprosy, and believed that "Every leper is a possible source of infection to whomsoever comes in contact with him." Before undertaking an exam Emerson would cram twists of cotton up his nose, and layer himself beneath lab coats. Even then he refused to touch his patients and often simply prodded them with a stick. When he packed his trunk to leave for the colony, Emerson added several pairs of rubber gloves and a heavy glass jug of disinfecting alcohol.

At 7:30 P.M. on January 4, 1879, Nathaniel Emerson strolled down the pier at the foot of Fort Street, in Honolulu, and climbed aboard the steamer bound for Molokai. With him was the current president of the board, Samuel Wilder. As they crossed the steamer deck, the men peered into a set of cattle pens at the head of the boat. The enclosure held a dozen people, including a dark-eyed young man with fine, appealing features. Emerson did not know the patient. Wilder, however, might have recognized a resemblance in the man—he was the spitting image of Wilder's predecessor on the board, Dr. Ferdinand Hutchison. The exile, in fact, was Ambrose Hutchison, the doctor's youngest son.

* * *

Every patient was not equal. Money and influence could often snip the nets of segregation, as Peter Kaeo had proved. Some persons found to have leprosy were allowed to seek a cure in Japan or flee quietly to Europe or America. At times the board slipped foreign patients $100 if they would return to their native country; the practice was a "positive economy," one board member declared, since every exile in the colony was costing about that amount each year. When the attorney general questioned the legality of the practice, however, it stopped. Foreigners found other means of escape. A German named Christian Bertelmann evaded the colony by dressing as a woman and sneaking on a ship bound for Japan; eventually he smuggled himself back to Kauai, where his family kept him hidden in a secret room in their house. A New Englander named Charles Derby managed to board a ship for the mainland before agents caught him. By the time Derby reached his hometown of Salem, Massachusetts, leprosy marked his nose, ears, and hands, and he was detained. "IS HE A LEPER?" the *Boston Globe Supplement* asked. Two medical students, in Boston for education after boyhoods in Hawaii, were called to identify "the insidious, incurable disease so prevalent and so much dreaded in their far-away home." Locked in the Salem almshouse, Derby went slowly blind, as a reporter from the *Salem Observer* discovered. "I am all right inside," Derby told the reporter. "If I could only shake off my skin"—Derby had made a motion as if shrugging off a coat—"I should be all right."

Flight was the most common method, but there were other ways to circumvent the colony. Occasionally the board allowed wealthy persons to avoid exile by agreeing to house arrest, as it had with a man named John Reeves. Though visibly diseased, Reeves had pled to remain at his Waikiki home, under treatment by his personal physician. The board relented, with the condition that "he did not mingle." When Reeves "grossly violated" this order, he was banished. Dr. Hutchison, who was still a board member at the time, gave his assent on the verdict, condemning Reeves to death in the colony.

By then, Dr. Hutchison had settled the fate of more than two thousand people. The work had a cost. When Hutchison's affiliation with the board ended, the doctor departed Hawaii for Australia, never to return. One morning while living in Queensland, Hutchison woke, stuffed some supplies in a rucksack, and vanished on foot into the outback.

The doctor left three surviving children, born to a Hawaiian woman named Malie Moa, the first of Hutchison's three wives. The couple had married after meeting in the early 1850s on the island of Maui, where Hutchison had maintained a medical practice in the port town of Lahaina. When

Moa died unexpectedly, Hutchison left Lahaina for Honolulu, handing his three young children—Christina, William, and Ambrose—to relatives of his late wife. Ambrose Hutchison landed in the home of a distant aunt and was soon sent away to boarding school. Years later he would write, "I have never had a true mother's care."

Although documents show that Ferdinand Hutchison maintained a relationship with Christina, Ambrose's sister, it is unclear if he made a similar effort with his youngest son. In letters and in the unfinished memoir he later wrote, Ambrose never mentions a father. The omission seems intentional and is perhaps Ambrose's attempt to shield his father from the stigma that settled on relatives of exiles, or a form of exoneration. He knew exactly who his father was, however: on official records, Ambrose accurately lists Edinburgh, Scotland, as his father's birthplace and physician as his father's occupation.

The pages of Ambrose Hutchison's memoir intimately detail the stirrings of his leprosy, which he detected in 1868—about the same time that Ferdinand Hutchison was trying to keep the exiles from murdering Donald Walsh. "The first symptoms I noticed were, absence of feeling over my right knee cap, either to touch, pinching, or needle prick, the loss of sensation gradually spread down to the ankle and foot," he wrote. Hutchison's aunt was a kahuna who specialized in herbal cures, and on several occasions she had treated a vividly infectious case of leprosy in the cottage in which Ambrose had briefly lived. He wrote, "I may have become a leper from contact with this man." By the time he entered boarding school Ambrose was likely already infected; he was twelve when the symptoms appeared.

It is probable that an agent or a doctor first reported Ambrose Hutchison's condition. The case would have come to the attention of Dr. Edward Hoffmann. Having learned the young man's name, Hoffmann would have gone to Ferdinand Hutchison. But if Dr. Hutchison tried to intercede on his son's behalf, the effort did not make it into the board's records. These show that in December 1878, twenty-two-year-old Ambrose Hutchison was arrested and locked in the leprosy detention station. He was held there for a month.

On the night of January 4 an officer took Ambrose and eleven other men and women and formed them in a line, two abreast. Each prisoner clutched a single sack of belongings. Policemen marched the group through the quiet city streets to the esplanade. At the end of the pier was the *Mokolii,* a "miserable little tub of a steamer," one physician later wrote. The group was funneled up the ramp and led into a series of open-air wooden stalls. Ambrose folded his blanket into a mattress and lay down on the deck. The steamer lurched away at six knots, and the passage was relatively calm, but Hutchison did not sleep. Shortly before 7 A.M. the *Mokolii* arrived at Kalaupapa. The newcomers climbed into a whaleboat that had slid alongside the ship and were rowed through the surf to shore. Clayton Strawn greeted them. "After our names, ages and places we hailed from were taken down," Hutchison later recalled, "[we were] left on the rocky shore without food and shelter. No houses provided . . . for the like of us outcasts."

Hutchison spent his first day resting in the cottage of a distant relative of his late mother's, Richard Una, who had been exiled several years earlier. Una had dispatched a rider to collect Ambrose from the landing, and Hutchison followed the man eastward across the peninsula to Una's cottage, where he was "received with open arms." He had barely settled when the shadow of the cliff slid over the settlement and "the pall of darkness closed in," Hutchison recalled. "[Thus] passed my first days experience of life in the Leper Settlement of Kalawao."

The next morning Hutchison started off on foot, "taking in the sights." While walking along a rutted dirt path that fronted the hospital compound, he saw a man hustling along behind a wheelbarrow. A white rag was stretched across the man's nose and mouth, like a bank robber in photographs of the Wild West. In the belly of the wheelbarrow Hutchison saw "a bundle which I at first mistook for soiled rags." The man advanced to a small shack, then "turned over the wheelbarrow and shook it." Suddenly the bundle let out an "agonized groan," Hutchison wrote, and began to crawl toward the shack, managing to cross the threshold before falling still, "with his body in and his legs stretched out." Hutchison had discovered the Dying Den. Patients in the last stages of leprosy were taken to the shed to spare the sensibilities of the other hospital inmates. "This spectacle of inhumanity," Hutchison wrote, "thrilled me with intense horror." He felt a "foreboding sense" that he too was destined to end up in the Dying Den, facedown and unattended at death. He continued, "God only knows."

Hutchison was hurrying from the shed when, as he later described, "there appears on the scene a priest, who had made his rounds of the inmates of this institution. A well knit stocky man of medium height, dark hair, prominent straight nose, plump round smooth face and wearing gold rim spectacles, garbed in black cassock with a rope girdle of the same color around his waist, on his head a black fur stiff brim hat held by four bands on the crown." In his right hand Damien carried a cane, with a heavy knot at its end. He introduced himself to Hutchison—the priest had not been present at the landing the previous day. After talking for a few moments Damien invited the young man to visit him at the rectory, and then hurried away. "Looking after him," Hutchison wrote, "consciously impressed, [I] muttered to myself—here is another found friend. This was the famed Father Damien Joseph De Veuster, the Christian Hero. Thus began an acquaintance which grew into an intimacy that lasted [to] the day before his death."

After Damien had disappeared down the road, Hutchison walked to the settlement store, bought a few supplies, and started for Richard Una's cottage. At the Dying Den he stopped to take "a sorrowful last look at the dying man still lying face down in the doorway." When he reached Una's cottage, Hutchison found that some neighbors had gathered for a visit. He told them what he had seen. "They heard me through and what I told them seemed not to move or surprise these stoic old timers for it was not new to see such inhumanity," he wrote. The scene was "a matter of fact well known to them," an "almost every day happening." Don't worry, one of the exiles told Hutchison. You'll soon be used to it.

In his description of Father Damien from that day, Ambrose Hutchison drew a portrait of a vigorous priest in abundant good health. Damien presented a stirring figure, as a visiting physician noted in his journal: "His features were regular, his face fleshy, round, and of good dimensions; the color of eyes brown, his hair black and abundant; his forehead of average breadth and height. He had a clear ringing voice, possessed a powerful barytone, and was a good singer. The view of his full face gave the onlooker the idea of force, harshness and sternness, due in part to the squareness of his chin and lower jaw. Having a wealth of hair, he roamed about bareheaded, resulting in his face becoming bronzed by exposure to the wind and sun's rays." The doctor added, "He was active and vigorous, of good physique, upright in his carriage, measured 5 feet and 8 inches in height, weighed 204 pounds, his chest was 41 inches in circumference, his hands and feet were shapely, although his fingers were stubbed and calloused from toil."

One of the projects Damien was toiling on was an orphanage, under construction adjacent to his two-story house, which doubled as a rectory. Since his boyhood in the Flemish countryside, carpentry had been a release for Damien—an enjoyable enterprise that yielded tangible results. In the settlement, where successes were elusive, laying down a lintel or finishing the joinery on a cottage was immensely satisfying. Damien rarely worked to completion, however. Sitting astride a beam with a hammer in his hand, he would gaze down and see a patient running toward him, carrying pleas from "the sick and dying," as Ambrose Hutchison recalled. Damien would "drop his tool, pull off his work clothes and put on his cassock [to] administer the last rite of the church." Afterward he oversaw the burial, often taking up the gravedigger's spade—by one account Damien personally dug 1,300 graves. The Catholic cemetery lay adjacent to his home. "Thus at night I am the sole keeper of this garden of the dead, where my spiritual children lie at rest," Damien informed Pamphile in one letter. "My greatest pleasure is to go there to say my beads, and meditate on that unending happiness which so many of them are already enjoying. . . . I confess to you, my dear brother, the cemetery and the hut of the dying are my best meditation books, as well as for the benefit of my own soul."

Damien's workdays typically lasted nineteen hours, and yet his roster of tasks never shrank. To one visitor he wearily complained, "My days are all too short, and I carry my works into my dreams." On an evening in 1879, at about the time Ambrose Hutchison arrived in the settlement, Damien sat at his desk and made a list of his daily routine:

> 5h: Get up without hesitation, short prayer, choose items for meditation, wash and dress neatly.
> 5.15h: In church: morning prayers, read about item for meditation, eliminate any form of distraction.
> 6h: Preparation for mass, wait for flock to arrive.
> 6–6.30h: Mass, on Sundays meditation till
> 7h: After the service, instruction about the theme of meditation, unvesting, tidying up, everything neatly in its place.
> 8h: Light breakfast, no meat or fish, only coffee, bread with eggs; smoke one pipe, discuss matters, arrange affairs, feed chickens, with the children, etc.
> 12h: Lunch . . . afterwards visit the sick. If they are far away on horseback, otherwise by foot. Before leaving short visit to Sacred Sacrament. No useless conversation. Be always friendly without being familiar. Don't waste time talking, return at the latest at 5 o'clock.
> 17h: Vespers and if converts are in church catechism.
> 18h: Early supper in winter, no staff around after nightfall (be strict with any woman or girl who stays in the compound after sunset).
> 19h: Rosary, then breviary, matins and laudes and spiritual readings.
> 22h: If not sleepy, read a chapter in the New Testament. To bed.

A few weeks after recording this schedule, Damien took his pencil and began to transcribe the medical histories of several patients, at the request of a visiting physician. From time to time Damien volunteered his help to leprosy researchers, in part because such exercises gave him a better understanding of his parishioners, and also because he was curious about the exact workings of the disease.

Damien had interviewed ten patients about their affliction. All eight had been photographed by a government physician more than a year earlier, and in his report Damien documented their current condition. Of David Ostrom, the fatalistic New Yorker who helped staff the hospital, Damien wrote, "Body covered with salmon-covered spots; hands and feet insensible to feeling; skin dry and shriveled." One of the female subjects had "both feet half gone, hands have no fingers, almost blind, mouth on one side, eyes always open, flesh wasted away, skin dry." Another patient was "deaf, has sore eyes, and asthma." When submitting the report, Father Damien included the following postscript: "Dr. F.H. Enders: I have taken the statements desired concerning the lepers who were photographed in 1878. Two of them are gone, eight still live; each one's history shown in the blanks the best I could." And though he was not part of the survey, Damien added the confession, "My own health continues to be the same as before; perhaps I have the germs of leprosy in system, I am not sure."

He had become suspicious three years earlier, after several small blemishes had appeared on his arm and back. A salve of corrosive sublimate helped fade the discolorations, but they always returned. Then, during the summer of 1878, Damien had begun to suffer what one physician later described as "true prodromal symptoms of leprosy . . . to wit, chills, osteal pains, slight swelling and tenderness of the joints, slight irregular fever, tingling numbness of the extremities, supersensitive and painful sensation in patches along the extensor surface of the upper and lower extremities; all of which . . . clearly indicated primary infection of Damien's system with leprosy." The doctor's conclusion was made in hindsight, however. At the time, Damien's probable infection went undiagnosed. Damien regarded his symptoms with anxious uncertainty, alternating between the mounting evidence that he was sick and the powerful hope that he had not yet fallen victim to leprosy.

From the moment he had stepped ashore in the settlement, Damien had disregarded the warnings made by the board and his superiors concerning infection. "Be careful not to expose yourself to catching this awful disease," his provincial had cautioned. Yet Damien could see no alternative. Every month, the settlers endured visits from skittish doctors, legislators, and clergymen whose detestation of the disease was obvious. Damien decided that he must not be seen as similarly fearful. How could he refrain from embracing the members of his congregation, or touching a dying patient with oil, or laying the host on the offered tongue of the communicant? To be a genuine priest, he concluded, he had to behave as if the disease held no power over him. Within days of arriving in Kalawao, Damien had abandoned all safeguards. A board physician later reported, "Fr. Damien took no precautions whatever. In the kindness of his nature, he never forbade lepers from entering his house; they had access to it any time, night and day. I named his house 'Kalawao Family Hotel and Lepers' Rest.'" Others observed Damien eating from communal bowls of poi, sharing his pipe with patients, and bandaging "the most frightful wounds as though he were handling flowers."

More than 125 years after Damien contracted leprosy, in early 2004, a team of Canadian scientists discovered the "genetic quirk" within a person's DNA that causes susceptibility to the disease. Researchers pinpointed a gene variant known as PARK2, which makes people vulnerable to infection by the leprosy bacillus, and a second gene, PACRG, which must also be present for the infected person to actually become sick. Even prior to this discovery, however, doctors noticed that susceptibility followed genetic pathways, concentrating along particular bloodlines, both familial and ethnic. Hawaiians were more disposed to the disease than many races. Certain French bloodlines showed a high susceptibility, including the colonists of Nova Scotia, known as Acadians; descendants of the group later carried leprosy to the Canadian province of New Brunswick, and from there to Louisiana, where it flourished. Often these lines of susceptibility were hidden among other, unrelated data. Four priests from the Paris-based Sacred Hearts order, all of whom served the mission in Hawaii, eventually contracted leprosy. Damien interpreted his infection as inevitable, and part of a divine plan. "Our Lord has willed that I be stigmatized with it," he wrote after the first symptoms appeared. "God certainly knows what is best for my sanctification and I gladly repeat: 'Thy will be done.'"

Several board physicians later suggested that Damien invited the disease to take him. He was willfully incautious, they charged, practiced poor hygiene, and was too familiar with obviously infectious patients. Had he been more careful, he might have been spared. Yet even the most meticulous of people sometimes caught leprosy, if they were among the unfortunate 5 percent with vulnerability. One such person was Dr. Edward Hoffmann, the much-loved physician from the now-demolished Kalihi Hospital. On a warm Friday one May the president of the board of health jotted a note in his journal concerning the doctor: "Sad news from Dr Brodie about Dr Hoffmann—he has leprosy." The president investigated the rumor and recorded his terse verdict: "Paid a visit to Dr Hoffmann—a leper." Edward Hoffmann died eleven months later, at his home in Honolulu.

Strange Objects

(Population 632)

The writer Charles Warren Stoddard first encountered leprosy in 1869, when he visited the colony in the company of Dr. David Lee, the physician briefly hired by the board to attend the exiles. The pair spent four days in Kalawao—Lee examining patients, and Stoddard observing the slow and sad implosion of the Walsh regime. Afterward they traveled by horse to the eastern tip of topside Molokai, where Stoddard hoped to visit a healthy young Hawaiian named Kana-Ana. Stoddard had fallen in love with the young man. When Lee realized the reason for the visit, "the doctor looked very grave," Stoddard wrote. "He tried to talk me over to the paths of virtue and propriety; but I wouldn't be talked over." Lee "never spoke again, but to abuse me," Stoddard reported, "and off he rode in high dudgeon, and the sun kept going down on his wrath." Charles Stoddard stayed on Molokai for several weeks with Kana-Ana. He later described the episode as the "sweetest idyl of my life."

Stoddard had been raised in San Francisco and as a youth had worked in a Montgomery Street bookstore. The city was a convivial place. By the time he was in his twenties, Stoddard was friendly with many of the authors of the books he sold, including Bret Harte, Walt Whitman, and Mark Twain, who employed him for a time as his secretary.

Critics who later dissected Stoddard's writing noted formidable talent, thinned by laziness. Stoddard would "rise with the idea of accomplishing a vast deal of writing, but it usually ends by my dipping into a book until I get tired, when I loaf [for] hour after hour," he once admitted. He took to authoring travelogues, easy work that allowed him to sprawl in the tropical sun, ideally with a lover. Stoddard's sexual preference had complicated his life. "I wonder if you are truly happy?" he once asked in a letter to a friend, a Catholic priest. "I am not; I cannot remember when I was for any length of time." A few years earlier, Stoddard had rejected Calvinism and joined the Roman Catholic Church, a conversion he described in *A Troubled Heart and How It Was Comforted at Last.* Any peace the Church could offer was years away, however. When he had first sailed for Hawaii, Stoddard held no illusions about its appeal: he hoped to live as his "nature" intended for him to live, he explained to Walt Whitman, and in a way not possible "even in California, where men are tolerably bold."

He discovered that travel dispatches paid very little. By 1880 Stoddard was broke and sick, living in a room in a decrepit mansion perched on San Francisco's Rincon Hill. He was thirty-seven years old, overweight, raccoon-eyed, with a beard that jutted forward like a plow. One spring morning he glanced out his window and saw a bone-white, painfully thin man sitting on his steps, sketching in a book. The next day he was there again. Stoddard later wrote that the artist seemed to like the "sagging and sighing cypresses," the "shaky stairway," and the "modest side door that had become my front door because the rest of the building was gone." When the stranger appeared for a third day, Stoddard went outside and said hello.

"What a background for a novel!" the man exclaimed, gesturing to the crumbling mansion. He introduced himself as Robert Louis Stevenson. Stoddard led Stevenson into the house, "where I sat presently in the midst of a museum of strange objects," Stevenson later wrote. On the walls hung Stoddard's bounty from the Hawaiian Islands: paddles, battle clubs, shells, baskets, and carved coconut bowls. "Evidence and examples of another earth, another climate, another race, and another (if ruder) culture," Stevenson wrote. At the time, the twenty-nine-year-old Scot was mostly unknown; *Treasure Island,* his first true success, was still several years away. Stoddard was the far more accomplished author, and his stories mesmerized the young writer. "It was in such talks," Stevenson wrote, "which we were both eager to repeat, that I first heard the names—first fell under the spell—of islands."

Stoddard confessed to Stevenson that he longed for Hawaii. He dreamed of returning to Molokai, he said, and as he lay in bed at night he pictured "the singular loveliness of the place . . . its abrupt walls, hung with tapestries of ferns." After that summer of 1880, Stevenson and Stoddard never saw each other again, although they continued to correspond. Through these letters, Stevenson learned that Stoddard's dream was going to come true. He was to make one last trip to Molokai.

The *Warwick* approached the settlement in high seas on a gray morning in October 1881. Father Damien waited onshore. When the men tried to bring whaleboats out to meet the schooner, surf pounded them back to land. The captain gave an order and the ship's crew started to shove the arriving patients over the outside rail. Residents rushed into the roaring surf, trying to pull the men and women to safety. They managed to save twenty of the newcomers, but two patients died—one while cradled in Damien's arms.

Rudolph Meyer claimed that something had gone terribly wrong with the ship, and that the deaths were an accident. The board reprimanded Meyer anyway and ordered that a board physician accompany all future patient transfers. The settlers were not as sanguine. Several predicted that the *Warwick* would be punished by the old gods. Two months after the incident, the schooner sailed from port and never reappeared. "She was given up as lost with all on board," Ambrose Hutchison reported. "Captain and crew and eight persons in all, not one escaped to tell the tale." A beachcomber later found a chunk of splintered wood on an empty stretch of Molokai's shore. He rubbed away the grime and saw a single painted word: *Warwick.*

In the weeks following the drownings, threatening pamphlets began to appear throughout the islands. "A punishment to the evil for evil deeds," one read. The tract lamented that the exiles were treated "like dogs thrown to the sea" and demanded the settlement be closed. "And therefore warning is hereby given [to] the Board of Health to immediately stay any further carriage of lepers to Kalawao.... If this is not heeded then the plantations from Hawaii to Kauai will be burned down at an unknown moment, until this warning is taken notice of. The Government had better consider." The subsequent arsons began on the island of Kauai. Men took oil-soaked rags, tied them to the tails of cats, and then lit the rags. The animals streaked across the plantation fields, leaving a trail of fire.

Attempting to appease the public mood, the board shuttered the jail-like detention station and opened a new leprosy hospital on the waterfront between Honolulu and Waikiki, in an area known as Kakaako. George Fitch, a gossipy, dangerously unskilled physician, was placed in charge. Dr. Fitch possessed a multitude of faulty medical beliefs, including that leprosy was the fourth and final stage of syphilis. This theory, wrote one physician, "assumed quite a popular topic of discussion amongst the laity and the medical fraternity in Honolulu." Although many clergymen agreed with Fitch's supposition, most doctors in the islands at the time did not. Neither did the local press, which routinely mocked the doctor. After one especially derisive article appeared in a Honolulu newspaper called the *Saturday Press*, Fitch sued for libel.

Testimony at the trial soon revealed that Fitch had attended medical school for less than five months, that his diploma was likely forged, and that he was unfamiliar with many basic medical techniques. Witnesses alleged that Fitch performed needless surgeries, including eye operations on four men who did not require them: all were left blind. In the courthouse halls during a recess, Fitch unsuccessfully tried to bribe one of the blinded men not to testify. During his summation, Sanford B. Dole, the lawyer for the paper, announced that Fitch "holds to-day the most important office under the Hawaiian Government.... [He] is the chief executive officer in the treatment of leprosy. He is an agent of the board of health, with the law and the police at his back." Dole then recited the language that Fitch considered libelous: "The article uses the words 'quack,' 'charlatan,' 'knave,' 'rogue' and 'ignorant pretender.'" Dole told the jury, "I leave it to you if the evidence does not show these words to have been correctly used." After ten minutes' deliberation the jury found that Fitch had not been libeled. Sensational though they were, the trial's revelations had little effect on Fitch's professional standing. The board left him in charge of Kakaako Hospital—and then gave him medical authority over the colony as well.

Charles Warren Stoddard climbed at midday down the cliff, after leaving Rudolph Meyer's home. "I slipped and grew weary and weak legged and many a time wished the tiresome descent over," Stoddard wrote in the small leather journal he carried. "Wild goats slid showers of stones upon us. Huge birds soared under us and over us and made me dizzy. The sea glimpse and the pali walls were glorious—a little white snowflake soil and the exquisite skylike sea—but the plain below us was sunburnt and sand colored."

Descending the trail with Stoddard was George Fitch and an aloof young physician from London named Arthur Albert Mouritz. The board had offered Mouritz the position of resident physician for the colony. Although it held few illusions about what a physician could accomplish, after Dr. Nathaniel Emerson's tenure had ended the board had sent a replacement to Molokai as a "concession to feelings." Within a few months of arriving in the settlement the physician, Charles Neilson, informed the board of his extraordinary opinion that leprosy was "essentially a neurosis: the principal factors productive of the disease are poverty, ignorance . . . and unwholesome diet." Having arrived at his conclusion, the doctor then conspired to spend much of his time in Honolulu, gambling on the horses at Kapiolani Park. Dr. Neilson, Ambrose Hutchison later recalled, was "a sporting man." His betting skills were poor, however. Deeply in debt, Neilson entered a Honolulu jewelry store, acquired $5,000 of gems on credit, and stowed away on a steamer bound for Australia, "leaving his creditors to mourn their loss."

In the absence of a resident physician, Fitch had been making monthly trips to the settlement. The board hoped Mouritz could be persuaded to take a full-time role. Mouritz and Fitch shuffled cautiously down the cliff, with the portly Stoddard lagging behind. After the trio reached Kalawao, Fitch broke from the group and "went whooping through the village," Stoddard reported, "kicking up his heels." Stoddard observed that Fitch made a habit of showing himself "in a ludicrous and not very agreeable light." Moments after arriving in the settlement, Fitch had let out a shout, and Stoddard turned to see "the energetic doctor spanking one of the larger wretches with a shingle."

That evening the visitors retired to the settlement guesthouse, a bare wooden cottage set behind a picket fence. When not in use the house was padlocked, to prevent contamination from the patients. Despite this precaution, Mouritz refused to risk using the mattresses or pillows. He spent the night "very unhappy and uncomfortable on the floor," Stoddard reported. While Mouritz tried to rest, Fitch read loudly from a volume of Walter Scott. Stoddard silently counted the number of words the doctor mispronounced. In his journal Stoddard wrote, "How funny it all is!"

At dawn Stoddard rose and stumbled stiffly onto the porch. Father Damien's buggy was waiting, to collect the author for mass. A white-speckled horse was hitched to the carriage. Damien had named the animal William. After a few minutes' trot William eased to a stop in front of a chapel. "The place was dingy and dirty," Stoddard wrote of St. Philomena, "the stations were tilted; the little interior painted in bad taste; the holy water font was a tin cup; some rosaries were scattered about, and a few torn catechisms. . . . The chalice was small, the altar decoration cheap and tawdry; the candles tilted all ways." Yet Stoddard found the humble setting unexpectedly powerful, animated by "the long, low slough of the sea-wind," which sounded to him like "a sigh of sympathy." Stoddard was similarly moved by the chapel's priest. "His cassock was worn and faded," Stoddard wrote, "his hair tumbled like a school-boy's; his hands stained and hardened by toil; but the glow of health was in his face, the buoyancy of youth in his manner; while his ringing laugh, his ready sympathy, and his inspiring magnetism told of one who in any sphere might do a noble work."

After Damien had concluded the sermon, Stoddard joined the doctors on their tour of the settlement, the party led among the cottages by Damien and Ambrose Hutchison. The good-looking Hutchison drew Stoddard's attention. "Him I might easily learn to like," Stoddard wrote. "He interests me unusually." In his months in the settlement, Hutchison had become an exemplary exile. He had managed to do what the board asked of every patient: make the best of the situation. Hutchison had taken a job in the butcher shop, become an enthusiastic member of Damien's church, and built a neatly kept cottage halfway between Kalawao and Kalaupapa, surrounded by low stone walls and gardens and colorful bursts of Christmas berry. "I lived a lonely life devoting my time to raising sweet potatoes and other vegetables," Hutchison would write. "I had plenty of every thing I wanted in the line of food except money which was a scarse commodity. . . . Nevertheless I was contented and happy."

As the party made their circuit among Hutchison's fellow settlers, they saw some who were coping very much as he was, and scores who were not. "Lepers were everywhere waiting to receive us," Stoddard reported, "they crouched under the thick banana hedges, or in the smallest of verandas, or squatted upon the floor within doors." He added, "I saw many horrible cases." Entering the hospital, the group came across "what seemed a little bundle of rags . . . or rubbish, half hidden under a soiled blanket." The doctors moved to examine the patient, but Damien held back Stoddard.

"You must not look!" Damien cried. "You must not look!"

Stoddard shrugged him off and stepped forward.

"A corner of the blanket was raised cautiously," he wrote, "a breathing object lay beneath; a face, a human face, was turned toward us—a face in which scarcely a trace of anything human remained." The patient was a child, nearing death. "The dark skin was puffed out and blackened; a kind of moss, or mould, gummy and glistening, covered it; the muscles of the mouth, having contracted, laid bare the grinning teeth; the thickened tongue lay like a fig between them." The child's eyes were open, the lids "curled tightly back and the eyes themselves now shapeless and broken . . . not unlike bursted grapes."

Stoddard hurried from the hospital and stood gasping in the open air. Trying to slow his rapid breath, he became aware of a rhythmic beat, beneath the melody of the surf. It seemed to arise from a small shed, which stood aslant just beyond the hospital gate. Finally it dawned on him. The sound, Stoddard wrote, was "the busy hammer . . . shaping the coffins which are to enclose their remains!" At the end of his time in the settlement, Stoddard would write, "That hammer seemed never idle."

Arthur Mouritz accepted the board's offer—he was engaged to be married and needed the $5,000 salary. With their visit complete, Fitch and Mouritz discussed the route they should take from the settlement. One option was to steer a canoe to a landing on the island's eastern tip, then travel by horseback to Kaunakakai, where the steamer touched. Such a method would take the party past the small village where Stoddard, years ago, had lingered with Kana-Ana. "I am hoping we may go [that way]," Stoddard confessed to his diary, "*strongly hoping.*" Mouritz favored a faster route, however: up the cliff, and then straight across the island to Kaunakakai. "I'll toss a coin," the doctor announced. "He tossed," Stoddard wrote, "heads, go around, tails, by the pali. It was *tails.*"

Aboard the steamer for Honolulu, the now-morose Stoddard recorded dark scenes: "A crazy woman was on board—a melancholy, handcuffed half-white who believed she was being prayed to death; a sick Chinaman whose friends brought him on board, went to sleep by his side, and found upon awakening in the morning that the poor fellow was dead." Earlier, Stoddard had filled his journal with sunnier comments, praiseful passages about Damien, and hopeful testimony to the power of faith. Stoddard had penned the observations while reclining happily on the veranda of the rectory, drinking Damien's wine as the priest prepared their dinner. "How charming he is," Stoddard reported, "how beautiful in his devotion, how sincere, how charitable." Stoddard noted the "miraculous" quality of Damien's work in the settlement, and the blessing of the priest's continued good health. He suggested that the Lord was shielding his servant from the disease.

Damien had not mentioned his fears about his health to the visitors. Mouritz suspected immediately, however. "The first meeting I had with Father Damien the dark copper color of the skin of his forehead attracted my attention," he later wrote, "it was the visible proof of the invasion of the Destroyer." Stoddard was more oblivious, although for one instant Damien forgot himself and hinted at the truth.

Stoddard had asked Damien for his portrait, to use in the book he planned to write about the settlement. Damien pulled a photograph from his desk. The image showed him in his dark cassock, clutching his prayer beads. The picture was taken several years earlier, and in it Damien was clean-shaven, and without the eyeglasses he now required. His complexion was ruddy from the island sun, and his serious expression was strangely pensive. "Looks like a leper," Damien had joked, handing over the photo.

Stoddard wrote, "And so it does."

Human Soil

(Population 680)

The dead Japanese carpenter was sprawled on a dirt road on the northern edge of the island of Hawaii, a half-burned cigarette smoldering beside his head. His distraught wife claimed that two white males in rubber overcoats had ambushed them and murdered her husband. She told the story to a doctor, L. S. Thompson, who had seen the woman leading a bloodstained horse. Thompson did not believe the woman, whose name was Kamaka. He sent for the sheriff, and Kamaka was arrested.

The next story she told differed from the first. She and a Hawaiian farmer named Keanu had become lovers, she said. When her husband had discovered the affair, he told Kamaka that they were immediately moving to the other side of the island, far from Keanu. The couple had set out at dawn. Three miles down the road, Keanu rode out from behind a screen of brush and said, "Aloha."

Kamaka's husband, known as Charley, answered, "Aloha."

Keanu stabbed Charley in the face, knifed him at the back of the head, pulled him from his horse and plunged the blade twice into his throat and once into his chest, then stood panting over his victim, who lay facedown in the dirt. "Charley did not say anything after being struck," Kamaka later testified. "Charley bled." A jury returned with a guilty verdict in two hours and thirty minutes, with one juror dissenting. At 1 P.M. on August 2, 1884, Marshal William Cooper Parke brought Keanu before Albert Francis Judd, chief justice of the Hawaii Supreme Court. An interpreter asked if the prisoner had anything to say before sentencing.

"I am not guilty," Keanu replied. "That is all I have to say."

Judd announced that Keanu was to be "hung by the neck . . . until you are dead. And may God have mercy on your soul!" A reporter from the *Advertiser* wrote, "During the delivery of the death sentence, the prisoner stood with his eyes cast downward, and apparently never moved a muscle. He evidently anticipated his fate."

Several weeks after Keanu was condemned to the gallows, Dr. Eduard Arning, a physician working on behalf of the board of health, asked that

Keanu instead be handed over to him to use as an "experimental animal." The men of the government Privy Council agreed to the request. To satisfy his own ethics, Dr. Arning later claimed, he explained in detail to the prisoner what was likely to happen to him. Keanu seemed not to care. In a steady hand Keanu marked his signature on the medical release. "With the prisoner's permission," Arning reported, "I commenced operations on the last day of September 1884."

A horse cart carried Keanu along the narrow causeway away from Oahu Prison. When the buggy reached Kakaako Hospital, an attendant led Keanu to a shed where the doctor waited, along with a frightened nine-year-old girl. Arning told Keanu to sit. A board physician later described Keanu: "48 years old, has physique massive, weight about 250 pounds, broad-shouldered, erect of carriage, 5 feet 10 inches tall." On a table next to Keanu was a short metal pipe fitted with a rubber hose, an apparatus invented by a German chemist who taught at the University of Heidelberg, where Arning had attended medical school. Arning was twenty-nine years old, a blue-eyed, golden-haired young doctor so intoxicated by the new science of microbes that he appeared to suffer from what was known at the time as "bacteriomania." While the convict watched, the doctor ignited the Bunsen burner.

Heating a scalpel over the burner, Arning used it to swell a blister on Keanu's right forearm. He then drew fluid from a leprous ulcer on the girl's chin, injected it into the blister, and rubbed the remainder onto a patch he had scarified on Keanu's left earlobe. Next, the doctor washed the girl's forearm, sprayed it with a diluted mix of carbolic acid, and, using his scalpel blade, split the skin. He sliced free a square of tissue and set it aside. After sewing closed the girl's wound, Arning turned to Keanu. Opening a deep incision on the Hawaiian's left forearm, the doctor exposed the marbled belly of the heavy radius longus muscle, which twitched in reflex to the cut. Arning transferred the material and stitched the tissue within the folds of Keanu's flesh. He swabbed the arm with disinfectant, touched it with ointment, and wrapped it in a sleeve of gauze. Then he waited.

Until the previous decade, doctors had no sure way to determine if someone had leprosy. Often they simply guessed. As a quick canvass among the exiles in the settlement would have shown, quite often these medical judgments were tragically incorrect. In the early 1870s, however, researchers pioneered new methods of studying bacteria by microscope. Various bacteria's physical characteristics began to be cataloged, including the distinctive shape of a germ that a Norwegian physician named Gerhard Hansen believed was responsible for leprosy. Using a small pair of scissors, Dr.

Hansen had snipped samples from the blemishes of several persons with leprosy and slid the unprepared biopsies beneath his microscope. He noticed barely visible masses of dark cellular matter, though he could not determine their composition. Then, in the winter of 1873, Hansen cut a tiny divot from the nose of a man named Johannes Gül. Peering through the barrel of his microscope, Hansen discerned a huge quantity of stick-shaped entities that were making "more or less lively movements." The same rod-shaped bacilli vibrated menacingly in biopsies taken from Hansen's next leprosy patient, and the next. These were *Mycobacterium leprae.*

By identifying the active leprosy bacillus, Hansen had found the first evidence that microbes—germs—could inhabit the human body as parasites and cause chronic disease. More important, Hansen established a link between leprosy and the presence in the victim of those specific rod-shaped bacilli. Hansen's breakthrough was at the vanguard of a scientific revolution known as bacteriology. In the coming weeks and months, scientists would identify the germs that ignited cholera, anthrax, diphtheria, and bubonic plague. These discoveries would change forever the practice of medicine.

One significant factor in this pathbreaking research was the invention of a process in which samples were washed with dyes before viewing beneath a microscope. The coloring attached to bacilli as a stain, throwing their various forms into sharp relief, and helping physicians to distinguish one germ from another. Hansen had identified *Mycobacterium leprae* without the benefit of staining—he had not yet learned the technique—but by the late 1870s the procedure was widely known among bacteriologists. By employing it, doctors could microscopically screen tissue for Dr. Hansen's signature leprosy germ and make their diagnosis with more authority. One critical research obstacle remained, however. Until someone absolutely proved *Mycobacterium leprae* to be leprosy's cause, the probability of discovering a cure for the disease was remote.

A bacillus is confirmed as the cause of a disease by meeting a series of conditions formalized by a brilliant German physician named Robert Koch, who is credited with discovering *Mycobacterium tuberculosis.* In 1877 Dr. Koch detailed the steps required to determine if a specific germ is in fact the origin of a particular disease. One of "Koch's postulates" states that "to prove that a microbe causes a disease it is necessary to extract the microbe from an infected person, introduce it into either an experimental animal or into a human being, and so reproduce the disease," as one medical historian later wrote. "Obviously in the overwhelming number of cases it is the experimental animal that is used. Human beings may on occasion volunteer for such experiments . . . but they are very much the exception to the rule."

Despite the alleged rarity of such events, however, both Robert Koch and Gerhard Hansen commonly used human test subjects—as did one of their colleagues, Albert Neisser, who had studied under both men. When Dr. Neisser had become established, he engaged a gifted young assistant of his own: Eduard Arning.

Dr. Arning's subsequent work with leprosy came to the attention of the Hawaiian board of health by a surprising source, Dr. William Hillebrand. Three decades earlier, Hillebrand had sounded the first alarm in Hawaii about leprosy. Now he was partially retired, residing in Switzerland and monitoring the field from afar. "Probably you have read in the papers of the discovery by Dr. Koch in Berlin of the bacteria which cause tuberculosis," Hillebrand wrote to the president of the board, Walter Murray Gibson. After sketching a brief picture of the stunning advances happening in bacteriology, he urged Gibson to engage Dr. Arning in an investigation of leprosy. "Only men in possession of all the specific knowledge obtained thus far, experienced in the use of the microscope and practically trained in the different methods of experimental research are competent to undertake it," Hillebrand advised. "Such a man offers himself to you."

Gibson replied quickly: "It gives me great pleasure to be able to assure you at once that if Dr. Arning comes here for the purpose of studying the natural history of the contagion of leprosy, he will receive from the Board of Health every assistance they are in a position to give him." Commission in hand—Gibson had offered $150 a month—Arning boarded a series of ships that brought him from Hamburg to Manchester to New York City. He traveled overland to San Francisco, found the city's medical supply shop, and filled a carefully packed crate with burners and autoclaves and several heavy brass microscopes. Satisfied that he was properly equipped, Arning climbed a ramp tipped alongside a hundred-foot iron-clad steamer, the *Mariposa.* The ship slid out through the pinched green fingers of the Golden Gate, and into the Pacific. Aboard the *Mariposa* were thirty-one first-class passengers, including Arning; thirty-two others rode steerage. After a week at sea, they sighted Hawaii.

At the esplanade in Honolulu a celebratory chaos prevailed, as it always did when a passenger vessel arrived from the mainland, a twice-monthly event. Souvenir sellers swarmed the wharf, toting trays of flower garlands and hollow-eyed idols, bouncing between the drays and the sightseers, who twirled parasols for shade. The Royal Hawaiian Band blared away beneath crescents of colored bunting. Drivers screamed at their teams of skittish horses, screamed again at loiterers to leap aside. Arning moved partway down the gangplank and paused, scanning the crowd. He had assumed the board president, Mr. Gibson, would be on hand to greet him. But he seemed to have been forgotten.

In fact, Gibson stood only a few yards away from Arning, a shambling, skeletal presence who shifted his feet upon the pier in nervous excitement. One Honolulu lawyer had recently recorded his impressions of Arning's host: "Walter Murray Gibson is a tall, thin old gentleman . . . with white hair and beard, a mild, cold blue eye, a fine patrician nose, and a tolerably port-wine complexion. . . . He is an unquestionably eminent-looking veteran, of smooth address, silky manners, and a somewhat fascinating mode of speech, in the estimation of the susceptible and sympathetic—a fine old fellow, I should say; wise as a serpent, but hardly as harmless as a dove." Had Arning held a description of Gibson, he could easily have spotted the distinctive older man. On the afternoon of the *Mariposa*'s arrival, however, Arning knew nothing about Gibson, and the board president made no effort to locate the doctor among the crowd. As usual, Gibson was caught in a drama of his own.

By the time Walter Murray Gibson appeared on the Hawaiian political scene, one out of thirty residents in the islands had been exiled. Thus segregation had affected almost every person in the islands, through the banishment of a family member, neighbor, or friend. Campaigning on an opportunistic platform of native rights and compassion for the exiles, Gibson had won a seat in the legislature, and his popularity eventually propelled him to the prime ministry, under King David Kalakaua. In short order, Gibson also connived to acquire each of the major ministry posts, and served—sometimes simultaneously—as minister of interior, minister of finance, and, though he lacked a legal degree, attorney general. The extraordinary consolidation lent Gibson his nickname in the press: Minister of Everything.

Even prior to his ascension in the political firmament of the islands, however, Gibson made for fantastic copy. He claimed to have been born at sea to English nobles, although in the confusion of an Atlantic storm he landed in the wrong crib and went home in the arms of a Northumberland sheep farmer. The Gibson clan later emigrated to Canada, and finally to New York City, where they settled in a Bowery tenement. At age fourteen Walter went south to find his fortune, and was quickly married, made a father, and then a widower. Placing his three children with his dead wife's parents, the twenty-two-year-old set out in search of a larger life. "My young widowed heart felt free to range again," he wrote. In Central America he befriended the dictator General Rafael Carrera, and soon agreed to help him found a Guatemalan navy. Returning to Manhattan, Gibson purchased a former U.S. revenue schooner, fitted her for combat, and loaded several tons of guns and ammunition aboard, hidden under eighty tons of ice. The *Flirt* was slinking from New York Harbor when an alert customs agent discovered the cargo and had the ship seized in violation of the U.S. neutrality acts. Gibson wrote, "[Thus] the pleasant and harmless scheme of the Centralian navy failed."

Later, an acquaintance remarked of Gibson, "He is a man of considerable talent, unhampered by any scruple." Within a year the *Flirt* showed up in Sumatra, with "Captain Gibson" at the helm. Dutch authorities arrested him, believing Gibson planned to spark a revolt and install himself as an island potentate. After a year in prison, he broke down and confessed, "I have allowed my fancy and my vanity to get the better of my judgment." Sentenced to hang, Gibson escaped and made his way back to America. He then convinced the U.S. secretary of state to press a claim against the Netherlands for false imprisonment. Though the *New York Herald* demanded that U.S. warships seize the Dutch island of Curaçao "as a guarantee for the payment of the indemnity," the Dutch ignored the government's threats. In a futile attempt to secure restitution, Gibson sailed for Europe and ultimately had to beg steamer fare home from the American consul in Liverpool, Nathaniel Hawthorne. The novelist wrote of Gibson, "The vicissitudes of his life appear to have tinctured him with superstition, inclining him to look upon himself as marked out for something strange."

Once more in the United States, Gibson had turned his attention to the Utah Territory. Aware of the Mormon community's difficulty in finding a homeland, he offered to help them establish "a Colony upon an island of Central Oceania," as Gibson proposed in a letter to the Mormon delegate to Congress. It seemed of little consequence to Gibson that he was not himself Mormon. But Brigham Young, the Mormon leader, found the detail inconvenient. Meeting with Gibson in Salt Lake City, Young suggested Gibson study the faith—afterward they could discuss a Pacific mission. On a freezing day in January 1860, Walter Murray Gibson was led though the Mormon baptismal ceremony and confirmed by Young himself. "I have invariably found him to be frank, kind hearted, intelligent, upright, and gentlemanly," Young wrote of the thirty-eight-year-old. Gibson was now free to investigate fields for the missionary work. Young suggested Hawaii.

For a mission site Gibson chose the island of Lanai, an arid speck ten miles immediately south of Molokai. "This is the nucleus of development," he recorded in his diary. "I set up my standard here and it goes hence to the islands of the sea." Quickly, Gibson created a fiefdom. He took the title of "Chief President of the Islands of the Sea and of the Hawaiian Islands for the Church of the Latter Day Saints," described Lanai as the "Hawaiian Zion," and insisted on being referred to as a "High Priest of Melchizedek." Soon he controlled a majority of the island. Ostensibly the property was for the Mormon Church, but Brigham Young discovered that the land titles listed only Gibson's name. With a little digging, the church found out that Gibson was commingling the mission's funds with his own. Two elders reported back to Salt Lake City that Gibson was presenting himself as the sole church authority in Hawaii, whose word was above that of Young. He began to sell church offices for $100 each. Rounding the male members of the ward into companies, Gibson began to train them as military recruits. At one point, the elders alleged, Gibson suddenly insisted that church members henceforth approach him on hands and knees. When Young heard the charges, he ordered Gibson excommunicated.

Forced out by the Mormons, Walter Murray Gibson took an oath as a Hawaiian citizen, moved to the port town of Lahaina, and entered politics. Fluent in Hawaiian and a spellbinding orator, he easily won election to the 1878 legislature, one of four white men elected to the twenty-seven-member assembly. Perhaps because disease had destroyed his own family—a childhood cholera epidemic had swept away three brothers—Gibson took particular interest in public health, and especially leprosy. He argued for additional funds for the settlement, and a less doctrinaire approach to exile. After leading a legislative committee on a fact-finding visit to the colony, Gibson raised the possibility of creating small satellite settlements on each island, so that families would not be completely torn apart by exile. Mostly, Gibson delighted in exposing the board's mismanagement of the settlement. "How can we vote for any measures for public improvements and neglect our unhappy lepers?" Gibson announced dramatically during one legislative session. "Their last cry to me and the members of the special committee as we passed from them at Kalaupapa was 'Do not forget us!' And we will not and cannot forget them."

Although the conservative white business leaders in the islands despised him, Gibson eventually won the respect of King David Kalakaua—in large part by his authorship of a handbook, *Sanitary Instructions for Hawaiians.* Printed in Hawaiian and in English, the manual offered a remarkably accurate description of germ theory and gave practical advice on how residents could avoid the infectious diseases that had been, and were still, carving away the Hawaiian population. After the book's publication, Kalakaua named Gibson to the board of health. "Gibson's persevering and humble bootlicking is producing fruit," Sanford Dole soon complained in a letter to his brother. "Kalakaua seems to be entirely given over to the devil." Kalakaua then brought Gibson into his cabinet, and from there Gibson began to collect ministry posts like a child pockets marbles. By the summer of 1883 he had claimed every major position, while also serving on the boards of immigration and education, and as president of the board of health. Though his political enemies decried the power grab, they grudgingly praised Gibson's skill. "It is months since we thought that each tomorrow would see our friend Gibson tumble from the premiership of the Pacific," one Honolulu resident wrote Dole, "and now really the octopus-like manner in which he hangs on to his various appointments is beginning to inspire me with admiration; he is a remarkable man."

Among the many ambitions Gibson held, however, perhaps the grandest was his desire to be written into history as the man who helped conquer leprosy. Convinced that Hawaii could become the world leader in "the treatment and understanding of the fearful malady," Gibson had arranged for Dr. Eduard Arning to undertake his research in the islands. Gibson also sought to improve the Molokai settlement. Despite the perpetually empty government purse, he hoped to transform the colony into the model facility of its type. Both the settlement hospital and Kakaako desperately needed competent nurses, but the board could not afford to hire professionals. The most practical solution, Gibson realized, was nursing nuns. Gibson wrote Bishop Hermann Koeckemann, soliciting "eight or more Sisters of Charity to come to the rescue of our sick people." Koeckemann, a stern, unyielding German who had recently succeeded Bishop Louis Desire Maigret, delegated the search to Father Leonor Fouesnel, Father Damien's superior in the Sacred Hearts' mission. On the board's behalf, Fouesnel sent inquiries to fifty different Catholic institutions in North America. Only one order agreed to take on the task.

On November 8, 1883, seven nuns from the Third Order of St. Francis at St. Anthony's Convent, in Syracuse, New York, arrived in Honolulu aboard the *Mariposa*. Gibson waited on the esplanade, along with a convoy of five royal carriages, intended to convey the nuns into town. The steamer sounded its whistle, and slid hard against the pier. Dockworkers wheeled a gangplank into place. Gibson mounted the ramp. On the steamer's deck stood six young women in black serge habits, wide white collars, and double veils. Knotted cord circled their waists, from which dangled rosaries. At the front of the group was Marianne Cope, the mother superior. Gibson approached Marianne. A head shorter than Gibson, the forty-five-year-old nun offered a study in contrasts to the board president: she full of face to his stark gauntness; her dark hair and gentle eyes to his colorless beard and icy gaze; her wide, red-lipped mouth to his tight and bloodless smile. Gesturing grandly, Gibson bowed before Marianne and announced, "Welcome to fair Hawaii." She offered him her hand.

Gibson was sixty-one years old. A widower at age twenty-two, he had never remarried. He was, he later confided to his diary, "too sentimental for my years." When he took the slender fingers of Marianne, curled them into his to place a kiss atop her hand, Gibson tumbled impossibly, absurdly in love. To his diary he exalted, "Great joy and delight . . . unexpected happiness."

Escorting the sisters down the ramp, Gibson eased Marianne into one of the royal carriages, bound for an elaborately planned reception. He scrambled into his own buggy, and the procession clattered away. Quiet resettled on the esplanade, as the last of the passengers slowly scattered. Beneath the pier shed a young man in a too-dark suit dug among the luggage until he located his bag. Dr. Arning glanced around one last time, then began to walk toward town. He wondered what had happened to Mr. Gibson.

While the board constructed a convent house on the grounds of Kakaako Hospital, Gibson installed Marianne and the sisters in a small mansion at the center of Honolulu, the renting of which he arranged personally, using the board's dwindling funds. For $4 daily he also hired a carriage to shuttle the sisters to mass, sparing them the five-minute stroll. When the convent house was complete, Gibson moved Marianne and the others into the whitewashed two-story wooden structure, which contained their living quarters, a chapel, and a modest visiting parlor—later Gibson had a conservatory built for the sisters, stocked with rare plants and flowers. He also ordered a phone line strung to the convent house and a telephone installed, a rare instrument in Honolulu. Marianne's most frequent caller was Walter Murray Gibson.

Kakaako Hospital was at the time still headed by Dr. George Fitch, and he had slowly allowed the facility to slide into squalor. The branch hospital stood one mile from the business center of town, on a sun-blighted shoreline that had historically served as a salt flat. "The site is most wretchedly chosen, and should be abandoned," Fitch reported to the board in the spring of 1884. Several times a year the sea overrode the low bank and flooded the grounds, and a recent storm had filled the compound three feet deep in water. "Only the most strenuous exertions by the Steward and the inmates saved the place from almost complete destruction," wrote Fitch. In the past, salt farmers would flock to the area following such storms, harvesting crystal from tidal pools as they bleached in the sun. Now a fence screened the property, and a locked gate barred outsiders. Behind the gate sat a dozen dormitories, a shabby hospital ward, cookhouse and dining hall, and the just-completed convent. The buildings rested atop wooden pilings above the swampy soil, and an unpleasant perfume of saline, rot, and overcrowding hung in the air. Kakaako was designed to accommodate one hundred patients; it currently held more than two hundred.

The board intended suspects to remain at Kakaako only long enough to have their leprosy confirmed and to receive simple treatment. Then they were to be exiled to Molokai. Yet Dr. Fitch permitted scores of patients to linger endlessly at Kakaako. Some bribed the doctor to evade exile, although corruption was only one factor in Fitch's shoddy execution of segregation policy. Despite the public repudiation it had suffered during his disastrous libel suit, Fitch still clung to his theory that leprosy was the fourth stage of syphilis. "Leprosy is an absolutely non-contagious and non-communicable disease," the doctor wrote. Thus segregation "has absolutely no effect toward checking" the disease. The board's concern should be preventing people with the disease from having sex. Fitch advocated closing both the Molokai settlement and Kakaako Hospital and opening a single replacement facility near Honolulu—"a perfect enclosure divided into separate yards" where men and women would be kept apart and abstinence enforced. The doctor hoped the board would hire him to oversee this chaste facility, at a salary above what he currently commanded. But for the scheme to come to fruition, Fitch needed Kakaako to fail as a treatment center and the colony to acquire a reputation as an immoral "leper manufactory," as he put it.

Fitch's laxity in enforcing exile—and Gibson's failure to correct it—infuriated Honolulu's business leaders. Kakaako had essentially become a second leprosy colony, a squalid camp visible to every reporter and tourist arriving from the mainland. "THE LAND OF THE LEPERS," screamed an article in the *San Francisco Chronicle,* after its reporter caught sight of the hospital from the rail of his ship. Mainland officials increased threats of a trade embargo unless the board proved it had leprosy under control. "It will not do to trifle with this terrible disease any longer," the *San Francisco Bulletin* announced. As Kakaako expanded, the Honolulu business community pressured Gibson and the board to act. "Health matters have claimed the attention of the thoughtful minded," wrote one Honolulu publisher, "and no little agitation has been given the subject in the public press at the inaction of the Board of Health . . . in carrying out the laws of segregation and isolation of lepers."

When Mother Marianne first visited Kakaako she was horrified. The dining hall and kitchen were "thick with filth and flies," one sister later wrote, and the living quarters "empty and cheerless." Patients "were crouched on the floor with their knees drawn up to their chins, and in every face utter despair not a smile from one of them." The hospital steward was J. H. Van

Giesen, "a pompous fellow whom everyone instinctively dislikes," one visitor later remarked. Van Giesen guided the nuns and Gibson on their tour. "Now let me show you the most interesting place," he announced, leading the group to a narrow building that teetered on pilings over the surf. The structure had been divided into three dingy cubicles, with warped floors and windows ghosted by salt spray. The first of the rooms was the "morgue." Van Giesen explained that when a patient's condition reached a certain point, he was forced into the morgue and remained there until dead. The body was then dragged to the second cubicle, where Fitch performed an autopsy. Finally the remains were moved to the third room, to await a burial team.

On the day of Marianne's tour, the morgue had one occupant. The young man lay in a stupor on the bare floor, shivering beneath a thin gray blanket. Dehydration had cracked his lips, and he had grown delirious. One of the sisters asked if the patient had eaten or drunk since entering the morgue. Such measures were pointless, she was told, since patients consigned to the morgue always died. A medical log kept at Kakaako recounts a typical experience, describing a ten-year-old boy who had been admitted two years earlier. As the leprosy bacilli became active, lesions erupted from the boy's chin to his ankles. "Entire body and face resemble the ancient portraits of the 'Satyrs,'" Fitch wrote. On July 27 Fitch reported that the boy was "very weak, but still eats. Is growing very thin and slowly wasting away." By September 23 his state had worsened: "Lips and eyes [have] good color, the latter bright and glistening; cannot walk of himself, but can crawl like an infant on his hands and knees." At this point, the boy was still under treatment in the dormitories. Fitch prescribed solutions of iodine, potassium, and ammonia. "Sol. Magn. Keeps him easy but he cannot last long," the doctor noted on October 14. The following week Fitch reported, "The end is coming fast." Fitch decided the boy's case was hopeless, and Van Giesen "removed him from ward to morgue." The room lacked beds or mattresses, and the boy lay atop the damp floor for seven days, mostly untended. When Fitch stopped in after two days, he reported, "Still cheerful, poor boy." Three days later Fitch wrote, "The candle is burning slowly out." The following day: "Still lives and this is about all: converses rationally, breathing labored. More inclined to sleep from which he wakes up every few moments with a start." At 2 A.M. on October 29 the boy, whose name was Kaaholei, "awoke, slightly delirious, with his mind wandering, talked of home and horse riding." He died an hour later, apparently alone. A worker dragged him to the autopsy room, and later that day a burial team carted Kaaholei to his grave.

As they gazed at the young man who currently waited to die, Gibson remarked to Marianne, "I had no idea that the sick were treated like this." Suddenly indignant, he ordered Van Giesen to return the patient "to his room and give him a nurse and plenty of milk and nourishment even if he should not get well." He roared, "Never treat any one like this again!" Gibson made it clear that Marianne was to assume control of the hospital. Van Giesen quickly had the patient carried back to his cottage. "With careful nursing," one of the nuns reported, the young man "soon recovered."

Mother Marianne had been born in Germany as Barbara Koob. When she was still an infant, her parents emigrated to Utica, New York, and Americanized their name to Cope. They settled Barbara and her siblings in a small house that faced the belching, block-long Utica Steam Woolen Mills. At fifteen years old, Barbara had trudged across Schuyler Street to begin work in the factory. "I was obliged to struggle and wait nine years," she later wrote, describing her career in the mills, "before it pleased God to open the convent gates to me." In 1862 twenty-four-year-old Barbara entered St. Francis Convent in Syracuse. She took the name Sister Mary Anna. With use, it became Marianne.

During the summer of 1870 Marianne had been installed as chief nurse and administrator of St. Joseph's Hospital in Syracuse, a surprisingly modern Catholic-run facility that served as a teaching hospital for Syracuse University's medical college. She remained in the facility for thirteen years, accumulating a remarkably complete set of medical skills. Physicians at St. Joseph's Hospital were among the first in the United States to follow the emerging European philosophy of antisepsis—pioneered by Louis Pasteur, Joseph Lister, and Robert Koch, among others—and Marianne embraced their techniques. These demanded strict cleanliness, absolute order, and frequent sterilization with solutions of carbolic acid, to keep germs at bay. A Syracuse newspaper reporter described St. Joseph's under Marianne's administration: "The hospital wards with their clean, well-aired beds, and the excellent ventilation; the lime-whitened walls and ceiling, and the healthful location of the institution presenting all that is advantageous." He added, "The same cleanliness, good order, care and attention pervades every department throughout the hospital."

In his initial entreaties to Marianne on behalf of the board, Father Leonor had suggested that in Hawaii she would be free to administer a similar first-rate facility. "The government supports the hospitals and defrays all expenses," he asserted—though at the time the priest wrote the letter the government treasury was essentially empty. At no point in his correspondence with Marianne did Leonor mention leprosy. "With regard to the other conditions I find it very difficult to develop them in a letter," he wrote, adding that he preferred to "explain verbally the matter to you."

As it happened, the priest did not need to be so coy. Before Father Leonor ever reached Syracuse to make his case in person, Marianne had reached a decision. "I am hungry for the work," she announced. "I am not afraid of any disease, hence it would be my greatest delight even to minister to the abandoned 'lepers.'" In fact, the prospect of the mission had become an obsession. "Waking and sleeping, I am on the Islands. Do not laugh at me, for being so wholly absorbed in that one wish, one thought, to be a worker in that large field."

Six volunteers from the order were chosen to join Marianne. They packed wicker baskets with jars of homemade ketchup, pickled peaches, and several roasted chickens, then set out by train for San Francisco, where they caught the *Mariposa*; Eduard Arning was already on board. As was the case with Dr. Arning, Marianne anticipated that she would accomplish her work in Hawaii in a matter of months or perhaps a year. Then she and the other sisters would return home. After seeing Kakaako Hospital, Marianne realized that she had been too optimistic.

Dr. Eduard Arning had finally met his new employer on his second day in town, when Gibson retrieved the physician from the Hawaiian Hotel and gave him a tour of Honolulu. Arning now saw the board president almost daily, when Gibson arrived at Kakaako for his visits with Marianne. Although separated in age by more than three decades, Arning and Gibson discovered they had surprising similarities: Each was slim and gangling, compulsively well-groomed, and convinced of the superiority of his own intellect. They soon disliked each other enormously.

The doctor had set up his laboratory in a small shed on a dry rise of the hospital grounds, within view of the sisters' convent house. Every day for several weeks following the inoculation of the murderer Keanu, Arning walked along the hospital's main gravel lane, passed through the gate, and rode to Oahu Prison. A prison turnkey allowed him into Keanu's cell. Arning snipped a divot of Keanu's skin at the point of the inoculations. "The microscope revealed the presence of the *bacillus leprae* in large numbers until the middle of March," Arning reported. "They have since gradually diminished in number, but a recent excision of a small part of the scar shows them present even yet." Though the leprosy germs lingered, they failed to multiply. Arning wrote, "There is nothing in the general appearance of the convict which would denote any development of leprosy."

Throughout the summer, as Marianne and the sisters set about remaking the hospital, Arning continued his "cultivation experiments." He acquired "a variety of animals of ages ranging from a few days old to grown up beasts, rabbits, guinea-pigs, rats, hogs, [and] pigeons," he wrote. One day he reported, "I have procured a monkey." The small, nut-colored animal was called Keko—the Hawaiian word for *monkey.* Slicing samples from the inmates of Kakaako, Arning injected and transplanted leprosy bacilli into the animals. "Not in a single instance," Arning wrote in frustration, did "any general symptom of leprosy" result.

Koch's postulates demanded that a causative link be shown between bacteria taken from a diseased body, and the same disease arising in an experimental animal injected with the pathogen. Until Arning accomplished this, or somehow managed to grow leprosy bacilli in a culture, he had no realistic hope of discovering the cure he desperately sought. "As regards treatment of the disease," he wrote, "I consider it altogether unwarrantable to call leprosy incurable, and simply to remove the afflicted out of sight. This is a remnant of mediaeval barbarism which every professional man ought to oppose."

Arning typically remained in his shed deep into the night, working by lamplight. Cages lined the laboratory wall; a collar and chain kept Keko within reach. Atop a wooden table sat ranks of glass slides, carefully labeled. During the day Arning used reflected sunlight to illuminate the slides beneath the barrel of his microscope; when the sun set, he pulled a burner near for light. In the beginning Arning could not spot the distinctive stick-shaped bacilli in tissue taken from patients, but he reported that after adjusting his method of staining and preparation, "I was able to prove the presence of the same microorganism which Hansen and Neisser first demonstrated as leprous tissue." He had then begun his experiments. "This work is of the most tedious and delicate nature," he informed the board, "and always associated with many discouraging failures." Months passed. Although not a single animal inoculation or culture attempt succeeded, Arning refused to be discouraged. "The recent experiments concerning the germ nature of the disease may be the means of showing us the path of rational treatment," he wrote. "They must and do give a new impulse and new encouragement to us to persevere in trying and experimenting."

In fact, Arning's experiments were fated to fail. As researchers later discovered, the leprosy bacillus has proved impossible to grow in a culture, and though Arning attempted to infect hundreds of mammals, he lacked access to the only creature ever proven vulnerable to leprosy: armadillos, whose core body temperature of 93 degrees mimics the ideal growth conditions of human skin. At times, Arning came tantalizingly close to decoding the complicated characteristics of susceptibility. "As every seed requires its peculiar condition of soil, atmosphere, etc., to allow it to strike," he wrote, "so does the leprous germ." His best hope for a breakthrough, Arning finally concluded, was his ongoing experiment with, as he termed it, "human soil."

Across the channel on Molokai, meanwhile, Arning's work had inspired Dr. Arthur Mouritz. Although Mouritz had no training in bacteriology and lacked both Arning's moral approach to science and his formidable intelligence, he believed he could find a cure. At the time, several hundred kokuas resided in the settlement. These people offered a "splendid field for experimental work," Mouritz wrote. "Stretching all questions of professional ethics, I did not hesitate to avail myself of the opportunities afforded me for testing the inoculability of leprosy." Over the next months Mouritz made more than one hundred attempts to induce leprosy in a healthy subject. He spent the bulk of his effort on ten men and five women. One kokua had arrived in the settlement four years earlier to care for his stricken wife. Mouritz carved a pattern of incisions on the man's forearm, neck, and navel, then coated the wounds with a serum brimming with leprosy bacteria. After the man failed to become infected, Mouritz sliced open his skin and dosed him again. Using a thick needle several inches long, the doctor injected four cubic centimeters of his "leper blister serum" into one test subject's right buttock; a month later he injected the man a second time. When the disease still failed to appear, an irritated Mouritz insisted the man return to his office regularly to be coated with a pungent salve of borated petroleum jelly and the blister serum—"my favorite application in such cases," Mouritz reported.

Another subject was a thirty-one-year-old man who had mistakenly been exiled in early 1883. Ten months into his banishment, the board reversed its decision and released him, but a few months later wrongly exiled him a second time. When Mouritz examined the man, he could find no bacteriological evidence of the disease. Hoping to create it, Mouritz repeatedly scored the man's skin with a scalpel blade and then inoculated him "with leper serum on a surface about the size of a half dollar over each lumbar region."

Mouritz also experimented on men and women who already had the disease. Using corn plaster, he fashioned two-inch-square boxes, open on one side. Mouritz then strapped the boxes to the arms, thighs, and abdomens of his patients, and filled these tiny cages with hundreds of bloodsucking insects: fleas, bedbugs, spiders, horseflies, and mosquitoes. The insects, his notes record, were "allowed many hours to feed." Afterward Mouritz etherized the engorged creatures and minced their abdomens, mixed the resulting pulp with alcohol, and centrifuged the solution. Spreading the bloody paste on a pane of glass, he checked for leprosy bacilli. He found no trace.

To explore the possibility of contagious "leper breath," as he termed it, Mouritz constructed an elaborate apparatus that fit atop the patient's head, with rods that projected forward at the ears. He hung curtains of antiseptic gauze from the rods, covering the subject's mouth. For the first twenty such experiments, Mouritz instructed the patient to breathe normally for several hours, so that their exhalations collected in the gauze like dew. On two comatose patients he found in the settlement hospital, Mouritz simply taped the cloth across their mouths for twelve hours. After removing the fabric, he sank it in a solution of carbolized water, let it steep six hours, then centrifuged the liquid. When he could find no bacilli he repeated the process, this time ordering the patients to cough continuously for hours.

On forty-two female patients Mouritz conducted gynecological examinations to determine if the disease might be sexually transmitted. Male subjects were asked to urinate and ejaculate, and their issue was checked for bacilli. Every week for more than a year, Mouritz hosted bizarre dinner gatherings in the hospital dispensary. Guests arrived to find the doctor had prepared a feast of salt salmon, mullet, and mackerel, all fish common to the Hawaiian diet. Before serving, Mouritz took the meal and reduced it to a paste, then tested the material for the bacillus. He portioned the food out in spoonfuls and instructed the patients to chew for exactly two minutes and then spit the pulp into a cup to be tested. Next, he served poi. Each guest was told to plunge his fingers deep within his mouth, coat the digits with saliva, then bury them into the communal bowl. When they had done this, Mouritz rushed in and pulled samples from the bowl. Circling the table, the doctor thumbed open his guests' mouths and collected additional samples.

To determine if bacilli traveled freely from the nose to the mouth and throat, Mouritz threaded long swabs through his subjects' posterior nasal passage, painfully forcing the object up the nose and then maneuvering it down the back of the throat before finally plucking it out of the patient's trembling mouth. The experiment proved nothing, although Mouritz was able to state conclusively, "The tears of the leper contain no bacillus leprae."

Whether Father Damien knew the full extent of Dr. Mouritz's experiments is unclear. Certainly Damien would have noticed the panicky reaction that a Mouritz sighting created among some residents, but if Damien objected to what the young doctor was doing at night in his dispensary, none of the parties involved ever mentioned it. And Damien had other concerns. The recent hard winter had taken an extraordinary toll on Kalawao. According to a report written by an English physician named J. H. Stallard, who toured the settlement in March 1884, the mortality rate in the colony was now "more than ten times that of any ordinary community of an unhealthy type." One hundred and fifty men, women, and children had died the previous year, and the death rate for 1884 was running 25 percent higher. "The excessive mortality alone condemns the management," Stallard wrote. "There is not a bandage in the settlement, nor even an adequate supply of rags." Residents were being "starved to death, imprisoned, and neglected," Stallard observed, and despite Damien's valiant efforts, the administration—specifically the board of health, Rudolph Meyer, and Clayton Strawn—was "defective and incomplete." After some quick calculations, Stallard determined that the settlement was receiving as little as half the food necessary for the population, a penury that Stallard claimed was contributing to the awful death rate. He wrote, "The leper cannot stand up against starvation."

In defense, Rudolph Meyer sent an angry letter to Walter Murray Gibson, refuting the remarks of this "stranger." The thrust of Meyer's argument was coldly familiar: no matter how generously the board provided for their needs, the exiles were going to die. Meyer pointed out that even under the best circumstances, the average life span in the settlement was five years. "There have been *many* lepers who had friends and means to attain the very best of living, and not *one* of them exceeded this period," Meyer wrote. "As instances, I will mention the names of a few: W. Williamson . . . Boehle . . . David Ostrom . . . W. Ragsdale . . . W. Humphries [*sic*] . . . Peter Kaeo . . . Kahoohuli . . . and many others." Given the board's limited resources, Meyer wrote, the situation was as favorable as one could expect. The residents, he announced during one board meeting, were "comfortable and happy." Their exile was "the very opposite of inhumanity."

Father Damien disagreed, and wrote Rudolph Meyer that the patients were greatly suffering and something must be done. Meyer responded with distressing news: the government was broke. Already in the current funding period the board's accounts had become overdrawn by $7,640, and vendors had stopped filling the board's orders. "Prospects are daily becoming worse," Meyer wrote. "There is no money, and I cannot even obtain a dollar to pay the bills on the food rations for this year nor the half of last year." As the food shipments dwindled, a rumor flared among the settlers: The government had decided to solve its budgetary problems by starving them to death.

At Kakaako, inmates also heard whispers that Molokai was being turned into a charnel house. Terrified that they would be sent there to die, several

Kakaako inmates announced that if the board tried to banish them, "blood would be shed." Then one morning six inmates "broke open the door of Van Giesen's house and made an assault upon him in his bed," the *Advertiser* reported. Splashing the hospital steward with kerosene, they threatened to burn him alive and destroy Kakaako. Walter Murray Gibson raced to the branch hospital and helped put down the uprising. After checking to see if Marianne was safe, he ordered Van Giesen to ready a large group of patients for exile.

Thirty-nine patients from Kakaako arrived in the settlement on March 8, accompanied by Dr. Arning. As he often did, Ambrose Hutchison had ventured to the Kalaupapa shore to meet the boat. Arning approached the young man. "I am telling you unofficially," Arning said, "but you will know before the day is over." He confided that the board had decided to remove the corrupt Clayton Strawn as resident superintendent. Hutchison was to succeed him.

Later, Hutchison would write, "The position of superintendent of the Leper Settlement of Kalawao was not a rosy one." He soon felt caught "between the upper and the nether stone of the grist mill." On one side were the board members "who sit in their wheeled office chairs in Honolulu." Opposite these men was an unhappy community of exiles, and the "lawless elements among [those] people." It was a delicate situation, Hutchison remarked, but "to clean an Augean Stable was a Herculean task which had to be dealt with a firm hand." Within a day of being named luna, Hutchison had ordered his first arrest. Later, Dr. Mouritz wrote of Hutchison, "He displayed marked ability and highly creditable administrative powers for a man so young." Although "the target for all the growlers and kickers" in the settlement, Mouritz remarked, Hutchison "stuck manfully to his post, and often alone and unaided met serious and unforeseen difficulties with commendable foresight and judgment."

By the time Hutchison came to power in the colony, he had fashioned for himself a surprisingly normal life. He had married, in a union blessed by Damien, and fathered a daughter. Although both Hutchison and his bride had leprosy, their daughter remained free from infection. More than a dozen similarly healthy children resided in the settlement, born to patients or kokuas or some combination of both. When their parents passed away, the children were typically taken in by other residents or placed under Damien's care in his Kalawao orphanage. An unlucky orphan might fall victim to sexual exploitation or be forced into servitude, but for many parents the most worrisome possibility was that their child would remain in the settlement and contract the disease. When David Kalakaua's wife, Queen Kapiolani, made a tour of the settlement, Hutchison held his daughter aloft and announced, "Here is a nonleper child, one of many other children like her, born of leper parents. Must she and the other children like her be left to their fate to become victims of the dread scourge?"

To outsiders, the sight of healthy children among the sick was one of the most disturbing aspects of exile. Dr. Arning had already mentioned the matter to both Marianne and Gibson, and when Queen Kapiolani became involved, more than $6,000 in private funds was raised to construct an orphanage in Honolulu. The facility was to house only girls; until a second home was funded, male orphans would remain with Father Damien. By the autumn of 1885, the Kapiolani Home for Girls, the Offspring of Leper Parents, was complete. It stood within a "clean" fenced area on the grounds of Kakaako, next to the convent. Gibson placed Marianne in charge of the home.

The steamer to collect the orphans arrived two hours after nightfall on October 29, 1885. Gibson had instructed Hutchison to have the girls packed and waiting, including Hutchison's own daughter. "All was in readiness and expectantly serene," Hutchison later testified.

As parents and daughters said their good-byes by lamplight, the foster father of an eleven-year-old named Abigail began to escort her toward the rowboat, carrying the girl's trunk. Board regulations forbade patients from coming in contact with the crews of ships, so a settlement constable reached for the trunk, to pass it to a crewman. Abigail's father resisted, as one resident later testified, "and in the struggle the lid of the trunk opened and its contents, the girl's clothes, fell into the sea." Describing events afterward, Dr. Mouritz wrote, "Then the bolt fell, and another leper tragedy happened in the twinkling of an eye."

Suddenly hysterical, Abigail's father pulled a butcher knife from his coat and began to stab the constable. Then Abigail's brother attacked two other officers, punching his knife deep into one man's stomach. The girls shrieked in the darkness. As Hutchison ran to the scene, one of the wounded men gazed at the pool of blood at his feet and announced casually, "I am hurt." Damien and Mouritz tried to stanch the officers' wounds, while Hutchison herded the screaming children into a rowboat. He knelt to kiss his daughter good-bye, and then he and his wife watched the steamer sail into the night. The girls arrived in Honolulu the next morning, in time for an elaborate dedication ceremony Gibson had arranged. To close the event Gibson led the girls in a rendition of "Home Sweet Home." Wrote one reporter: "The voices of the children were sweet and melodious, and they apparently entered into it with much spirit."

Two of the wounded officers died—one of them Ambrose Hutchison's brother-in-law. A third constable recovered after six weeks. The subsequent murder trial took place in Lahaina. Fifteen witnesses were called to testify, including Hutchison, Mouritz, and Damien. Sheriff Peter Treadway met the group when they landed and led Hutchison and the other patients to the island's prison; Hutchison thought they were going to visit the killers. Then a guard took the witnesses inside and locked the gate. "We were as much prisoners as the other persons were," Hutchison wrote. When he asked about food and blankets for the witnesses, the guard only shrugged. With a touch of grim irony, Hutchison remarked, "Hard luck for us outcasts."

The witnesses were imprisoned for a week. On the fifth day Hutchison was called to testify, and lawyers asked a single question before returning him to his cell. Both defendants received ten-year sentences, though Abigail's foster father died before serving his term. On the morning that Abigail's brother was released from prison, a health agent arrested him and dragged him back to the settlement.

After the murders, Gibson had sailed to Kalaupapa to investigate. Resentfully sarcastic, Dr. Mouritz reported the result of Gibson's inquiry: "The priest got into hot water, the doctor also, and deputy superintendent Hutchison, because we all had willfully and stupidly disobeyed the clear (?) instructions of the Board of Health." The Honolulu press blamed Gibson for the disaster, however, and uncoiled a merciless round of attacks. By now, Gibson was an extraordinarily polarizing figure—beloved by some yet reviled by an increasing number. His most dangerous antagonist was the Hawaiian League, a shadowy group of prominent businessmen led by Sanford Dole and his colleague Lorrin Thurston. The league's primary goal was to topple the Gibson-Kalakaua regime and install a pro-business democracy, and the unending profligacy of the administration made for an easy target: According to the most recent budget, the government had fallen more than $2 million in debt. Since assuming the prime ministry, Gibson had fed both the king's and his own extravagant whims—all at government expense. The outlays included a lavish royal palace, a pair of custom-made crowns costing $10,000 each, and a grandiose coronation ceremony for Kalakaua, despite his having been in power for almost a decade. As the league's attacks eroded his public support, Gibson clung to office by further indulging the spendthrift royal. "Yet an empty treasury," Gibson lamented to his diary, "and the King wants so much."

To narrow the budget gap the government sold rights to an opium monopoly and licensed brothels. Dole and Thurston, both sons of Protestant missionaries, denounced the measures. David Kalakaua then decided that Hawaii required a navy, one that would allow him to subdue a vast Pacific empire. Gibson scraped $20,000 from the threadbare treasury and bought a former British guano steamer, rechristened the *Kaimiloa*—"Far Seeker." Once the vessel was fitted with Gatling guns and cannons, Gibson gathered a dozen teenaged boys from a Honolulu reform school to serve as her crew. Gibson then dispatched the *Kaimiloa* to Samoa, as the first step toward realizing Kalakaua's dream.

Dole and Thurston stepped up their campaign. Upon being elected to the legislature in 1886, Thurston launched a series of partisan assaults from the assembly floor. "Bitter spirit of opposition in the House," Gibson complained to his diary. At Thurston's urging, the legislature sent a committee to investigate conditions in the settlement, hoping to impugn both Gibson and the board. "An unsatisfactory reception by the lepers at Kalawao," Gibson wrote after returning from the trip, during which the exiles assailed him with angry complaints. "I feel they have been prompted by the Opposition from Honolulu."

In an effort to distract his enemies, Gibson had begun to assemble a massive volume chronicling the board's fight against leprosy. He intended his report, "Leprosy in Hawaii," to climax with the sensational details of Dr. Arning's experiment with Keanu. But when Gibson asked the doctor to submit his findings, Arning replied, "I do not consider my experiment with Keanu concluded, or mature for scientific publication." Annoyed, Gibson demanded that Arning release his research notes. Arning again refused, and Gibson had him fired: "You will vacate the offices situated in the Kakaako Hospital enclosure," the board informed Arning, "leaving therein such articles as have been supplied to you by the Board." Arning swept the supplies from his desk, packed his microscope and other personal items, and caught the next steamer home. After they realized that the doctor had departed for Europe, patients released the experimental animals he had left behind, keeping possession of several large hogs. During the previous months, Arning had repeatedly injected the hogs with a serum teeming with leprosy bacilli, to no visible effect. The patients roasted the hogs in a pit, and served the pork at a luau.

Dr. Mouritz took over the study of Keanu. Much to Arning's frustration, the prisoner had not exhibited any signs of infection, and the doctor departed believing that his experiment had failed. Only a few weeks later, however, blemishes erupted on Keanu's face and trunk. "Twenty-five months after [his] operation," Mouritz reported, "Keanu showed the maculation of nodular leprosy all over his body." A board photographer hung a sheet on a wall and posed Keanu in front of it, to document the scientific breakthrough, and the image shows Keanu's face disfigured with a series of deep ridges and fleshy waves. Keanu frowns unhappily, and his eyes are cold with anger.

Officers took Keanu from Oahu Prison and brought him to the colony, where Ambrose Hutchison had him locked in one of the settlement's two small jail cells. After learning that his subject had contracted the disease, Eduard Arning contacted the board. "Of course I do not know whether the reports of Keanu's leprosy are based on facts," he wrote, "and I feel most anxious to know what particular symptoms, if any, have developed." If Arning could prove that his inoculation of the prisoner had caused the infection, then he would have met one of the conditions of Koch's postulates and could proceed toward a cure. There was also the equally pressing issue of Arning's guilty conscience: "I consider it my duty to do my best in helping to arrest the disease I myself have inflicted," he wrote. Arning asked the board to send Keanu to him in Germany, where he would attempt a cure. The board declined the offer. Keanu remained on Molokai, imprisoned in a windowless cell.

Later, when he discussed the Keanu episode, Arning defended his behavior. "Will it not stand as having been done in the interests of, not against, the laws of humanity?" he asked. The case shadowed him for years, in both academic and popular circles, and Arning eventually stopped responding to questions about Keanu. Then one day the doctor contracted pneumonia. His heart started to fail. Physicians at a Munich hospital kept the organ beating by using a series of new, mostly untried remedies. "For 6 weeks . . . his suffering [was] prolonged due to the administration of cardiotonic drugs," one of Arning's relatives later reported. Arning's heart finally stopped one warm August morning. After they had buried him, his three children complained angrily about "the way their father had been artificially kept alive," one relative later wrote. "They found the way he had been treated '*unmenschlich*'—inhuman."

With his hold on the government weakening, Walter Murray Gibson rushed around Honolulu in a frantic effort to forestall his fall. "A strong opposition feeling has been aroused, that is turning the popular current of thought against me," he reported in his diary, adding, "I can correct this." He cut an odd figure, dressed formally in a long black coat with gray silk vest, a top hat farther stretching his elongated frame. Every day, Gibson whipped his buggy from his home on King Street to Iolani Palace, raced to do battle on the floor of the legislature, dashed off to a cabinet meeting, then a tense session with the government's bankers, and finally back to the palace. Soon he stopped presiding over the regular board of health meetings. Then the board meetings stopped altogether. Segregation ground to a halt.

Even in the midst of such political chaos, Gibson found time to make daily, often twice daily, pilgrimages to Kakaako Hospital. His love for Marianne had become obsessive. On Sunday mornings he would hurry to the cathedral, hoping to sight her. He phoned the convent repeatedly, wrote her note after note. Gibson dispatched endless gifts to Marianne and the sisters, delivered personally or via a servant: "Sent to Convent at noon a chicken pot pie & custard pudding, with note. No reply—disappointed." Page upon page of his diary chart the emotional chaos of Gibson's romantic pursuit. "A few sweet minutes at Br. H. [Branch Hospital] this morning," he wrote. "Sent a bot. of wine and some flowers to Convent. Got a sweet note in return." At times the only detail he considered worth preserving after his busy days concerned Marianne. "With M. this aft.," one day's entry reads in its entirety; another remarks, "Another very happy day at Kakaako." Following one visit, Gibson joyfully wrote, "A happy hour with my little girl—so faithful to her duty—so good—so pure. What a noble character. I reverence as well as love her."

Though his original plan had called for several of the sisters to be stationed in the settlement to assist Damien, Gibson now felt hesitant to send any of the women away. The prospect of Marianne on Molokai, exiled among the sick, alarmed Gibson, and he confided to his diary, "We will never be separated." When Damien made a rare visit to Kakaako, to meet with the sisters and try to speed up their dispatch to Molokai, Gibson behaved like a jealous lover. "I called on Father D.—and still have some misgivings—he talks too much." Two days later, after Marianne purportedly confided to being exhausted from the demands of Damien's visit, Gibson exalted as if he had bested a rival suitor. "S.M. [Marianne] told me she was completely wearied out with Father Damien's talk—will be content when he returns to Molokai."

From the accounts several of the sisters later offered, Marianne apparently endured Gibson's smothering attention with kindness and patience. Most of their meetings included a chaperone, usually one of the sisters. Marianne seems to have given Gibson little on which to pin his romantic hopes, yet Gibson invested every utterance and action of Marianne's with soul-shaking importance. "Annoying event at Kakaako," he wrote one evening. "I am afraid I am becoming tiresome." Two days later he gushed, "At Kakaako—all happy again. My misunderstanding." After Marianne encouraged Gibson to write to a former female acquaintance in London, he apparently believed that she was trying to divert his attentions from her. "I did not like it," he wrote. A few days later he had forgiven the slight. "S. M. telephoned me to come—took my lunch to the convent—a happy and inspiring visit."

Even as the viability of his government narrowed and his health declined, Gibson remained focused primarily on Marianne. "An invalid today," one day's entry reads. "Sent turkey to Kakaako. The King distresses me with a Nicaraguan canal scheme." By the winter of 1886–87, Dole and Thurston had the Hawaiian League positioned to roust Gibson from power, yet on February 12 he wrote simply, "At Kakaako this P.M. about half an hour—very happy with my little girl." Two days later, when Marianne told Gibson that "she was ready and cheerful to go to Molokai" to aid Damien, a wounded Gibson wrote, "This expression annoyed me—that she was cheerful to go—but I suppose a mere expression of willingness." A few weeks later Gibson arrived at the branch hospital bearing a small box, which he offered to Marianne. Inside, she discovered a gold ring. Engraved on the band were the initials *W.* and *M.*, separated by the figure of a heart. Inside the band an inscription read, "Ruth 1:6, 17." Marianne knew her Scripture: "Entreat me not to leave thee, or return from following after thee: for whither thou goest, I will go; and where thou lodgest, I will lodge."

Gibson did not record Marianne's reaction to the gift in his diary. She apparently decided to insert some emotional distance into the relationship, however. In his entry five days later, Gibson describes sending a "tender note" to Marianne at the hospital. "Messenger went at 3 P.M.—no answer—no return message not even by telephone. I was disappointed. About 9 P.M., M. telephoned to me about a supply of fish for the sick tomorrow. Was at prayers when my messenger came. Had not thought to send a message afterwards. More disappointed after the explanation. Did not go to Kakaako." His "unsatisfied and painful yearning," as he had described it, remained unfulfilled. "I need a companionship she cannot give me."

Through it all, Sanford Dole and the Hawaiian League pressed ahead. "The tempest seems to be rushing to a climax," Gibson wrote. "I am weary, languid, listless, oh, so weary." By early summer the league had formed an armed military wing, the Hawaiian Rifles, and its uniformed officers included Lorrin Thurston. Frightened that the coup would toss him from the throne, the king signaled that he was ready to meet their demands. These, Thurston announced, included dismissing Gibson "from each and every office held by him under the government." At the height of the revolution, Gibson appeared at Kakaako, where one of the sisters found him, "his bowed white head, drooping shoulders and snow white beard." She went to get Marianne. The sisters gathered around to comfort him. "His words were not many, but very kind," one of the sisters later wrote. "'You need not fear,' he said, 'they will not harm you, it is only me they are after.'" When darkness fell, a mob trapped Gibson in his home, and at dawn a detachment of the Rifles marched Gibson to the esplanade, intending to hang him. When Gibson saw the noose, he snatched a scrap of paper from his breast pocket, shoved it into his mouth, and swallowed—it was a note from Marianne.

The mob did not follow through with their threat. Sanford Dole caught wind of the lynching, interceded, and allowed Gibson to flee Hawaii on the next boat. He died in San Francisco just six months later. "A LIFE FULL OF ADVENTURE, PERIL AND VICISSITUDE," the *New York Times* headlined his obituary. Walter Murray Gibson's remains were carted aboard a steamship and returned to Hawaii for burial. The casket cleared the Honolulu customhouse with the rest of the ship's cargo. On the outside of the crate, a customs officer wrote, "W.M. Gibson. One Corpse. No Value."

"A Strange Place to Be In"

(Population 1,144)

Yellow blemishes bloomed on Father Damien's back and arms, and the surface of the spots turned rough, like lichens adhering to a stone. Short sips of sarsaparilla seemed to fade and smooth his skin, but only briefly. Next, a deadness began to swallow his left leg, which for several years had periodically flamed with sciatic pain. Mouritz prescribed an opiate powder for relief, but the doctor's drugs were weaker than the disease. One evening while the settlement slept, Damien slid off his dusty cassock and glided a fingertip down his leg toward his left foot. The outside edge was numb to his touch, as if sculpted from a chunk of wood or bone. Partway across the rise of the arch a sharp tingle of feeling remained, however. Damien drew a line in ink along his skin, mapping the disease's advance. "Soon I will be disfigured entirely," he wrote.

During a visit Damien made to the mission house in Honolulu to confer with his superiors, he filled a shallow tub with bathwater. Then, he later explained, "I had the stupidity to put my foot into almost boiling water causing the skin to burn and blister." Yet he felt nothing. One of the priests summoned his personal physician, Dr. Georges Trousseau. The doctor examined Damien's scalded foot, noting the lack of sensitivity that extended high up the priest's left leg. Trousseau telephoned a colleague, a physician also working for the board. When the doctor arrived, he pushed an electrically charged platinum needle "deeply into the flesh of the foot and leg of [Damien], causing him no pain," his report reads. "This discovery indicated that the peroneal nerve and its branches were dead due to leprosy."

Ambrose Hutchison was waiting for the schooner when Damien returned from Honolulu. After the skiff surfed ashore, Hutchison took the priest's arm and helped him alight. "He had his left foot bandaged," Hutchison later wrote. "Naturally I asked the Father how he hurt his foot." Damien said that he had foolishly burned himself and, "with a touch of irony," as Hutchison recalled, confessed that he had the disease. Before he limped away, Damien announced, "It is the beginning of the end."

Though Damien revealed his condition to few in the settlement, his symptoms were familiar to every resident. "In May 1885, there were no striking changes in his face, except the forehead," Mouritz reported. "In August 1885, a small leprous tubercule manifested itself on the lobe of the right ear, and from that date to the present, diminution and loss of eyebrows, infiltration of the integument over the forehead and cheeks is slowly, but certainly going on." Damien's hands grew knotty as bacilli engorged the nerves, and a cloud of red and gray passed over his eyes, which the disease caused to become "weak and at times very much inflamed," one resident recalled.

Aware that the details would leak, Damien decided to let certain people know about his condition. "There is no more doubt about me, *I am a leper*," he wrote one colleague. "Blessed be the Good God!" To another he announced that his leprosy "was the natural and recognized consequence of a long journey among the lepers.... My robust constitution resisted it for a long time. It has been undermined; now the bacilli have attacked my members." Charles Warren Stoddard, who had accepted a teaching position at the University of Notre Dame, opened a letter from Molokai and read, "Those leper microbes have finally nestled themselves in my left leg and my ear.... I feel myself calm, resigned." Responding to a note in which his brother Pamphile complained of feeling sick, Damien replied, "I was sorry to hear of your illness.... As for myself, I cannot hide from you for long that I am threatened by a yet more terrible disease." After explaining, Damien told Pamphile, "Let's not go shouting this out, and let's pray for each other."

In reaction to Damien's infection, the Sacred Hearts order issued new guidelines for its Hawaiian missionaries. Priests were "to avoid touching the lepers, not to breathe their breath, not to use nor receive what has been used by them." When confessing a sick parishioner, they should "breathe camphorated vinegar ... and if by accident, they have touched them, to wash themselves at once with a solution of carbolic acid." These rules were to apply when dealing with all lepers—Damien included. "I have never been so isolated and excluded from all communication with my confreres," Damien soon lamented to Pamphile. "I am always alone."

Though both the Sacred Hearts mission and the board of health held private discussions about Damien's condition, neither publicly acknowledged his leprosy for many months—in part because they feared the effect it would have on the government. Of late, the board had been insisting that it had leprosy well under control. But the gossip soon spread, quickened by the celebrity Damien had acquired following publication, the previous summer, of Charles Warren Stoddard's *The Lepers of Molokai.* Stoddard's slender book about the priest and the colony had become a worldwide bestseller.

By autumn of 1886 newspapers around the globe were reporting that the "martyr" of Stoddard's book had leprosy. Damien continued to try to shield his elderly mother from the news. "Thanks to God, my health is passable," he wrote in a typical letter. "I am just about the same, except that my beard which is about a finger in length is beginning to get gray." She learned the truth, however. "Belgian papers announced the leprosy of my brother Damien," Pamphile later reported. "It is clear that they exaggerated his state, for among other things they said his flesh was falling from him in rags." A neighbor recited the article for Damien's bedridden mother. "Well then, we shall go to Heaven together," Anne Catherine de Veuster announced, then fell dead.

Six days earlier, on March 30, 1886, a board of health official had retrieved the leather folio containing the name of every exile, his or her nationality, age, and last place of residence. Board officials maintained a similar list of all nonpatient residents, and for thirteen years Damien de Veuster had occupied a spot on this separate roll. The board decided it was time to acknowledge his actual status. Laying open the ledger, the secretary found a single line on the half-filled page and in sweeping script wrote, "Father Damien—Belgian—45—Kalawao." Damien was now patient 2886.

That summer in a library in a convent house in New Orleans, a neatly dressed man named Ira Dutton sat silently reading a Catholic newspaper. The articles in the paper included a brief report from Molokai, describing the settlement and the efforts of Father Damien. "I had never heard of him," Dutton later wrote. The report, filled with details of Damien's service and his subsequent infection with leprosy, had caused Dutton's heart to race. He went to a convent official and asked how he could learn more about the settlement. The official replied with a name, and Dutton immediately hopped a paddleboat up the Mississippi, then traveled by rail to the small town of South Bend, Indiana, where he walked briskly across the campus of the University of Notre Dame. Charles Warren Stoddard was in his office when the stranger knocked. Dutton introduced himself. Then he began to explain why he had come.

He had been born in Stowe, Vermont, he said, and raised in Janesville, a farm-girded village forty miles below Madison, Wisconsin. His was a standard if bookish boyhood: he was interested in gymnastics and reading, and clambered happily along the shelves behind the counter of Sutherland's Bookstore. He had clerked at the store since age twelve; people in Janesville called him the Bookstore Boy. Had a war not begun, he might have acquired Sutherland's Bookstore and never again set foot outside the town. Instead, on September 9, 1861, nineteen-year-old Ira Dutton joined Company B,

Thirteenth Wisconsin Infantry Regiment, and headed south to engage the Confederacy. "Dutton was a handsome fellow," a Union officer later wrote. "And one of the best and bravest officers in our army."

In short order Dutton won a commission and then lieutenant's bars, and rose to brigade quartermaster. He was to carry the $22,000 payroll and protect supply lines from the marauding Nathan Bedford Forrest. "I had a busy time keeping out of his hands," Dutton later wrote. A string of small skirmishes propelled him across Kansas, Kentucky, Texas, and Tennessee and kept him safely distant from the calamitous battlefronts of the war. As he curved across the country, Dutton managed to acquire a fiancée, and a few weeks after Robert E. Lee surrendered, they were wed. Dutton's fortune immediately turned. "My marriage was the first serious mistake," he later confessed. "All was quite horrid." Within the year his wife was living in New York with another man, leaving Dutton to reconcile her considerable debts. He retreated to the army. When he asked for hard duty, the government assigned him to "the gathering of the dead." Battlefield fatalities were to be unearthed from hurried graves, identified, and properly interred. "So far as possible I made it a rule to be present at the disinterment of every body," he remarked. "I thus made record of about 6,000 bodies." Dutton added, "While I was burying the dead what I had in life was cast adrift. And then I drifted."

He soon formed a "fierce and reckless" addiction to whiskey. "John Barleycorn," he exclaimed, "my friend John B." The next years he described as his degenerate decade. "Conditions that were repugnant I submitted to without resistance," he explained. "Even going of my own will into them." Dutton drifted between towns and jobs, and when two ex-army friends found him and offered work, he accepted without a single question. Taking a train to Alabama, Dutton arrived at the address and discovered he was now manager of a whiskey distillery. "This was, of course, a surprise," he wrote. In the months to come he would have fractured recollections of furious women and drunken brawls; often he awoke with torn and reeking clothes, and the uneasy apprehension that something terrible had transpired.

One afternoon Dutton had become curious about the exact number of glasses in a barrel of whiskey. He began to count. When he arrived at the figure, he decided to estimate how many barrels he had drunk during the year. Then he tallied ten years—and recoiled in shock. Filled with self-loathing, Dutton renounced whiskey. He wrote, "I was not entitled to any more." On the occasion of his fortieth birthday he joined the Catholic Church, and a short time later Dutton appeared at the door of a Trappist monastery in Gethsemane, Kentucky. He meant to make "reparations" for his sins, he explained. "The remainder of my life should be devoted to that, and to nothing else." The Trappist order is among the most severe in the Catholic Church, a discipline of work and prayer and perpetual silence. A member of the order once wrote, "It is the loneliest of human habitations."

The monks showed Dutton to a cell six feet square, with a shelf slotted into the wall as a bed. He took the new name of Joseph. "[I] was laying aside the 'Ira B.,'" he later wrote. "I was Joseph, stepping out to a new life." For almost two years Brother Joseph remained at the monastery. Among the tasks required of novitiates was to scythe hay in St. Mary's Field, and Dutton was slicing through the field one warm spring day when a noise drew his attention. The writer James Lane Allen wove the details of what happened next in his story "The White Cowl." Allen wrote, "Suddenly his eyes were drawn to the road below. Around a bend a horse came running at full speed, uncontrolled by the rider. He clasped his hands and breathed a prayer. Just ahead was the slippery, dangerous footing. Another moment and horse and rider disappeared behind the embankment. Then the horse reappeared on the other side, without saddle or rider, rushing away like the forerunner of the tempest." A postulant from the Kentucky monastery also described Brother Joseph's actions, although he lacked Lane's flair for drama: "The rider, a young girl, fell off as the horse went by. He picked her up and carried her to the monks' school."

The injured girl was treated and sent to town, and the abbey again grew silent. Then a few days later Brother Joseph suddenly vanished. "When he left the monastery," one brother wrote, "the rumor went around that he had gone off to marry her." If his departure was related to the young woman, Dutton never admitted it. The nearest he came to an explanation occurred years later, when he suggested that he had realized his penance needed more active form. "I wanted to serve some useful purpose during the rest of my life without any hope of monetary or other reward," Dutton said. "The desire grew upon me with a forcefulness that is difficult to explain." Exactly how or where he could apply this devotion had been a mystery until he had read about the settlement. He exclaimed, "There is the very work that I have been looking for!"

Charles Warren Stoddard simply stared at Dutton. He was not sure what to make of the stranger's story. Dutton seemed sincere, however. And Stoddard knew from Damien's last letter that the priest was faltering. Stoddard jotted several brief letters of introduction for Dutton, including one to the president of the Hawaiian board of health. Dutton asked a final question: "Do you think I can be of service there?" Stoddard answered, "Oh, yes."

Joseph Dutton went by rail to San Francisco and boarded a broken-down bark called the *Eureka,* which left the coast and became becalmed, drifting for thirty days. Dutton read his Bible to pass the hours. On Tuesday, July 20, 1886, he appeared unannounced at the board of health offices in Honolulu. The board president's diary reads: "Capt Ira B. Dutton called—a religious enthusiast—volunteers to assist at Leper Settlement." The president was skeptical. After learning that Dutton expected no salary for his labors, however, he quickly wrote a pass granting Dutton permission to enter the colony. An interisland steamer landed Dutton at Kalaupapa on July 29. Dr. Mouritz described the man who stepped ashore: "He wore a blue denim suit, which fitted his well-knit, slim, lithe, muscular figure. He stood about five feet seven inches tall, had dark brown hair and grayish blue eyes, low voice, placid features, and pleasant smile."

Dutton saw a priest near the landing, sitting atop a buggy hitched to an ancient white horse. He walked over.

"You are Father Damien?" Dutton asked.

"Yes," Damien replied.

"I am Joseph Dutton, a lay brother . . . and I have come to help you."

Damien was silent a minute, looking at the newcomer. Then he said, "I need you. Jump up here alongside of me and we will ride over to the settlement." Dutton would write, "I was happy as we drove over that morning. The Father talked eagerly . . . he was full of plans that morning, talking of what he wished for his lepers, the dreams he had always had." Twenty minutes later they reached Kalawao. Dutton took Damien's hand and gently helped him down.

In the Kentucky monastery the monks maintained a book with the dates of admission for members of the order, and details on postulants who had departed. After he left the abbey, no further information about Dutton had been marked. A monk later completed the entry, and in the space next to Brother Joseph's wrote, "He has gone to Molokai."

Dutton discovered that leprosy had tripped a clock in Damien. The priest seemed desperate to accomplish everything he could before becoming incapacitated. The most ambitious of Damien's undertakings was a new Boy's Home, to shelter the young men in the settlement. Damien envisioned two long dormitories, deep porches, an office and dispensary, and neat picket fencing. He had sketched a blueprint of the facility, and asked his new helper to manage the details. "'Off I am, Brother Joseph,' he said to me daily, almost hourly," Dutton later wrote, "and this was coupled with the request that I finish what he was doing. It seemed sometimes that he tried to do more than one person could expect to finish."

Mouritz began to teach Dutton basic medical skills so that he could also assume Damien's nursing duties. Dutton "was methodical and accurate in his work," Mouritz reported, "and quick to learn the rudiments of medicine and surgery." Later the doctor wrote, "Brother Dutton soon demonstrated that leprosy had no power to instill fear in his mind. He possessed a DIVINE temper, nothing could ruffle it, no vulgar or angry speech ever emanated from his lips." In addition to his nursing and carpentry chores, Damien turned over to Dutton the care of altars and sacristies in St. Philomena. He could not continue, Damien explained, "being myself now on the list of the unclean." Dutton accepted every task willingly, as Mouritz reported. "I enumerate some of Br. Dutton's manifold duties performed daily: Fr. Damien's companion, secretary, servant, nurse . . . sexton, sacristan, verger . . . hospital steward, dresser, clinical clerk . . . sanitary engineer, architect, landscape gardener." Mouritz added, "Br. Dutton was also postmaster."

Years later, Joseph Dutton would write, "In taking up a new life in this faraway place, in which I found as expected many things naturally repugnant and very 'different,' I was firm in at least one resolve—to 'get along' with everything; to ask no special favors; to not make any one the slightest difficulty that I could reasonably avoid, and to do what I could to help my neighbor in every way." Not long after arriving on Molokai, Dutton sent a message to Charles Warren Stoddard: "I believe my vocation is found."

After Walter Murray Gibson was chased from office, Dr. Georges Trousseau had been appointed president of the board of health. The new government, headed by Sanford Dole, instructed him not to yield on segregation. Trousseau took the order to heart. In the final eighteen months of Gibson's administration, the board had exiled only 35 patients; the new board swiftly banished 767 men, women, and children, including most of the inmates of Kakaako Hospital. In the settlement, people scrambled to accommodate the surge of newcomers. Workers began to construct a proper pier at Kalaupapa, and using dynamite, they blasted rock hazards from the ocean floor and built a short breakwater to shield the landing. At the end of the blunt pier the workmen erected a massive scaffold and boom, to pluck cargo from whaleboats and swing it to land. Rudolph Meyer managed to finally remove the last healthy holdouts in Kalaupapa, people who had never considered the exiles a health threat and had thus been reluctant to vacate their longtime homes. The board now controlled the entire peninsula. Slowly, the settlement population migrated westward, toward the warmer, drier, bustling village of Kalaupapa. Next, Meyer and Damien scouted a location for a convent, and a dormitory for orphan girls. Released by Gibson's death, Marianne and the sisters were finally coming to Molokai. The Bishop Home for Girls was built atop a rise in Kalaupapa, a few minutes' walk from the landing, with a sweeping view of the settlement. Marianne was placed in charge.

Among the many projects unfolding in the settlement was an insignificant one, yet Damien seemed particularly eager about it. It involved a tiny cottage near the Boy's Home, in Kalawao. The priest explained he wanted it swept clean, to prepare for a new occupant: Clayton Strawn. Damien's former nemesis had undergone an extraordinary transformation. Shortly after he was removed from the settlement and sent to Kakaako, Strawn had begun to pine for Damien. He began to write pensive letters to his "dearest and best friend," announcing, "I have to hear a letter from my good old friend Damien." In one note Strawn wrote, "Father, I have been to confession and holy communion a number of times. I am altogether changed since I left Kalawao. As I am now [I] feel a great deal more composed, better in spirit and body." He described a dream in which he landed in the colony and Damien warmly welcomed him. "Well, Strawn, you want to stop with me, do you?" Damien said in the dream. "I will hunt you up a house." Strawn returned to the settlement on August 6, 1888. The disease had left him blind. Hutchison and Damien met him and guided him to his new home. "A cute little cottage," one resident later described it, "with a cute little yard."

By the end of that summer Damien had shed thirty-five pounds, and "he tottered in his walk, his clothes appeared like bags hung on his figure," one doctor wrote. A kona storm struck the peninsula, and the screaming winds lifted St. Philomena's steeple and dropped it a hundred feet away. Surveying the wreckage, Damien worried that he was too frail to rebuild. He soon crouched atop the chapel, however, barking instructions and swinging a hammer. A visitor wrote of the "wild activity he was directing, giving his orders now to the masons, now to the carpenters, now to the laborers . . . you would have said he was a man in his element and perfectly healthy." After a similar sighting, a visiting priest remarked, "What a man! What energy he still has!" When the priest faltered in the afternoon heat, Damien hurried over with a piece of fruit. "You must eat this," Damien said. "It will do you good. Don't be afraid. It hasn't been touched by a leper." Then he remembered.

Dr. Arthur Mouritz left the settlement that season to open a private practice. His replacement was Sydney Bourne Swift, a morphine-using Irishman who claimed to be descended from the writer Jonathan Swift. The new resident physician also bragged of a medical degree—it was later revealed to be for veterinary medicine. Shortly after Swift arrived, an epidemic of influenza struck the settlement. Seventy-five patients died in one week. By the time the epidemic passed, one-third of the residents of the Boy's Home had succumbed, a mortality that deeply shook Joseph Dutton.

One afternoon he turned abruptly from his work and started hiking up the cliff, climbing to clear his head. He stopped midway up the rock face. Below him, riders trotted along the lane that linked the two villages, now known as Damien Road. Mother Marianne and the sisters were outside Bishop Home, the wind in their robes. Canoes bobbed offshore, filled with patients fishing. In the yard of the Boy's Home knots of children played. They "have a great way with their games," Dutton had written a few days earlier. "A week of kites, then of arrows, then of marbles, and so on, like boys the world over." In the same letter Dutton had mentioned Damien's perseverance: "Father Damien is suffering very much now, though he is out and about every day. He says Mass every day, has missed only two mornings since I came here and these on account of his eyes—they are growing very weak. One of his ears is swollen to an enormous size and covered with lumps of many colors; on his forehead ridges and lumps, also on the face, hands and arms, and yet he is very active and cheerful, one of the most powerful men physically to be found." Dutton watched the light deepen across the peninsula, nightfall coming on fast. Soon the trail would be too dark to travel, in either direction. In a letter to his brother, Damien had once remarked, "The only way out of here is by the cemetery road." Dutton started to descend. When he reached the base of the cliff, he hurried toward the home to see about dinner for the boys. It was very late.

In October 1888, Father Damien collapsed while saying Mass. "I know that my days are numbered," he wrote. "My illness progresses quickly. Both my face and my hands are beginning to decompose." To his brother Pamphile he confessed, "I think I am the happiest missionary in the world."

By the next spring he was having difficulty breathing. He could walk only with help. At night he slept fleetingly and trembled beneath the sheet. Marianne came from Kalaupapa to comfort Damien and collect the orphaned girls still in his care. "My children," Damien told the girls, "I shall die soon but you will not be abandoned. The sisters whom you see have come to care for you." One nun later wrote that two of the children refused to abandon Damien: "Clinging to his feet they cried, 'Father, we want to stay here until your death.'" Marianne allowed them to remain, and then led the others away.

He spent his days on the second floor of the whitewashed rectory, and on warm afternoons Dutton would carry him to the porch to feel the sun. Damien showed Dutton the cubbyhole in the rafters where he kept the church funds hidden, so that Dutton could find the money after Damien's death. On March 10 Damien recited his medical history to Dutton, detailing his leprosy as it repeatedly attacked and then fell back. The document concludes: "Now, since the disease has spread over the body, it becomes strong again."

On March 11, Damien received an invoice from the vendors J. T. Waterhouse and Co. for a final gift he had arranged for the boys; the cost of two large sacks of colored marbles was $8.50. Dr. Swift arrived and began a medical log, itemizing Damien's last days. "8.00 A.M., Temp 103, Pulse 96," Swift wrote. "At 8.30 eat 4 ozs raw hamburger steak." Two entries later he reported, "Refuses to take quinine," and "Prescribed egg nog." Beneath Swift's entry Dutton wrote, "Will have no more egg nog."

Damien made his last confession on March 30 to a waiting Sacred Hearts priest. The next morning he exclaimed, "Look, all my wounds are closing up, the crust is becoming black. It's the end. I have seen too many lepers die to be deceived. The Lord is calling me to celebrate Easter with him." Three days later he received extreme unction, the final sacrament, during which the dying person is anointed with oil. He protested that he wanted to hold on until Easter and join Christ in death. Later he whispered that he was tired and wished it over with. Rudolph Meyer ventured down the cliff to visit Damien. He wrote, "Even Saints and Martyrs have to exercise sometimes a little patience."

On April 10 at 9:14 in the morning, Damien's pulse was 104, and that afternoon he experienced "a pronounced chill." Swift recorded that Damien "had one ounce whiskey at that time." Ambrose Hutchison visited and joined Dutton at Damien's side. Marianne and several of the sisters arrived from Kalaupapa. "Oh! How sad it was to see that holy priest," one nun later wrote, "lying on that poor bed tossing to and fro with pain and fever. . . . How cheerful he tried to be, forgetting awhile his own suffering to think of others." Kneeling beside Damien's bed, the sister asked, "Will you pray for us when you go to heaven?" Damien replied that he would pray for everyone in the settlement, "if I have any credit at all with God."

On Palm Sunday, Damien grew delirious. He insisted two figures were standing in the room with him, hovering near enough to touch. Dr. Swift entered the room with a camera to take deathbed photographs, copies of which he later sold, despite the board's objections. When the startling image was displayed in a London shop window, police had to be summoned to control the huge crowds. Swift had placed his camera at the foot of the mattress and instructed Dutton to steady Damien, so that he would have a better shot. Dutton held the feverish priest upright. An instant before the shutter tripped, Swift yelled for Dutton to step from the frame.

Three pillows elevate Damien's head. A quilted and striped blanket is pulled high to his chin, almost covering a white nightshirt. His large and mottled hands lie in his lap, the tips of his long fingers lost in folds of cloth. His black hair is tousled and gray at the temples, his mouth slightly open and slack, and his eyes are strangely bright. They stare at Swift's camera, seemingly unaware. Father Damien de Veuster died at 8 A.M., on Monday, April 15, 1889, passing away "like a child going to sleep," one observer wrote. He was forty-nine years old.

At 11 A.M., Damien's body was taken to St. Philomena. Marianne lined his coffin with white silk and draped it with black cloth woven with a cross. The funeral was held the following day. Pallbearers carried Damien to a grave dug beneath the tree that had sheltered him on his first night in the colony, sixteen years earlier. "On the day of his burial it was sad to see the children near his grave," one of the sisters later wrote. "The smallest boys circled around his grave, then the next size behind them and the taller ones in the back of them forming three or four rows." She added, "their sad little faces looked as though they had lost their best friend." Several boys shimmied high into the trees and watched the service from above.

Afterward, Joseph Dutton gathered Damien's belongings, to be forwarded to his family. According to his notes, Dutton found:

1 Cape—Part of the Religious habit.
1 Writing desk—with trinkets inside.
1 small Card board folder with 2 pictures "Ecce Homo" and "Bearing the Cross."
4 Photographs of Father Damien in youth—one not mounted.
1 Old pipe—showing Fr. Damien's tooth marks.
3 smooth old copper coins.
1 Record Book—leper cases.
1 physician's hand book—with Father Damien's medical formulas.
8 Copies of Mr. Stoddard's "Lepers of Molokai."

Before Dutton could safely collect them, Dr. Swift managed to pilfer some of the priest's belongings, which Swift's family later put up for auction, along with the deathbed photos. The doctor acquired Damien's knotted wooden cane, his meerschaum pipe, and a piece of the priest's treasured rosary. One other memento was also offered for sale: a final handwritten note from Damien. The letter urged Swift to check on a sick patient Damien had been worrying about. The dying priest had written: "Please spare a moment to go and see him—at the second house after that of Jack Lewis—and oblige your friend."

Joseph Dutton took over Damien's work in Kalawao. A succession of Sacred Hearts priests handled the religious duties. Dutton's main task was to oversee the Boy's Home and, with the sisters' help, care for a hundred boys and young men. In the evenings Dutton wrote letters describing his changed life. "Have just blown the candle lights out because the sun is making a light," he reported. "Began at the desk at 9:00 P.M. and shall continue until about 6:30 A.M. Four nights that way this week—dozing one hour in the chair." Correspondence from Dutton landed on the desks of newspaper editors, clergymen, physicians, and politicians; in time his address book swelled with four thousand names. He inked notes on the frontispiece of books, in the margins of news clippings, and on the back of photographs—then promptly mailed them away. After a photographer persuaded him to sit for his camera, Dutton posted copies of the image, narrated on the back with the story of "the little gentleman" who posed beside him. The child, Dutton wrote, was Peter Akim, a boy with a British mother and a sister named Cecelia, who lived with the Franciscan sisters at Kalaupapa. "Peter is smart and active," Dutton reported, is a good tailor, helps with the cows, and hopes to be a carpenter. "Though small he is hardy, and strong."

In the coming years Dutton came to call Kalawao "my penitentiary—a very happy one for this ragged remnant of life." The pace of his work and correspondence never slowed. He appeared once to be on the brink of exhaustion, and someone suggested a vacation. "Nothing else could make me so miserable," he replied. "Why, I have vacation all the time, every blessed moment of all these blessed years—in doing what I like—what I think my soul needs—the work I like to do. Anything else would be slavery." He added, "As it is I am enchanted. The people here like me, I think, and am sure I like them."

Among the many recipients of Dutton's frequent notes was Dr. Nathaniel Bright Emerson, who had been named board president after Georges Trousseau. Emerson typically worked on board matters in the morning and spent afternoons writing in his diary. He was at his desk one day in May 1889 when Robert Louis Stevenson strolled into the office. Emerson recorded that Stevenson then requested "of all things, the permission of the Board to visit Kalawao! Naturally I refused. But with that pleading look he is so well known about town for I almost gave in."

As Stevenson began to make his case, Emerson stopped him—all would-be visitors had to file a written request. The appeal arrived the following morning. "I beg to apply for permission to visit the Leper Settlement on Molokai," Stevenson wrote. "I am aware how much you must look askance on such a proposition; but I trust you will consider that I scarcely belong to the same class, and that I visit the settlement with no design to make capital." Put off by Stevenson's presumption, Emerson decided to bury the application.

The next morning Emerson found a note waiting from the king. He hurried to the palace. David Kalakaua explained that he would consider it a "personal favor" if Stevenson was allowed into the settlement. "I stated my feelings in the matter, that once we make exception to him others will want to also go over and play tourist," Emerson complained in his diary. "My opinions were to a deaf ear."

Kalakaua told Emerson that the visit would announce to the world "how safe it is to live in the islands." Emerson thought otherwise. The king's argument, he wrote, sounded "like an Oceanic S.S. travel poster—much good for Hawaii can come from this—! ! ! Bah." But the matter was settled. A single entry in Emerson's diary reports: "Stevenson to have his letter."

To prepare for the visit, Stevenson took a steamer to the Kona coast, on the western side of the island of Hawaii. Board agents had been concentrating on the area, emptying the coast with relentless efficiency. On the day Stevenson visited, suspects were being held near a village called Hookena, detained in a hut atop a dead lava flow. Among them was a nineteen-year-old girl. She had covered her face with a shawl. "Perhaps she had been beautiful," Stevenson wrote, "certainly, poor soul, she had been vain—a gift of equal value." Suddenly the shawl slipped, and the girl snatched it closed. "But this time I had seen her face," he wrote, "it was scarce horribly affected, but had the haunting look of an unfinished wood doll, at once expressionless and disproportioned; doubtless a sore spectacle in the mirror of youth." He watched agents load the suspects into a boat, pulling them from sobbing relatives. "At length the scene was over," he reported. "The whaleboat was urged between reefs into a bursting surge, and swung next moment without on the smooth swell. Almost every countenance about me streamed with tears." He wrote, "I had seen the departure of lepers for the place of exile; I must see their arrival and that place itself."

Robert Louis Stevenson reached the settlement on May 14, 1889. He arrived aboard one of two whaleboats that bucked toward the Kalaupapa landing from the weekly steamer. A dozen patients crowded the first craft; the second held a pair of Franciscan sisters and Stevenson. As the shore drew near, one of the nuns began to weep. Stevenson noticed the nun's fright and also burst into tears. Later that day he wrote, "My horror of the horrible is about my weakest point."

"A great crowd, hundreds of (God save us!) pantomime masks in poor human flesh [were] waiting to receive the sisters and the new patients," Stevenson reported. Residents milled around the arriving sisters, welcoming them to the settlement. Although he had earlier insisted to Dr. Emerson that he was no tourist, Stevenson suddenly felt like one: "Shame seized upon me to be there, among the many suffering and few helpers, useless and a spy." He slipped away from the pier, carrying his bag, a camera, and a small black flute.

The road skirted Kalaupapa village and then looped east, as Stevenson later described: "Beyond Kalaupapa the houses became rare; dry stone dykes, grassy, stony land, one sick pandanus; a dreary country; from overhead in the little clinging wood shogs of the pali chirruping of birds fell; the low sun was right in my face; the trade blew pure and cool and delicious; I felt as right as ninepence." Patients on horseback raced past, to join the celebration at the wharf. Stevenson waved. A man rode up, leading a second horse. Stevenson saw that his face was mildly damaged by disease, his mouth slightly crooked.

"Are you Stevenson?" Ambrose Hutchison asked.

Hutchison helped the writer into the saddle. When they reached the guesthouse, Stevenson let the horse loose in the garden, stumbled inside, and collapsed on the bed. He woke after dark. "As yet, you see, I have seen nothing of the settlement," Stevenson wrote that evening to his wife, Fanny. In his journal he remarked, "This is a strange place to be in. A bell has been sounded at intervals while I wrote, now all is still but a musical humming of the sea, not unlike the sound of telegraph wires; the night is quite cool and pitch dark, with a small fine rain . . . one cricket whistling in the garden, my lamp here by my bedside, and my pen cheeping between my inky fingers." He had noticed "one light over in the leper settlement." He wondered who was up so late. A few hundred yards away, Joseph Dutton was writing letters of his own.

The next morning, Stevenson introduced himself to Dutton and asked to see the hospital. When they reached the entrance to the long, narrow building, Stevenson froze. In a letter to his editor, he had once remarked that "the ideas of deformity and living decay" had been "burdensome to my imagination since the nightmares of childhood." Stevenson imagined the Kalawao hospital to be filled with "gorgons and chimaeras dire." Standing at the hospital threshold, he admitted, "Horror and cowardice worked in the marrow of my bones."

Dutton, however, merely pushed through the door and ambled down the hall, making gentle jokes with the patients. Stevenson stuck his head inside and watched: "His pleasantries, which might have scattered a dinner party at home, were given and received with kindly smiles." Stevenson took a deep breath and followed Dutton into the hospital. As they went among the patients, Dutton noticed a change in Stevenson. His manner became "one of intense sympathy . . . quick to feel, quick to love," Dutton later wrote. "He sought out the cases most in need of sympathy, those beyond all hope of relief, and he seemed more and more interested, more and more moved with compassion."

When they emerged from the hospital, Stevenson spotted a tiny shack, leaning slightly into the wind. He found Clayton Strawn inside, bedridden and blind. Strawn told Stevenson stories about his early days in the colony, and about his beloved Father Damien. He recited a poem he had composed—then blurted in embarrassment, "It's doggerel, that's what it is." When Stevenson thanked him for his time, Strawn replied, "I've got nothing to do but sit here and think."

Afterward, Stevenson quizzed Dutton about the disease. He asked about the infectiousness of leprosy, and what risk it posed to a person with tuberculosis—Stevenson did not mention that he had tuberculosis himself. Later, Dutton pieced it together. "He knew, of course, his physical condition," Dutton wrote. "In some ways I got the impression that he was looking for a spot to end his days. Was he thinking of Molokai? I do not know. But he could hardly have settled here, even if such had been his wish." Before they parted, the two men discussed faith and the salvation of service. Stevenson made a comment about the fortunate rarity of a place such as the settlement, where so many felt loss. Dutton looked at Stevenson a moment. Then he replied, "There are Molokais everywhere."

Sister Leopoldina Burns was crossing the yard of the Bishop Home when she spotted "a strange looking man hanging on the fence," as she wrote in her diary. For an instant she thought he might be a tramp. Leopoldina moved to the fence. Stevenson wore a gray suit, with a red silk scarf tied around his waist. He held a large hat. As she drew near, she saw that he was beaded with perspiration, and "his remarkable eyes were sunk with dark rings around them." He introduced himself; she did not recognize the name.

Stevenson asked if he could meet Mother Marianne. Leopoldina opened the gate, then glided away. Stevenson entered. The compound comprised four whitewashed cottages and a small convent house, white with green shutters. Every building faced the sea. When Marianne emerged from the convent and saw Stevenson's flushed face, she was immediately alarmed. "The poor man is subject to hemorrhages," Marianne told Leopoldina. She knew the signs: Marianne also suffered from tuberculosis and recognized the "galloping consumption, cold sweats, prostrating attacks of cough . . . all the ugliest circumstances of the disease," as Stevenson had once described his malady. Marianne begged Stevenson to rest in the parlor, but he refused. He wanted to meet the girls.

That morning many of the patients were on a guava hunt, and the dorms were unusually quiet. Only the weakest girls remained. Marianne narrated their histories. "I was told things which I heard with tears, of which I sometimes think at night, and which I spare the reader," Stevenson later wrote. Their rooms were decorated with photographs and pictures torn from magazines, and the walls were colored with Christmas cards several years old. Handmade dolls sat on the neatly made beds. A few weeks earlier, Stevenson had sent a croquet set to Marianne, for use at Bishop Home. Now, he announced, the girls needed lessons. Marianne tried to talk him out of the idea, worried that he might overexert himself and end up dead. But Stevenson insisted. The next morning Marianne had seven girls waiting on the lawn.

"It was interesting to watch them," Sister Leopoldina later recalled. "Mr. Stevensen stripped off his coat and hat and working so that every now and than he would throw himself on the soft grass to rest until it was his turn to play." Marianne felt certain he would have an attack. She tried to get him to sit on the porch and merely explain the rules. Stevenson wrote, "I said 'they would not enjoy that'—'sh,' said she, with a smiling eye, 'you say that, but the truth is you enjoy playing yourself!' And so I did."

He came to Bishop Home every day for a week. The girls began to keep watch. When they spotted him heading down the lane, they "met him with joyful welcome," Leopoldina wrote. Stevenson later told his mother, "The croquet helped me a bit, as I felt I was not quite doing nothing. I used to have an easy conscience when returning from those croquet parties."

On his final day in the settlement Stevenson stopped to say farewell. "The children crowded to the fence and hailed and summoned me with cries of welcome," he wrote. Several of the girls offered their mallets and begged Stevenson to play. He wrote, "I wonder I found the heart to refuse the invitation." When he started for the landing, to board the departing boat, the girls ran inside and began to strip the sheets from their beds. They then raced to the highest point on the lawn. Sister Leopoldina recalled that the girls "waved the sheets until the boat turned the corner and was lost to view."

On board the steamer, Stevenson organized the notes he had made while in the settlement, writing on a lined journal warped into waves by humidity. On one tearstained page he had written, "I have seen sights that cannot be told, and heard stories that cannot be repeated: yet I never admired my poor race so much nor (strange as it may seem) loved life more than in the settlement."

Part Three

You never know beforehand what people are capable of, you have to wait, give it time, it's time that rules.

José Saramago, *Blindness*

Kalaupapa circa 1900.

Kindred Dust

(Population 1,123)

When she emerged from Kalalau Valley in 1896, Koolau's widow hid from the government in her mother's home. Piilani believed that she would be charged as an accomplice in the killing of Deputy Sheriff Louis Stolz. "After some time in this quietude," Piilani wrote, "the rumor began to spread amongst some people that I had been seen, and as little trickles of water become a stream, thus the rumors spread until it became widely known and came to the ears of the government watchmen."

Sheriff John H. Coney went to see Piilani. He asked her if Koolau was alive. Piilani explained "the truth from beginning to end," she later wrote, "the story of his deeds, from our wandering existence with our beloved child in the mountainous regions of the unforgettable valley of Kalalau, until I returned his clay and that of our child to sleep in the enduring peace of mother earth." At the end of her testimony Coney expressed his "complete belief" in the story. He assured her she would not be prosecuted. "On this day I triumphed over my doubts as to the effects of the government's power over me," Piilani wrote.

The people arrested in Kalalau Valley had long ago passed through the system and arrived at Kalaupapa. Ambrose Hutchison would have met them at the landing. By this time the settlement consisted of 423 buildings, "arranged in reference to streets, rather than in the usual haphazard style of most Hawaiian villages," one newspaper reported. Patients' cottages "show very plainly the characters of the residents. Some are untidy and cheerless; others neat and attractive; some have not the slightest appearance of any care; others have flowers, and grass plots, and fruit trees, and vines, as if they were the abodes of taste and comfort." In the Boy's Home, now called the Baldwin Home for Boys, Joseph Dutton oversaw 96 residents; at the Bishop Home Marianne shepherded 116. Although the board still kept an eye on outlays, the Hawaiian economy had improved enough to significantly increase the settlement's budget, and as the Honolulu paper the *Friend* remarked, since "the Gibson-Kalakaua period of misrule came to an end, the administration of affairs at the settlement has been conducted on better business principles."

Every week a white-hulled interisland steamer delivered supplies to the Kalaupapa landing. Residents received three pounds of poi daily, seven pounds of beef or five pounds of salmon weekly, salt, a half pint of kerosene, and matches. The board had increased the patients' yearly allowance to $10. Since the beginning of exile 4,904 persons had been sent to the settlement; 3,491 had died. Of late, the patients were perishing less rapidly, however—a consequence of better food and medical care, and the simple fact that most exiles with the lepromatous form of the disease had already expired, leaving a majority of milder tuberculoid cases. The board had built a new branch hospital in Honolulu, on the site of the original Kalihi Hospital. The facility contained a small research laboratory where a team of doctors studied leprosy. "The virulence of the disease is apparently abating," one report concluded. "When it first broke out, five years formed the limit of duration of the disease. There are some lepers who have been at the settlement 25 years." A Honolulu publisher had made a recent trip to the settlement and wrote of the residents, "They are comfortable, well-housed, clothed, fed, and cared-for. In case of illness, the Government Physician attends them, and if disease takes an acute form they are moved to the hospital and cared for, until relieved by medicine or death. If they are well, and wish to work, they are paid for it; if they are unruly, there is a prison; if religious, churches; if scholarly, schools; if rambling, beautiful valleys." Of the settlement's most famous resident, the visitor wrote, "Father Damien [sleeps], and other laborers now occupy the field, and still life and death go on as before."

That winter, one of Damien's replacements had arrived on Molokai: his brother Pamphile. In the final years of Damien's life, his well-publicized martyrdom had prompted an extraordinary outpouring of donations. Eager to capitalize on the charity-inspiring notion of one brother taking up for his fallen sibling, Sacred Hearts officials had pulled Pamphile from his academic post and dispatched the fifty-eight-year-old to Molokai. "He laid aside his cherished books and left the famous college in which the best years of his life had been spent in study and teaching to go forth to the succor of the miserable denizens of Molokai," the *Brooklyn Eagle* reported. When the writer inquired about the motives for his mission, Pamphile "simply responded that he had been asked to undertake it, and that it was his duty to obey." He lasted twenty-one months in the settlement, before hurrying back to Europe.

One morning after Pamphile had departed, a patient named John Unea canvassed the community, recording a census. As he went door to door, Unea wrote down each resident's name, age, house number, and job. Most entries give no occupation, but those that do are recorded as machinist, Horse-man,

Teamster, cook, painter, Notary Public, Steward, fishermen, School Teacher, and jailor. Four people are identified only as "Prisoner." House number 287, in Kalawao, was noted as the residence of "Dutton, Joseph . . . Manager for Boys Home." A thirty-six-year-old Pennsylvania man, John Wilmington, was listed as "Store Keeper." At house number 267, John Unea found a forty-one-year-old man and his forty-two-year-old wife: the occupation of "Hutchison, Ambrose" was said to be "farmer."

A Honolulu reporter recently wrote of Hutchison, "The Government is fortunate in having as the Acting Superintendent a half-white of marked ability. Almost helpless from disease, semi-paralyzed, half blind, his good judgment and quiet decision give him great control of the unfortunates under his charge." In the years since Damien's death, Hutchison had become increasingly devout, embracing a rigid Catholicism in tribute to his friend. The intensity of his faith created administrative problems. If a steamer arrived on Sunday, Hutchison refused to allow it to be unloaded, to protect the Sabbath. Some residents claimed that he showed favoritism to the Catholics in the settlement, and bias toward others. The board repeatedly cautioned Hutchison that the settlement was to be run "on a secular basis, [with] no church influence to interfere with the administration of the place." He replied that he was "giving the best that was in me to fill the arduous duties of my office."

In September 1897 Hutchison opened the weekly mail packet and read his latest orders from the board. Its members had voted "to instruct Mr. Hutchison at the Leper Settlement that all dogs except poodles be killed." One of the antimongrel movements that periodically swept Honolulu was in force, and the press was lamenting the number of "cur dogs" in the islands: "the great unknowns and small snarleyyows, untaxed, unclaimed and unfriended." The board had decided that dogs were a nuisance in the settlement too. Hutchison was told to destroy any male dog that weighed more than twenty pounds or stood higher than sixteen inches, and all female dogs. Reluctantly, he began to measure and weigh his neighbors' pets. He shot 157 animals, cremating the carcasses in an oven. Several months later Hutchison resigned as superintendent. He decided to work in his garden instead.

By the time Hutchison gave up power, Rudolph Meyer had also vanished from the scene. Meyer had grown big-bellied over the years, bald and sallow-eyed. After thirty years as manager, he was tired of the colony. "His position is not one which would be sought by most men," the *New York Times* had commented, and Meyer finally reached the same conclusion. The place seemed to bring him bad luck, and had almost from the very beginning. In 1866, just weeks after the first exiles landed, an epidemic of typhus killed

Meyer's six-year-old daughter, Bertha. He carved a family plot on a flat piece of land set back from the cliff; Bertha was the first to be interred.

Over the coming decades the graveyard filled with dozens of Meyer's descendants, who appeared to be spectacularly cursed. One grandson was beaten to death on the Kaunakakai waterfront, then thrown into the sea by his unknown assassins. Another grandchild, fifteen-year-old Otto Jr., ventured out to hunt spotted deer and never returned; they found him in the topside brush with an errant bullet in his head. Meyer's grandson Harvey became unbalanced and died in a sanitarium, and another descendant was working in a sand pit on a Molokai beach when the walls collapsed, smothering him alive. "He was trapped for many hours before they were able to free his body," a relative reported. One spring morning Emma Meyer, Rudolph's three-year-old granddaughter, plucked an oleander from a hedge in the yard, popped it in her mouth, and was poisoned. The family buried Emma in the Meyer cemetery too.

On June 12, 1897, seventy-two-year-old Rudolph Meyer had passed away unexpectedly while visiting his daughter Elizabeth at her home in Honolulu. He was placed in a casket and loaded on a steamer to Molokai. A storm caught the ship as it crossed the channel. When it finally reached Kaunakakai at 6:45 A.M., the waves were thundering. "There was much trouble landing the passengers," the *Honolulu Evening Bulletin* reported. "First they were landed on the ship boats, then transferred to flat bottom scow and again transferred to lighter draught scows and finally the women and children were carried by men over the muddy flats until reaching the sandy beach." An ox-team hauled the coffin to the homestead, and his children laid him out in the parlor while the grave was prepared. "The body was carried out by his stalwart sons and borne through a pathway densely shaded with fruit trees down to a luxuriant tropical glade," reported the *Bulletin,* "and the body of the honorable patriarch was committed to its kindred dust." The board announced, "The Hawaiian government has lost an officer whose services were invaluable, while the Hawaiian people have lost a wise and sympathizing friend."

Dr. Eduard Arning's experimental animal, the prisoner Keanu, spent four years in the settlement, locked with a patient named Daniel in "two cells each 6 ft by 9 ft square," Ambrose Hutchison later reported. The jail stood next to the Dying Den, now unused. Eight years and fifty days after being inoculated by Dr. Arning, Keanu passed away. His death yielded no scientific insight. After investigating the case, a board physician discovered that Keanu's guard at Oahu Prison had had an active case of leprosy while he served as

Keanu's jailer. The doctor then learned that Keanu's nephew, cousin, brother-in-law, and son all had leprosy, and that as a young man Keanu "had lived in the same house with these leper relatives." The findings suggested that Keanu had become infected "previous to his inoculation," as the physician noted. Concluding that Arning's experiment was flawed, researchers subsequently ignored the case. No successful inoculation of a human subject with leprosy bacilli has ever been proved.

As the century drew to a close, the board's understanding of the disease began to incrementally improve. Among the first of the board's physicians to recognize that the exiles were being needlessly isolated was Dr. Georges Trousseau, once the most vociferous advocate of banishment. One day Trousseau brusquely severed all his relations with the board. "Accompanying his resignation was a long private letter," the *Advertiser* reported, "in which the doctor stated his reasons for his course." Trousseau wrote that he had concluded that leprosy was only feebly contagious: "Hence my resolution to be no more a party to a measure that I think useless and unscientific."

The doctor had another reason for his change of heart, although it would not be revealed for several years. In the interim Honolulu newspapers cruelly mocked Trousseau's flip-flop, dubbing him "Dr. Anti-Segregationist Trousseau." He fell into a chronic depression, which grew darker after the death of Kaaepa, the other male member of Trousseau's plural marriage with the Hawaiian woman named Makanoe. Following Kaaepa's burial, Trousseau made out his will, leaving everything to Makanoe. "As far as I am concerned I am tired of life and wish for death," he wrote. Two months later, at age sixty-one, Trousseau committed suicide with an overdose of sedatives; he was buried alongside Kaaepa. When his widow, Makanoe, died several years later, estate lawyers began to search for two of the children produced during her union with Kaaepa and Trousseau. After much investigation, they discovered the heirs. Emilia and George both had leprosy, and had been exiled.

Following David Kalakaua's death in January of 1891, his sister Liliuokalani had been made queen. She attempted to regain the monarchial powers that had been stripped from her brother during the final days of the Gibson-Kalakaua regime, but the increased power of Sanford Dole and other members of the Hawaiian League stymied the queen's efforts. When Liliuokalani had tried to force into law a new constitution, her opponents seized the main government building and declared the monarchy abolished. They then established a provisional government, "to exist until terms of union with the United States of America have been negotiated and agreed upon." On July 4, 1894, the Republic of Hawaii was officially created. Sanford Dole was named president.

Dole's lushly gardened residence in Honolulu was on Emma Street, near the home where Peter Kaeo had died. Dole's wife believed leprosy hung over their residence like a thunderhead. Anna Dole wore her gloves indoors, and used her dress hem to turn doorknobs. She begged Sanford to be careful of what he touched and ate when he was outside, and when he returned home in the evenings she insisted he scrub his skin until it bled. "I fear I have made a fool of myself by my fear of leprosy," Anna confessed in a letter to her mother. "But it is such a dreadful disease."

Although the dilemma of leprosy still occupied many of Dole's constituents, his primary goal was to arrange for America to annex the islands. The idea that Hawaii was riddled with disease had slowed the campaign. Dole and his colleague Lorrin Thurston huddled frequently to discuss how to efface that notion. The mainland mood seemed to run against their cause, however. "Shall We Annex Leprosy?" the *American Monthly Review of Reviews* asked in a typical article. Quoting "a Hawaiian Government School Teacher," the story described leprosy so rampant that teachers were in perpetual flight from infected pupils. "There is scarcely a city in the United States without some lepers," the article announced, "and [there is] reason to believe that these islands contribute a majority of them all."

Writing in the *North American Review,* a New York physician named Morrow, who had visited the settlement, insisted "there remains to be considered the practical question of the danger to the health interests of this country involved in Hawaiian annexation." If annexation took place, Morrow wrote, "many lepers would, in their desire to escape Molokai, emigrate to this country." He concluded, "There would seem to be no reasonable doubt that the annexation of Hawaii would create conditions favorable to the dissemination of the seeds of leprosy in this country."

With public and political sentiment in America turning negative, Thurston assembled "A Hand-Book on the Annexation of Hawaii," a sixty-three-page rebuttal of every objection against annexation. Thurston listed the most common arguments, then explained why they lacked merit. "It is unconstitutional because Hawaii is not contiguous to the United States," stated the second of Thurston's twenty straw objections. "It is contrary to the Monroe Doctrine," read the ninth. Thurston buried the most volatile issue deep within his brief, as the seventeenth objection: "There is leprosy in Hawaii." He answered, "This is, unfortunately, true." However, "no cases are seen at large" and annexation would present "no more . . . danger to the people of United States than there is now." All of the leprosy patients "are most carefully cared for by the local government," he wrote. "Moreover, I have yet to learn that political relations existing between two countries will increase the danger arising from diseases existing in either."

The matter eventually became moot. On May 1, 1898, Commodore George Dewey entered the Philippines' Manila Bay with a fleet of six U.S. warships and launched the first major battle of the Spanish-American War. Dewey's vessels destroyed the Spanish fleet that had been anchored in the bay, and with the harbor under Dewey's control, the United States dispatched additional ships to maintain a blockade. The strategic value of the Hawaiian Islands quickly became obvious. Challenges to annexation melted away, and on August 12, 1898, Sanford Dole signed over sovereignty to U.S. minister Harold Sewall. Hawaii was now an American territory.

In Kalawao, Joseph Dutton had his American flag ready. He had taught the boys to play "The Star-Spangled Banner" on their tin flutes, but would not allow them to perform the piece until Hawaii had officially joined the United States. At 12 P.M. Dutton raised the flag and signaled for the boys to play. He performed the color guard every day for the remainder of his life.

When word of Dutton's patriotism reached the mainland press, strangers began to mail American flags to Kalawao. They arrived in bunches, more flags than he could possibly use. Dutton stayed up nights writing notes of thanks, rewrapping the gifts, then forwarding them to a school or a church in some town he had never seen. Inevitably another newspaper story would appear, and additional flags arrived. Dutton scanned the papers looking for possible recipients. One day he read about St. Catharine's Industrial School, a struggling orphanage in Memphis. Dutton sent the orphans a flag. Then he quietly arranged for his army pension to go to the orphanage too.

With annexation, the settlement became the official responsibility of the U.S. government. A California representative proposed in Congress that the settlement be made the national leprosy colony, and all mainland cases sent to Molokai. Control would fall to the U.S. Public Health and Marine Hospital Service, which operated quarantine facilities at U.S. ports of entry, screening for "all idiots, insane persons, paupers or persons likely to become public charges, and persons suffering from a loathsome or dangerous disease." The idea was not well received in Hawaii. In an editorial titled "Hawaii's Future," the *Advertiser* urged the Chamber of Commerce to hurry to Washington and quash the proposed bill, which the paper claimed would destroy trade. Responding to a second, similar proposal, one Honolulu newspaper wrote, "Hawaii will become marked off as the great Leper Reservation of the United States, and will become an object of contempt and loathing. Instead of being the Paradise of the Pacific, to be sought by tourists, we shall get the evil repute of being a leprous Gehenna, a place to be shunned, an infected region."

One man especially incensed by the idea was Lorrin Thurston. For years, Thurston had warned Honolulu business leaders that the word *leper* contained a terrible power. Its mere mention could collapse the islands' fledgling tourism industry, which Thurston oversaw as the founder of the Hawaiian Bureau of Information. He believed that much damage had already occurred. Stop a man on the street in New York City and quiz him about Hawaii, and he was sure to blurt something about leprosy, and probably Father Damien. Thurston had experienced this frustrating phenomenon in person several years earlier. In one of his early promotional efforts Thurston had created the Cyclorama Company and secured space on the midway of the 1893 Chicago World's Fair, intending to introduce Hawaii as a vacation destination. His lure was the active volcano Kilauea, viewable in person for the price of a steamer ticket. To whet tourist appetites, Thurston had commissioned an artist to sketch Kilauea in action. He then had a cyclorama built, 60 feet high and 420 feet long, rotated by hidden motors. Colored lights and fans threw stylized lava into the sky, rumbled the ground, and hissed steam; it was, he wrote, "a wonderfully realistic spectacle." Thurston printed fifty thousand copies of a brochure, "Paradise of the Pacific and Inferno of the World," to further set the hook.

Just as the cyclorama began to turn, however, Koolau had murdered Deputy Sheriff Louis Stolz and escaped into Kalalau Valley. Mainland press pounced on the lurid tale, quickly forgetting Thurston's volcano. From that day forward, it seemed to Thurston that every time a newsman wrote about Hawaii, he felt compelled to mention leprosy. "Everyone visiting the Hawaiian Islands has been cautioned against leprosy," the *New York Times* remarked in April 1894, "and no doubt has looked round very carefully at first, expecting to see lepers at every turn." The article was not an anomaly. For a period at the end of the century clerks compiling the yearly index of *Times* stories would leave the entry beneath the heading "Hawaiian Islands" blank, with the notation "see 'Leprosy.'"

Over the years Thurston had launched multiple schemes to recast Hawaii as a place of healthful rest. He created advertising pitches centered on Hawaiian music, the hula, and the temperate climate. Eventually, however, Thurston resigned himself to the fact that the colony would not remain out of public view—its morbid attraction was too strong. Acknowledging the reality of the situation, Thurston argued that the board should stage-manage the inevitable stories. One way to accomplish this was to invite authors sympathetic to the board to tour the settlement. Thurston helped to select one of these sanctioned writers: Jack London.

London had commissioned a private yacht, intending to sail around the world. The adventure had begun as a well-publicized fiasco and had never fully recovered. Shipbuilders gleefully swindled the famous author, overcharging for shoddy materials and suspect labor. What London had initially envisioned as a $7,000 pleasure craft quickly consumed more than $30,000 of his savings and remained unfinished at the Oakland docks. In a panic over finances, London decided to sail anyway; he needed to start filing the magazine articles he had presold to fund the trip. London reported to one friend, "We shall complete the boat when we get to Honolulu."

The *Snark*, as London named the yacht, was forty-five feet long, a two-mast ketch that required only six crew members. London had no trouble choosing four: himself, his wife, Charmian, her step-uncle Roscoe, and London's Japanese cabin boy. Two slots remained open, which London filled shortly before departing. One went to Martin Johnson, a twenty-two-year-old from Independence, Kansas, who had sent an earnest five-page letter offering himself as the *Snark*'s chef, omitting the detail that he did not know how to cook. The final crew member, London informed Johnson, "is a young fellow your own age, an all-around athlete from Stanford University. He is shipped, in reality, as an after-thought, and largely to do that portion of the sailorizing that would otherwise fall to me." London did not know the young man well, but he was strong and seemed capable. People mentioned that as a boy he had lived in Hawaii, and that his mother was a widow. London reported to Martin Johnson that his fellow crew member was called Bert. In fact the young man's full name was Herbert Stolz. He was Deputy Sheriff Louis Stolz's son.

Civic Duty

(Population 857)

The ailing man checked into the Salvation Army Industrial Home in Washington, D.C., on a sweltering summer evening. He was five feet nine inches tall, tautly built, and he claimed to be thirty-four years old. When a physician arrived, John Early complained of short breath, fever, and kidney ache. The doctor noticed discolored patches on Early's forehead, and sores on his hands. He telephoned health officials.

At 12:30 P.M. on Friday the city's bacteriologist declared that Early had leprosy. Police officers took him to a mud flat on the Potomac River and placed him in a canvas tent. Three guards kept watch. From descriptions later made on his case, John Early apparently had a mild case of tuberculoid leprosy; he almost certainly was not infectious.

The morning newspapers announced Early's arrest, and the stories "stimulated the appetite of man to 'see a real leper,'" the *Washington Post* reported. Sightseers streamed to the riverbank. "They began to arrive in the neighborhood soon after 9 o'clock in the morning," one reporter wrote, "and from then on until sunset the stream of the morbidly curious was unceasing." People stood six deep along the perimeter fence, "peering through the chinks and cracks across the meadow at the prison tent."

Officials were uncertain what to do with Early. At the time, federal law forbade the "Transportation of Lepers in Interstate Traffic." Persons known to have leprosy could not cross state lines without written permission from every locality being traversed. State officials rarely consented. Recently, a young Chinese student named Mock Sen had been preparing to return home from the United States after attending school when he was diagnosed with leprosy. Officials stuck him in a freight car and used a pole to push food in after him. Sealing the car, they sent it down the tracks toward the next state. Local agents had the car decoupled and routed back to its point of origin; authorities there promptly sent the railroad car away again. Mock Sen was shuttled around the country in a sealed boxcar for almost two weeks. Finally, a physician insisted on entering the car. Mock Sen had been dead for days.

Washington officials decided to hold on to Early, and notified his wife.

Lottie Early was five feet tall, weighed ninety-five pounds, and had, one reporter wrote, "grave, brooding, deep-set eyes of wistful sorrow." By the time she arrived from their home in North Carolina, that state's attorney general had announced that neither she nor her husband were welcome to return—if they did, their entire family would be placed in permanent quarantine. The news "came as a shock to Mrs. Early," the *Post* reported. "Tears flooded her eyes, and for a long time she could not speak." After several minutes Lottie exclaimed, "Our lives are linked together more firmly than ever before. What's the use of love if it's afraid to help the one it loves best in the world?" She claimed to be willing to follow her husband anywhere, "even to that island of lepers."

Dr. William Fowler, the city's senior health officer, arranged for Lottie Early to occupy an abandoned house at the foot of E Street Southeast, a few hundred yards from her husband's tent. She and their son, Emmanuel, were allowed to see Early for thirty minutes each day—although guards prevented Early from touching his wife and child. One morning Lottie and the boy set off down the sloping riverbank for their visit. She stopped a dozen feet from the tent; the boy continued toward his father. Early grabbed a stick and began to sweep it from side to side.

"Go away, Manly!" Early shouted. "Go away from Papa!"

A reporter at the scene wrote, "Manly hesitated, wavered, laughed a little gurgling laugh of bewildered mischief, and ran back to his mother." Early told the reporter, "That's the worst thing that happens to me here. I have to scare my baby boy away from me with a stick."

In January agents moved Early into a wing of the abandoned house, then sealed the doors and hall with bricks. At night, he and Lottie sang to each other through the walls. "I could hear his voice," Lottie later recalled, "and it wasn't so lonely during the winter evenings."

While Early was in custody, the U.S. surgeon general sent a cable to the board of health in Honolulu. "Can you care for leper there?" he wrote. "What monthly expense?" Legally the U.S. government could not exile Early to Hawaii, as the *New York Times* had noted: "Though virtually a part of the United States, the leper colony on Molokai cannot recruit its population from this country." The colony "is strictly a territorial enterprise . . . there exists no precedent to warrant the removal of a leper from any State . . . to the settlement." A congressman proposed changing the law and suggested offering to pay the board $360 a year to imprison Early on Molokai, and $360 for every additional mainland patient it accepted. The board was not eager to establish such a precedent. John Early, relayed the *Maui News*, "is not wanted at the Molokai home."

Early's plight received wide publication. Strangers began to write Dr. Fowler requesting Early be released into their care for experimentation. One Iowa man, Daniel David Palmer, claimed leprosy was the result of "subluxations," and that he could cure Early with "the science of chiropractic," which Palmer had discovered in 1895. Palmer's request was denied. Eventually, however, Fowler did agree to allow a New York dermatologist to examine Early. After the proper transport papers were filed, Early boarded a train heading north. In Manhattan, at the New York Skin and Cancer Hospital, doctors decided that Early's disease was lupus vulgaris. They elected to treat Early with a device known as a Finsen Ray. "[An] ultra red ray," the *Washington Post* informed its readers, "the most powerful of all the hot rays."

The machine was a shiny metal cylinder a foot and a half in length, filled with ice water to keep it from exploding. Doctors placed Early in a chair, strapped the apparatus to his head, and pointed the lens at his blemishes. The nurse hid behind a door. Someone flipped a switch. Instantly, the Finsen Ray began to warble and shriek, and the room filled with the "blinding glare of the great arc light," the *Post* reported, "far more dazzling than even the X-ray." Each session lasted an hour.

After several weeks doctors declared John Early cured. He moved his family into a second-floor tenement apartment in Brooklyn. Early's fame preceded him, however. Harassed by neighbors, the family quietly made their way to a small town in Connecticut, but locals chased them away when they discovered their identity. They lasted only a few months in Virginia, their next stop. Fleeing across the country, Early and his family eventually settled in Los Angeles. He began to use the name John Western. To a confidant he announced, "The John Early that was is dead to the world."

The autumn that John and Lottie Early arrived in Los Angeles, leprosy researchers gathered in Bergen, Norway, for the Second International Leprosy Congress. Among the attendees was the discoverer of *Mycobacterium leprae,* Dr. Gerhard Hansen. During the congress, Dr. Hansen revealed that he had tested a sample of John Early's tissue, which Lottie Early had sent to him. The test confirmed the presence of leprosy bacilli. Reacting to Hansen's announcement, the *Washington Post* charged that doctors in New York City had made a "serious blunder" by releasing Early. The reporter failed to address the most curious aspect of the diagnosis, however: Why was Lottie mailing away pieces of her husband's flesh?

After Hawaii came under the United States' jurisdiction, President McKinley had authorized the U.S. surgeon general to make "a complete report on leprosy in the Hawaiian Islands," as well as a census of the number of persons with leprosy in the United States. Officials found 278 cases on the mainland—although, as the *Brooklyn Eagle* reported, "the members of the commission are convinced that this represents only a small proportion of the total cases that actually exist." Segregation was recommended for these people, and as the *Eagle* pointed out, "Now that we control Hawaii it is an easy matter to continue the leper station at Molokai, not merely for the present members of the colony, but for all other victims who may be found within our borders. Absolute segregation is absolute safety, and we cannot afford to intrude sentiment into the matter."

A congressional subcommittee subsequently recommended "control and management of the lepers" on Molokai be transferred to the "government of the United States, Treasury Department." Hawaii's colony "was admirably adapted as a location for a national leprosaria" and could easily hold as many as three thousand exiles. Upon hearing of the committee's finding, Honolulu business leaders began to lobby furiously against the move, papering Washington with urgent cables decrying the "federal supervision and transfer of lepers from Mainland," as one read. Island press, marshaled by Lorrin Thurston, joined the campaign. "Is Hawaii to be the dumping ground for lepers of the mainland?" one Honolulu paper asked. As a team of Hawaiian legislators headed for the capital to protest, others filed lawsuits to scuttle such a development. The outcry killed the committee's proposal. Eventually President Theodore Roosevelt recommended instead that Congress appropriate funds to build a research center on Molokai, to study "the cause and cure of leprosy." No mainland patients would be sent to the settlement, however.

Acting on Roosevelt's wish, Congress voted to acquire one square mile of land in the settlement, on which to build "the most modern laboratory in existence," as one public health official wrote. Blueprints for the U.S. Leprosy Investigation Center depicted a series of huge multistory structures and a half dozen outlier buildings, including a storehouse, generator station, animal lab, barn, and, "of course, the housing for the Chinese workmen" who were expected to build it all, as one observer wrote at the time. The proposed federal facility was larger than anything in the settlement—larger than any complex in all of Hawaii. Washington officials disregarded warnings about attempting such an ambitious project in one of the most inaccessible locations in the world. "The conviction is rife that only success can attend an undertaking backed by so much professional enthusiasm," one federal official wrote. The board knew the reality, however. Remarked one sardonic board member, "Certainly the operations of the [federal] government will tend to relieve the monotony of the Settlement."

Surveyors chose a site in Kalawao, now almost deserted by the exodus of residents to Kalaupapa. "The [station] grounds had to be cleared by burning rows of houses formerly used by lepers," wrote Emma Gibson, the young wife of one of the federal researchers. Interisland steamers delivered lumber, tile, fencing, iron beds, mattresses, and an electric dynamo. "Uncle Sam furnished us with the best of everything: fine linen, good furniture, Haviland dishes, silver . . . our own water system and even a Jersey dairy and a flock of chickens," Gibson reported. Curious residents hiked to Kalawao and spent hours watching crates being unpacked. The federal government was installing "the first electric lights, flush toilets, and ice machines on the island," one official reported, and constructing "one of the most complete laboratory outfits in the world."

A thirty-two-year-old Harvard Medical School pathologist named Walter Brinckerhoff was placed in charge of the federal investigation station. "Young, modest, patient, persistent, enthusiastic, he is described as a born investigator," the *Advertiser* reported. The doctor was also hypersensitive to the notion of deadly microbes, a phobia acquired during the 1902 smallpox epidemic in Boston. Fearful that exiles would scatter bacteria throughout his facility, Brinckerhoff ordered that the entire station be surrounded by a double fence. "These two fences were 10 feet apart to ensure no contact whatsoever," Emma Gibson wrote. "It was dogproof and kept birdproof also, no birds being allowed to even build nests. Dr. Brinckerhoff was even so germ conscious that he wouldn't have any rugs or draperies in his house." On his visits to Molokai to check the station's progress, Brinckerhoff stuck cotton up his nose, and he employed gloves to shake hands, even with Mother Marianne. "His precautions became offensive," a medical historian later wrote, "as well as ridiculous."

After receiving his commission, Brinckerhoff had wed an East Coast society darling named Nellie White, the daughter of multimillionaire Nelson White. When the New England papers learned Nellie was "giving up wealth and privilege to live among the lepers," they were aghast: one depicted her doing battle with a salivating dragon—the artist's visual metaphor for leprosy. Nellie, however, told her husband that she would "never set foot on [Molokai]" and intended to live in Honolulu. Thus, while the station was being built, Brinckerhoff worked out of a laboratory at Kalihi Receiving Station. He began his research by conducting "experiments with . . . serum on several patients" at Kalihi, as the *Advertiser* reported. The doctor also ordered a crate of apes from East Africa to use as test subjects. At the end of each workday he vigorously scrubbed, changed his clothing, then hurried from Kalihi to his home in Waikiki. Brinckerhoff planned to relocate to the settlement when the station was complete, but before that day arrived, Nellie White passed away during childbirth. A distraught Brinckerhoff resigned his position and returned to Massachusetts. Two years later Dr. Brinckerhoff also died abruptly. Boston papers initially cited the cause as pneumonia. Subsequent reports suggested that the doctor took his own life—having become certain that he had leprosy.

As officials in Washington hunted for a replacement director, Emma Gibson's husband, Leighton, tried to keep the complex from falling apart. Mildew bloomed in the damp Kalawao air and "made the fillings in one's teeth rust overnight," he complained. When one of the annual kona storms struck, it lifted the hospital from its foundation and started it toward the sea. The Gibsons' house "rose and fell with each battering gust," Emma wrote. The confused young couple tied their toothbrushes to their necks with twine and ran outside. "[We] clung to the grass and dug our fingers into the earth to keep from being blown into the ocean," Emma reported, "crawling along our stomachs like snakes." In the morning, workmen used a block and tackle to wrench the hospital back into place.

Joseph Dutton sent a message through the double fence, asking Emma if he could be of service. Gibson later recalled that "the note began: 'Dear Next Door Neighbor' and hereafter that was always his name for us. He jotted his thoughts down as they came, putting in all kinds of puns, with almost childish delight whether they made sense or not. He punned continually when he talked, chuckling over his small jokes, probably as a relief from his deadly serious work." Dutton told Emma that if she needed anything to let him know, and if she wanted to tour Damien's church, he would be pleased to guide her. He also asked permission for the Franciscan sisters to visit the station—the nuns had never seen "modern sanity plumbing." Describing the sisters, Dutton wrote simply, "They are nice."

At the time, the settlement held slightly more than eight hundred patients, and the doctor in Kalaupapa, a Canadian named William J. Goodhue, struggled to keep pace with their medical needs. In Goodhue, the board had finally secured a caring, competent resident physician. "He is the best physician we have had at the Settlement," Ambrose Hutchison told the *Advertiser*, "and he has helped me more than any doctor we have ever had before." The young doctor was athletic and tall, with an overhung brow and a bowl of dark hair, trimmed neatly above the ears. His hands were enormous, spanning ten notes on the organ he played in the evenings for relaxation.

Goodhue maintained an exhausting schedule. In a typical six-month period, he reported that he had filled 14,600 prescriptions and handled a total of 20,770 medical incidents. During a similar stretch he amputated five legs and three arms, and performed 267 major operations. Goodhue had one assistant, and for additional help relied on the nuns. Meanwhile, the federal facility across the peninsula was staffing up with twenty-three people, including a stenographer, a seamstress, a pharmacist, and three surgeons. Although the government had spent more than $300,000 on the investigation station, federal law required that the sixteen-bed facility remain independent of the board's treatment efforts. The station was intended to be a national research laboratory, not a caregiving hospital. And though Goodhue coveted the station's bountiful supplies and equipment, he had no access to them. Nor could the federal employees aid Dr. Goodhue in emergencies, such as during the periodic outbreaks of a mysterious illness that Goodhue referred to simply as "Swollen Head Fever." As Joseph Dutton had remarked, the settlement now boasted "the greatest institution on the islands, or in the world, probably of its sort . . . everything present day science can provide." Yet two miles away, Dr. Goodhue still shredded sheets to use as bandages.

Another condition of the investigation station was that treatment had to be voluntary. When the research hospital was finally ready to open, however, patients had taken note of the high double fence and the strange machines and Dr. Brinckerhoff's apes. "An irrational certainty [was] expressed by some patients that they were being 'rounded up'" for "use as experimental animals," a medical historian later wrote. Only nine patients volunteered. They passed through the gate and were locked inside.

"Unused as they were to the restriction of hospital life," Emma Gibson later wrote, "they had little liking for it and proved uncooperative. One by one the volunteers left. . . . When the last one departed, Washington decided to close the Station." Leighton Gibson padlocked the gate, with all of the costly equipment still inside, and he and Emma sailed home to California. Every year on his birthday, Joseph Dutton received a chocolate cake and a card from Emma, addressed "Dear Next Door Neighbor." She would ask if the station was still empty. It was, Dutton always answered.

The facility grew haunted, "dry-rotting from lack of use," one visitor reported. The same visitor lamented the awful waste of the project: "Three hundred thousand dollars of our public money was spent in building a laboratory where a laboratory was of no use—like building a full-rigged ship on top of Pike's Peak & then finding no way of launching the ship into the sea!" Once or twice a year the settlement superintendent rode over and wandered the grounds, eyeing the lumber. He sent a note to the board asking permission to disassemble the buildings. The board informed him that the federal boundaries remained in effect. Eventually Washington relented, as the board later reported, and "the old Federal Leprosarium [was] torn down." Patients scavenged the wood and used it to build beach houses.

Congress held hearings to dissect the costly failure. They again expressed the need for a national leprosarium. At present, New York City segregated leprosy victims on North Brother Island, in the East River; Massachusetts banished its sick to Penikese Island, a seventy-four-acre speck in Buzzards Bay. In San Francisco cases were locked in a brick annex next to the City Pest House; and in Louisiana people with leprosy were held at Indian Camp Plantation, which came to be known as the Louisiana Leper Home. These were the largest detention sites. Others, like a camp near Seattle called Diamond Point, were small, squalid affairs in which only a few sick people were imprisoned. Such places, one federal report concluded, were "unfit for either the treatment or comfort of their inmates."

Having decided that Hawaii was inhospitable, the U.S. surgeon general proposed Penikese Island as the next most likely site for a national colony; citizens staged a violent protest and thwarted the idea. Congress then considered the camp in Louisiana, and neighboring residents vowed to prevent the development "by a force of arms," as one paper reported. At various times legislators discussed turning Angel Island, in San Francisco Bay, into a colony, and one congressman suggested an island in Alaska's Aleutian chain, where the sick "could be put to gardening and homesteading. The climate there is good; perhaps a little damp in winter." Lawmakers were still debating options when Dr. William Fowler, the chief medical inspector for Washington, D.C., received an anonymous telephone call. A man named E. J. Watson had registered at the Shoreham Hotel, the caller said, and he appeared to be dangerously ill. Fowler wondered if the call was a prank. The vice president of the United States lived at the Shoreham, however, as did several senators. Fowler decided to investigate.

A house detective let him into the room registered to Watson. Three nervous-looking men stood opposite a slender man dressed in a boxy new suit. As the *Washington Post* later reported, Dr. Fowler smiled at John Early.

"Hello, John," Fowler said. "What are you doing here?"

The reporters explained that they had responded to a tip Early had phoned in. When they arrived at the room, he had greeted each warmly, then announced, "You have just shaken hands with a leper." Several of the reporters were now near tears. "I called you newspaper men up here to my room so you would write stories about me," Early had explained, "and tell the public that unless the Government takes care of us in hospitals we'll continue to go freely among you and spread the disease." He knew Congress was debating the leprosy issue.

Dr. Fowler took the reporters to the public health laboratory, where, one later wrote, "we were properly disinfected." They then went to interview Early, now held in a brick jail cell surrounded by barbed wire, not far from where he and Lottie had been imprisoned years before. "You are now treating him practically as a wild animal?" a senator later asked Dr. Fowler.

"Practically, I am afraid," Fowler replied. "We have to, in order to keep him."

Early and his family had lived for several months in Los Angeles. They were next spotted in Oregon, and then in Washington State. After running out of money, Early wrote to the Veterans Administration, demanding to be placed on disability. The government instead offered Early a job as superintendent of the Diamond Point leprosy camp outside Tacoma, Washington. He accepted. Lottie and the children moved into a cottage adjacent to the camp.

Lottie Early found frequent excuses to travel into town. Then one day she packed the children and moved to Tacoma permanently. John sent flowers and wrote fumbling love notes. She sent back an attorney, who explained that Lottie intended to marry a town clerk. The news turned Early "insane," the *Washington Post* later reported, and he became "increasingly violent." He helped an inmate escape from the camp, with instructions to "wreck vengeance" on Lottie and her new husband. Hearing of the plot, police encircled their home. Inside, Lottie was "prostrated from fright," a reporter wrote. He poured a glass of sherry and watched as Lottie drained it. He then asked her to "bare to the world the nightmare life which she led with her afflicted husband." Lottie agreed.

She said that the moment she married John she knew it was a mistake. The magnitude of her error became obvious after he was diagnosed. He had turned irrational, racked by a spiteful paranoia that extended even to his children. "He seemed to detest . . . Manley," Lottie recalled. "Once he struck the boy such a hard blow on the head that a bunch of hair, the size of an egg, was torn from his head. The baby brought the hair to me, and cryingly told me, 'Papa hit me.'" During the months they were detained in Washington, D.C., John had managed to convince one of the guards to smuggle him whiskey, and at night he would shriek in drunken fury through the farmhouse walls. Lottie said she suffered dreams in which John exploded past the bricks and grinningly choked her to death.

She said that after John was freed things became better. But he had quickly grown embittered, obsessed with the way the government had treated him. He sat awake nights poring over law books, searching for a way to sue. Early was a "bright man," she said, "but he would not use his brains." He refused to hold a regular job—Lottie earned their meager income.

She came to suspect that John had known about his leprosy before he married her. She feared he still had the disease, even after New York doctors declared him cured. She worried he might infect the children. One night when he had passed out drunk, Lottie clipped a piece of his skin and posted it to Europe. When Dr. Gerhard Hansen's verdict arrived, she held the proof before John's eyes. "He was compelled to admit he had leprosy," Lottie recalled. Nothing changed.

By the time they reached California, Lottie had begun to think about taking the children and fleeing. But she did not know how to manage it. "I didn't have enough sense," she said. "I thought, once married, you must stand all that comes with it." At Diamond Point, John had started to suspect her intentions. He had become desperate and mean. Lottie said that she was aware that her husband's abuse was born of his circumstances, but she no longer cared. They had been on the run for almost five years. She was twenty-two years old.

Police soon captured the man John had dispatched to murder Lottie. They returned the would-be killer to the Diamond Point camp, where Early was under heavy guard. For the next year Lottie heard nothing from the camp. Then one spring day her new husband came home with disturbing news: John Early had escaped.

Perched on a chair in his brick cell in Washington, D.C., John Early told reporters a story of his own. After his wife divorced him, he had gone briefly insane. When he emerged from his madness, he had a clearer view of things. Lottie, he realized, deserved no blame; it was a miracle that she stuck with him for as long as she had. He also now understood that his leprosy was not the government's fault. What officials could be charged with, however, was cruelty—toward him and everyone with the disease. Early explained that in the midst of his loneliness and alienation he had had an epiphany: he would become an advocate for patients' rights. He would "serve as a great national example and bring about the proper treatment of unfortunates." But why infiltrate the Shoreham Hotel? one reporter asked. Early replied, "I knew that if I mingled among the well-to-do and the rich and exposed them to contagion . . . they would arise out of self-protection and further my plan."

Early had escaped from Diamond Point two weeks earlier to embark on what he described as a "deluxe tour." Using money from his pension, he had purchased a first-class train ticket to Manhattan. On arriving in the city, he ate in fine restaurants, attended Broadway shows, and "saw all the sights in that week that I could." He added, "And I enjoyed them too." Early treated himself to a baseball doubleheader, Giants against Athletics. He then boarded a southbound train and spent several days in Washington, roaming the galleries and dining in establishments favored by congressmen and senators. Early said he hoped to trigger panic in both cities. His plan worked. When a rumor went around Washington that Early had passed a $2 bill to a shopkeeper, the *Post* reported no merchant in the city would "accept a bill of this denomination."

Washington authorities sent Early to the Louisiana Leper Home, a leprosy camp near the small town of Carville. He escaped several times. Once, when Washington police received word that Early was heading their way, they mobilized the largest manhunt since Abraham Lincoln's assassination. Officers were staking out the train station when Early strolled into a congressional committee room.

"I am John Early," he announced. "The leper."

"What are you doing up here?" a congressman asked.

Early replied, "My civic duty."

He was arrested and sent back to Louisiana. Then one spring day Early again appeared unexpectedly in the capital. Entering a meeting of the Senate Committee on Public Health and Quarantine, he said, "I am John Early, a patient from the leper colony at Carville, Louisiana. I have come to tell you gentlemen something about how much we patients need to have that colony made over into a United States hospital." A short time later Congress voted to federalize the Louisiana Leper Home and place it under the control of the Public Health Service. It appropriated $645,000 for "expansion and modernization" of the facilities, and within a few years the home was the foremost leprosy hospital and research center in the world. Early remained its most famous resident. One patient later wrote, "I remember the first time I saw him, a tall, gaunt, hatchet-faced, bug-eyed individual who was preaching hellfire and brimstone to the open-mouthed sinners under the oaks."

Despite the improvements, however, Early still bridled at his enforced isolation. He ran away from the hospital several times more—once to see his dying father. Nine federal agents surrounded Early and his brother at the family's North Carolina home. Early hid with a rifle. The agents called for him to surrender. "Haven't they kept me cooped up long enough?" he screamed. "I only want to be left alone! I won't harm anybody!" They captured Early and returned him to Carville. Reporting on the episode, the *Washington Post* wrote of Early: "His eccentricities have at least served to keep the public apprised of the fact that there is a leprosy problem in the United States."

Good Breeze

(Population 810)

Jack London's boat *Snark* finally set sail from Oakland on April 23, 1907, more than six months behind schedule. Life at sea swiftly became an ordeal. On a routine inspection several days out, London found seawater bleeding into his yacht from a dozen different spots. The ship's food had been improperly stored and was now slick with rot. The *Snark*'s engine sputtered and the fuel tanks fouled; the head became inoperable after the first day. Twelve days into the voyage London fired Roscoe Eames, the ship's navigator. "He was incompetent, a shirker, a whiner, a demoralizer of the crew, and no more a seaman than I am an Egyptian dancing-girl," London reported to Eames's wife. "As regards his incompetence, the boat is a botch from beginning to end. It isn't one item, it isn't two items; but it is a thousand items that are botches."

Taking the charts and a sextant, London began to teach himself how to navigate, while Eames hid belowdecks. The *Snark* slid miles off course. London might have asked for help from one of his crew members, had he not concluded that the entire group was inept. Not only were they useless in sailing his yacht, they were also lousy passengers. Martin Johnson and London's Japanese cabin boy had gotten seasick within an hour of leaving Oakland and were waylaid for a week. Herbert Stolz, the sixth crew member, tried to bathe himself by dangling off the bowsprit and was almost taken by sharks. Another day Stolz mistakenly left a sea cock in the engine room open and came close to sinking the *Snark*.

London soon realized that the only able person on board—beside himself—was his wife. When the first of several storms struck the *Snark*, however, even Charmian began to panic. During the blow the *Snark*'s jib snapped and her sea anchor crumbled. London had barely begun to make repairs when a second storm hit, stripping away the ship's gaff and collapsing her mainsail, to the horror of the crew. Johnson became so distraught that he cried that they would never live to see Hawaii.

"Never mind, Martin," London had replied. "We are not more than two miles from land now."

"Which way?" Johnson asked, suddenly hopeful.

"Straight down, Martin, straight down."

Twenty-seven days after they departed Oakland, the *Snark* wheezed into Pearl Harbor, towed along by a pair of tugs. In a letter to a friend in California, London omitted the details of the ill-fated passage and his bungling crew. "We had a beautiful voyage down; lovely weather; and the Islands are delightful," he wrote. "Mr. Eames went back from here. He was getting too old." In the same letter, London reported, "Bert Stolz leaves us here, also."

Herbert Stolz's father was buried in a grave in downtown Honolulu, a twenty-minute carriage ride from where the *Snark* was tied. Stolz had not seen the grave since he was six years old, when his mother had fled with the family to California in the aftermath of her husband's murder. Now Mary Rowell Stolz urged her son to again hurry away from Hawaii. She wrote Bert to abandon the cruise and return to Stanford University, where he had been studying medicine. London accepted Stolz's resignation with only minor protest. Although the young man had proved to be a poor sailor, London enjoyed the stories he had told on board, and he took notes. By the time Herbert Stolz stepped from the *Snark* for the final time, Jack London knew every detail of the tale of Bert Stolz's father and the outlaw Koolau.

While the *Snark* lay in a berth getting painted and caulked, Jack and Charmian London rented a cottage at the eastern end of Waikiki. Early in their stay the couple held a dinner party, and the guest list included the board president, Lucius Pinkham. Charmian later wrote, "[He] seems anxious for us to see Molokai." In fact, Pinkham was desperate for London to visit and write about the settlement. A few months earlier Pinkham had told the legislature, "It is time to cease crying 'Unclean, Unclean' to the lepers and refrain from painting dark pictures for literary or sensational effect, thus making avoidance and segregation more cruel than necessary."

During the past several years the board had made an extensive effort to, as Pinkham wrote, get "the Leper Settlement into up to date shape so that the Lepers will find life better worth living." It had allotted extra funds to the settlement and had finally found a capable superintendent, to serve alongside the talented Dr. Goodhue. As was board policy since the time of Ambrose Hutchison's retirement, all superintendents were now civil servants: healthy, nonpatient employees of the board. John Devine McVeigh, known as Jack, had accepted the position five years earlier. McVeigh was French Canadian, thick-necked and beetle-eyed. As a boy he had been on a round-the-world voyage with a private tutor and had jumped ship in Honolulu. "They looked for him everywhere," one descendant later recalled, "and they couldn't find him." Many years later a stranger knocked on the door of the family's home, claiming to be Jack's brother. "This man looked exactly like [Jack]," his granddaughter later recalled. McVeigh went to the door, told the man that there had been a mistake, and swung it closed.

Jack McVeigh's administration of Kalaupapa had begun with a vengeance, and after five months on the job he had reported to the board that the "beer makers, drunkards and law breakers" were now under control. He achieved this in part by arresting forty-five of them, and brawling with many others. During one dustup a patient bit McVeigh, and he burned the wound out with acid. "Improvement followed his fists and his feet," the *Advertiser* remarked of McVeigh. "He made himself respected and earned his way to be loved." As one Franciscan sister later wrote, "When Mr. McVeigh took charge, how different it was—little by little he managed to have everything fixed up just as it should be."

With McVeigh overseeing the settlement, and Dr. Goodhue, Mother Marianne, and Joseph Dutton managing their respective areas, the board felt it had dramatically improved every aspect of the colony. The settlement was now "a peaceful, contented and happy place," as Pinkham explained in a letter to a friend. Yet the press still often rendered it "as a place of confinement, abandoned hope, a chamber of horrors, [and] the impression is very incorrect." Encouraged by Lorrin Thurston, Pinkham had decided to combat this public portrait. He invited the Londons to visit Kalaupapa, "in order that the world might be apprised of the facts as they exist." Pinkham instructed McVeigh to make certain that London saw the settlement in a positive light.

Before London left for Kalaupapa, Pinkham passed him a pamphlet that gave information about the settlement and the board's segregation policy. Pinkham had written the tract himself. "He who seeks sunshine will find and transmit it," it read, "and he who chooses to dwell on the dark spots only will so darken his picture it will be untruthful."

Jack and Charmian London sailed for the settlement on July 2, 1907. McVeigh accompanied them on the steamer. Before the ship left Honolulu, twenty-five patients were brought aboard from Kalihi Hospital, bound for Kalaupapa. McVeigh stood at the inboard rail beside the Londons, narrating the scene. He had been told to stress to London the board's obligations, which often got lost in the gothic drama of the moment. Jack London duly wrote, "But the means of segregation of the lepers on Molokai is not the horrible nightmare that has been so often exploited by *yellow* writers. . . . He is given ample time—weeks, and even months, sometimes—during which he stays at Kalihi and winds up or arranges all his business affairs." In her diary, Charmian was less circumspect: "We are not merry, Jack and I, for what we have witnessed during the past two hours would wring pitying emotion from a graven image." She wrote of her gaze being drawn to "the huddle of doomed fellow-creatures amidst their pathetic bundles of belongings on the open after-deck of the plunging inter-island steamer bound for Molokai."

The ship arrived before sunrise. McVeigh took the Londons to his cottage and gave them the best room. The next morning they rested on the veranda, Charmian rocking in McVeigh's hammock, Jack sprawled on a rattan lounge. McVeigh put a cool drink in London's hand. Then he went to his telescope. He usually kept the instrument pointed at the cliff trail, to see if anyone was entering or exiting the settlement; now he let the Londons use it to scan the scenery. London wrote, "The Settlement has been written up repeatedly by sensationalists . . . who have never laid eyes on it." He recounted an article in which "McVeigh [was] crouching in a grass hut and being besieged nightly by starving lepers on their knees, wailing for food." The only wailing he had heard, London reported, was "the serenade which the glee clubs always give Mr. McVeigh whenever he returns from a trip to Honolulu," London wrote. "So much for a lie that should never have been printed."

McVeigh proved to be an excellent tour guide. He took the Londons on a careful circuit of the board's improvements in the past five years: the new hospital building, the horse-racing track, baseball field, visitors' quarters, steam laundry, the vegetable gardens and coconut groves. Aware of London's interest in guns, McVeigh steered Jack and Charmian to a neat building near the base of the cliff, where the Kalaupapa Rifle Club just happened to be conducting a shooting contest. London fired a few shots. Charmian wrote, "Both of us were duly decorated with the proud red badge of the Club bearing 'Kalaupapa Rifle Club, 1907,' in gilt letters."

Arriving at the Bishop Home, the Londons were introduced to "plucky aged" Mother Marianne, as Charmian recorded in her diary, which she later published as *Jack London in Aloha-Land.* "Like a tall spirit she guided us across the playground through the schoolrooms and dormitories." Marianne asked the Londons if they would like to hear the girls sing. Charmian wrote, "*Like* was hardly the word; I would have fled weeping from what could only be an ordeal to every one. But we could not refuse good Mother Marianne."

One of the sisters went to fetch the girls. "Draggingly enough they came," Charmian wrote, "unsmiling, their bloated or contracted features emerging grotesquely from the clean holokus. Every gesture and averted head showed a piteous shame over lost fairness." One girl awkwardly plinked the piano that Robert Louis Stevenson had sent to the home as a gift. Charmian wrote, "But play she did, and weep I did, in a corner, in sheer uncontrol of heartache at the girlish voices gone shrill and sexless and tinny like the old French piano."

The next afternoon McVeigh took the Londons to see a patient known as Major Lee, an American who was formerly a steamship engineer. "Give us a good breeze about how we live here," Lee told Jack London. "For heaven's sake write us up straight. Put your foot down on this chamber-of-horrors rot and all the rest of it. We don't like being misrepresented. We've got some feelings. Just tell the world how we really are in here." London would write, "Man after man that I met in the Settlement, and woman after woman, in one way or another expressed the same sentiment. It was patent that they resented bitterly the sensational and untruthful way in which they have been exploited in the past."

After leaving Major Lee, the Londons rode to Kalawao. There they "met up with Brother Dutton [who] has immolated himself for years among the leper youth," Charmian wrote. "We found him very interesting, as he found Jack, with whose career he proved himself very well acquainted." Dutton took them "across the road to a little churchyard, [and] we stood beside the tombstone of Father Damien." Charmian reported that the grave was "just a little oblong plot of carefully tended green, enclosed in iron railing, with a white marble cross and a foot-stone . . . appropriately simple for the simple worker." The next morning, Jack woke Charmian with a question. "Quick!" he cried. "First thought! *Where are you?*"

During the visit, McVeigh made certain that the Londons observed Goodhue at work in his operating room. The doctor advocated the aggressive use of surgery as a remedy for the disease. "Leprosy is emphatically a surgical disease," Goodhue wrote. "Surgical treatment of clinical manifestations can do more for the comfort of the patient and in staying the progress of the disease than any medical treatment so far discovered." London spent most of one morning in the hospital, watching the doctor excise ulcerous tissue and necrotic bone from three patients. "In each case Doctor Goodhue put an immediate and complete stop to the ravage," London wrote. His wife also described the scene: "Although the details are not pretty, and I shall not harrow with more of them, I wish I could picture the calm, pale surgeon, with his intensely dark eyes and the profile of Ralph Waldo Emerson, whose kinsman he is, working with master-strokes that cleansed the fearful cavity of corruption; for it was an illustration of the finest art and beauty of which the human is capable."

The last full day of the Londons' visit was July 4, the most celebrated holiday in the settlement. The previous year, the *Advertiser* had sent a reporter to describe the festivities: "No day was ever known there when the conditions of misery inseparable from the place were more effectively submerged by the elements of joyousness." In Kalawao, Joseph Dutton commemorated Independence Day with songs and flags, but most of the day's activities occurred in Kalaupapa. They began just before dawn, when hundreds of residents would gather for a costume parade of "Antiques and Horribles," as it was known. Slipping homemade fright masks over their heads, the patients transformed themselves into monsters and ancient crones, then went hooting through the village while a band played "The Star-Spangled Banner." McVeigh conspired to have the extraordinary procession pass his cottage, so London could snap pictures with his Kodak.

Throughout the holiday residents staged contests in marksmanship, pie eating, pole-vaulting, horse racing, and bicycle racing. They pursued one another on stilts, in gunnysacks, and blindfolded, while holding the legs of an outstretched partner and rumbling him along like a barrow. Jack London and Charmian served as judges of the equine events, one of which had McVeigh, atop a donkey, nipping Goodhue for first place. McVeigh then quietly donated the prize money for the next race, so a patient would win the $10. "He is not the man to go about with his heart's good intentions pinned on his sleeve," Charmian wrote of McVeigh. "Indeed, a supersensitive character would be out of place as manager of such an institution." When the parades and concerts and fireworks were finished, McVeigh hosted a dinner to bid the Londons farewell. Toward the end of the meal, a choir of patients assembled outside the cottage to serenade the visitors. As their voices built, McVeigh raised a glass of wine and declared, "The Londons—Jack and Charmian, God bless them!"

Jack London's "The Lepers of Molokai" appeared in the January 1908 issue of *Women's Home Companion*. The piece begins: "When the *Snark* sailed along the windward coast of Molokai, on her way to Honolulu, I looked at the chart, then pointed to a low-lying peninsula backed by a tremendous cliff varying from two to four thousand feet in height, and said, 'The pit of hell, the most cursed place on earth.' I should have been shocked, if at that moment I could have caught a vision of myself a month later, ashore in the most cursed place on earth, and having a disgracefully good time along with eight hundred of the lepers who were likewise having a good time."

In the article, London describes "a happy colony, divided into two villages and numerous country and seaside homes, of nearly a thousand souls. They have six churches, a Young Men's Christian Association building, several assembly halls, a band stand, a race track, baseball grounds and shooting ranges, an athletic club, numerous glee clubs, and two brass bands." London's piece was blissfully free of gruesome description, and in its narrative the board is benevolent, Dr. Goodhue gifted, and Jack McVeigh tough but fair. London wrote, "If it were given to me to choose between being compelled to live in Molokai for the rest of my life, or in the East End of London, or the East Side of New York . . . I would select Molokai without debate."

Lucius Pinkham and Lorrin Thurston were ecstatic. "The article is highly approved by Mr. Pinkham," Charmian reported, "and Mr. Thurston avers it is the best and fairest that has ever been written." London's words, declared Thurston, were "of a value to Hawaii that cannot be estimated in gold and silver." Thurston was so pleased he invited the Londons on vacation with him. Thurston, his wife, and the Londons spent a week on Maui. Each morning, Thurston watched as London sat at a table writing his daily quota of one thousand words in longhand. As Thurston later recalled in his diary, every day at noon London would "throw down his pencil, and say, with a sigh: 'Well, my job's done for today!' Once I said to him: 'Jack, I should think you would run out of subjects for stories.' 'Run out of subjects!' he exclaimed. 'Why Thurston, I have so many subjects in the back of my head that, if I continued writing a thousand words a day for the next hundred years, I couldn't begin to cover them all.'"

Some months after "The Lepers of Molokai" was published, Jack London started a story titled "Koolau the Leper." It had emerged from shipboard talks with Herbert Stolz. Although London had shown restraint in his depiction of the disease for his article on the settlement, with fiction he felt no such restriction. "They were creatures who once had been men and women," he wrote. "But they were men and women no longer. They were monsters—in face and form grotesque caricatures of everything human. They were hideously maimed and distorted, and had the seeming of creatures that had been racked in millenniums of hell. Their hands, when they possessed them, were like harpy-claws. Their faces were the misfits and slips, crushed and bruised by some mad god at play in the machinery of life. Here and there were features which the mad god had smeared half away, and one woman wept scalding tears from twin pits of horror, where her eyes had been."

Thurston was furious. Writing in the *Advertiser*, of which he was now publisher, he called London "a sneak of the first water, a thoroughly untrustworthy man and an ungrateful and untruthful bounder." London had "made the worst out of the leprosy situation here, distorted facts, invented others when the truth was not enough to suit his purpose and thoroughly misrepresented conditions."

"Dear friend," London wrote in reply to Thurston. "I think Hawaii is too touchy on matters of truth."

A Terrible Mistake

(Population 791)

During the spring of 1907 the U.S. Supreme Court declined to take up case No. 172, which had originated as a lawsuit filed against Lucius Pinkham and the board by a woman named Mikala Kaipu. The court gave its reason for not hearing the case: "Death of Mikala Kaipu having been suggested, and the case abated, appeal dismissed." A Canadian-born civil rights attorney named C. W. Ashford had filed the original suit, and also one on behalf of a young girl named Ellen Freeman. At the time, both were being held at Kalihi Hospital. Ashford asserted his clients were wrongly detained. Ellen Freeman had been committed as a leper on the basis of a single sore, which Ashford claimed was "the result of a wound . . . from a certain marine growth known as *unaoa.*" Mikala Kaipu had shown true symptoms of the disease, but they had improved to a degree that Ashford felt warranted "a change of opinion" on her status.

The Hawaiian Supreme Court had already ruled on similar cases. A decade earlier, in a habeas corpus filing, justices were asked to decide if the segregation of lepers was constitutional. Citing "the law of overriding necessity," they determined it was. In summary, the justices, led by Chief Justice Albert Francis Judd, had asked, "Is it a crime to be afflicted with leprosy?" It was not, they decided. Leprosy, their decision reads, "is a disease." Anyone unlucky enough to have caught this disease could not in any legal sense be considered a criminal. Yet he or she would have to be treated as one.

"It was decided that both Mrs. Mikala Kaipu and Miss Freeman were lepers," the board ruled during executive session, "and that this fact had been fully and legally established." Ashford continued to file lawsuits on behalf of patients, however, as did other lawyers. Such suits eventually exposed an actionable flaw in the segregation policy, which the board was forced to correct rather than risk having its exile powers stripped away in federal court. In essence, Ashford and other attorneys successfully argued that their clients were being declared lepers without substantive due process. Often the medical finding of leprosy was made after the briefest of investigations, "so extremely superficial as to scarcely deserve the name of an examination,"

Ashford wrote. Exile could be initiated upon the decision of a single board doctor, no formal challenge mechanism existed, and the suspect's personal physician rarely had a say in the final diagnosis. None of this was legal, Ashford suggested.

Members of the legislative assembly drafted a new set of procedures, which were signed by the governor and written into the books as "Leper Law, Territory of Hawaii." These guidelines came in response not only to the legal challenges, but also to political pressure on the lawmakers, as Dr. Carl Ramus, the head of the Federal Honolulu Quarantine Service, remarked: "The lepers are all voters, who, with their relatives (practically the entire population), will vote for those who treat lepers most leniently." The exile process was now rigidly prescribed. Once identified, every suspect was to be examined by the government physician in their district; the person had the option of being checked by their personal doctor as well. If the government physician decided the person did not have leprosy, the board "furnish[ed] him with a certificate setting forth such a fact." If either physician believed the person had leprosy, however, he or she was sent to Kalihi. There, a bacteriologist checked for leprosy bacilli, while the board assembled a case file, detailing medical and family history, clinical symptoms, and bacteriological findings. When the file was complete, the person appeared in front of a panel composed of five physicians, including two bacteriologists. Before the suspect could be exiled, four of the five examiners—including at least one of the bacteriologists—had to declare that the person had an active case of leprosy.

Not long after the regulations took effect, a number of patients in the settlement asked to be reexamined. Of the first eleven to be tested, ten were immediately determined not to have leprosy. "VICTIMS OF A TERRIBLE MISTAKE," the *Honolulu Evening Bulletin* cried. The ten patients, all male, had spent between three and twenty years in exile. "The long years during which they have awaited in fear and trembling the outward appearance of the dread disease which they had been told was in their flesh, have been wasted, and worse than wasted," the *Bulletin* announced. The following morning the eleventh exile, a forty-one-year-old woman named Augusta Freitas, was examined and also declared healthy. "How many more unfortunate victims of a terrible mistake are there on Molokai?" the *Bulletin* asked. "Her youth lies behind her—the best years of her life, the years of joy and hope and love. . . . Now Augusta Freitas is free. But who is to repay her for all she has lost?" At the end of the account the *Bulletin* remarked, "Eleven supposed lepers re-examined and every one of them found to be well. Truly a fine record." Reporters pressed the board president for comment, which he eventually gave to the *Hawaiian Gazette.* "The results," he said, "show that much is being learned in connection with the disease."

At the time, the primary treatment for leprosy was an oil derived from the seeds of a tree common in East India, known as a chaulmoogra tree. Doctors had long believed the oil had germicidal properties and had tried slicking it on blemishes or spooning it into patients, with little result. Then a physician injected the sick person with the oil. The patient improved. A drug company refined the mixture and began to market it under the name Antileprol. At Kalihi Hospital and in the settlement, doctors administered Antileprol and other chaulmoogra oil mixtures. The oil was viscous, burned like fire, and when injected moved visibly beneath the skin, a phenomenon one doctor likened to a snake slithering under a sheet. Injections were "extremely painful," one patient at Kalihi recalled. "The women fainted, and the men trembled." Some patients required three hundred shots a week.

In many instances, chaulmoogra oil therapy appeared to dramatically relieve the patient's symptoms. Physicians were uncertain if this had occurred spontaneously or resulted from the oil. But whatever the reason, the board felt it could no longer justify leaving a seemingly recovered person in permanent exile and announced that it had rethought its segregation policy. "In the earlier decades there was little attention given to the possibility of . . . recovery in the disease," a board-affiliated physician wrote. "The dictum prevailed that 'once a leper, always a leper,' and segregation was to be permanent." As a result of their bacteriological investigations, however, the board now recognized that some cases "become temporarily quiescent or arrested, or recover."

The board began to grant "temporary release" to select patients "deemed non-infectious and not a menace to public health." The name the board gave to this procedure was "parole." Describing the new policy, the *Advertiser* remarked, "Its adoption means that hereafter treatment is to be considered of more importance than segregation, and that segregation is to be incidental only to treatment, an almost complete reversal of the policy which has been in force in these islands for the past 43 years." Within the first few years under these new rules, 249 people were freed from exile.

Among the patients released were James Harvey, age seven, and John Ku, age six. Joseph Dutton had taken care of both at the Baldwin Home. The boys packed the few belongings they owned, then bounded down the steps from the porch of the home and into the yard. They ran to Dutton's cottage to say good-bye. Emerging from his tiny home, which was also his office, Dutton shook each boy's hand. Then he watched as they raced to Kalaupapa to catch the steamer home.

Although the other village was only two miles distant, Dutton had not visited Kalaupapa in almost twenty years. He rarely even stepped from the yard of the Baldwin Home, a well-kept sward of lawn and garden in the middle of Kalawao. By now the settlement population had almost entirely moved to the western shore; fewer than two hundred people remained in the original village, half of them residents of the Baldwin Home. While the home had originally served as an orphanage for boys under eighteen, its current occupants included older men, the blind and infirm, and some who simply enjoyed Dutton's company. All were referred to as "boys," no matter their age. If a boy fell sick, Dr. Goodhue rode over to attend him, otherwise Dutton dealt with the daily scrapes. He read to the boys, led them in games, scolded and comforted them. On Sundays he walked them to St. Philomena, where everyone sang. Afterward Dutton would visit Damien's grave and sometimes found Ambrose Hutchison already at the site, leaning against the stone wall, absentminded in prayer.

During the past several years the occupants of the Baldwin Home had gradually begun to leave Dutton, freed from Kalawao by death or treatment or through the correction of monstrous error. "Things have changed, advances are being made, and are still being made," Dutton wrote one friend. "The settlement is not what it was 20 years ago." His own routine remained unchanged, however. Inside his cottage Dutton had built a "crude, homemade desk, homemade table and bookshelves," a visitor reported. "Everything was bare and plain. There was nothing indicating luxury, and few things indicating even modern conveniences. . . .There was a large number of books, several well-thumbed encyclopedias, a small statue of Saint Francis, an American flag, a large map of Europe." Dutton drank only milk with water and kept a cool bottle handy. His desk was a warren of cubbies, "stuffed with letters and papers, all neatly folded and bundled." Every month he penned hundreds of letters. When the replies came back, the mail bags sometimes weighed fifty pounds. He maintained two hundred regular correspondents and still wrote until dawn, beset by insomnia. Through the letters and the magazines he received, Dutton monitored the outside world. Soldiers were a good news source, he discovered, as were schoolteachers. Emma Gibson wrote Dutton frequently from her home in California and sent him a cake on every birthday. She still addressed her cards "Dear Next Door Neighbor."

In the summer of 1908, Dutton wrote a letter musing about how it would be interesting to see a warship. The wish was relayed until it reached the president. Teddy Roosevelt sent a cable to the commander of the U.S. Atlantic Fleet, then steaming across the Pacific on a circuit of the globe: "Divert from course. Pass Molokai Island in battle formation. Show naval power to Brother Dutton. Dip colors. Then continue to Japan."

When the boys from the home spotted the massive white-hulled ships on the horizon, they ran to alert Brother Joseph. Raise the flag, one boy screamed—Dutton already had. The fleet "sighted the flag and headed straight for it," Dutton later reported. He stood silently on the shore, holding a salute as the sixteen warships passed. When the last had vanished, he hurried to his desk. "This visit is so exceedingly wonderful as to make the blood tingle and the heart grow warm," he wrote. Dutton offered thanks on behalf "of all in the leper asylum, a place having in it some suffering, it cannot be denied, but it is the home of sensible and contented people whose lot has become, after many years of labor and improvement, a condition not so difficult to bear." He added, "As thinking of myself, 'Did ever one deserve so little and get so much?'"

That summer a team of workers landed at Kalaupapa to erect a lighthouse. Federal surveyors had realized that almost every ship bound for Honolulu from the mainland threaded the narrow channel between Molokai and Oahu, skirting the treacherous shelf that comprised the settlement. Several smaller ships had already wrecked off the peninsula. "There is not a single light on the whole northern coast," a surveyor wrote, to "warn them of their approach to land." Surveyors chose a site at the peninsula's northernmost tip, creating a triangle in which Kalawao and Kalaupapa were the other points. When it was complete, the concrete tower rose 213 feet above the surf, one-tenth the height of the cliff. Just before sunset on September 1, 1909, James Keanu, one of the lighthouse keepers, lit the oil-vapor lamp and started the clockworks spinning.

Three keepers were required to maintain the light. The government built a trio of stone cottages at the base of the tower, with a fence surrounding. Keepers and their families were not allowed to mix with patients, but often did, visiting across the low fence. Only once did the board intervene and enforce total quarantine, when an assistant lighthouse keeper's daughter developed chickenpox. During the outbreak Dr. Goodhue cautioned patients to stay clear of the keepers since they carried a dangerous infection. James Keanu was working with dynamite one day when a stick exploded and took his right hand. Patients gave him tips on how to compensate. Before long, one resident marveled, "He could use a shovel, a pick, an axe; he could even wring out sheets!" The patients then taught Keanu to handle a baseball glove, so he could play in their Sunday games.

The light's three-ton lens rotated in a lagoon filled with fifteen gallons of mercury, which had to be drained and filtered every six months. Its lamp was the brightest in the entire Pacific, and could pierce the darkness for twenty-one miles. The beam made three revolutions every minute, glittering across the water and sweeping the switchback cliff trail. On a dark, moonless evening an unhappy patient made use of the light to escape the settlement, racing up the cliff in frenzied bursts, timed at every twenty seconds.

One autumn day Dr. Goodhue and Jack McVeigh also made their way to the top of the cliff, then crossed the meadow to the Meyer homestead. There, Goodhue wed one of Rudolph Meyer's granddaughters. In the coming years, the couple had three children, all born in Kalaupapa. Although the Goodhue children were exempt from the policy, the board required that every infant born in the settlement be removed from its parents at birth and placed in the Kalaupapa nursery. With a permit from McVeigh, the mother could visit her child once a week, but was never allowed to hold the baby. Newborns remained behind "specially constructed hermetically sealed glass panels," and after the board arranged placement with foster parents or in one of the two government orphanages in Honolulu, the child was bundled in blankets and taken out of the settlement.

Mother Marianne and the sisters staffed the Kalaupapa nursery. Marianne was now seventy-two years old. Arthritis had bent her spine, and the tuberculosis she had battled for years still manifested as "repeated hemorrhages and continued racking cough," Sister Leopoldina Burns reported. Despite the complications, Marianne remained surprisingly active. "She was never known to complain," Leopoldina wrote, "but [was] always at her post." A quarter century had passed since Walter Murray Gibson had first greeted Marianne and the sisters on the deck of the *Mariposa.* At the Kapiolani Home—which had been spared when the board disassembled Kakaako Hospital—three sisters oversaw fifty-six girls; at the Bishop Home in Kalaupapa, Marianne and four sisters took care of more than a hundred girls and young women, in addition to their duties in the sick wards and the nursery. "[We] have our hands full," Marianne admitted in a letter to her superior in Syracuse. A writer named Katharine Fullerton Gerould visited the Bishop Home and found Marianne "in her little parlor . . . an old, old woman who had seen many things. It was only when one stopped to think of the precise nature of those things . . . that the breath failed for an instant."

Like many in the settlement, Marianne attempted at times to keep a daily diary, only to abandon the effort without explanation. Others were more successful, although their acts of self-expression served differing purposes. Ambrose Hutchison collected scattered fragments of settlement history, which he would later attempt to weave together as a personal narrative. Joseph Dutton reconstructed his days in the form of cheerful letters to others; Dr. Goodhue's journal was a medical log; Jack McVeigh's a police blotter. "May 17. Geo. Kauoa. Assault and battery. Fined $1.00," McVeigh wrote. "July 28. W.J. Freary Jr. Disturbing quiet of the night. $2.00; August 1. Tina Thielmann. Violating Sunday Laws. $2.00; September 8. Ah Kee. Selling spirituous liquors. Fined $100."

A Sacred Hearts priest named Father Maxime Andre, who spent two decades in the settlement beginning in 1905, maintained a tersely vivid account of life in Kalaupapa. Writing in his native French, the priest noted the day McVeigh was thrown from a horse, shattering his leg, and the happy morning when Dr. Goodhue "swore off his Protestant beliefs" and joined the Catholic Church. When an altar boy accidentally set St. Francis Church ablaze, Father Maxime recorded the frantic effort to smother the flames, and itemized the $10,000 required to rebuild. He documented a storm that crashed waves onto his rectory windows, and the sad theft of his wallet, stolen from his room while he was ringing the church bell. The arrival of fifty-five patients from Kalihi, a census of 316 Catholics in his congregation, and the twenty-fifth anniversary of Father Damien's death all merited entries.

In 1916 Maxime's diary revealed that he had performed thirty-six baptisms, attended nineteen births, and married eight young couples. McVeigh's journal from the same year details the construction of a social hall, and yet another fierce storm that "overturned a number of the smaller buildings, stripped the shingles off the houses, smashed windows and doors, and broke down several thousand feet of fencing." Goodhue logged the return of the mysterious swollen head fever, which struck 107 residents in the settlement, killing one. The doctor described how he averaged six amputations annually, and although a few patients "have hoarded their savings, little by little, until enabled to secure an artificial limb . . . the majority can not do so." The following April, Maxime reported that Goodhue had cleared thirteen patients for parole, and the priest registered a marriage between the settlement's mail carrier, a patient named David Kupele, and a young woman named Annie. And on September 18, 1917, Father Maxime remarked in his diary that Mother Marianne had fallen ill. He wrote, "We fear the worst."

"There is nothing can be done," Dr. Goodhue told the sisters. "Make her as comfortable as you can." They lifted Marianne into a wheelchair, and in "the lovely cool evenings" Leopoldina rolled her onto the veranda to take the air. By the next summer Marianne was bedridden, unable to rest. "During those sleepless nights she used to cry out loud, 'Sweet Heart of Jesus, pity me, pity me,'" one sister told a reporter. "She used to say it so pleadingly." On Friday, August 9, 1918, Maxime arrived to give last sacraments. That evening the sisters gathered around Marianne. "Mother looked so peaceful," Leopoldina recalled, "her eyes and mouth were closed, and they never opened again, not a muscle in her face moved and her breathing so easy one could scarcely know she was living only for the slight movement of her hand when we would stop praying." Mother Marianne Cope passed away at 11 P.M. She was eighty years old and had spent thirty years in the settlement.

Every month a mainland newspaper would print the news that Joseph Dutton had also died and give its pages over to eulogy. A week or two later the editor would open his mail and find a note of aggrieved protest from Dutton. One spring day Dutton got a letter from the Kentucky governor's office. "We were especially glad to receive your Easter greeting today," wrote the governor's wife, "as we had read in the papers that God had taken you home."

Newspapers began to call Dutton the Hermit of Molokai. The modern world held no fascination for him, they reported. When Jack McVeigh offered to connect Dutton's cottage to the settlement generator and string a light over his desk, Dutton refused; he feared the brightness would blind him. Although McVeigh had installed a movie projector in Kalaupapa, to the delight of residents, Dutton refused to leave Kalawao to see the show. He turned down the gift of a radio and might never have encountered an automobile if Dr. Goodhue had not one day decided to expose him to the wonders of technology. The physician drove his sputtering black Ford straight into the yard of the Baldwin Home. "Before Brother Dutton knew it," a reporter recalled, "his eyes had beheld the modern juggernaut." In a fit of high spirits, Goodhue chased Dutton across the lawn with the car.

When war in Europe drew America in, Dutton engaged in the only discussion he would ever have about leaving Molokai. He thought he could reassemble his old army regiment, the Thirteenth Wisconsin Infantry, and he asked the president to send them to the front, "as a body of independent sharpshooters." Dutton had no illusions about the sort of soldiers they would make: "Not that we would do much good at the front—the Army would be stumbling over us; but for the example to the youngsters at home." The army gently declined his offer, and Dutton fought the war with colored pins on a wall map of Europe. "I am an old, old relic," he wrote, "still on duty."

He helped to organize a Red Cross effort, working with McVeigh and Goodhue. "The gift of nearly $250 by the lepers of Molokai . . . to the relief of suffering in Europe is one of the most remarkable and touching incidents of the great world war," one local paper wrote. The writer then added, "The lepers are a public charge. They have no money to speak of, and any contribution . . . represents a sacrifice they should not be permitted to make." Patients responded to the editorial by buying $4,255 worth of war stamps.

When the legislators' biannual inspection tours landed in the settlement, they always ventured to Kalawao to look in on Dutton. "He is an aged man," one visitor wrote, "with a face rimmed on brow, chin and cheeks by white hair and beard . . . his open joy at meeting the newcomers showed how he, too, is affected by the immense loneliness of Molokai." The same writer remarked that Dutton seemed eager to hear "things of the world that lies beyond the rearing white breakers of the Pacific."

As the years passed, the story of Dutton's selflessness spread. One morning Dutton opened his mail and found a letter from the president, Warren Harding. "The other day a friend of mine spoke of the work of Father Damien and yourself," Harding wrote. "I had known, through the writings of Robert Louis Stevenson, something about the story of Father Damien, and more recently of how you had carried that work forward. I do not know why I have been moved to write a letter to you. I am very sure that nothing I can say can possibly add to the satisfaction which you must feel in having thus carried on a service to the bodies, the minds, and souls of men and women, for which we find few parallels. I hope you may be spared many, many more years to carry it forward." Dutton replied, "My dear President: It was a beautiful letter, yours to me . . . am wishing to be really so good and useful as you think."

By 1920 the population in the settlement had fallen to 546, the lowest since the year prior to Damien's arrival. For almost two years, no patients had been sent from Kalihi Hospital. The majority of patients at Kalihi were receiving treatment with a purified form of chaulmoogra oil, developed by a young chemist named Alice Ball. Responding to a request by a physician at Kalihi, Ball had managed to isolate the active component in the fatty acids of the oil. The refined formula seemed to have miraculous effect. A Kalihi inmate named Rosalie Blaisdell was among the first to receive treatment, enduring weekly injections of between one and three cubic centimeters. "On March

5, 1915, I was declared a leper," *Leslie's Illustrated Weekly* reported Blaisdell as saying in July 1921. "I wish I had with me the picture that was taken of me then so that you could see the different woman I am now. I am sure you would not know me for the woman in that picture." After the board paroled Blaisdell, the *Leslie's* reporter visited her. "I have seen Mrs. Blaisdell since and been in her home, and although there are still the scars of her wounds, they are only scars, the memories of the treatment. She is cured."

The board planted a chaulmoogra orchard, importing two thousand of the rare trees. Seeds harvested from the trees' fruit yielded a liquid, which was processed, cut with iodine, and injected into the patient's hip. By the fall of 1921, 50 percent of the inmates receiving treatment at Kalihi had "recovered and been paroled," the *Honolulu Star-Bulletin* reported. Because of the oil's scarcity, Dr. Goodhue could treat only a smaller number of settlement residents. In 1921 he paroled seventeen of his patients, several of whom had endured exile for more than twenty years. "LEPROSY NOW UNDER COMPLETE CONTROL IS PHYSICIAN'S BELIEF," trumpeted the *Star-Bulletin.*

All transfers of patients to Molokai stopped. As had happened fifty-five years before, when Dr. Edward Hoffmann had opened the original Kalihi Hospital, patients again began to come willingly to the facility. "Because . . . entrance to Kalihi hospital does not necessarily mean a life of exile, there is now little tendency to conceal [themselves]," reported one paper. The board announced, "In no equal in the whole history of the segregation of leprosy [patients] in the Hawaiian Islands, extending over half a century, has there been so many voluntary surrenders. . . . Not only have adults come and asked to be taken in for treatment, but parents and guardians have brought their children and youths as soon as the nature of the disease was suspected." Despite the seeming miracle, the board sounded a note of caution: "As has been pointed out, there is no way of demonstrating that any person has been cured absolutely of leprosy."

In fact, although chaulmoogra oil had a palliative effect, it had not actually cured anyone. Medical historians later suggested that the majority of "cures" were simply instances of spontaneous remission. Such events occurred fairly often, and in about one-quarter of those patients the disease later reactivated. Before long, patients who had been paroled began to show renewed symptoms of leprosy. They were returned to Kalihi. One board official complained that "the patients might as well be fed sugar pills."

On June 12, 1923, the board resumed the exile of patients to Molokai. Seventy-three men and twenty-one women arrived at Kalaupapa aboard the

Likelike. The women took rooms in the Bishop Home. Men were assigned to a housing compound called McVeigh Home, which consisted of several dozen bedrooms, a small sick ward, a dining room, and a social hall. Built in 1910, the home was initially to house "white lepers." When too few American patients took up residence, Jack McVeigh allowed a dozen Portuguese inmates to move in; shortly thereafter, it became an ordinary dormitory.

Over the past several years the board had gradually reduced the number of residents assigned to the Baldwin Home, with the intention of closing the Kalawao facility overseen by Joseph Dutton. Dutton was eighty years old, and at times he struggled to maintain the home. His long beard now fanned over the blue chambray shirt he always wore, the cloth faded to match his eyes. By 1923 the average age in the settlement was thirty-five. Dutton and Ambrose Hutchison had resided in the settlement longer than anyone else—although Dutton was quick to add that he was Hutchinson's senior by a dozen years. The two old men brought up the rear of the yearly Ascension Day parade, each helping the other along the meandering path.

Sometime earlier, a board physician had asked Ambrose Hutchison to chart his medical history, to preserve it for the record. "I think the leprosy has exhausted itself in my system," Hutchison wrote. "My present condition—I am physically maimed and weak, and a wreck to what I was. [Though] I am without pains, sores, or ulcers on any part of my body, my hands and feet are much mutilated from the ravages of the disease in the past." He added, "It is with great reluctance that I take my pen to write about this matter, for it recalls to memory the pathetic side of my life as a Condemned outcast and prisoner."

In 1925 the board decided to revise the segregation laws yet again, partly in response to pressure by the business community. It reasserted the government's right to arrest any person suspected of having the disease, raised the threshold for parole, and announced that anyone "whoever shall knowingly . . . conceal or secret, or assist in concealing or secreting," a suspect would be charged and fined $100. The attorney general of the territory, Earl McGhee, then ruled that the settlement would again become "quasi-penal." McGhee offered a suggestion to ease the sting of banishment, however. Exiles, he wrote, should be referred to in government documents as "patients," and the colony itself as the "leprosarium."

In the coming months thirty-eight Kalihi inmates clambered over the fence, wormed beneath the wire, and dashed past inattentive guards, hoping to avoid being sent to Molokai. Police officers hunted them down and brought them back to the facility. The board then restored a disciplinary provision at Kalihi, allowing the immediate exile of any misbehaving inmate.

Nineteen patients were swiftly banished. One person summarily shipped to Molokai was a teenager named Stephen Dawson. At Kalihi, Dawson had become celebrated for his frequent escapes. More than a year had passed since his last breakout, but when the harsher regulations went into effect, the board sent Dawson to Molokai. From Kalaupapa, he argued that he had been punished retroactively and demanded a legislative hearing. A special investigatory committee subsequently found that the "deportation of Dawson had been a mistake which should be rectified." Dawson was returned to Kalihi. The board soon found another excuse to exile him.

When Dawson landed at Kalaupapa, he spotted a woman he had known from Kalihi: Rosalie Blaisdell, the subject of the cheerful profile in *Leslie's Illustrated Weekly.* Blaisdell's leprosy had reactivated, and she had been sent to Kalaupapa. Shortly after arriving in the settlement, Blaisdell had spoken to another reporter. "I like the place," she had confessed. "It is not so dreadful or horrible as pictured to me from what has been written."

As the public battles over segregation policy continued, news spilled into mainland newspapers. "HAWAII IS TROUBLED BY LEPER PROBLEM," blared the *New York Times* in a typical account. Such articles distressed the Honolulu business community, which feared depressed tourism and trade in the booming canned fruit industry. Kalihi Hospital abutted the island's canning factories, a detail that the press did not fail to notice. The pineapple consortium, led by James Dole, the young cousin of the late Sanford Dole, advocated moving the leprosy facility to some hidden valley far from Honolulu. One of Dole's colleagues in the campaign was his late cousin's cohort, Lorrin Thurston. The elderly Thurston was now the owner of the *Advertiser* and dean emeritus of Hawaii's tourism industry. As a means to blunt the flurry of leprosy-related press, Thurston encouraged local business leaders to generate uplifting stories—promotions that reflected positively on Hawaii. The news they ultimately created was not what Thurston had in mind.

On May 23, 1927, James Dole tore open a Western Union cable. "From angle advertising islands and yourself we believe an exceptional opportunity [exists]." The message came from two Honolulu newspaper editors and had reached Dole in San Francisco. "In view of Lindbergh's Atlantic flight the Pacific remains one great area for conquest aviation. This moment ripe for someone offer suitable prize non-stop flight Hawaii." In the contest they proposed, the first aviator to fly from Oakland to Honolulu would win $25,000. Such a race, the editors promised, would bring Hawaii upbeat coverage "from every newspaper in the world."

Dole quickly agreed, and the North American–Honolulu, Hawaii, Trans-Pacific Flight was born—it came to be known as the Dole Derby. Although Dole had hoped that Charles Lindbergh would participate, the pilot declined to enter. In his place swarmed a motley group of barnstormers, stuntmen, wing walkers, and backyard aviators. Would-be racers bolted together ramshackle planes, and several attempted to enter aircraft lacking even crude instrumentation. The pilots argued this would not present a problem, since they couldn't read instruments anyway.

Two days prior to the start of the contest a pair of navy lieutenants wheeled onto an airstrip in San Diego to fly north to join the race. Moments after liftoff the plane plowed into a cliff. When a British war ace named Arthur Rogers took off from a Los Angeles field, his plane stalled and began to cartwheel toward the ground. Rogers kicked open the cockpit door and leapt free, but his parachute snagged the gear of his plane and he died on impact. By race day, three pilots were dead, three aircraft destroyed, and four other entries had reconsidered and abandoned the race entirely. Eight entries remained. On the morning of the contest, fifty thousand spectators lined the Oakland airfield, clutching ukuleles and sporting flower leis. A priest moved down the line of aircraft and handed each pilot a Bible. Several racers seemed to be fighting tears.

At noon on August 16, 1927, the starter flapped a checkered flag. Men shoved the first plane, *Oklahoma,* into the air; she rose gently and headed out the Golden Gate. The second plane roared along the runway, lifted a few feet, and slammed back to earth. Then the *Pabco Pacific Flyer* thundered down the strip but never rose an inch. The next aircraft soared away beautifully: her sponsor, William Randolph Hearst, had paid $12,500 for one of the first Lockheed aircraft built, a sleek shaft of yellow called the *Golden Eagle.* As she vanished westward, the four remaining planes took off in turn. Three promptly limped back to the airfield, crippled by mechanical problems. While their pilots made hasty repairs, the *Pabco Pacific Flyer* lined up for her second attempt. She managed an altitude of fifty feet, belched smoke, and crashed.

The last to leave was a plane called *Miss Doran,* an entry that held huge fascination for the press. Its three-person crew included a twenty-two-year-old Sunday school teacher from Flint, Michigan, Mildred Doran, whom reporters had dubbed "the prettiest little pigeon on wings." Doran was entered as a publicity stunt by the millionaire owner of the Flint airport. When asked if she was nervous, Doran had replied, "No, truly, truly I'm not in the least bit worried or anxious." Reporters later wrote that Doran was clearly petrified. "They ought to tell her not to go into that thing," a spectator yelled. One observer remarked, "I know she was scared to death. . . . But no one was going to call her a quitter." A chase plane followed the *Miss Doran* out over the water. Mildred Doran mimed plucking a carnation from the lei she held and tossing it through the sky to the other plane, whose pilot pretended to catch the flower. Then Doran smiled and waved good-bye.

The next morning in Honolulu, thirty thousand people idled in a two-mile-long traffic jam, trying to reach Wheeler Field. Military radiomen gave updates on the fliers' progress, relayed by seven navy vessels strung along the route. Ham operators fiddled the dial to pluck detail from the air. In the settlement, patients gathered around the radio in the hospital ward, listening to a minute-by-minute account of the race. Several residents placed bets on which pilot would pass Molokai first, while others headed to the lighthouse point to watch for the planes. At Wheeler Field, James Dole turned to a reporter and said with satisfaction, "Hawaii is on the lips of the world today."

Shortly after noon, a two-hundred-horsepower monoplane skirted Maui, hugged the length of Molokai, and buzzed noisily toward Oahu. As he neared Honolulu, the pilot dropped flares and smoke bombs from his window to celebrate the victory. Twenty-six hours and seventeen minutes after leaving Oakland, Arthur Goebel brought the *Woolaroc* to a wheezing stop to claim first prize. One hour and fifty-eight minutes later, a Hawaii resident named Martin Jensen landed in the *Aloha,* for second place. He had four gallons of fuel in his tanks—less than twenty minutes' worth.

Dole watched for the remaining two planes, Hearst's *Golden Eagle* and the *Miss Doran.* One hour passed. Then another. An engineer did a calculation and broke the news: neither plane could possibly be aloft. Forty-two ships and aircraft scrambled to search for the missing fliers. Almost immediately an army rescue plane crashed, killing both men aboard. Two more pilots died when their plane, the *Dallas Spirit,* plunged into the sea. She had been among the original eight race entrants to take off from Oakland, but a fuselage rip had forced her to abort. When the crew learned about the downed planes, they patched the rip and joined the search. Later that day a navy ship picked up a distress call from the *Dallas Spirit*: "S.O.S.—We are in a tailspin!" Seconds afterward the plane's navigator announced with relief, "We came out of it okay but we're sure scared." An instant later he screamed, "We are in—!" Then only silence.

The search continued for ten days. When it was certain that no survivors would be found, the effort halted. James Dole's promotion had claimed twelve lives. The story filled every newspaper in the United States and many around the world. "DOLE'S RACE TO DEATH," cried one account. Another called the Dole Derby "an orgy of reckless sacrifice," and another described Dole as a "publicity-mad promoter leaving a trail of carnage." Dole went into hiding.

Lost in the grief over the disaster was the fact that the Dole Derby had chased a false prize. Two men had already made the first civilian crossing of the Pacific by air, more than a month earlier. Earnest Smith and Emory Bronte had left Oakland on July 14, 1927, carrying one compass, a rubber life raft, sandwiches, coffee, and four carrier pigeons, in case their radio gave out. They flew due west without incident for twenty-five hours, realized that they could not clear the massive sea cliffs blocking their way, and ditched their plane in a stand of stunted trees on Molokai. When mainland reporters subsequently recounted the pilots' achievement, the writers took care to explain that the island was the locale of a leper colony.

All a Man Holds Dear

(Population 510)

Lawrence Judd's memory of that morning remained crisp, despite the three decades that had passed. He had been eleven years old, pedaling his bicycle along the Honolulu esplanade. The wheels ticked on the planking, and Judd had been following along with the rhythm when a strange noise sounded. "A wail," Judd would write, "trouble of some kind." He hopped from his bike. An interisland cattle boat was tied at the end of the pier, screened by a white fence. Policemen ranked the fence, holding back a group of distressed men and women. The crowd "clung to the picket barrier, their bodies rocking, as they gave way to spasms of grief," Judd wrote. Just then two guards began to escort a group of people past the audience.

Judd approached one of the uniformed men. "Who are they?" he asked.

The man replied, "Kalaupapa."

A health officer pulled patients from a canvas-sided van and steered them to the gangplank. Another officer, wearing dark gloves, took hold of each patient and towed him or her aboard. Judd noticed a woman emerge from the van, leading a small girl. "As these two appeared, the crowd, which had been momentarily silent, burst again into a long wail," Judd wrote. "I wanted to cry myself, without knowing why." The woman cleared tears from the girl's eyes, then tucked her handkerchief into the child's dress, but it fluttered to the ground. A guard hurried over with a sheet of newspaper, dropped the paper atop the handkerchief, crumbled them into a ball, and tossed both aside.

Again Judd asked, "Who are they?" The guard said that the people being taken aboard the ship had leprosy.

"But they look all right," Judd insisted.

The guard answered, "You cannot always see."

Lawrence Judd was one of nine children born to Albert Francis Judd, chief justice of the Hawaiian Supreme Court. In his years on the court, Albert Judd had ruled on many cases involving the disease. He had presided over the murderer Keanu's trial, heard Dr. George Fitch's libel complaint, and authored the 1884 decision that leprosy victims be treated "as criminals." When Lawrence

Judd raced home from the pier, he found Albert Judd sitting in the parlor, reading the *Advertiser.* Lawrence asked his father if he knew anything about the disease. "His brow knotted," Lawrence later recalled. Then Albert had replied gravely, "Yes, I know a little about leprosy." The judge explained to his son about Leviticus and the pariah status of the Molokai exiles, and then began to recount the Keanu case, and Dr. Eduard Arning's experiment with the prisoner. "Father stopped suddenly," Lawrence later wrote. "I had the idea that he felt he should not have talked so freely upon such a serious topic with a small boy. He picked up the newspaper. I was dismissed. The wailing of the bereaved at the pier was still in my ears."

Justice Albert Judd died two years later, in May 1900. Lawrence was sent to the mainland to attend school at Hotchkiss, and then the University of Pennsylvania. He returned to Honolulu in 1909 and was elected to the state legislature. In April 1929, Herbert Hoover appointed forty-two-year-old Lawrence Judd territorial governor of Hawaii. Judd wrote, "Almost my first thought was the necessity of a thorough study, followed by action, to alleviate the conditions at the leper settlement at Kalaupapa."

Judd appointed a committee to investigate the exile policy "in all its phases," as the *New York Times* reported. On October 16, 1930, the governor's Advisory Committee on Leprosy in Hawaii submitted its findings. "Your committee has studied the subject of leprosy in this Territory and has reached the conclusion that a continuation of effort under conditions as they now exist offers very little, if any, hope for the eradication of the disease." The report was a sweeping indictment of the segregation policy. Although the government's motives had been honorable, the committee declared, all that the original board of health and every succeeding board had managed was to warehouse the sick. "The leprous population has averaged 760 for the past 20 years—the annual influx of new cases and the average annual number of deaths among patients in segregation being practically equal. All things being equal therefore, it is safe to assume that our leprous population will remain at that figure indefinitely."

Segregation had to be entirely rethought. The committee presented Judd with a six-point plan to eradicate the disease. Among its proposals was that no more cases be exiled to Kalaupapa. Current residents could be allowed to remain, and facilities at the settlement could be improved—but otherwise the settlement should be gradually depopulated. At the same time, facilities at Kalihi Hospital must be enlarged and improved and made capable of providing "the very best care and attention for the patients of the future." The committee recommended starting a social welfare program, to "add to the happiness of patients and their dependents." And most critically, the board had to focus on early detection of the disease. It suggested hiring an epidemiologist to assemble case histories of "patients in segregation, [and] of patients on conditional release and new patients. These case histories will furnish a means of determining 'backwards' the previous exposure—hereditary, familial, contact or otherwise, and 'forwards,' the individuals, familial or otherwise, who have been exposed." If all of these measures commenced, the committee wrote, the leprosy rate in the islands would fall.

Shortly after Lawrence Judd received the committee's findings, he removed control of the settlement and Kalihi Hospital from the board of health. Believing the board to be too political to effectively manage Kalihi and Kalaupapa, Judd created a new administrative body, called the Board of Leper Hospitals and Settlement—and soon had "leper" dropped from the official title. Then he traveled to Molokai. Both Jack McVeigh and William Goodhue had retired, after twenty-three years in the settlement. The current superintendent was a popular forty-three-year-old Kentuckian named Robert Cooke.

"Could you spend three hundred thousand dollars in Kalaupapa if the opportunity presented itself?" Judd asked Cooke.

Cooke thought Judd was teasing and sarcastically drawled, "Yep."

"But he wasn't joking," Cooke later explained in a letter to friend. "Very promptly he unearthed certain funds that made good his threat." Judd then addressed the residents. "Your problem is one of my main interests as governor," he told them. "It was difficult to get the people to realize the need here. But now we are ready to stop blowing bubbles and to do definite things for your welfare."

Very quickly, Judd began to push through an ambitious slate of improvements. Both Kalihi and Kalaupapa received new hospital facilities and new dispensaries. The board hired a social worker, an epidemiologist, more bacteriologists, and a nutritionist, who charted menus for the inmates months in advance, with meals of pounded rump steak, shepherd's pie, baked macaroni, and instructions to cooks to "serve a dessert at least once a day."

The governor ordered cottages at both facilities torn down and rebuilt, and a two-thousand-foot-long airfield constructed at Kalaupapa. Work crews in the settlement enlarged the concrete landing and outfitted it with an industrial-sized boom and erected a new general store, warehouse, and laundry. Government laborers installed an ice plant, a bakery, a diesel power plant, and streetlamps. "The pall of hopeless tragedy which formerly hung over [Kalaupapa] like the motif of a Greek tragedy has lifted," one paper reported, "thanks to the beneficence of the taxpayers of Hawaii, awakened to their duty by Governor Lawrence M. Judd and his admirable board of hospitals and settlement."

After the work was complete, the advisory committee returned to Kalaupapa. "For the first time in the history of leprosy in Hawaii there has been a definite, constructive plan to handle this disease and its unfortunate victims—a plan completely divorced from politics," they reported. "The accomplishments and purposes of the last 10 months speak for themselves." Although the members of the committee did not realize it, in their enthusiasm they reached for an analogy that Ambrose Hutchison had also once employed, almost half a century earlier. "The Augean stable," the committee informed the governor, "is finally clean."

Hutchison had survived fifty-three years in the settlement. He had moved from his cottage in the heart of the peninsula to a newer place, near the center of Kalaupapa. Outside his window cars carved into hot rods by the young men in the settlement raced each other down Damien Road. As he sat in his chair, Hutchison would hear them roar past, and also the planes trimming speed to land at the airfield, and the shrill whistle of the supply barge as it began its turn toward the wharf. At 7:00 A.M. on January 5, 1932, the steel-hulled steamer *Kaala* sounded a distress signal and was driven by a storm onto the rocks. The ship cracked in half, spilling its cargo and crew into the sea. Residents fought their way across the waves in canoes to rescue survivors. Two men drowned; the captain refused to abandon his ship.

Throughout that winter Hutchison worked on the story of his life, using a fat pencil and a schoolboy's ruled pad. His once crisp penmanship had grown shaky with age. "The writer of this memoir," his first sentence reads, was "exiled from all a man holds dear in life by force of the law." Hutchison was now a widower, and he passed his sleepless nights in prayer. On the Catholic holy days he would climb into someone's automobile and make a rattling pilgrimage to Kalawao, to visit Damien's grave and check on Joseph Dutton, his partner in endurance.

A reporter had recently visited Kalawao and spent the day at the Baldwin Home. "Brother Dutton and I chatted in his little office during the greater part of the sunshiny mornings," he wrote. "Outside the majestic stillness was broken now and then by the songs of birds, or the softly spoken words of leper boys passing by. Once I heard the tap-tap of a stick as a blind leper felt his way along to his cottage. Far away could be heard, dimly, the pounding of the surf on the cliffs at the sea edge."

Dutton told a story about a midnight storm that had ripped Kalawao not long before. Gullies had filled with tumbled boulders, and the runoff rolled cottages from their foundations. On the cliff the waterfalls merged into a single furious stream, which leapt far into the air. "It was grand!" Dutton recalled. "I crept like a little mouse down the steps of my cottage—the oldest building here—like myself, the oldest person." The raging water trapped him on the final step. Brother Jules, one of the Sacred Hearts missionaries, waded through the torrent, lifted the old man onto his back, and carried him to the safety of St. Philomena.

Dutton led the reporter to the chapel and knelt to open a trapdoor, exposing a room hidden beneath the floor. "It was lighted by one tiny, oblong window on a level with the surface of the ground," the visitor wrote. Dutton explained that he had built the crypt decades ago, while helping Father Damien repair St. Philomena after a storm. He had done so, the reporter wrote, "for the special purpose of housing his own body after death." The visitor laughed and told Dutton that the way he was going, he would live to be one hundred. "Do you really think so?" the older man asked brightly. And then, the visitor wrote, Dutton smiled, "rather wistfully, I thought."

One August evening Dutton went to lower his flag and felt "a bit tired, and suddenly cold." He collapsed in a heap on his cottage steps. Brother Jules ran over and gathered him up. The brothers carried him to Kalaupapa, and the settlement doctor put Dutton aboard the next steamer, bound for the hospital in Honolulu. For the first time since 1886, Joseph Dutton left the settlement.

The steamer tied off at Pier 25, and an ambulance collected Dutton. It sped through traffic to St. Francis Hospital. "Honolulu!" Dutton said, looking out the window. "So this is Honolulu again. Everything goes like a whiz these days." At the hospital he was "put to bed in a cheerful room," one of his visitors reported. The nurses stuck a green eyeshade on his white-haired head, to shield his eyes from the electric lights. "I guess," Dutton announced, "that I have come to the end of the trail—that my work is finished. I hope God approves."

The post office began to forward Dutton's mail, fat sacks filled with well wishes. A Catholic nurse took down his replies. "One of the sisters here has answered nearly two hundred letters for me," he informed one acquaintance. "You see, my old eyes won't let me read anymore, and these old fingers can't hold a pen." He soon lost his hearing, and then the last shards of sight. When Lawrence Judd came to visit, he tapped hello atop Dutton's frail hands.

The newspapers stationed reporters to file daily updates on Dutton's condition. "I forget so many things now," Dutton announced. "They are in my mind and now and then they come back to me." One day Dutton softly declared, "I regret nothing in the world but evil, nothing but evil." Another reporter was present in the hospital room when Dutton awoke and mumbled, "Was selfish. It was not for the benefit of humanity, but selfish."

For his birthday Emma Gibson arranged to send Dutton a chocolate cake with yellow candles, and a letter that ordered him to get well soon. "Dear Next Door Neighbor," her note began. The present arrived too late. At 1:50 A.M. on March 26, 1931, the eighty-eight-year-old Dutton let out two short, sharp breaths and died. "A noble life, rich in achievement for humanity, came to its end peacefully and quietly, when Brother Joseph Dutton passed to his reward," one newspaper reported. They put him in a casket draped with American flags, and a detachment of soldiers conveyed him through the city. A navy ship carried Dutton back to the settlement, where he was laid to rest.

Kalawao began to vanish. At the Baldwin Home, after Dutton had departed, the Sacred Hearts missionaries had packed their belongings and those of the remaining boys, and everyone moved to Kalaupapa. Lantana brush now inched along the grounds, swallowing paths worn smooth in the dirt by a thousand shuffled feet. Cottages moaned in the wind, made fragile by vacancy, until suddenly, one by one, they tumbled. Roots and vines shattered gravestones, disassembled stone walls, and began to encircle St. Philomena, intending to wrench it back to earth.

Only Damien's grave remained untouched, guarded with an iron fence and shaded by encroaching trees. When creepers crept close enough to finger the grave, someone arrived to snip back the assault and nurse the zinnias that colored the site. For many years the caretaker had been Ambrose Hutchison, but no longer. A year after Joseph Dutton passed away, on July 17, 1932, Hutchison also died. He was seventy-six years old. A worker found the curled sheets of his manuscript. The memoir was unfinished, frozen in midsentence halfway down one page, the story stuck in the autumn of 1888.

Months now passed without a visitor to Kalawao. In Belgium, people believed that Father Damien, their most famous native son, was being neglected. The Belgian consul sent a petition from the king that Damien be exhumed and returned, to occupy a marble crypt. The bishop of the Hawaiian islands, Father Stephen Alencastre, agreed to the request.

On January 27, 1936, a crew of gravediggers arrived in Kalawao. They used a curved pickax to crack the concrete tomb, sunk seven feet into rocky soil. From atop a wall Bishop Alencastre prayed aloud. Workers "came forward bearing a long object which the sunlight revealed to be an aged, wooden coffin," one man present at the exhumation recalled. Someone slipped a crowbar into the coffin lip and pulled. Everything fell silent. Father Damien lay before them in the light.

After forty-seven years his vestments "still retained some color, and the heavy embroidery had not fallen to dust," reported the *San Francisco Examiner.* "In the hands of the martyred was a rosary, the metal parts of which were green with corrosion." The crowd moved closer, "as though they hoped to draw some spiritual virtue from its nearness," a witness wrote. Minutes elapsed as ecclesiastical officials made formal identification of the priest. Several members of the church's tribunal of canonization, the men tasked to judge Damien a saint, encircled the casket and peered down at the body; Father Patrick Logan, the current Sacred Hearts priest in Kalaupapa, had been named by the tribunal as devil's advocate, to argue against the cause. When they had finished their inspection, the casket was resealed. One patient began to sing, and another, and the song echoed off the cliff: "Aloha oe, aloha oe. Until we meet again." Then Damien was gone, in a hearse trailing dust.

The body was to be flown to Honolulu and loaded aboard an army transport ship to San Francisco. From there it would sail to Europe. An army pilot named Phillips Melville drew the assignment of flying Damien's body from Molokai. When the hearse arrived at the Kalaupapa airfield, workmen heaved the casket through the plane's bomb bay and tied it down with rope. Melville fired the engines. He turned the bomber into the steady wind and brought the Keystone B-6A Panther aloft. Banking the plane over Kalaupapa, Melville leveled off at five hundred feet, passing above St. Francis Church. He had just finished the flyby when suddenly the plane began to shoot skyward. Checking his altimeter, Melville later recalled, "I was astonished to see that we were still gaining altitude at over a thousand feet a minute." He could not explain it nor immediately slow the plane's ascent.

Many residents had bitterly protested taking Damien from the settlement. "Talk to any man anywhere on the globe and if he has heard the name Father Damien he at once associates it with the leper colony," a letter to the editor of the *Advertiser* argued. "If ever there was a case that cried out against removal, it is this." Some warned that to violate a grave was a fearsome kapu. Older Hawaiians in the settlement, who knew the stories of Paniku Hua and the kahunas, cautioned that disturbing Damien would have consequences. Their belief in sorcery seemed to have merit. One week before the exhumation, the army had dispatched bombers to shell the flanks of the sacred volcano Mauna Loa, on the island of Hawaii. The volcano was erupting, and engineers thought they could blast the lava flow away from the town of Hilo.

Military planes emptied five tons of explosives on the volcano, and residents insisted the fire goddess Pele would exact her revenge. Several days later two of the planes from the mission collided over Honolulu, killing all six men aboard. Their remains were to be carried to San Francisco aboard the army transport ship *Republic*, the same vessel on which Damien's body would travel. The convergence of ill omens did not pass unnoticed in Kalaupapa.

Captain Edgar S. McClellan was in command of the *Republic*. He had twenty-six years' experience in the service. His ship left Honolulu and on February 10 steamed in view of the lighthouse on the Farallon Islands, granite outcroppings thirty miles west of San Francisco. The sea was calm and the skies clear. Captain McClellan came onto the bridge of the ship, checked the horizon, then asked to be notified when the *Republic* reached the San Francisco light—he wanted to be at the helm when the ship passed beneath the Golden Gate Bridge, almost complete after five years' construction. At 5:45 A.M. the lookout sent a man to the captain's quarters. McClellan was not inside. A frenzied search of the ship yielded no clues. The second-in-command brought the *Republic* into San Francisco, where Damien's remains lay in state for a week before being shipped to Belgium. During that week an army board of inquiry conducted a secret investigation into McClellan's disappearance. Officers searched the ship for evidence of foul play, but "everything in his cabin was in perfect order," according to one account. Only one thing was amiss: all the pictures in the cabin had been turned facedown. McClellan's wife insisted to a *New York Times* reporter that "it was not suicide," and the captain's colleagues testified that "they did not believe he would have left his transport voluntarily." In the end, the board of inquiry found no logical explanation. McClellan had simply disappeared.

Olivia

(Population 459)

In the late autumn of 1934 the most popular song in the islands was a nonsensical tune called "My Little Grass Shack in Kealakekua, Hawaii." Stores sold thousands of copies and sheet music with the lyrics. Olivia Robello put the record on her phonograph one Thursday morning, as a soundtrack for her chores. Olivia was eighteen years old, a willowy girl with cascades of thick brown hair and dark luminous eyes; at the carhop where she sometimes worked, boys jockeyed for her station and beeped their horns until she looked their way and laughed. She lived with her parents in a working-class neighborhood in Honolulu, and on weekends Olivia and her sister would walk the paths of Moanalua Gardens, talking about the men they would marry and the children they might raise. "So many dreams," Olivia would later write in her memoir, *Olivia: My Life of Exile in Kalaupapa*. "We both had them and they sounded so possible—all within reach."

Olivia was to be wed in two months. She had met Les when she was sixteen, and he soon began to mention marriage. They had decided to have a holiday wedding, so Olivia could be a Christmas bride. On that warm morning in October, Olivia spun around the room, singing along to the phonograph. "It won't be long 'til my ship will be sailing," the song's main stanza declared. The doorbell rang. She opened the door and saw a tall, skinny man in a dark suit standing on the porch. Olivia thought he looked like a skeleton.

He announced that he worked for the board of health. Olivia invited him inside. The agent moved to the couch, sat down, and cracked open his briefcase. He studied something inside the case, then glanced up at her. Olivia grew aware of the silence, and of being alone with a man she did not know. She wondered where her sister had gone.

The man said that he had instructions to escort Olivia to Kalihi Hospital.

"I got scared," Olivia recalled. "My parents were not around. Then he told me it was a leprosy hospital. I got icy cold. My whole body stopped working. I couldn't talk. I couldn't think. It was the worst day of my life. I was never going to be the same again—ever." Believing she would vomit, she ran to the bathroom. After the nausea passed, Olivia searched frantically beneath the sink for the bottle of disinfectant her mother kept, intending to drink it and kill herself. But the cabinet was empty.

When she emerged, she saw that her older sister and one-year-old niece, Lenora, were now sitting with the man. Lenora spotted Olivia and ran to her, but Olivia pushed the girl away. "See, I already felt like a 'leper,'" she later wrote, "belonging no longer with the ones I loved."

The agent who had appeared at Olivia's door was well-known to many people in town: they called him the bounty hunter. That morning he drove Olivia and her mother to the office of one of Kalihi Hospital's consulting physicians. The doctor used the blade of a razor to excise samples from Olivia's shoulder, back, and earlobes. When he returned from his lab, the doctor informed Olivia that he had found no trace of leprosy bacilli. There was a problem, though. Earlier that month a doctor had taken samples from Olivia while she was at a different hospital to have her tonsils removed. Those snips did show leprosy bacilli, the doctor explained. Olivia now had to be examined by the full panel of board physicians.

The panel convened at 9 A.M. every Friday. Olivia arrived with little hope. "I knew already that the Wheel of Medicine was grinding me down and there was nothing I could do to change my situation," she later wrote. "Nothing." A nurse had Olivia remove her dress and led her into the room where the doctors waited. Climb onto that, the nurse said, pointing to a wooden platform that rotated, like a lazy Susan. One of the doctors was a young man, not much older than Les. When she climbed onto the platform, Olivia used her hands and arms to cover herself. The doctor remarked to Olivia that her hair was lovely. Then the nurse began to slowly turn Olivia, like an item on display. She shut her eyes until it was over and staggered from the room.

In an adjacent office a secretary fed a form letter into a typewriter: "We, the undersigned, having been duly designated as the examining physicians to examine __________, and to determine whether or not, in our opinions, said person is a leper, do hereby report that, in our opinion, <u>said person is a leper</u> as shown by full and complete examination of said person made by us on this date." The secretary aligned the paper and in the blank spot typed *Olivia Robello.*

Olivia went to the bed in the infirmary she had been assigned, and crawled beneath the sheet. She was terrified—afraid of the other patients, afraid of what was going to happen to her. She wanted to weep, but she was unable to get started. "My heart felt so heavy and frozen," she later wrote, "it seemed like I was never going to cry again."

A few days later a nurse took Olivia to have her entry photograph made. The board photographer had strung a white sheet in the hospital yard and set his camera in the soft light that filtered through the trees. When he was ready, the photographer turned to Olivia and asked her to smile. "You stupid man," Olivia recalled thinking. "I am dying on the inside and you want me to smile." He snapped the shutter twice, once with Olivia staring into the camera and another with her standing in profile. The nurse held a small board beside Olivia's cheek in the photograph, marked with the date, October 19, 1934, and a number: 3306.

After ten days nurses moved her to a room in one of the dormitories. Narrow shelves were nailed to the walls, and the furniture was an iron bed, a tiny table, and an uncomfortable wooden chair. The dorm had no janitorial staff, so the residents served as maids. Olivia took a job in the sewing room, repairing sheets and making pajamas for the hundred or so patients at Kalihi. She earned $9 a month.

Les had been on the mainland during this period, arranging his discharge from the military and making plans for their wedding. Olivia was too ashamed to phone him with the news. "I felt so sure that if he knew, he would run away as fast as possible," she later wrote. By the time he returned to Honolulu, Olivia's family had fled to a different neighborhood, to escape the inevitable stigma. Les asked the family's former neighbors if anyone knew what had happened to Olivia. He canvassed the neighborhood, yet failed to discover what had become of his fiancée. Eventually he stopped coming around.

Olivia knew it was likely that he would decide she had rejected him or had found another man. He would be hurt and angry, she knew, but that was preferable to his knowing the truth. "I never saw him again," Olivia wrote. "Let him hate a lost love."

Her family moved three times, but the neighbors always learned about Olivia's leprosy. The board insisted on screening relatives of patients for the disease several times each year, and the bounty hunter would appear at the Robellos' door to remind them of their exam. Usually he drove a gleaming sedan with a government insignia stenciled on the side, but even when he made his rounds in an unmarked car, everyone knew his purpose. Although the board no longer credited chaulmoogra oil therapy, it now recognized that some cases of leprosy did become inactive, and the patient posed no risk. Such cases were paroled. As part of Lawrence Judd's initiative the board had "humanized" the language of exile; "parolees" were now referred to as "patients on temporary release." By late 1933 the board had 145 temporary releases on its books. At the time, an agent named Cecil Kiilehua monitored their location and retrieved them for their quarterly exams. If a patient on temporary release vanished or escaped from Kalihi, it was Kiilehua's job to hunt him or her down. When a Kalihi patient named Robert Purdy fled, Kiilehua and eight Honolulu police officers swarmed the city bus he was riding, locked Purdy in handcuffs, and threw him on a steamer for Molokai. Purdy swore in a subsequent affidavit that he had been kidnapped and "as an American citizen" demanded "humane, and not forcible, treatment."

Kiilehua, a social worker named Ethel Paris, and several other board agents kept track of every known case of leprosy in the population, both active and inactive. Under the new board Judd had assembled, early detection of the disease had become a priority. Every month the Kalihi medical director, Dr. Newton Wayson, gave workshops for general practitioners on how to identify the disease—patients, the reluctant stars of such events, called the clinics the Monkey Show. The spectacles served their purpose, however. "Hawaii's physicians, as a group, are for the first time becoming proficient in the diagnosis of leprosy," the board reported. An epidemiologist began to map the contagion of every patient, tracing the possible point of first infection and identifying "individuals, familial or otherwise, who have been exposed . . . and who in the future should be observed for the earliest signs of the disease."

The web of statistics showed that leprosy spread within some families more easily than in others. In 1932, Dr. Wayson had scrutinized the genealogy of 420 patients and found 30 percent had multiple cases among their family members. Seven decades later, genetic predisposition to leprosy would be positively established. At the time, however, the board simply knew that children born into a family with a history of the disease seemed at higher risk. If it could shield such children from exposure, the number of cases in Hawaii would likely drop. The board had hired Ethel Paris in part to monitor children in the homes of current or former patients. After Olivia entered Kalihi, the board added her relatives to the watch list.

Olivia's leprosy, however, was not part of a family cluster. She had suffered a random infection with no traceable origin. None of her relatives had the disease, and none subsequently caught it—her infection seemed like a lightning strike from a cloudless sky. But the specifics of the case meant little to the family's neighbors. One worked at Kalihi Hospital, and when Olivia's mother encountered her in town or at the store, the neighbor would say, Watch out, her daughter has leprosy. Shoppers in the store would begin to back away.

Within a year of her daughter's diagnosis, Olivia's mother had neared the brink of a nervous breakdown. When the board's agent arrived for his inspections, Olivia's father chased him from the property, screaming that the man had already stolen one of his children from him. Olivia later wrote that her older sister, Mary, seemed unbothered by the gossip, but it shamed her younger sister. Once during a double date she offered her lipstick to the other girl, who recoiled and refused to accept it. Everyone knows your family is diseased, the girl announced. When this sister later married, she kept Olivia a secret from her new husband, and sent word to Olivia that if she had anything to tell her, to route the news through Mary. "I think she disowned me," Olivia later wrote. Eventually Olivia's mother also began to selectively hide her daughter's existence. When the family finally settled on a street where no one suspected them, Olivia later wrote, her mother "never told any of her new friends about me again."

In the two and a half years she spent at Kalihi Hospital, Olivia Robello ran away a half dozen times. She usually returned on her own, before the bounty hunter had a chance to pursue her. The escapes were excursions, an assault on the sameness of isolation. Often another young female patient snuck away with Olivia. They would take wire-cutters and snip a hole in the fence and then bend it closed behind them. The girls would take the bus into downtown Honolulu to see a movie or linger in the aisles of Liberty House, the city's largest department store. Sometimes they simply strolled along the sidewalks, watching people.

Late in the day Olivia would creep down Puuhale Road and climb back through the fence. Then she would walk toward her dorm, acting nonchalant. The guard had usually spotted her, however. He would alert the matron at Kalihi, a hard-nosed woman named Bessie Clinton. "Special Incidents," reads Clinton's report of one of Olivia's escapes. "The 'French Leave' of Olivia Robello . . . was the first of its kind since Oct. 22nd of this year." After another escape Clinton cornered Olivia and warned her that if she continued to escape she would be sent to Kalaupapa. The settlement was thick with male predators, Clinton insisted, men who lived to abuse young girls. "When you get off the boat," Olivia recalled Clinton saying, "those men will lasso you."

During the early summer of 1937, Olivia again snuck away, her absence detected at the nightly bed count. The next day a staff member handed her a notice from the board—she was being sent to Molokai. On the morning of June 29, Olivia waited for the right moment, then brazenly walked out the front gate. She ran to her parents' house. The police had already phoned. If they discovered Olivia in hiding at the house, her father could be arrested, charged with violating Section 1193 of the penal code, and fined hundreds of dollars. She decided to return voluntarily. Her father was driving to Kalihi when a patrol car approached. Olivia scrambled from her father's vehicle. The cruiser pulled alongside, and the officer told Olivia to climb in.

Olivia asked whether the policeman was nervous about having a leprosy patient in his patrol car—it might become tainted.

"Be quiet," he replied gently. "Get into the car and we'll take you back."

The police handed her over to Bessie Clinton. The next morning Olivia pinned her hair in a shining wave, put on a long, dark skirt and blouse, and stepped into a pair of white high-heeled shoes. She looped three flower leis around her neck, farewell gifts from friends. At 11 A.M. guards began to load the patients for the trip to the docks. "Suddenly I loved my ugly mattress and my room was so dear to me," Olivia wrote. "I wanted to hold the railing so they couldn't take me away." At the time, patients at Kalihi believed exile was a death sentence. "You could see grown men cry because they were going to Kalaupapa to die," one recalled. Another remarked, "Going to Kalaupapa was the end—the finale—you weren't expected to return again to society. It was a one-way trip. You went there to die."

In her memoir, Olivia described what happened next. Guards led her and the others getting transferred that day to the stern of an interisland steamer, the *Hawaii.* The vessel rode heavy in the water, its deck level with the pier. Someone had strung a canvas tarp along the aft portion of the deck, to keep the exiles from view. She stood on the deck, trying not to cry.

"Olivia," someone called through the canvas. Then a corner of the tarp peeled away, and her uncle John's face appeared.

"Don't worry," he told her. "You will come back."

As the steamer churned away Olivia carefully lifted the garlands from her neck. Honolulu was receding, the buildings blurring into patterns of brick and glass. She flung the leis overboard. The flowers floated in the harbor, riding atop the wake. If they made it to shore, Olivia told herself, it was a sign that her uncle's words were true—*You will come back.*

When the *Hawaii* reached Kalaupapa, it anchored two hundred yards offshore. Although smaller craft could slide into the expanded wharf, interisland steamers were too large. Olivia landed in the old way, aboard a launch rowed over the waves. The pier had concrete steps carved to the waterline, and the oarsmen tied off at their base. Olivia stepped free of the launch and mounted the stairs. Then she spotted them. The men were on horseback, just as Bessie Clinton had warned, and their saddles dangled lariats. A dozen cowboys surrounded the landing, watching the women arrive.

Before the crossing, Olivia had hatched a plan with a young Kalihi patient named Jim, who was also being transferred. They would claim to be a couple, so that no one would see Olivia as fair game. The ruse must have worked, she decided, since none of the men had lassoed her and dragged her to his home. Later, Olivia learned that a man named John Breitha had hoped to do just that. Breitha confessed that when he saw her climb to shore, he had fallen in love. John Breitha was a lean, deep-voiced horse trainer who had once handled polo ponies and now operated the settlement chicken farm; he was seventeen years Olivia's elder. By the time Breitha revealed to Olivia the story of his instant infatuation, the two were already dating. "Of course I didn't believe him," Olivia later wrote. She married him anyway.

Six months after Olivia arrived at Kalaupapa a writer named Ernie Pyle spent two weeks in the settlement. "Many of the things that have been written about Kalaupapa are not true," Pyle soon reported. "There is drama here—intense, awful drama. But it is not the sinister, cursed place that fiction gives us. It is a human place. Once you are here, there is no mystery about it." Pyle was thirty-seven years old and traveled the country for the Scripps-Howard newspaper chain, writing a six-times-a-week column for its syndicate. Flirting with alcoholism and unhappily married to a woman crippled by depression, Pyle expressed an affinity for stories of hardship and exile. "I have no home," he once wrote. "My home is where my extra luggage is, and where the car is stopped." He would earn the Pulitzer Prize for his coverage of the war already building and die just afterward, shot by a Japanese sniper.

The plane that delivered Ernie Pyle to Kalaupapa sat ticking in the heat on the rolled-grass airstrip. Robert Cooke drove up in his new Chevrolet sedan. Pyle slid in and the superintendent aimed the car toward the village, a mile and a half away. Almost immediately Pyle noticed the graves. Headstones appeared several hundred yards shy of the lighthouse and hugged the wandering shore almost to the edge of town. "There is cemetery after cemetery," Pyle wrote. "They adjoin, and they stretch on and on until they impinge upon your consciousness like the beating of a funeral drum."

By 1937 more than seven thousand people had been exiled to Molokai, and the majority had never left. The bones of thousands of exiles remained, in neat plots in Kalawao or Kalaupapa, and in unmarked places now overgrown or forgotten. Almost every week another patient was interred, buried on the day he or she died because the settlement lacked a morgue. Sometimes the deceased was placed on the table in the settlement's pool hall and a brief wake held. Relatives rarely reached the island in time, so patients took turns as mourners, knowing they would be repaid in kind.

Cooke kept driving. Just where the graves stopped, the town's buildings began: a Mormon church, jail, social hall, Catholic church, visitors' quarters, warehouse, store, gas station, Protestant church, hospital. Residents lived in small private cottages, or in one of four group homes. Young men resided in the new Baldwin Home, the name transferred from Kalawao. Single women and girls occupied the Bishop Home, where four Franciscan nuns, successors to Mother Marianne, still maintained order. Elderly and blind patients resided in a dormitory called Bay View Home, and single men lived at McVeigh Home. Married couples dwelled in scattered cottages with three tiny rooms, a bath, a kitchen, and a railed porch overhung by flowers. "Kalaupapa is not regimented in appearance, like an institution," Pyle wrote. "You see no rows of cottages all alike, and no great prison-like dormitories. Nothing is crowded together. There are gardens and vacant lots and shrubbery and space everywhere."

A hundred patients owned automobiles, lifted to land from the barge by the massive boom. The board required no driver's license, insurance, or plates. Sometimes a constable caught a blind patient driving happily, steering by instructions his passenger shouted. Ten partly paved streets crosshatched the village, and dirt roads sliced across the peninsula to the airfield or to Kalawao. One rutted road angled up the western flank of the Given Grave, ending at the crater's lip; lovers parked there on moonlit nights. The entire spit of land held only about twelve miles of road, but some residents drove them every day, circling until the spotted deer and wild pigs crept from the brush and froze in the headlamps, eyes aglow.

Robert Cooke installed Ernie Pyle in a private room in the staff compound, a fenced collection of cottages across the path from the parade ground. On the bathroom sink sat a fat bottle of rubbing alcohol. "After we've prowled around we always use some of this on our hands," Cooke explained, splashing his palms. When Cooke departed, Pyle washed and slipped into the narrow bed, the sheets acrid with fumigant. "The darkness was terrifically still," Pyle wrote. "No sound was in the atmosphere but the roar of the ocean on the rocks, and the occasional crow of a patient's rooster. The pali was darker than the night."

During his long tour in 1937, Pyle paced around the village, trying to capture the mood. Usually Cooke or a member of the settlement staff accompanied him, pointing out the sights. On movie night he visited the theater, sitting in the low balcony, where patients were not allowed. The film that evening was *San Quentin,* starring Pat O'Brien. "It doesn't seem an especially apt picture to be showing here," Pyle wrote. "But the patients laughed and reacted the same as anybody else." In his columns from Kalaupapa, Pyle wrote of the myth "that there is an atmosphere of dejection and impending doom in the Settlement. It is, as a matter of fact, a rather happy community. Not exactly hilarious, but there is gayety here. The patients have their clubs, they play games, they form cliques and gossip around, they have dances, they go to the movies three times a week, they even have cocktail parties."

The board enforced no daily regimen. Residents were free to do whatever they liked with their days, or nothing at all. If a patient wanted to work, the board found a job and paid a wage, which at the time averaged $18.50 a month. Some worked as fishermen or stockmen, others as carpenters, clerks, and nurse assistants. A sunny-tempered man named Kenso Seki trained himself as a barber, practicing on the thirty blind patients in the settlement, "so if I make a mistake, they no worry," Seki later explained. Another patient ran a small bar, selling bottles of beer and glasses of wine. The patient David Kupele ferried mail and the movie reels up and down the cliff; if the weather was bad he would send the mules up the trail by memory. Over time, Olivia worked as a dishwasher and a waitress, and as an orderly in the hospital. Later she helped John with the chicken farm.

Almost every day as he walked, Pyle saw the manager of the settlement store, a patient named Shizuo Harada. The store sat opposite the wharf, next to St. Francis Church. The single-story building had a shallow porch where residents gathered to talk. Harada was a dapper, keen-eyed athlete who had been diagnosed with leprosy in 1925, three weeks after graduating with honors from the University of Hawaii. "For a long time I kept on reading in economics and agriculture, which is a sort of hobby of mine," Harada told Pyle. Now he read only magazines. He said, "There isn't much point in trying to keep on learning."

When Cooke had introduced Pyle to Harada, the patient was suspicious. Before he agreed to answer questions, Harada later wrote, "I asked Ernie Pyle ONE favor, and that was to write the TRUTH in his column. For others have written false reports, and did us more harm than good."

Pyle would recall, "For privacy we stepped into the warehouse back of the store, and I asked some questions about the volume of sales and so on. Our conversation drifted from the store to Harada himself, which was what I wanted." Harada's leprosy had appeared as a tiny patch on the far finger of his pitching hand. The board doctor told him what it was and announced his exile. "I just couldn't believe it," Harada said. "I thought the doctors were wrong. I thought for years they were wrong." In the first decade he spent in the settlement, the disease never advanced beyond Harada's hand—he looked perfectly healthy. "But three years ago it broke out," he told Pyle, "and once it started, it came on fast." Harada was quickly disfigured. Dr. Eric Fennel, one of the board's physicians, had known Harada for years and visited Kalaupapa just after that time. "I went down to the Store and asked the first person I saw where I might find Harada," Fennel later wrote.

"I'm Harada," Shizuo had replied.

Pyle confessed to Harada that he had arrived at Kalaupapa expecting to find "a place of great gloom and dejection." And yet, Pyle said, the residents "tell me it is really a happy community, and it seems so to me." Harada replied, "Well, I guess it depends on the individual. We get down in the mouth, and then see somebody in worse shape than ourselves, and then pick up a little and say, 'It could be worse.'"

When he returned to his cottage that evening, Pyle sat at the typewriter and wrote, "I shall always have a mental picture, to the end of my days, of us sitting there talking. Sitting in chairs, face to face, not three feet apart—one 'clean,' and one 'unclean' as Harada would put it. The truth would be, one 'lucky' and one 'unlucky.'"

Olivia's work in the hospital took several hours each day. The facility was a wood-framed, H-shaped structure that stood five hundred feet back from the shoreline, facing west. Long ramps led into each ward, wide enough for wheelchairs and low steel gurneys. Rows of beds lined the walls, with room between for a table and chair. Sometimes the patients who knew Olivia from Kalihi would brighten and announce, "Hello, Olivia!" But Olivia could not recognize the person. "Even voices had changed," she later wrote. "I cried inside when they told me who they were."

One morning an elderly patient lay in her hospital bed while a nurse washed her face with a cloth. The day was humid, and warm air had collected in the corners of the ward. The patient had lived in the settlement for almost her entire life. Doctors thought she would not survive beyond the week. That morning, however, the woman seemed cheerful, even happy. One of the nurses commented on her mood, and the patient answered that she had been thinking that she would soon be in heaven. "And when I get there," she said, "I'll be pretty again."

Years later Olivia began a journal, which would later grow into her memoir. When she wrote about the women in the hospital, Olivia exclaimed how they "just a few years ago [were] beautiful in body and full of hope—like me. Look what happened to them." She added, "This disease was really unstoppable."

Olivia filled the pages with her thoughts and with news from the world outside, gleaned from the radio or—in time—her television: a hurricane in Tahiti, earthquakes in China, war in some place that she would never see. She talked to her journal as if it were a living thing, a friend who had joined her on Molokai. Olivia recalled how someone poisoned twenty of John's white leghorn chickens, and how they lost more birds after someone snuck a dog into the coop. Then John was asleep one Sunday morning, after Olivia left for mass, and someone poked a pistol through the bedroom window and squeezed off a shot. The bullet missed John's head, exploding his feather pillow. Constables tracked down the shooter, a forty-six-year-old patient named Sacarias Decalan. He had worked as a handyman at the Breitha chicken farm, but Olivia had fired him after he had tried to kiss her. Decalan told the constables that he was in love with Olivia. He reasoned that if John Breitha died, he might have her.

Police charged Decalan with assault with the intent to maim. The circuit judge held the trial at the top of the cliff, with a folding card table as her bench. "There, in the open air, overlooking one of the most spectacular views in the world," reported the superintendent, "the defendant upset the proceedings by pleading guilty." Decalan served five months in the tiny Kalaupapa jail before the judge suspended his sentence. She released Decalan into the superintendent's custody. "Since he, like all the other patients in the settlement, was already in my custody," the superintendent wrote, "the problem was settled with a minimum of inconvenience to all."

After she married, Olivia had begun to imagine having a child with John. The board had no official policy preventing patients from becoming pregnant, although it took steps to dissuade such births. In 1931 the legislature had ruled that any child born to parents with leprosy was a ward of the state until the age of twenty. The Kalaupapa nursery had closed in 1930, and from that date newborns were typically removed to the Kapiolani Home for Girls or the Kalihi Boy's Home. If the child showed signs of infection, it was transferred to Kalihi Hospital—about 10 percent of children born in the settlement eventually developed the disease. By 1937 the board had 129 healthy children of patients in its care. Believing a home environment preferable to the orphanages, the board decided to close both facilities. It instructed Ethel Paris to find the children foster homes. She placed the last child on October 5, 1938.

Sometimes the foster home was located by the child's parents, utilizing what the board described as a "grapevine system." When a patient in Kalaupapa became pregnant, word went out among friends and extended family, asking if anyone would take the child. Stigma slammed many doors, however, and the board closed others; it disallowed some adoptions by relatives in the belief that it was disrupting "family clusters" of disease. Often the child went to strangers, with unhappy results. Many were beaten, used as servants, and abused. One girl, identified in records only as D, was removed from three foster homes after being repeatedly mistreated. When one foster mother became angry with the eleven-year-old, she screamed that D's parents were lepers, and that no one would ever love her. A social worker visited the girl and found her cowering in a corner. "I wish I were a dog sitting in the sun," the girl had said. "Then maybe I would be happy."

Olivia knew that if she had a child, the board would take it from her. It was possible, however, that they would allow Olivia's family to raise the boy or girl. Then when the child was old enough he or she could come to Kalaupapa, and Olivia could talk to her child through the fence that bisected the visitors' house. A number of children who had been born in Kalaupapa later returned to see their parents—the board allowed healthy children who were sixteen or older to make brief visits. Patients would hurry to the pier on visiting days, to meet the arriving steamer and glimpse their sons and daughters. Despite the emotional hardships, some patients elected to have large families. One couple had twelve children, all born in the settlement and subsequently taken from them to be raised by foster families or in one of the government homes.

Such situations had eventually become a sensitive issue for the board, however. Over the years, politicians in Hawaii had frequently pressured the board to outlaw births in the settlement. "In permitting the physically diseased to breed and propagate their kind," declared the Report of Special Committee on Leprosy Investigations, "we are vitiating and blocking the likeliest of all paths of human progress, and if individuals that are diseased could be made to remain childless, nothing would be irretrievably lost to the race." During the previous decade, a number of eugenics programs had taken hold in the United States; by 1933 twenty-seven states had passed laws allowing "unfit" citizens to be made infertile, and sixteen thousand sterilizations had been performed. "Isn't the time now ripe for [Hawaii]?" asked Dr. Nils Larsen, medical director of Queen's Hospital. "Is it possible that this community will continue not to take legislative measures to correct the evil that indiscriminate breeding brings upon us?"

Larsen advocated sterilization for the criminally insane, and any person whose intelligence tested below a certain level—"morons," Larsen termed them. Persons with leprosy also made the sterilization list, in part for economic reasons. "The 140 [children] that are now in the Kalihi Boy's Home will cost the taxpayers $1,053,500," a legislative committee had reported in April 1932. "This money can be saved by a simple operation." Declared the *Star-Bulletin*, "HAWAII PAYING HIGH PRICE FOR UNFIT CITIZENS."

Although the legislature did vote to establish a eugenics board, Lawrence Judd managed to derail the policy as it applied to residents of the settlement. In its place, the board began to strongly encourage patients to volunteer for surgical sterilization. One tactic was to set sterilization as a condition for a visit to Kalihi Hospital. Since many residents were desperate to visit Kalihi, either for elective medical care or to be near their families in town, they agreed. "You had no choice," one resident later recalled. "That's the only way you could go. So I submitted and I went and I saw my only son."

On the pages of her memoir Olivia would state, "I am of the opinion that there are two reasons for the good life: love and bringing up children. Otherwise, life has no meaning at all." She added, "Parents in Kalaupapa were denied the joy of bringing up their children." Some couples never had the opportunity—among the men who had been sterilized was John Brietha.

Part Four

How can the prisoner reach outside except by thrusting through the wall?

Herman Melville, *Moby-Dick*

A resident's beach house, on Kalaupapa's western shore.

Attack

(Population 349)

The disease struck Bernard Punikaia when he was six years old. A school nurse had noticed the blemish on his cheek and alerted Bernard's mother and the board. One week later the bounty hunter delivered Bernard to Kalihi Hospital. "I was taken into the examination room, stripped naked, and placed on a little revolving platform," Bernard would recall. "I was spun around slowly, to be observed from all angles by various doctors in that room." When it was over, a nurse led him into the yard. The photographer framed his shot while the nurse held a slate with the number 3441. He tripped the shutter. Bernard's denim overalls are rolled to his waist, exposing thin arms and a narrow, freckled chest. Someone has drawn a wet palm across his brow, flattening his thatch of flyaway hair. A faint red streak marks the right corner of Bernard's down-turned mouth, and he wears a searing expression of sadness.

Moments later, a young male inmate appeared at Bernard's side to escort him to his room. Bernard's mother had been allowed to stay with him until that instant, and she swept him into a last embrace. Then a nurse pulled her away and she climbed into a car. "I stood along the roadside as they drove her off," Bernard would recall. "Then I was alone. And so it began."

On Sundays his mother would come to see him. The visiting area at Kalihi was a pair of low fences with a hibiscus bush between. "Although the separation was just three or four feet," Bernard later said, "it seemed like it was thousands of miles away." At Kalihi, children spent their weekdays in class at what was called Mount Happy School. The school was part of a grouping of buildings formed around a central yard, defined by four gravel drives. One corner held a basketball court, another the baseball diamond, a third was given over to a playground. Across the lane from the playground was Building 13, a small cottage with three single rooms and a bathroom. "This is known as the detention cottage and is set apart for disciplinary purposes," plans for the facility read. Bessie Clinton determined who was locked in Building 13.

Physicians at Kalihi at the time employed a variety of experimental animals, including rats, guinea pigs, mice, and rabbits. Researchers would inject them with serums derived from the blood of horses, goats, donkeys, and healthy human hearts. Some animals suffered identical treatments as the patients—doctors used them as controls. The cages containing the animals were marked with patients' names and numbers. Bernard soon began to sneak into the research building, to look at the caged rabbits. In time he found the one that carried his name. He visited his rabbit often, to see how it was faring. Sometimes whatever the doctors had done had made his rabbit sick; on other visits it seemed just fine. "They lived and they died," Bernard later recalled. "If they made it, we believed that we would too."

The waters of Kalihi Bay fronted the leprosy hospital on two sides, to the west and south. Across the bay lay Hickam Field, the army's bomber base. Just past Hickam was Ewa Field, where marine pilots operated. Immediately between Hickam and Ewa spread the natural anchorage that had been called the Pearl Lochs and was now known as Pearl Harbor. Aircraft flying from downtown Honolulu to the heart of Pearl Harbor passed over the hospital yard. In a report warning of the facility's vulnerability, one official wrote that Kalihi Hospital sat "in the shadows of the bomb-release line."

Just before dawn on Sunday, December 7, 1941, five Japanese midget submarines approached Pearl Harbor from the southeast, skirting Kalihi Bay. At 6 A.M., 183 planes took off from a fleet of 31 Japanese military vessels, 200 miles directly north of Oahu. One hour and fifteen minutes later, 170 additional Japanese planes lifted off from the decks of the carriers. The focus of their attack was the 96 American warships within Pearl Harbor, army and navy planes parked at Hickam and Ewa fields, and various military installations elsewhere on the island of Oahu. When the Japanese formation reached the island's northern tip, it broke in multiple directions, intending to converge on Pearl Harbor from the north, south, east, and west. Attack plans called for torpedo planes to strike first, followed by high-level bombers, dive-bombers, and the fighter planes. A communication error muddled the sequence. The aircraft struck simultaneously, from every direction. The first bomb fell at 7:55 A.M.

Bernard was playing in the Kalihi Hospital yard, biding time until his mother's visit. By 1941, Bernard had lived at Kalihi for more than four years. Hospital staff considered him uncommonly bright, unruly, and a natural leader: even the older boys at Kalihi seemed to follow the eleven-year-old. Years later, Bernard would remark: "I was not shy, but always outspoken. Sometime, that got me into difficulty, because I would speak my mind about different matters. I guess that part of my personality formed very early."

Bernard saw a dark shadow race across the grass and looked up to see a streak of metal. Then the bombings began. In the sky to the west columns of smoke started to rise, visible over the tops of the hospital buildings. At 8 A.M. a U.S. communications officer sent an urgent radio message to the chief of naval operations, the commanders in chief of the Atlantic and Asiatic fleets, and all the forces at sea: AIR RAID ON PEARL HARBOR. THIS IS NO DRILL. Ten minutes later a bomb from a Japanese plane struck the battleship *Arizona,* punched through the forecastle, and detonated five hundred pounds of ordnance in her forward magazines. The explosion blew out windows a mile away and erupted a five-hundred-foot-high fireball. A thousand men died almost instantly.

The concussion from the blast washed as an oily wind over the hospital yard. Patients ran for the chapel, believing it safe from attack. Sixty patients resided at the facility, including twenty-five children. Hospital staff herded the boys and girls into the church and told them to pray. Bernard remained outside. He scrambled up a tree for a better view of the events. Just then a fighter plane bore down on the hospital. "The plane was very low, just above the treetop," Bernard later recalled. "I could see the pilot's face looking down at us, smiling. His bullets made a double line, starting about one hundred and fifty feet from my tree, thumping and kicking up dirt onto the fishpond beyond. I remained in my hau tree, high in its branches, hidden in the leaves."

Aircraft strafed the roads leading to Pearl Harbor, targeting servicemen as they rushed back after a night of leave. Japanese high-level bombers quickly destroyed 188 American planes and disabled Hickam and Ewa fields. Servicemen hid in aircraft hangars and died when the buildings were blown apart. At one base the cooks closed themselves inside their freezer and were killed by the vacuum of a nearby bomb. In the neighborhoods around Kalihi people hid in their closets, curled into bathtubs, and held pillows over their heads. Drivers slammed on their brakes and dove under their cars; others sought safety in drainage pipes and beneath bridges. Soon the planes began to pepper residential streets, circling in widening loops. Panicked American soldiers finally began antiaircraft fire, but in their confusion many gunners forgot to light the fuses on the artillery shells and launched missiles over the city that exploded on impact, opening holes in the streets as far as Waikiki.

Elroy Malo was shooting marbles when he heard the screaming. The Malos lived in a simple two-story house in a neighborhood north of Punch Bowl. Elroy was seven years old and called most often by his Hawaiian name, Makia. He looked up and saw neighbors streaming past the house. A bridge spanned the narrow valley that separated the neighborhood from the rest of town, and from its high reach it was possible to see Pearl Harbor. People were running toward the bridge. Makia started in that direction.

He spotted his mother and father among the neighbors. "A noise caught my attention and I looked over to my left," Makia later recalled. "You know when bullets hit the ground? That's what caught my attention."

Makia watched the bullets advance toward him. Suddenly somebody scooped him from his feet. A moment later Makia was on the floor in his kitchen, huddled with his parents as fighter planes howled by outside. As the panic spread, people phoned a Honolulu radio station to ask if the bombings were a drill. "This is the real thing," the announcer yelled. *"The real McCoy!"* In Kalaupapa, Olivia had just returned to her cottage from church. She clicked on the radio for some company. "*This Is the Real McCoy*!" it shrieked.

Burning oil covered Pearl Harbor, and hundreds of bodies floated in the flames. During the two hours of the attack, 2,403 persons had been killed, 68 of them civilians. Another 1,178 had been wounded. Buses were commandeered as ambulances, and casualties brought to Queen's Hospital and other triage sites. Dr. Forrest Joy Pinkerton, former head of the board, filled his car with bags of plasma and raced them to emergency rooms around the city. When supplies ran out, Pinkerton went on the radio and asked people to donate more. Nurses emptied bottles of Coca-Cola and used them to store the blood.

The board immediately began to discuss what to do next. No one at Kalihi Hospital had been hurt in the attack, but the board believed the facility was still at risk. It decided to transfer most of the adult patients to Kalaupapa, and all of the children. For more than a decade the board had been housing minors with the disease at Kalihi Hospital, and few children resided in Kalaupapa. The settlement school was long-since closed, and facilities that had been established as orphanages, such as the Bishop Home for Girls, now served older residents. At the time of the Pearl Harbor attack only seventeen of the more than three hundred patients at Kalaupapa were minors.

The boys and girls from Kalihi Hospital landed at Kalaupapa off the steamer *Hawaii,* the largest single arrival of children in settlement history. Bernard rode one of the first launches and scrambled up the stairs of the pier. Prior to coming to the settlement, few of the children had seen patients badly disfigured by leprosy. Such patients were typically sent to Kalaupapa, and at Kalihi most people still appeared fairly healthy. About half of the residents in the settlement also showed no serious signs of the disease. In addition, the community held more than fifty nonpatient residents, including nurses, administrators, physicians, electricians, gardeners, carpenters, and other staff. Thus it was possible to walk the main street of the village without ever encountering a disfigured person. Yet it was equally possible for a person to glance up and be abruptly confronted by the disease in its most terrible form.

Newcomers reacted differently to the scene. Some nurses lasted only hours, then begged to use the telephone, to arrange an escape. Olivia, on arriving, had forced herself to smile pleasantly through the day. One board physician, George Tuttle, later confided to a visitor that his first morning in the settlement had exceeded his imagining. "He had to go home in mid-forenoon and go to bed," the visitor wrote of Dr. Tuttle. "He was absolutely sick." Among the crowd waiting to see the boys and girls arriving from Kalihi were many disfigured patients, including mothers long separated from their own children. In their excitement, the women rushed forward in greeting. As Olivia later recalled, "Those kids turned and ran as fast as they could go."

The board opened a school for the children, with classes from eight in the morning until noon. One of the teachers, a woman named Cecelia Akana, had taught public school in Honolulu. While brushing her hair one day she had noticed that her forehead was numb. "I sterilized a needle, pricked my skin, and could not feel it," Akana later recalled. "I knew what I had." Akana had said good-bye to her two young daughters, then told her husband, "I give you your freedom."

Every day after school let out, the children scattered around the village. Shizuo Harada would find them in his store, hidden underneath the counter. Dr. Norman Sloan would drive home at lunch and spot them peeking out from the tall grass, playing cowboys and Indians. The boys formed a Boy Scout company, Troop 46. "THEY SCOUT ALONE," one magazine reported, recounting the activities of the unusual group. The troop learned to tie knots and make fire from sticks, and once a year held a camping retreat in Kalawao. The boys pitched their tents on the grounds of the old leprosy investigation station, where Emma Gibson's home once stood.

As the war progressed, the board imposed gas rationing on patients and halted cash sales at the settlement store. Residents carried quota cards instead: $6 a week for food, $32 a year for clothes, $20 a year for "spending money." When he inventoried supplies, the superintendent determined they had enough to last eight weeks. But if shipping lanes were cut, there would be trouble. The board flew an air raid siren in from Honolulu, and workers began to carve a bomb shelter, but abandoned their labor when they hit volcanic rock. They covered roofs with camouflage instead, and painted a large red cross atop the hospital. The village civil defense officer gave the

Boy Scouts fat sticks and told them to hike the shoreline; he hoped enemy submarines would mistake the children for soldiers. A captain from the army's chemical warfare division arrived and outfitted every resident with a gas mask—"with the exception of eight patients," the superintendent reported, "whom we were unable to fit on account of facial deformities." The captain took molds of the patients and told them he would send custom masks.

Keepers extinguished the lighthouse, and navy pilots practiced bombing the strip between the light and the Given Grave. Sometimes their aim was off, and shells thumped in the yard of McVeigh Home, scattering residents. Several airmen crashed on maneuvers, including Ensign Earl Hansen, who plowed his plane into the surf off the lighthouse point—residents rowed out to pluck him from the water. Eleven patients registered for the military and volunteered for the front; the government replied that they would be of more use growing vegetables in the settlement's victory garden. The Kalaupapa flower nursery, run by Harry Murakami, also turned toward produce. "The flowers have not been neglected," the board reported, "but there are times when a head of lettuce is more beautiful than a rose."

A rumor spread that the Japanese had captured topside Molokai and would come spilling down the cliff. Another suggested that frogmen lurked offshore, awaiting dark to land. One story claimed that the Japanese planned to use Kalaupapa as a staging ground for a second Honolulu attack. Another insisted that saboteurs had already infiltrated the settlement—they were hiding in the Given Grave. When a supply shed was burglarized of dynamite, a general panic ensued. Then a resident sheepishly came forward with the missing explosives and explained he had merely hoped to blast fish for his supper.

Shizuo Harada posted bulletins with war dispatches, so patients without radios could follow the news. On February 19, 1942, these reported that 200 people, including 175 of Japanese descent, had just been shipped under guard from Honolulu to California. Their banishment had been planned for months. In the hours after the Pearl Harbor attack, army intelligence officers, the FBI, and Honolulu police had begun to apprehend men and women of Japanese, German, and Italian heritage. In time they arrested 1,569 island residents. Authorities imprisoned 1,250 in Sand Island Detention Camp, which was the board's former quarantine camp, across from the old Leper Detention Station. Military authorities created a colony on the marshy island, segregating internees by sex and nationality. Then they began to exile the prisoners. The ships left Honolulu and curled past Molokai, heading for the mainland; 700 prisoners had been sent to the California internment camps by the end of 1943, along with 930 relatives who agreed to go as helpers. On the porch of the settlement store residents discussed the matter. No one deserves to be treated so cruelly, someone remarked. Shizuo Harada agreed.

One winter afternoon Harada pinned a fresh clipping to the bulletin board, though it held no military news. It concerned a doctor whom some of the oldest patients knew, Arthur Mouritz. The settlement's former physician had spent his declining years in Honolulu, living in a cottage a few miles from Kalihi. Mouritz passed his days writing, a solitary expiation. He poured the bulk of his effort into a rambling examination of the history of leprosy, which he titled *The Path of the Destroyer*. When the massive volume failed to sell, he became convinced that the government was suppressing the book. In time he turned paranoid, drew his shades, and sat in darkness, leaving the doorbell unanswered. Mouritz began a journal on lined brown paper, scratching in pencil as he quietly went mad. "RATS IN ATTIC," he recorded one day; on another, "WAX CLEARED FROM EAR." He reported that people were attempting to break into his house, phantoms who tapped at the windows. He composed lists of the dead he knew, hundreds of entries long, the names typed neatly and amended in smudged lead. The ledger ran for pages. He left a single space unfilled. Mouritz died December 1, 1943, at age eighty-seven. "Dr. Mouritz's life was an unselfish one," his obituary read, "and one of good deeds."

Olivia discovered that she knew many of the boys in the settlement from her years at Kalihi Hospital. There they had always been underfoot, dragging her into games. One of her favorites was Henry Nalaielua, a witty four-foot-tall sprite who used to beg toast from her breakfast tray. Henry had entered Kalihi in 1936 as a ten-year-old and had two sisters who preceded him into exile. By the time Henry reached Kalaupapa, both of his sisters were dead.

The boy Olivia now encountered was seventeen, handsome, and amusingly droll. He ran with a boy the others called Bataan, and sometimes Bernard—although Bernard was five years younger. Olivia saw Henry everywhere in the settlement, always up to something. "If people were going out fishing," Henry later recalled, "I'd go even if I didn't want to. Hiking, hunting, swimming, anything to be active. It was the only way to keep my mind off things, to stay hopeful and release the anger." He added, "Otherwise, the anger would kill you."

On movie night Henry was usually first through the door, and when the Scouts started for Kalawao, Henry often took the lead. Henry and Bataan clambered around the Given Grave, hunting the eight-inch dummy bombs the navy fliers dropped. He rode up the cliff with David Kupele, ferrying movie reels and the settlement mail. If the weather was poor Henry retreated indoors, and his friends would find him sketching in an artist's pad, or lost in a paperback by Zane Grey. One day the Sacred Hearts priest in the settlement loaned Henry a biography of Father Damien. When he handed it back, Henry announced, "If he can go through all that, I can handle it too."

Once a month the children in the settlement went before Dr. Norman Sloan for inspection. If a boy's fingernails were dirty, Sloan gave him a spanking, but the primary purpose of the visits was medical. Henry usually sailed through these checkups; he had developed only a mild case of leprosy. Other children were not as fortunate.

When Dr. Sloan opened the file that the board had sent with Bernard, he would have seen a record of misery. Bernard had the disease in its most devastating form, and at Kalihi doctors had passed him through many of the standard protocols: serums, pills, and thick needles of medicinal oil. "I remember getting experimented on," Bernard later said. "I remember the chaulmoogra injections, extremely painful." No matter what the doctors tried, however, Bernard had continued to decline. When the children were being readied for the voyage to Kalaupapa, doctors had debated if it was worthwhile for Bernard to go—he seemed likely to die within months. But he had sailed with the others to Molokai, and for a time in Kalaupapa it appeared that Bernard was improving. Then he abruptly turned worse.

The board had long ago determined that leprosy was not fatal. The disease engendered conditions that could result in death, however. These included nephritis, an acute inflammation of the kidneys, and "leprous laryngitis," in which the throat and nasal passages ulcerate until the person is unable to cough them clear—unless relieved by a tracheotomy, the patient suffocated. Perhaps the most perilous event was a reactive attack known as *erythema nodosum leprosum.* During these episodes, the "temperature sometimes reaches 105 F . . . the patient is acutely ill, and skin lesions tend to exacerbate," wrote Dr. Norman Sloan. Crops of "transitory nodules" appeared, scarlet red and "extremely tender to touch." Nodules swarmed the "ears, alae nasi, cheeks, and forehead," Sloan wrote, "but they may occur anywhere." Legs and feet might turn crimson, and the limbs could harden like wood. As the reaction deepened, the features deformed, as had happened to Shizuo Harada. Many patients did not survive these events, and those who did sometimes wished that they had not. Physicians referred to such attacks as "lepra reactions." Patients employed more descriptive argot, and when a case of leprosy turned especially disfiguring they spoke of it as "blowing up" or "exploding." Not long after he arrived at Kalaupapa, twelve-year-old Bernard began to explode.

Like a Pebble Thrown

(Population 312)

John Early managed to free himself a final time from the Louisiana Leper Home. By then he was in his fifties, hollow-cheeked and wild-eyed. The home was now under federal control, officially known as U.S. Public Health Services Hospital #66—everyone called it Carville. Patients at Carville frequently won parole if doctors decided their leprosy had turned inactive. When Early's disease appeared to be arrested, physicians pronounced him cured and let him go. At the news that their tormentor no longer posed a threat, legislators in the nation's capital "heaved sighs of relief," the *Washington Post* reported. The paper added, "The name of John Early will go down in history as another of those men who, either voluntarily or unwillingly, have aided materially in the advancement of medical science." Across the Pacific, the *Advertiser* offered that Early "goes forth now to mingle among his fellow man."

His liberty lasted only months. Early's leprosy reactivated, and agents returned him to Carville. There he spent his days scribbling political pamphlets, jeremiads of protest against the policy of exile. The last such publication, forty-eight pages long, offered himself as crowning evidence of man's inhumanity. He titled it "John Early: World-Famous Leper."

Early died in April 1938, at age sixty-four. He was buried with military honors at the National Cemetery in Baton Rouge, Louisiana. In Washington, D.C., congressmen who had been the target of Early's furious rhetoric had already approved vast changes for his asylum. They routed millions of federal dollars to Carville, intending to create, one government official wrote, "the finest institution of its kind in the world." Construction began just months after Early's death. The subsequent transformation was so striking, one resident later wrote, "old-timers could not believe their eyes." Improvements included modern research facilities, an increased scientific staff, and a new medical director, a young Tulane graduate named Guy Faget. "He wore spectacles, a small toothbrush mustache, and had the poise of a bantam rooster," one resident wrote. "But he was above all a brilliant physician, and a scientist of imagination and courage."

Prior to his tenure at Carville, Dr. Faget had worked at a tuberculosis hospital in the high New Mexican desert, battling *Mycobacterium tuberculosis.* In Louisiana, his focus shifted to *Mycobacterium leprae.* Faget soon noticed that the two bacilli behaved similarly; the germs even resembled each other, when properly stained and examined through a microscope. Faget began to wonder if they shared vulnerabilities as well. At the time, tuberculosis researchers were working with a number of powerful antibacterial drugs known as sulfonamides. One drug from this synthetic group, Promin, showed encouraging results when tested on guinea pigs infected with tuberculosis. The physician conducting the experiment published the findings in a medical journal. Faget kept current on his former field. He wrote the company that made Promin and requested a supply.

Sulfones, as the drug family to which Promin belonged is commonly called, can be dangerously toxic. When Faget started six volunteers at Carville on the medication, their bodies' violent response quickly halted the trial. Faget tinkered with the mix. Then one of his staff, Dr. Raymond Pogge, combined Promin with small amounts of glucose, calcium, vitamin B, and penicillin—a concoction residents referred to as the "Pogge cure-all cocktail." Adverse reactions mostly vanished. Patients now "flocked to try it," a Carville resident wrote. Faget began giving daily intravenous injections of Promin. The results were exciting: "Slowly . . . open sores began to heal, nodules disappeared, and the patients began to feel almost cured," reported one Carville physician. "Cautious after the innumerable failures of the past, the medical staff refused to jump to conclusions. But the patients knew. We had reached a turning point."

Initially, doctors at Carville limited sulfone therapy to persons with lepromatous leprosy, the most active form of the disease. Dr. Faget revealed to *Time* magazine that though sulfones could not repair existing damage, they stopped "even the most hopeless cases in their tracks." Instead of a slow daily decay, the health of a patient held steady, then began to improve. When Faget took snips from his volunteers and examined them by microscope, he saw sample fields littered with dead and dying bacilli. Of the twenty-two patients initially placed on Promin, Faget reported that five soon showed no trace of leprosy bacilli, ten had the germ in smaller numbers, and six remained the same; only one patient had grown worse. "Now it is possible to report," one of Faget's colleagues wrote, "that the use of promin in the treatment of leprosy results in improvement in all major, chronic manifestations of the disease."

In a short time, 179 Carville patients were taking Promin, and another hundred were on Diasone and Promizole, two similar sulfone-based drugs.

Almost every case improved remarkably. Doctors signed release papers for more than a tenth of Carville's population, crediting the work of the drugs. A patient who used the name Stanley Stein reported that the effect of sulfone therapy on Carville morale was "striking." Stein added, "Chaulmoogra oil had been nothing like this."

Stanley Stein's legal name was Sidney Levyson, although to spare his family shame he no longer used it. A charming, elegant Texan, Stein had dreamed of being a Broadway actor. He was sent to Carville in 1931 and had entered its gates clutching copies of the *New Yorker* and *Theater Arts.* When the staff assigned him a cottage, he christened it Wit's End.

Once settled at Carville, Stein founded a newspaper, *The Sixty-Six Star.* "It seemed to me that a local weekly devoted to common problems and common interests would relieve the tedium of our lackluster existence," he later wrote. Stein had a storyteller's eye and harvested material freely, reporting on everything from what the patients were served at Thanksgiving—oyster cocktail, stuffed Spanish olives, roast western turkey, candied Puerto Rican yams—to Carville's other wonders, which came to include a nine-hole golf course, a private lake stocked with bass, a ballroom, and a theater with reclining, cushioned seats. Photographs in the *Star* showed exam rooms gleaming with equipment, teams of white-smocked scientists, and grand research buildings of light stucco encircled by mossy oaks. News of medical breakthroughs filled Stein's paper, as did his editorials insisting that the victims of leprosy had value. "We realize that we will reach only a small portion of the reading public," Stein wrote in volume one, number one, of the *Star,* "but, as a pebble thrown in a pond causes ripples in an ever-widening circle, our message will be carried." Under Stein's editorship, the paper grew into arguably the most influential publication on leprosy in the world, read by medical professionals and also laymen. At a time when the population at Carville totaled less than four hundred patients, the *Star*'s circulation exceeded fourteen thousand.

Copies of the *Star* reached Kalaupapa by mail. Residents would collect on the steps of the store and pass around the pages. Kalaupapa was now a well-run, comfortable place, but in contrast to the fabulous reports emerging from Louisiana, it seemed almost a pesthole. Everything at Carville sounded superior. Reading about the facility, many Kalaupapa residents became despondent with envy. Then Stein printed the news about Promin.

"Our patients were naturally eager to try it," reported Dr. Norman Sloan. When patients burst into his office waving the latest issue of the *Star,* Sloan would calmly explain that the board was concerned about the toxicity of the drugs. It had decided to wait before attempting treatment with sulfones. After the drugs had been thoroughly vetted, the board might then make them available. Sloan wrote, "Preliminary work on such a drug should be done by an institution with adequate clinical and medical staff and equipment—a situation that has never existed at Kalaupapa." By the spring of 1942, doctors at Carville already knew that sulfone therapy idled the disease within weeks of its initiation. For someone hurtling toward disability and death, Dr. Faget reported, every day without treatment was a lost opportunity.

During the early morning hours of April 1, 1946, an earthquake ripped the ocean floor in the Aleutian Trench, twenty-five hundred miles north of Hawaii. The resulting tsunami slammed into Kalaupapa just past dawn. Drawing backward the length of a steamer, the sea fell flat and then heaved forward, gathering speed. It swept over the peninsula. "We thought it was the end of the world," Henry recalled. "The whole airport area went under. Water rose up the stairs of the store and covered the ball field." Olivia had just finished brushing her teeth when she heard someone scream, "Tidal wave!" She thought the person was playing an April Fools' joke.

Along the cliffs the ocean climbed fifty feet high. Glancing out his cottage window, the superintendent watched in shock as his office building was "spun off its foundation and [deposited] in a different direction." Surf overwhelmed the village's western flank, setting sail to a dozen cottages. Homes "floated into the ocean," one amazed patient reported—but by luck no residents were still inside. The wave drove two hundred yards up a riverbed and shattered the pipes that supplied Kalaupapa's drinking water. One patient sprinted to the shore with his movie camera, to capture the turmoil on film. Much of the tsunami's impact landed on the dead. "The long line of cemeteries was left a shambles," wrote one resident. "Massive grave stones were carried hundreds of feet from their original foundations, long lines of fences and stone walls were destroyed. Fortunately no graves were uncovered." That evening, when authorities in Honolulu tallied information from the other islands, they counted seventy-nine dead and fifty-one missing. After a quick canvass the Kalaupapa superintendent reported, "There was no loss of life nor serious injury."

Workmen were still repairing graves when a plane touched down on the sodden airfield. It carried the settlement's first supply of sulfones. Even at this late date, more than four years after sulfones were introduced at Carville, the Hawaiian board of health was leery to begin their use. Promin's strength made Dr. Sloan nervous, and he disliked the delivery method. "I have never been satisfied with the idea of intravenous therapy," he wrote. Preferring to introduce an oral sulfone, the board had initially decided to give patients

Promin's sister drug, Diasone. "But we could not get it!" Sloan reported. "Requests for experimental supply were refused, and it was not yet on the market." Turning reluctantly to Promin, the board placed its order. The manufacturer replied that they had just consigned their full inventory to Carville. Three more months elapsed.

Sloan commenced sulfone therapy in the settlement in May 1946. He chose six test patients. After swabbing their skin with alcohol, he slapped until a vein swelled, then injected five grams of Promin. "Nausea is common," Sloan wrote of the side effects. "Vomiting may occur. Some patients . . . sneeze regularly after each injection." But the results showed promise. "Appetites improve and patients gain weight," Sloan reported. "Nodules flatten and small ones disappear; long standing ulcers heal; eye, nose, and throat conditions improve." Within twelve months 70 percent of the patients were taking sulfones. "Oh joy, for most of us," Olivia wrote. "The medicine worked!"

Although Sloan cautioned that it was too early to "speak of a 'cure,'" he did admit that the drugs furnished "real optimism regarding eventual solution of the ages-old problem of leprosy." His colleague Dr. Eric Fennel was less reserved. "Dr. Sloan is conservative and not carried away by enthusiasm," Fennel wrote in the aftermath of a three-day inspection of the settlement. "But for me it all was more than startling." Fennel had gone to the Kalaupapa store to visit Shizuo Harada, whom he had last seen a year earlier. "He was heavily nodular at the time," the doctor wrote, "and it must have taken hours to apply all the dressings to the ulcers of his hands and fingers." After a course of sulfone therapy, however, Harada's face had become "relatively smooth" and Fennel reported that "there was not a single dressing on his hand—only new, pale epithelium." He wrote, "Now I believe in miracles; almost a beneficent God."

As quickly as it could, the board upped the number of patients on the medication. Introducing several additional sulfone types into their arsenal, physicians pushed the success rate for the drugs to more than 80 percent. "Patients develop a sense of well-being, have more energy, sleep better, and in general feel they have a new lease on life," one physician wrote. In almost every case, Sloan observed, "bacilli disintegrate and eventually disappear." By the end of 1948, Sloan and the board's physicians had finally concluded that Dr. Faget's breakthrough of six years earlier was legitimate. They wrote, "Now . . . we are ready to agree with others that a new day has dawned in the history of leprosy."

Bernard Punikaia was now seventeen. Germ action and leprosy attacks had left him permanently damaged. Much of the injury had taken place in the past five years. His eyes were weak, feet and hands impaired, and his handsome features changed. "My early days at Kalaupapa were mostly a matter of suffering," Bernard later recalled. "They are not cheerful memories. It was a very serious sickness I had. I was literally covered with raw ulcers, my hands, feet, face. I became so hypersensitive to touch even the changing of dressings caused extreme pain." When sulfones arrived, doctors began to pump Bernard full of the drugs. "The turning point in my life was 1948," he later said. "I started to improve and get better. After I got well, I did all the things I was not able to do as a young kid, a lot of sports, hiking, hunting—everything." Sulfones, he announced, were "miracle drugs."

In the spring of 1949, Dr. Sloan and the board medical staff published their findings regarding the first wave of sulfone therapy in Kalaupapa. They wrote: "Hope for complete arrest of the disease . . . and for avoidance of deformity and blindness is much greater when treatment is begun early."

Makia

(Population 290)

Makia Malo was walking home from school when he decided that his foot hurt. He limped the rest of the way. In the kitchen he filled a bucket with warm water and Lysol, balanced his way into the yard, and began to soak the foot. Makia's father, William, examined his son's right heel the next morning. Before Makia knew what was happening and could squirm free, his father clicked open a pocketknife and started to dig into the heel. A piece of cinder popped out. His father cautioned Makia to be more careful where he stepped. Then he added, Don't mention this to anyone.

The following fall, Makia's eighth-grade teacher called to him in class.

"Elroy," Mrs. Moore asked. "Why is your eye so red?" She said that it looked bloodshot, as if someone had poked it.

Makia answered, "I've been swimming a lot."

A few days later William Malo came into the yard while Makia was playing. We're going to see the doctor tomorrow, he said. Makia asked why.

Don't ask questions, his father replied.

On the morning of September 26, 1947, Makia climbed into his father's car. They drove to the offices of Dr. Edwin Chung-Hoon "We went inside and sat down and my dad still hadn't said why we were there," Makia recalled. William Malo told his son to sit, then vanished with the doctor into the back. A short time later he emerged. Chung-Hoon called Makia into the room.

Several years earlier, Dr. Norman Sloan had formalized the board's exam procedure. "The entire skin surface, including the soles, should be examined in good indirect daylight," Sloan wrote. "Male patients should be naked. Women may be permitted a two-piece undergarment (shorts and brassiere) or similar arrangement, which can be moved as needed." Sloan had typed an outline of the exam.

GENERAL

1. General Health
2. Nodules
3. Macules
4. Diffuse thickenings
5. Anesthesia
6. Ulcerations
7. Muscular atrophy
8. Thickening of nerves
9. Paralyses
10. Loss of hair
11. Loss of perspiration
12. Contractions
13. Other deformities

LOCAL

14. Eyes
15. Ears
16. Nose
17. Mouth and throat
18. Lymph nodes
19. Hands
20. Feet
21. Genitalia
22. Internal organs

LABORATORY

23. Bacteriological examination
24. Biopsy

Chung-Hoon usually began by testing sensibility. Sloan recommended using "two test tubes containing water . . . one cold—preferably ice cold—the other hot, but not over 107 F., as one does not wish to test *pain* at this time. The patient closes his eyes (if malingering is suspected, a blindfold may be used, or hands tested behind his back) and he is asked to say 'hot' or 'cold' when touched. When the test is positive, some patients will guess, but wrongly; others, perhaps more conscientious, will say, 'I can't tell' or 'I can't feel anything.'" To assess feeling, Sloan suggested using "a feather, a wisp of cotton, a fine camel's hair paintbrush, or a twist of paper." To test pain the doctor used an ordinary pin pushed through a wooden tongue depressor: "The patient is touched lightly, and asked to call 'sharp' or 'dull.' Sometimes one may draw the point of the pin lightly over the anesthetic area and see the patient wince as sensitive skin is reached." Such a method, Sloan advised, "may be of value in small children."

The doctor held the lobe of Makia's left ear between his thumb and index finger. "You'll feel a little nick," Chung-Hoon said. He sliced an incision five millimeters wide and three millimeters deep. Makia yelped. Then Chung-Hoon told Makia he could go sit with his father. An hour later, the doctor joined them.

Chung-Hoon announced that William Malo showed no bacteriological evidence of the disease. Makia, however, was infected with leprosy. He would have to enter Kalihi Hospital immediately.

William asked the doctor if it was possible for Makia to be sent straight to Kalaupapa. He explained that two of Makia's brothers and his older sister were patients in the settlement.

Chung-Hoon answered, The plane leaves next Friday.

In 1939, after Makia's sixteen-year-old brother Bill was sent to Kalaupapa, the board social worker began to visit the Malo home frequently. Three years passed before the next child showed signs. One day, however, several small blemishes appeared on Earl Malo's left forearm. Mary Malo handed her youngest son a sweater and told him to wear it at school, but a teacher noticed Earl's symptoms. Makia rode with his parents when they delivered Earl to Kalihi. "We drove through the gates and stopped in front of a long building," Makia remembered. "Dad gave him his small suitcase. And we left him there. He was only seven."

The board transferred Earl Malo to the settlement twelve months later. In 1945 Makia's older sister, Pearl, joined Bill and Earl in Kalaupapa, leaving her two young daughters with Mary Malo. Makia remained at home. His parents did not mention his absent siblings. Nor did they speak about leprosy. Kalaupapa, Makia believed, was merely a place where Earl got to ride his bicycle all the time. Makia was jealous of the bike, which his parents had purchased for Earl.

When he realized that he was going to Kalaupapa, Makia felt excited. "I didn't know what leprosy meant," he recalled. "It was just a word." He imagined the trip would be like a vacation. He wondered if his parents would now buy him a bike too. Makia began to assemble the things he would need for the journey: comic books, a slingshot, some Indian arrows that he had fashioned from sticks and tenpenny nails. On Thursday evening his mother cooked a special meal, but Makia was uncertain if his departure was the reason. "My family never explained anything," Makia later said.

In the morning they drove to the airport. The board had contracted Andrews Flying Service to transport patients to Kalaupapa; the flight lasted twenty-five minutes. A pilot beckoned Makia toward the tiny plane. Makia waved at his father, standing near the hangar. Then Makia hugged his mother. "Mama's tears were falling on my face," Makia recalled. "And she whispered, 'Oh God, why me?'"

As the plane approached Molokai, Makia lifted in his seat and peered out the window. Below him spread a small village, with empty narrow streets, a hundred scattered cottages, and a white-steepled church. The plane bounced twice and rolled to a stop.

Makia looked for Pearl. He waited nervously for an hour, sitting in the shade. Then there she was—clattering toward the airfield in a rusted jalopy streaked with orange paint. With Pearl was a strange man and a boy he did not recognize. Pearl shouted hello. He ran to her and she took him in her arms. Makia then heard the boy speak—it was Earl. "Then I started to cry," Makia later said. The man with Pearl was her boyfriend, Johnny. Everyone climbed into the car, and Johnny started for Kalaupapa.

As they drove, Makia began to see men on horseback, wearing bandannas around their necks. Some of the women also wore handkerchiefs. "I thought, what a town," Makia later recalled, "filled with cowboys and cowgirls!" Pearl explained that the kerchiefs covered openings that Dr. Sloan had made into their throats when the people had difficulty breathing. "I wasn't frightened by what I learned and saw," Makia later said. "And I didn't feel any shame or stigma. I knew that on the outside, leprosy was not something you should talk about. But here, on the inside, there were so many of us. So leprosy was just a way of life. I just began to live another life."

Several months before Makia arrived at Kalaupapa, the superintendent had resigned. Confronted with the vacancy, the board had proposed to former governor Lawrence Judd that he take the position. Judd surprised them by accepting. On a clear morning in June 1947, he arrived at Kalaupapa. Judd was now in his sixties and beginning to stoop with age. "I wouldn't say he was good-looking," Makia later wrote, "more leaning to the other side. But he was a nice man." Most of the community had assembled to greet his plane. Cars idled in rows two deep along the airstrip, and when Judd's head popped into view, a chorus of horns erupted. "Never will I forget the first few hours of my return," Judd later wrote. "I fumbled for words to tell them, without sounding presumptuous, that I had come to live among them in the hope that I could better their lot."

Judd had not visited the settlement since the advent of sulfone therapy. "I was struck by the fact that the younger men and women looked almost normal," he wrote. "The ravages of the disease had finally been arrested." By now doctors had raised the sulfones' success rate to 92 percent, and would soon clear almost a hundred patients for temporary release. A majority of residents "could have returned to their homes," Judd observed, "without danger to others." Yet many had refused to leave, and Judd understood why: "They preferred to live out their remaining years in the pleasant peninsula where life was semi-secure, and where nobody stared." The most reluctant patients were longtimers in the settlement, having endured since the turn of the century. "Their readjustment to normal life would have been difficult," Judd reported, "often quite impossible." Judd believed he could help ease the transition for many of the younger inmates, however. If existence within Kalaupapa were made as commonplace as life outside, their daily experience would become normalized, and they might be more willing to brave reentry into society. As he walked with his wife, Eva Marie, heading for the superintendent's cottage, Judd announced, "I'm going to shake this place up. I'll probably get tossed out eventually. But I'm going to make changes fast, before [they] can catch up with me."

By 1947 the government had been exiling people to Kalaupapa for eighty-one years. Evidence of its attitude toward patients abounded. "Wherever we went," Olivia later wrote, "there were signs telling us where we could or could not go, and what we could not touch. . . ." Residents were prohibited from mailing money to relatives, for fear of tainted bills. Outgoing mail was disinfected. If a visitor toured Kalaupapa, a policeman accompanied him, to keep patients and nonpatients apart. The board banned photography on the peninsula, unless for scientific purpose. If a patient departed the island, his luggage was steeped in formaldehyde; if the patient left by air, the pilot dusted him with fumigant. One government committee recommended that persons working with patients receive hazard pay, since "submarine rescue, experimental diving, handling of lepers, [and] demolition of explosives" were fraught with equal danger. In Kalaupapa, rules forbade physical contact between staff and patients, and the cottages, dining areas, and offices of government personnel were off-limits. Even the chapel at Bishop Home had protective dividers. They had been made to look decorative, Olivia recalled in her memoir, but "its real purpose was obvious—to keep patients separated."

Within days of his arrival, Lawrence Judd started to hammer away at the barriers. He dispatched work crews to collapse the twenty-foot-tall fence that cordoned off the guest quarters, and rip down the wire mesh dividing the visitors' house. Judd removed dozens of "No Patients" signs and sent a worker up the cliff to unhinge the gate that sealed the trail. For decades a railing had split the administration office, separating the superintendent's desk from a bench where patients sat. "I tore it out," wrote Judd. The changes had an immediate effect. "This place isn't like a jail anymore!" one patient exclaimed to a reporter. Olivia cataloged the transformation in her memoir. "You cannot imagine how much a simple thing like a fence and railing coming down meant to me," she wrote. "That gave us a feeling that we . . . almost belonged to the human race again."

Judd next decided that residents required something to do with their days—treatment for their "souls as well as their bodies." He invited the Lions Club to found a Kalaupapa chapter and arranged for a beauty salon to begin operating in the settlement, offering "instruction in cosmetology, hairdressing, and personal grooming," as one paper reported. Judd flew in psychologists, social workers, and vocational counselors, who helped institute classes in auto shop, cooking, carpentry, typing, and shorthand. When Eva Marie Judd formed a crafts club, twenty residents signed up, including Makia and Earl Malo. Makia joined the theater group, and one of the community's bands, which Lawrence Judd occasionally conducted. Although Makia looked forward to the excitement of the concerts, he never actually learned to play his alto horn. During performances he would mime the action while Judd urgently whispered, "Blow, boy. *Blow!*" "Mr. Judd was a man of *great* compassion," one patient later wrote. "He was a man ahead of his time."

Makia had moved into a cottage with his siblings. The house had two bedrooms and a kitchen and a closet-sized bath. One day shortly after he had arrived in Kalaupapa, Pearl barged into Makia's room, dragged him from bed, and steered him toward the door. Makia was saddened to discover that his vacation included school. He trudged to class, held in a small building near the village center. "Perhaps the only difference between these students and those in other schools," a teacher explained to a reporter at the time, "is that along with their mid-morning snack of milk and crackers they must take their vitamins and sulfone." The board had outfitted the tiny Kalaupapa school with materials donated by the public system. In Honolulu, Makia had been in the eighth grade, and a promising student. Opening the battered textbook Mrs. Akana handed him, Makia recognized it as the book he had used in class four years earlier.

When Mrs. Akana released the class at the end of the day, Makia began to explore Kalaupapa, kicking rocks along the quiet streets and stepping shyly aside if another resident walked by. Some of the men and women he passed were startling, and Makia tried not to stare. "For Mama taught me always to be kind," he later wrote, "to respect." He came to a small store run by a patient named Katie. "The dark yawning inside of the open door intrigues me," Makia later wrote, in a poem he published describing his first days in Kalaupapa. Makia noticed a face in the door. "An almost featureless face," he wrote. "Then it smiles." The patient crooked an arm and waved.

"Come, boy."

Makia began to cry. "I am but a boy of twelve," he would write. "And not prepared." The man had a ravaged voice, "like that coming out of a grave calling."

He said he wanted to treat Makia to ice cream, to welcome him to the settlement. Makia entered slowly and sat at the table. The man brightened with the company and began to tell stories. He explained that he had been in Kalaupapa for a very long time. In the beginning, his face was smooth and his body strong. He hiked and he swam, and his hands could play the guitar; he had a fine, clear singing voice. All that was now gone, the man said. He showed Makia an awkward grin. Makia ate his ice cream. Then the man announced: "You know boy, first time I come Kalaupapa I look juss like you."

By the autumn of 1947 all but a dozen men, women, and children in the community were undergoing sulfone therapy. To gauge their progress, patients presented themselves monthly to Dr. Sloan. The goal of every patient was for the leprosy bacillus to vanish from their bodies. Sloan took samples, called smears, to determine their status. "We seek the organisms where it seems likely they will be found," Sloan wrote. Using a scalpel, he would make a small notch in the skin, then angle the blade and scrape a tiny amount of tissue from the underside of the cut. "Bleeding is avoided if possible," Sloan advised. The smear was fixed with acid and stained. Sloan then slid it beneath his microscope. Every smear yielded a bacteriological index. These ranged from 0.0 BI, in which no bacilli were found, to 6+ BI, where a thousand or more bacilli crowded the microscopic sample field, suggesting trillions of germs beyond view. To be classified as an inactive or "negative" case, a patient's smear had to test as 0.0 BI for twelve consecutive months.

That autumn Olivia had had her first smear tested. Sloan announced that it was 0.0 BI. The next test also showed no leprosy germs, as did one the following month. After nine more examinations Dr. Sloan told Olivia that her leprosy was inactive, and that she had earned temporary release. Olivia decided to go see her family. "I packed my clothes and then I took my bags to the hospital fumigation box," Olivia wrote. When she donned the treated clothes, the chemicals made her flesh sting. The disease had left Olivia almost unmarked; she looked the same as she did on the day she had entered Kalihi. At the Kalaupapa airfield, the pilot assumed that she was a guest who had been touring the facility. He asked how long she had been visiting.

Olivia smiled and replied, "Thirteen years."

When the plane landed her sister Mary was waiting. Olivia asked to see the new supermarkets, and the high-rises in Waikiki. The family had a celebration that evening. In the middle of her Welcome Home dinner Olivia burst into tears. "I was so homesick," Olivia later wrote. "Imagine that. I had come to Honolulu and found out that, after all, my home was in Kalaupapa where Johnny was."

* * *

Less than a year into his appointment, Lawrence Judd began to issue "tickets of leave" to select patients. "It would be a humane action," Judd wrote, to allow residents "to make sightseeing trips" aboard one of the Andrews Flying Service planes. Many patients had not left Kalaupapa in decades; most had never flown. The idea was that the pilot would circle the island and then land again at Kalaupapa. Since the patients would have no contact with outsiders, Judd could not see the harm. "So we loaded several patients into one of the small planes," he reported, "and gave them a whirl around Molokai."

Soon the tours extended farther, to Maui and Hawaii. These longer jaunts required refueling. "That gave me an idea," Judd wrote. "When the pilot stopped . . . would it not be a good idea for relatives of the patients to be on hand to greet them?" Judd began to phone ahead to families of patients, and the sightseeing tours now included brief airport reunions. "Without," Judd later stressed, any "physical contact." Soon more than a hundred patients had flown. "Then," Judd wrote, "the roof fell in."

During the most recent legislative session, lawmakers had decided to dissolve the Board of Hospitals and Settlement and hand its duties back to the board of health—the body that Judd, as governor, had decided was too political. One board member was a physician named Marie Faus. When Dr. Faus learned that these "dangerously diseased patients" were making airplane excursions, she demanded they stop. Faus also insisted that the current governor "censure" Lawrence Judd. Then Dr. Sloan weighed in. The doctor had long advocated that Kalaupapa function foremost as a treatment hospital, with strict but necessary rules. Judd, however, seemed to allow patients to do as they pleased. Upset at the disregard for board procedures, Sloan declared that if Judd remained at Kalaupapa, he would quit.

Inevitably an "intolerable situation" developed, as one board physician reported. "The friction between the medical side . . . and the administrative side has become so unbearable that certainly, Kalaupapa is not large enough to hold both Mr. Judd, an ex-politician, and Dr. Sloan, an eminent leprologist." Both men insisted the board decide who was to remain. A majority of patients backed Judd, and Shizuo Harada wrote to the governor informing him of their feelings. The settlement medical staff aligned with Sloan and threatened to resign if the doctor lost the power struggle. "That would be one of the worst calamities that could affect our lovely islands," Dr. Eric Fennel wrote. "And with real success just around the corner!" He added, "The decision will be up to the Board of Health—God help it."

The board chose Sloan. "If I am not wanted here," Judd announced, "I won't stay. I have never stayed where I am not wanted." Serenaded by a choir of more than a hundred patients, Lawrence and Eva Marie Judd climbed into a small prop plane and flew from Molokai. Some time later, Lawrence received a telephone call from an official in Washington, D.C. The man oversaw the appointment of governors for the territory of Samoa. He asked, Would Judd like to be a governor again? Judd replied, Yes, I would. When the paperwork was completed, Judd boarded a flight for Samoa, landing along the way in Fiji. Across the channel from the Fijian capital of Suva was an island called Makogai, site of a leprosy settlement. Judd asked to visit the island. There he encountered a group of anguished Samoan patients who "pleaded to be allowed to return . . . to be near their families, instead of being condemned to perpetual banishment," as Judd later recalled. "I could make them no promise," he wrote. But he felt hopeful that he could secure their release. "After all," Judd remarked, "I was now governor." A few months later, a U.S. Navy ship stopped at Makogai, collected the patients, and carried them home.

When You Start to Make a Fist

(Population 243)

Henry went to Dr. Sloan's office twelve times in 1949. Every smear showed a 0.0 BI. He hurried to the Baldwin Home and threw his belongings onto a sheet, then tied the corners. "I was like a hobo from some movie," he recalled. Later Henry confessed, "I was scared as hell." He was twenty-three. When word of his release circulated among his family, one of Henry's uncles offered a place to stay. The relative lived in a small town on the northern side of Oahu, about twenty miles from Honolulu; he owned the local bar.

By January 1949 the board had granted temporary release to 204 Kalaupapa residents. Of the men and women eligible to leave, 52 chose to stay in the settlement. "There are many reasons why," explained Dr. Fennel. "They have a good home, good food . . . and are away from prying, hostile, fearing eyes." Unschooled in the minutiae of immunity and bacterial indexes, the public disliked the idea of patients running loose. "Do you want your children in a crowded movie house while some [patient] sits next to them?" a housewife asked in the *Advertiser*. In rebuttal, a resident wrote: "Mrs. Weltmir, it is your hysterical fear upon a subject of which you apparently know very little that is dangerous." Commenting on a score of such reactions, the board remarked, "Unfortunately, no 'educational sulfone' is available to change the attitudes the public holds toward the disease."

Newly released patients were often traumatized by their experiences outside. "It is in this stage in many cases that the hopes of a new life are broken, and the patient is thrown back into despair," one leprosy specialist wrote. "He returns back to his family; he tries for employment, but he is met with fear and hostility. He produces the certificate which states that he is not infectious, that his disease is cured, but his prospective employer points to the clawed fingers, to the hairless eyebrows or collapsed nose and says, 'That means leprosy.' He may say that he would like to employ this man, but that his other employees would leave, or that the customers would not come to his shop." Discussing the pitfalls that awaited him, a patient observed, "They have some sort of program for prisoners when they are through. That would be good for us." The board recognized that there was little it could do, however. Describing for a reporter the upcoming release of an "attractive girl in her twenties," one board physician remarked, "[We] know that the success or failure of her return to society will depend quite a bit on the acceptance Mary gains from the public. The sulfone drugs made Mary well. Society's attitude can keep her happy."

Henry discovered that his uncle's town was smaller than he had expected. Everyone seemed to know his story. When he passed the open door of the bar he imagined that gossip hung in the air, to resume when he passed out of sight. Henry soon moved to Honolulu, seeking urban anonymity. He told the board that he would like to attend art school. There is no such thing, they replied. Eventually Henry joined a construction crew, assembling furnace boilers. He lived with his older brother, and in the mornings he would pull on his coveralls, travel to the worksite, and wriggle into the machines, to piece together the strange-looking parts. Henry's leprosy had done little damage; its past existence was apparent mainly on his left hand, which he usually tried to conceal.

Many evenings after work Henry went to the movies. He held his money in his right palm, and learned to peel bills with his thumb. The ticket seller grew accustomed to Henry, buying a single for the 10 P.M. show. The movies let out at midnight, when the sidewalks were safe in shadow. Henry liked to arrive a few minutes late and take a seat in the back row, near the exit. If someone sat too close, Henry would often leave. It didn't matter much—he could come back the next day. After a year of this, Henry's brother stopped him at the door.

"Henry," he said, "what are you doing with your life?"

Henry replied that he worked. And he went to the movies.

"Do you see any friends?" his brother asked. "Go on dates?"

No, said Henry.

"Henry, you made it out," his brother remarked, "but you might as well be back inside."

Henry thought about that.

One day Henry started chatting with one of his coworkers. The man mentioned that he belonged to the YMCA and often went there after his shift. He asked if Henry wanted to tag along. "That's where I started meeting other people," Henry later recalled. "Lawyers, clerks, musicians, doctors. They became my friends." An untapped charisma suddenly seemed to rise from somewhere within Henry, and he perfected a deadpan stoicism that made people laugh. He joined a community choir, and also a musical band. If he went to the movies, Henry now sometimes brought a date and strolled through the lobby before the lights went dim. Afterward they would eat and talk about the actors they liked, and in which roles their favorites had excelled. One June several of Henry's friends invited him to join the Kamehameha Day parade. He made his way along the crowded avenues waving, smiling at the strangers who waved back. Later, Henry found himself crossing the same streets the parade route had taken, as he headed to the board physician's office for his regular exam. The doctor cut a sample, fixed and dyed it, and checked the smear beneath the microscope. He saw the bacilli's distinctive shape. Henry's leprosy had reactivated. He would have to go back.

For the first five years that released patients were outside, the board required them to submit to monthly screenings. If their bacteriological index rose above 0.0, the board rescinded their release and sent them back into isolation. About one in five released patients reactivated. Doctors would set to work on the returned patient's sulfone therapy, altering dosages and drug types until they again overwhelmed the germ. Occasionally they tried new medications, in untested form. One, known as B-663, effectively suppressed the bacilli, but turned the patient's skin a wine-dark red. "When you went out in public," one woman wearily admitted, "people would notice."

Some patients shifted repeatedly between active and inactive states, and entered a medical limbo. If doctors happened upon an effective therapy for the patient, they then had to repeat the yearlong smear test ordeal. "It was heartbreaking," one resident recalled. "Sometimes people would be negative [every time] and then fail the last one. So many patients broke down and cried, even the adults." One man claimed he did not require an exam to know his status. "I used to feel the leprosy germs inside me," he recalled, "bucking like a wild horse."

Every time a case reactivated, something was lost. A patient would venture outside, find a job, buy a car, sign his name on an apartment lease or mortgage. When the germ reappeared he was swiftly torn away. Years could pass before he again won release, and by then the job was gone, car repossessed, lease broken, and mortgage in arrears. Friends vanished during stretches of absence; lovers and spouses disappeared. One man left the settlement, married, and fathered a child. Then his leprosy reignited. His wife divorced him and "never let me see my daughter [again]," he later recalled, "even after I became negative."

Although many residents had no intention of leaving Kalaupapa, the idea that they could not was devastating. "A friend was leaving and I went to the airport to see him off," a resident recalled. "I watched his plane depart, and I said to myself—I'm going to die in this fucking hole." One New Year's

Eve, a patient named Hiyashi hanged herself in her cottage bathroom; her grief-stricken husband then tried to stab himself to death. "It is believed the couple was hindered in attempts to return to Japan," a newspaper reported. Another resident became unbalanced, ran screaming through the hospital, and shot a patient, who died three days later. At the time, the board followed exacting directions from the Bureau of Vital Statistics regarding deaths in the settlement. "'Leprosy' is given as the principal cause of death on all death certificates," one board official reported, "even though leprosy may have been only a contributory cause of death. Thus all persons dying of whatever cause, who have leprosy at the time of their death, are treated statistically as though dying of leprosy." The policy extended even to victims of murder or suicide, a practice that annoyed the settlement superintendent. He wrote, "This causes leprosy to bear greater weight than is due it."

On average, the board now diagnosed only thirty-eight new cases of the disease each year. In about half these people, the bacilli already tested as inactive, and the board was confident that sulfones could quickly render the remaining half negative. It announced that "no more patients will be sent to Kalaupapa," the *Advertiser* reported in 1949. Instead, newly diagnosed individuals would be treated as outpatients or held in Honolulu until their disease became inert. To accommodate this approach, the board decided to close the aged Kalihi Hospital and open a "modern" treatment facility, which could also serve as a halfway house for patients transitioning out of the settlement.

The new hospital rose on an eleven-acre plot in an area known as Pearl City, some ten miles from downtown Honolulu. During the war, the navy had housed its female reservists on the site; when the government offered the board a favorable long-term lease on the property, the board leapt at the deal. Kalihi was dismantled and "every usable" item moved, the board proclaimed proudly, including "doors, windows, and toilets." Old navy barracks were patched and painted white and green, and fitted with the Kalihi detritus. Workers dragged outbuildings and Quonset huts onto the site, then fashioned them into an office, an auto garage, a chapel, a school, a recreation hall, and a theater. When construction was complete, the board began to christen the buildings, in tribute to its distinguished past employees. One dormitory was named for Bessie Clinton, the strict disciplinarian at Kalihi. Another honored Dr. J. T. Wayson, a frequent participant in the Kalihi "monkey shows." The theater carried the name of Dr. Arthur Mouritz. And for the facility itself, the board selected the "most apt and cheerful" moniker it could imagine: *Hale Mohalu*, "House of Comfort."

* * *

Dr. Sloan maintained the patients' records in a tan-colored file, one of several copies—another was sent to Hale Mohalu. Information was usually written by hand, then typed on sandwiches of carbon paper and foolscap. Some patients had slender files, but most inmate dossiers burst with grim documentation: scribbled notes, annotated photographs, full-body diagrams with sites marked by an X.

The file that held Bernard Punikaia's history would have been fat with the story of his struggle to become well. By 1950, however, Bernard's leprosy was in retreat, and his health had stabilized. In the decade preceding sulfones 378 people had died in Kalaupapa, and the average life expectancy of a person with the disease was less than ten years. After the drugs arrived the figure shot up to forty years, and often longer. Bernard was now twenty years old, and wondered what to do with his restored life. "We can all go around nonchalantly not even realizing the things happening around you," Bernard later said. "Then all of a sudden, *bang,* you realize there are a whole slew of things that have been committed against you. And all along, you have been a happy idiot!"

Bernard decided he wanted to fight for patients' rights. "[The government's] perception of us is that we are mindless," he said. "That we are zombies, incapable of thinking, of feeling." Believing that he could help shape policy, Bernard joined Hawaii's Democratic Party and rose to precinct chairman. He captured the presidency of the Kalaupapa Lions Club, which functioned as a sort of local government for the community. After he was elected to the Patient's Advisory Council, Bernard began to pepper the board with complaints, arguments, advice and occasional praise, all on behalf of the other residents. During the day he labored on a Kalaupapa work crew, earning fifty-five cents an hour. In the evenings after work Bernard played his autoharp, sang Hawaiian songs, and studied. In time he earned his high school equivalency degree, making up for the classroom hours stolen by disease. When he got the diploma Bernard began to think about attending college, an ambition that was rare in Kalaupapa. Later a reporter visited the settlement and commented critically on the education level of the patients. Bernard responded angrily. "We aren't drop-outs," he exclaimed. "We had nothing to drop out of."

After Hale Mohalu opened, the board decided to close the settlement school. Students would be transferred to a new school on the grounds of Hale Mohalu. Most would remain at the facility for the school year, then return to Kalaupapa for summer vacation. At first Makia did not want to go. "I chose to remain at Kalaupapa," he recalled, "since I got used to the place as my home." When he discussed this plan with his family, however, they urged him to finish his education. In 1949 he moved to Hale Mohalu, and graduated from high school three years later.

During the summer months Makia would return to Kalaupapa. In time he acquired a car, a 1936 Chevy modified for island living. The doors had been removed and the sedan's rear half cut away, so that the car could function as a pick-up. Makia would load his gear and drive to Kalawao, spending the day hunting and fishing. On other days he would dive the wreck of the S.S. *Kaala*, or explore the lava tube caves, or comb the coastline for the hand-blown glass balls that had worked free of fishing nets and now gleamed amid the black volcanic rocks. In the evenings he sometimes went roller-skating with the other young people in the community, turning lazy circles on the wooden floor of the social hall. The trick was to time each revolution until you drew alongside the girl you liked, and then act as if it had happened by chance.

Makia discovered that he was interested in one particular girl. She lived in Bishop Home, with the Franciscan sisters. Olivia worked as a waitress in the home's main dining room. In her memoir she wrote, "The windows were all curtained. The tables had checkered tablecloths, oil cloth for daily use and white cloth with appropriate color trim for special days, such as Valentine's Day." Although the nuns tried to keep close watch on their charges, the sisters were getting old. When they dozed off in their chairs the girls would tiptoe past, silently cross the sloping lawn, and race into the night.

Kalaupapa, Makia later recalled, "was a small sleeping town. Everybody knew everybody." In such a place privacy was elusive. Every action drew knowing eyes, and the sense of familiarity could be stifling. Over the years residents had devised ways to create space for their behavior to shield it from their neighbors' scrutiny. Some retreated to vacation shacks, tiny boxes that faced the sea. Others blanketed their windows with newsprint or heavy drapes. Olivia had a rule to never enter anyone's house, even when asked, and to extend no such invitations herself. "I need my space," she said, "and people need theirs." A few men spent days secreted away in their automobiles; others hid in their cottages, emerging only if they required supplies. When the biannual supply barge arrived, people nosed through the pallets as they sat upon the pier, seeing what had been bought. Reporters did the same: "Thirteen pieces of furniture ordered by a patient for her cottage," the *Advertiser* announced. "Twelve umbrellas . . . 200 pounds parakeet seed, tropical fish food [and] 24 bottles of dog shampoo." John Breitha had purchased "1,093 bags of chicken feed," the paper reported, explaining that Olivia's husband "has a chicken farm and sells eggs and poultry to the settlement." The dispensary received 22,000 tablets of sulfones. And 182 cases of canned vegetables, 980 pounds of coffee, and 106 cases of fruit and tomato juice landed at the settlement store.

As workers at the store began to shelve the goods, they took care not to disturb a small arrangement of wooden roses that sat behind the counter. Beneath the roses was a plaque, painted with the name "Harada." In 1952 Shizuo Harada's leprosy turned inactive. He had earned temporary release, but had chosen to stay in Kalaupapa. "He knows he will never be accepted outside," a reporter wrote. "He says he will never leave." Harada died two years later, of pneumonia. He had spent his final days in a Honolulu hospital. His family flew his ashes to Kalaupapa, "for burial among his longtime friends," a paper reported. Someone tacked the clipping to the wall of the general store. "In Memory of Shizuo Harada," the obituary read. "Life Beat But Never Bested Him."

Every day in the summer the boys in the settlement went swimming at the pier, waiting for their girlfriends to appear on the concrete landing. "You never really dated," Makia later said. "You walked them to the movies, or went swimming. I didn't know how to land the girls. I felt clumsy." Eventually he found he was spending most of his time with the young woman from Bishop Home. It felt to Makia as if he loved her, although when he quizzed himself he found he did not know what such love entailed. Even among his family, the word was seldom used. "We just never learned to do that," he recalled. Makia knew he loved his brothers, and Pearl, and his parents. He loved his friends too: Jimmy and Eddie and Frank, whom everyone called Donkey because of his laugh. But in this new context the word *love* was powerfully strange. Also Makia thought, How could anyone love me?

After they had married, Makia tried to say the words as often as possible. But for a young couple stranded in the settlement, love could be difficult to nurture. Kalaupapa had two men for every woman, and the state of the community's unions was closely monitored. "About two-thirds of the town is laughing at you," Makia recalled, "and the others don't give a damn." One day Makia and his bride had a bitter argument, and she moved back to Bishop Home. By the time Makia decided to apologize and ask her to return, she had begun to see another man. Makia recalled, "There was always someone ready to step into your place." She ended up in a cottage a few minutes' walk from Makia, married to Henry.

Makia tried to distract himself from the loss. Fashioning a surfboard from a discarded ironing board, he spent hours adrift, not caring if a wave drove him under. "I would be crying while I was surfing," Makia later said. "I didn't give a damn if I died." Bernard helped him land a job on a settlement work crew, collecting garbage and trimming hedges, but when he missed work too often the crew boss fired him. Bernard pronounced him a fool. "I felt pain all over," Makia remembered, "and it eased only when I was drunk."

His behavior exacted a toll. A healthy person typically suffers four thousand minor injuries in his lifetime—about one per week. "The fingers and thumbs account for 95 percent of these wounds: paper cuts, cigarette burns, thorns, splinters," wrote one physician. "Leprosy patients, without the safeguard of pain, experience wounds much more frequently." Makia would return from hunting scored by branches, his shoes filled with rocks pounded deep in the soles of his feet. Fishing trips brought punctures, and swimming earned him scrapes. Even in sleep he was not safe. "Insensitive persons tend to lie on the same spot hour after hour," one doctor wrote, "shutting off the blood supply, and after about four hours of unrelieved pressure the tissue begins to die." Makia knew the hazards of his condition and tried to avoid them, but the damage happened nonetheless. It did to every patient. During one twelve-month span the settlement medical staff dressed 49,514 wounds.

In time, the injuries wrecked Makia's hands and feet. His fingers curled inward, "the way they do when you start to make a fist," he recalled. Despite years of treatments, the bacilli in Makia's body had not been arrested. When physicians encountered patients with sulfone resistance, they typically adjusted dosages and sulfone types until they overwhelmed the germ. "But they didn't work for me," Makia said of the treatments. "The disease never got any better for me."

Often when doctors tried to find a combination of drugs to combat resistant cases, the patient's system responded violently, becoming racked by scalding fevers. In a minority of patients, the drug had this effect. "It is definitely toxic," reported one board physician, "producing at times hemolytic anemia; severe itching, sometimes with allergic dermatitis; nausea and vomiting; headache; dizziness; and exacerbation of leprous lesions." The drugs could tint the skin scarlet and color the patient's urine. In a few instances the body felt suddenly molten, as if the flesh might slip from the bones. Board physicians had learned to settle such reactions with steroids. Usually, they could then work past the impasse toward an effective therapy. But some cases thwarted their efforts. Makia's was one. "I kept going," Makia later remembered, "from bad to worse." One morning he went to wash his face and saw that swellings had begun to form across his forehead and cheeks. "There was nothing left to feel but despair," Makia recalled. "I knew my face was going to get all fucked up, that it was hopeless. I had reached the limit." Then the disease began to take his eyes.

Stand Up Straight

(Population 174)

One of the first outsiders to live in the colony, the former British officer Donald Walsh had believed that blindness was an immediate precursor to death among the exiles. Walsh offered this theory to the board in May 1868, shortly before he himself became blind and died in his son's arms. Blindness, however, was simply a common symptom of untreated leprosy; in the early period of the settlement as many as 80 percent of exiles had eyes damaged by leprosy. Even as the virulence of the disease lessened, vision problems persisted. By the 1940s, just prior to sulfones, a third of the 350 residents had impaired sight, and 30 patients were blind.

Seeking a cool field in which to multiply, leprosy bacilli invade the cornea, destroying its sensitivity—a disastrous loss. "No pain sensors are more sensitive than those on the surface of the eye," one leprosy specialist wrote. "A stray eyelash, a speck of dirt, a flash of light, a puff of smoke, or even a loud noise will trigger an instantaneous muscular response." Without a blink reflex to protect and wash the cornea it becomes damaged, clouded with scar tissue. Doctors tried training patients to blink on schedule, using a timer or some other device. The technique worked in some cases, but only if the patient was physically able. Leprosy bacilli also attack the nerve controlling eyelid muscles, creating a condition known as lagophthalmos, in which the person cannot close the eyelids. In such cases surgeons rigged a thread of muscle from the jaw to the lid, which caused the person to blink as he chewed—doctors then handed them a pack of gum. With most patients, however, the most critical lesson physicians tried to impart was never to rub. For a person with no feeling in his hands, it was all too easy to grind the eyes into oblivion.

As the bacilli attacked his corneas, Makia developed iritis, an ailment one physician described as "one of the most agonizing afflictions in the world." At Carville, the editor Stanley Stein was also struck by iritis. He wrote that he "would lie awake nights, dreading the dawn, for sunlight stabbed my eyes with burning needles. I'll never know how I got through those eight months. I would clench my teeth and dig my fingernails into the mattress to keep from screaming with pain." Makia likened the sensation to "somebody screwing my eyeballs out."

Eventually Makia's right eye became badly impaired. When he was accidentally struck in the face by a volleyball, further damaging the eye, doctors decided to remove it. Three months later the sight in his left eye began to fade, leaving him with vision that was "like looking through smoke." His sight vanished completely while he was onstage during the annual Christmas pageant. When the curtain dropped he stumbled offstage. He told no one what had happened.

At the time, Makia was again living at Hale Mohalu, where he had been transferred for the surgery on his right eye. Fearing that he would be warehoused among "the blinds," as they were known, Makia tried to hide the truth. The blinds were "a separate people even among the leprosy patients," he later recalled. "They had their own little community, left to themselves by other patients." For Makia, to descend into the domain of the blinds would be to enter "a final place, a place I could never leave."

Makia began a charade. He memorized the number of steps from his bed to the door, then to the bathroom, lounge, and outside doors. He stopped taking meals in the cafeteria, since he could no longer find the food on his plate. "I would eat alone in my room and try to feed myself," he later explained. "But I had no sensation in my hands, so the forks would fall from my fingers." He sat with the plate at his mouth, shoveling the meal. "That was the only way I could eat," he said. "But nobody saw that."

At night while the others slept, Makia practiced maneuvering the grounds of Hale Mohalu, freezing if a person approached. Then he would return to his bed and weep. During the day Makia hid from the staff, hoping to forestall his exile to the blind ward. He learned to glance expectantly toward the nurse if she entered his room, and to feign clumsiness when he thumped into furniture. If someone tried to draw him into a card game, Makia pled exhaustion or pretended to be absorbed in a book.

The drug regimen that doctors had placed Makia on required that he swallow as many as thirty pills a day. A nurse delivered them in the morning, mixed together in an envelope. Usually, patients divvied their allotment of pills into four servings. Makia could not manage the task and worried he might overdose. He asked the nurse to separate the pills in cups.

"What's the matter, boy," she asked, "are you blind?"

"I was shocked she used the word *blind*," Makia later recalled. He wasn't blind, he thought: he simply could not see. Makia later confessed to feeling an inexplicable guilt over his condition, as if carelessness had caused him to lose his sight. At times he had imagined that his leprosy was also self-inflicted, brought upon him for reasons he did not understand. Now he felt doubly ashamed. He resisted telling his mother about his blindness. Yet he did not want her to hear the news from someone else. One night, while the other patients were in the Mouritz Theater, Makia groped his way to the telephone in the hall. Then it struck him: how to dial? He tried to make the motions from memory. A moment later Mary Malo said, "Hello?"

"Mama," he asked, "can you and Daddy come down tomorrow?" She asked him if anything was the matter.

Makia replied, "I just want to see you."

His parents arrived the next day. Mary Malo entered the room and sat on the edge of the bed.

"Mama," Makia said. "I'm blind."

His mother began to cry. Makia felt his hand being lifted and held. He said the words again: I'm blind, Mama. "Then she kissed me," Makia remembered, "and I heard her whisper, 'Lord, why me?'" A few weeks later they moved Makia onto the blind ward.

"Without a doubt, blindness is the most feared complication of leprosy," wrote Paul Brand, a physician who had made a lifelong study of the disease. This dread, he reported, "leads many patients to attempt suicide." Brand quoted one man who had lost vision in one eye and awaited the loss of sight in the other. "My feet have gone and my hands too, but that didn't matter much as long as I could see," the man had said. "Blindness is something else. If I go blind, life will mean nothing to me and I shall do all I can to end it."

For almost a year, Makia rarely emerged from his room. "I closed myself off completely," Makia later said. "I left the world before my friends left me. That was how I intended to protect myself." He sold his rifle and spent the money on a radio and a set of weights. "I began to drink heavily," Makia recalled. "To escape. To feel frustrated, and feel sorry for myself. My world was Hale Mohalu Hospital, the blind ward. I tried to break free, but it was so hard."

In December 1957 the last living patient with memories of Father Damien passed away in Kalaupapa. Mele Meheula had been exiled sixty-nine years earlier, at age nine—at age twelve she had stood by Damien's grave and watched workers lower his coffin into the ground. Shortly before her death, the board and the *Honolulu Star-Bulletin* had launched a public campaign to find Meheula's relatives so that they might reconnect in her dwindling days. The paper ran a series of stories about Meheula, sent its reporters across the islands to knock on doors, and printed a phone number to call.

But no one had come forward to claim her. The *Star-Bulletin* remarked: "Miss Meheula [has] never heard a word from her family from the day she was taken from them." At her funeral, her mourners were fellow patients.

A short time before Meheula's death, a reporter visited the settlement and wrote, "You couldn't, at first glance, tell Kalaupapa from any other island community. Choral music filters through the night from the Father Damien Memorial Hall as the chorus rehearses for Christmas. The gray ghost light of television filters out of darkened homes. A man quarrels with his wife." The piece was titled: "Kalaupapa, Once a 'Graveyard,' Can Now Face Future with Hope." The article concluded, "The prayers are the same as yours or mine—for good health, for love, and for a little human dignity."

That survivors of leprosy deserved respect was a sentiment that resonated with Bernard Punikaia. He had been struggling to promote that simple idea, and arguing against the stigma associated with the disease. Bernard had additional goals as well. For the past several years, he had been huddling with the islands' political leaders. "The objective was statehood," Bernard recalled. "These were exciting times for the Territory of Hawaii." Granting state status to Hawaii had been proposed as early as 1849, but the idea did not gain force until the 1940s, when modern aircraft cut travel time to the islands. This, one historian wrote, "[destroyed] the old argument that Hawaii was too far away from the rest of the nation." Statehood had come tantalizingly close in 1948, only to be stalled by the "deep conviction that international revolutionary communism [has] a firm grip on . . . the territory," as a U.S. senator claimed. Following the senator's assertion, an investigative team from the House Un-American Activities Committee was dispatched from Washington. A year later it filed its report: "Evidence shows . . . the people of Hawaii have successfully cast [out] communistic influence." Local politicians renewed their push for admission to the union, but years passed before the effort took hold. Finally, on August 21, 1959, Dwight Eisenhower signed the proclamation declaring Hawaii the fiftieth state. Residents expected sweeping changes to result in Kalaupapa. Instead, one relatively minor one occurred: the Territorial Board of Health was recast as the Hawaii State Department of Health. When Bernard filed grievances on behalf of the residents, he made certain to use the new name.

At the height of the island's red scare, John Wayne had arrived in Kalaupapa to film a scene for a movie called *Big Jim McClain*. Henry watched the crew as they worked. In the movie, Wayne plays a federal investigator who discovers a Communist cell in Hawaii. Tracking a clue, Big Jim flies to Kalaupapa. "Lonely. Desolate," he intones in voiceover. "No bars—but escape-proof." Big Jim climbs from the plane and spots a half dozen patients loitering at the edge of the airstrip. "Frankly," he narrates, "leprosy scared me." But Jim summons the courage to enter the settlement nonetheless. Barging into the Kalaupapa hospital, he finds his suspect's ex-wife, a former Communist, tending the patients' babies. She has renounced her politics, she tells Big Jim, and exiled herself to Kalaupapa to "atone for the injury I had done humanity, by helping these unfortunates."

From a distance, Henry studied the crew while they filmed a scene, the huge silvered reflectors shining light onto the actors. He would have liked to meet John Wayne, but patients had been instructed to keep distant from the star. Henry did sidle close enough to hear Wayne speak, however: "He sounded exactly like he did onscreen—'*Hey, pilgrim.*'" Wayne looked awfully uneasy, Henry thought. Whenever anyone approached he would skitter away anxiously, and then hide near the director of the film. "For a tough guy," Henry later said, "he seemed pretty nervous."

Henry had discovered that Kalaupapa was a strangely fine place to be a fan. Producers sometimes shipped reels of their movies directly to the settlement, allowing the patients an early look. When *Gone With the Wind* was released, Kalaupapa got one of the first prints in the islands; people from topside Molokai had streamed down the cliff on movie night. Celebrities also frequently visited, most out of simple generosity, but some because of the press such a gesture guaranteed. The board often solicited the visits, as they had years ago with Jack London, believing they could help collapse myths. "They thought if I went over it might help publicity-wise," recalled Shirley Temple, who entered the settlement for several hours in 1950. "That the public might now know it was okay, that leprosy was not contagious." Red Skelton, Edgar Bergen, Bud Abbott and Lou Costello, Irving Berlin, Edward G. Robinson, and many others landed at the airstrip, were driven to the social hall to perform, then whisked away. Some made an effort to tour the settlement and form with the residents a fleeting though authentic connection. Others simply used the visit as material or as an opportunity to impart spiritual lessons. In the spring of 1952 a plane carrying the Trapp Family Singers had landed. "With all our travels, our only encounter with lepers had been through the Gospels," wrote Maria Augusta Trapp in *A Family on Wheels*. "Now we were to meet them face to face." At the time of the Trapps' visit to Kalaupapa the majority of residents had been cured by sulfones, and many showed no significant damage from the disease. Nonetheless, Trapp wrote, "the poor featureless faces smiled at us, [and] their whole bearing signaled, 'We are the untouchables.'"

By the time Hawaii became an American state, 139 patients were eligible for release. The health department tried to encourage the residents to leave:

costs for the facility ran $1 million a year. When the department hired Booz, Allen & Hamilton to advise it on its budget, the firm recommended dissolving the community. "They might have talked to us," complained one resident. "This isn't about cold figures." The department considered paying the residents to vacate the land, "a guaranteed payment for life of $10 or $15 per month for each year the individual resided in [Kalaupapa]." Patients who had already departed, however, "would receive no payment."

As the department pressed, residents grew more stubborn. "Where the problem once was getting patients to come to this semi-isolated, 12-acre peninsula," the *Advertiser* reported, "now the problem is getting them to leave." One resident, who had been exiled in 1925, explained, "It's too late to start all over again." Another added, "I wish the powers-that-be would stop begrudging us what we earned with heartache, tears and anguish."

Over the years, Bernard had studied the patients who had challenged the government, one of whom was Stephen Dawson. Although Dawson had ultimately been exiled, his initial besting of the board in 1926 had been stirring; residents still spoke of it. When he had arrived at Kalaupapa, Dawson had begun to take correspondence courses on the law and earned a license to practice. He soon "became a watchdog for patients' rights, writing letters to the . . . legislature [and] anyone, in fact, who he thought might help," the *Advertiser* reported.

Dawson was now elderly and infirm, living at Hale Mohalu. Bernard took over his role. "If I don't speak out for my people, who will?" Bernard asked. He began to demand the department change policies that demeaned the residents. "Sometime, I hope that the Health Department will be able to accept us as human beings rather than as a disease," Bernard said. "They forget that we're no different than other people, that we also laugh, cry and are sad; that we love and get angry. We have all the emotions that everyone else has. All we are asking for is dignity."

At the time, all patients continued to "abide by rules that could be called ancient by modern medical standards," a Honolulu paper noted. "Patients and staff do not dine together here, or drink together. Staff personnel are not permitted to eat food prepared by patients (including those classified as temporary released) and patients are not allowed into staff homes." Patients could not offer rides to staff members, nor have family under the age of sixteen visit, even if the patient's leprosy was inactive. Residents' outgoing mail still got fumigated, and departing patients continued to endure disinfection in a cloud of formaldehyde. The department tracked the movements of patients out on temporary release as if they were criminals, and they were subject to arrest if they failed to show for exams. State laws and penalties concerning the reporting of suspects and released patients, as Bernard complained, had created "a system of informers."

For patients who had not yet earned temporary release, rules were even stricter. The editor of the *Honolulu Star-Bulletin,* Adam Smyser, wrote, "If a 16-year-old girl were recognized in Hawaii today as having communicable leprosy she would be compelled by law [into] treatment that would last three to four years. She would be taught not to shake hands with people who came to see her. She would eat only with other patients. If she left . . . before getting a discharge she would be brought back by health officers and face the possibility of a fine or even imprisonment." Smyser pointed out that on the mainland persons diagnosed with leprosy were treated as outpatients and hospitalized for as little as three months. "If I were to suspect that I had the disease myself, I would fly to the Mainland to be diagnosed," Smyser admitted. "I would not take the risk of a long confinement here."

Doctors could now almost immediately determine if a person had a contagious case of leprosy. In addition to having established a bacteriological index for patients, researchers had discovered a method of determining the viability of individual bacilli. Leprosy germs with low viability were not infectious, even in high numbers. Mainland hospitals were already using this clinical tool, called a morphological index. Vaccines, or prophylaxis, that could safeguard families against a possibly infectious reactivated case were also now in use. All of these developments argued for the abolishment of mandatory isolation. "It is readily evident that enforced hospitalization . . . is not necessary for the protection of the public," the head of one group of experts insisted. The "laws dealing with leprosy [should] be rewritten."

Over the course of four months beginning in November 1968, a Citizens Committee on Leprosy studied the state's administration of both Hale Mohalu and Kalaupapa. Bernard was selected to be on the committee. "I think leprosy patients are frightened to stand up and speak out, to fight for their rights," he later explained. "Myself, I am not awed by authority."

When the committee completed its study, its recommendations were far-reaching. Hospitalization should be voluntary, it wrote, "as is the case with other diseases." The committee advocated that all patients be discharged as soon as they had been "satisfactorily established on therapy," and that newly diagnosed cases be treated exclusively as outpatients. Kalaupapa ought to exist only "as a retirement home for older patients." To enlighten the public and the medical community in the islands, the state must undertake "an intensive education program" about the disease. Lastly, the members of the committee suggested cleansing all state laws of references to "segregation."

Over the next weeks officials debated the proposals and drafted a revised set of laws applicable to leprosy. When they had finished, Part 40 of Section 326 of the Public Health Regulations read, "The legislature finds that Hawaii's Hansen's disease victims have in many ways symbolized the plight of those affected throughout the world. Those patients who settled in Kalaupapa remain a living memorial to a long history of tragic separation, readjustment, and endurance. It is the policy of the State that the patient residents of Kalaupapa shall be accorded adequate health care and other services for the remainder of their lives. Furthermore, it is the policy of the State that any patient resident of Kalaupapa desiring to remain at the facility shall be permitted to do so for as long as that patient may choose." On June 30, 1969, the revised laws went into effect. After 103 years, exile had officially ended.

In the settlement, residents reacted mildly to the news. "They just change the words," one man said. "There are no real changes." Several people gathered timber and lit a bonfire, and a few residents climbed into their cars and sounded the horn. "People got a little drunk," Henry recalled. "But then again people always got a little drunk." After the bonfire died to embers, everyone returned to their cottages and went to bed.

One Sunday morning that July, three Honolulu broadcast stations sent out the live network telecasts of the Apollo 11 mission, during which Neil Armstrong and Edwin Aldrin Jr. walked for slightly more than two hours on the surface of the moon. Their reentry capsule splashed down twelve hundred miles southwest of Molokai. There, the *Star-Bulletin* reported, a Hawaii-based naval lieutenant named Clancy Hatelberg was dropped into the water to retrieve them: "[P]rotected by a biological isolation suit, [he] will be the first to welcome back the returning explorers and pass them similar suits. He will then assist in decontamination procedures required before the astronauts can board the *Hornet.*" After being lifted from the sea, Armstrong, Aldrin, and Michael Collins entered a hermetically sealed container, which newspapers referred to as "the astronauts' plush prison." NASA scientists hoped the precautions would prevent the spread of unknown lunar infectious agents. This fear of contamination, Walter Cronkite informed an estimated fifty million viewers, required that the men be "quarantined like lepers."

With the gate officially unlocked, residents began to make travel plans. Henry wanted to see Europe and visit art galleries. Bernard was curious about Asia. A large number of residents hoped to experience Las Vegas. Few people had the money for extravagant trips, however, and most merely booked interisland tickets. About eighty residents took trips in the first year after the exile law was repealed. The board reported that the typical foray outside was surprisingly brief. One resident remarked, "After three or four days on leave with family or friends, I feel uncomfortable due to the repeated deceits necessary to prevent divulging that I'm a former leprosy patient who lives in Kalaupapa."

A few months after the laws changed, Olivia's mother died. Olivia decided not to attend the funeral, to preserve the secret her mother had kept. She composed a letter to her late mother, which she later included in her memoir. "As you must know from where you are now," Olivia wrote, "my face is in pretty good shape but the rest of me is not. But, I have become a pretty good person. In that way I'm not a disgrace to you, Mama." Olivia was fifty years old, and had lived in exile for thirty-three years.

Over the years, Olivia's mild case of leprosy had damaged her feet, and she could hardly put weight on her right foot. She used crutches to walk and sometimes employed a wheelchair. Olivia decided to travel to Carville, to have the foot operated on. She and John boarded a plane at the airfield and then transferred to a commercial aircraft in Honolulu. Nine hours later they landed in Baton Rouge. A van awaited to shuttle them nineteen miles southeast across levees and through cypress swamps. The vehicle swung sharply toward a low plantation that spread behind a wrought-iron gate. A guard waved Olivia and John inside.

After they were settled into separate rooms in the hospital ward, the couple went to see Dr. Paul Brand, Carville's chief of rehabilitation. Brand was a quiet, intensely religious man, and a specialist in orthopedic surgery. He had spent two decades in southern India, pioneering techniques to restore function to hands and feet compromised by leprosy. In her memoir, Olivia published a letter she later wrote to her afflicted foot, which had again begun to bother her. "Dear Right Foot: This letter is to you. I tell you, everyone tells me I should get rid of you but, as much pain and trouble as you have been to me, I do love you and hope to keep you. [But] I want to be rid of the wheelchair. I want to walk to the door to look outside. I want to stand up straight."

On first impression, Carville resembled the campus of a pleasant, rural college, with ranks of neat dormitories, and greenswards, and well-maintained administration buildings. Nuns in blue-and-white habits pedaled three-wheeled bicycles down gravel paths, and patients steered golf carts to the course or climbed into their cars and headed out the gates. "We don't tell them where to go or where not to go," Dr. John R. Trautman, the administrator of Carville, explained to a reporter from Hawaii. "But we do suggest they use some judgment."

Those from Kalaupapa found the sense of easy freedom exhilarating. At the time, about a half dozen residents from the community were visiting Carville, to have surgery or simply to experience the place. Olivia would see her Hawaiian neighbors as she wandered around, familiar faces that smiled and stopped to talk. One of the patients who came to Carville for Dr. Brand's surgery was Henry. Although the impetus for his visit was the rehabilitation of his foot, soon after arriving Henry decided to postpone surgery. Now divorced, he had become smitten with a Carville nurse and didn't want to be distracted from his pursuit. When he finally submitted to the operation, Henry spent his recovery painting scenes of Kalaupapa. Later Henry tried his hand at nudes, including an oil painting he titled *Red Blanket,* which depicted a languorous, unclothed model.

At Carville, Henry began to take classes again, a schoolboy approaching middle age. He learned to speak Spanish and studied history, literature, and art. He read whatever he could find about leprosy. The Carville library archived every issue of Stanley Stein's *Star,* and Henry paged through them. Stein had died in 1967. Toward the end, his leprosy became resistant to sulfones, and doctors had resorted to a powerful alternative drug, which sometimes caused deafness. "A visit to see Stanley during the last months of his life was nearly unbearable," Dr. Brand wrote. "Unable to see, unable to hear, unable to feel, he would wake up disoriented. He would stretch out his hand and not know what he was touching, and speak without knowing whether anyone heard or answered. Once I found him sitting in a chair muttering to himself in a monotone, 'I don't know where I am. Is someone in the room with me? I don't know who you are, and my thoughts go round and round. I cannot think new thoughts.'"

Henry discovered that the library at Carville shamed its counterpart in Kalaupapa. In the early 1970s the settlement library held mostly paperback adventure stories, potboilers, and romance books. A few dozen works of literature and several medical journals sat on its shelves, but the facility was primarily a place to read magazines: *Tropical Fish Hobbyist, American Home, Baseball Digest, Better Homes and Gardens, Car & Driver, Ladies' Home Journal, Life, National Geographic, TV Guide.* At Carville Henry found the classics, philosophy, poetry anthologies, and hundreds of works relevant to the disease. One such book was titled *Through the Leper-Squint,* a reference to the slits carved into medieval church walls to allow the sick a glimpse of paradise. A chapter began: "It is the leper's fate that he is never the hero of a story." Henry wasn't so certain about that.

Olivia's surgery took place at the end of November. Surgeons opened her right ankle and leg, reconfigured tendons, and stripped away wasted tissue.

Doctors then wheeled John Breitha into the operating room to correct his clawed hand. Their rehabilitation continued for several weeks. By Christmas it seemed that both surgeries had succeeded. Then John's condition abruptly turned worse, the difficulties unrelated to his operation. Nothing seemed to help. Olivia watched John turn ashen. On the afternoon of February 22, 1973, she entered his room and found him in what she thought was a deep sleep. Grasping his leg, she tried to wake him. "He took one deep breath," she wrote, "and then it seemed such a long time before the next." Olivia frantically tried to rouse her husband. "*Please* hurry," Olivia cried. "I can't wake John." The nurse told her to wait outside. After a few minutes the nurse approached Olivia, carrying a glass of pink liquid. She said, Drink. Then the nurse announced, "He has gone to God." As the news spread, patients from Kalaupapa appeared in Olivia's room. They embraced her in turn, each touch releasing more tears. One of the physicians entered. Olivia turned to him and said quietly, "I want to go home."

She buried John in one of the cemeteries on Kalaupapa's western shore. They had been married twenty-nine years. The priest recited a prayer and then it was over, and the mourners began to file away. Olivia returned to her cottage, unlocked the door, and entered her empty home. She wrote, "I knew that my aloneness was very real and permanent."

Orientation

(Population 146)

Makia learned to dress by touching clothes to his lips, where a small spot of sensitivity remained. He could identify his shirts by the slickness of the fabric and tell his shorts from his pants by the weight. When he found the shirt's waist, by pressing his lips against the seams, he would work his way down to the collar and sleeves. Once the garment was identified and properly oriented, Makia began to slowly tug it on, taking care not to become trapped. Sometimes it took him thirty minutes to get dressed.

In the middle of the night he would take a cane and practice walking the grounds, acres of area that he memorized and mapped. Frequently he became disoriented, stuck between buildings or in the maze of a hedge. "Of course, I had to fight off the panic, lost in my dark, in the dark," he recalled. "But I kept a cool head, and would try to retrace my steps. Where did I go wrong?"

With no sense of feeling, Makia could not touch the obstruction in front of him and determine if it was a wall or tree or man. Nor could he employ his toes to find a curb or the edge of a cliff. He used hearing instead—the nuanced sound of his cane as it swept smooth concrete, which indicated sidewalk, or rough asphalt, which signaled road. He could approximate time from the tones of traffic, which surged and fell like surf at rush hour. Intensely attuned, Makia learned to locate building corners by noting where the wind changed octaves, and to gauge buildings' height by the music of their echo. His proximity sense improved. And as the weeks went by, his hearing became acute, filling his head with snatches of overheard conversations, birds singing, and chatter from distant televisions.

One day after he became blind, Makia's brother Earl died, his heart failing on an operating table at Queen's Hospital. Earl had asked to be buried at Kalaupapa. Makia flew back for the funeral. After the service, he decided to stay in the village for a time. Counting steps, he paced from the landing to the store, the store to the church, the church to the McVeigh Home compound, where he and his brothers had lived. Makia found the cottage where he had lived during his marriage, and the bar where he had sat in the evenings listening to stories. As he walked, Makia could sense the gaze of the residents on him, taking notice of his blindness. But nobody much cared: they had seen these things before.

Makia had returned to Hale Mohalu and was navigating its halls one morning when he smacked into a wheelchair, steered by a patient who had lost his legs to the disease. His arms were tired, the man said, and now he was stranded. Makia offered to push him. "Just tell me which way," Makia said, "straight, right, left, whatever." The patient said he was embarrassed to be steered by a blind guide. Makia replied, "Don't be ashamed. If I don't push you around, no one else will." The man thought about that, and then said, Okay. "We became a pair," Makia recalled, "a blind man pushing a legless man."

By the 1970s, Hale Mohalu had grown dingy, a consequence of government economizing. The lease was soon to expire, and the health department did not want to sink money into the facility. In a report itemizing capital improvements made to department facilities, the entry beside Hale Mohalu read: "None, ever." Despite the wear, the hospital had retained a peaceful, homey air, its buildings "set off from the hustle of the normal world by lush foliage," as one reporter wrote. A highway abutted the compound, and homes and businesses crowded the surrounding blocks, but most patients welcomed the nearness, in contrast to the quiet of Molokai. At the time, 143 residents lived at Kalaupapa, and in all but 3 the disease was "under complete control," the department announced. "Reportedly, the 3 have not cooperated fully in following medical instructions." In the past year 32 new cases had been diagnosed, 90 percent of them recent immigrants from other countries. All began drug therapy, and most were allowed to go home. Persons who "react unfavorably to anti-leprosy drugs or to interactions between the drugs," the board reported, were detained at Hale Mohalu "for a short time [to] adjust the type and dosage of medication." The average stay was two months. Makia sometimes heard the newcomers arrive, their strange footfalls following the familiar steps of the nurse, as she rattled off the rules.

Two decades earlier, Dr. Norman Sloan had written, "It will be seen that while no age, except earliest infancy, is exempt, leprosy is primarily a disease of later childhood, adolescence, and early adult life." Late onset was rare: when Sloan wrote those words, only 7 out of a population of 568 patients had been between the ages of 65 and 70 when first diagnosed with leprosy. Even so, it did sometimes happen.

Makia was in his room one day when Mary Malo walked in and announced that she was now a patient. "Mama used to tell me she had a red spot on her cheek that she suspected," Makia later recalled. "But then she would say nothing more." Doctors started Mary on sulfone therapy and assigned her to a second-floor room, on the ward opposite the blinds. "Mama was comfortable in there," Makia said. "She didn't sit and worry." After several months doctors released Makia's mother as an outpatient. He remained at Hale Mohalu.

The department had established a vocational program at Hale Mohalu where patients took lessons in sewing, auto mechanics, ceramics, cosmetology, and television repair. Officials imagined that patients could use the skills to make a living when they were released. Most of the program was impossible for Makia, however, and he passed his days in boredom. Then a counselor suggested talking books. Makia listened to one straight through, went back for another, and then another. The counselor then proposed to Makia that he emulate the authors and compose stories of his own. The first tale he wrote started as a play unfolding in his head. It was an adaptation of an island legend, about a homely but willful pig that tries to win a beautiful woman. When he had it ready, Makia spoke the story aloud, and his counselor took it down. Without Makia's knowledge, she then entered the piece in a literary contest sponsored by a national magazine called *Dialogue,* which was published in Braille. It won first prize. "This is for real?" Makia cried when a reporter called with the news. The reporter asked how someone in Makia's condition could write. It was easy, Makia explained. First you imagined something wonderful, and then you worked to make it real.

Doctors had placed Makia on an improved drug regimen, which drove down his bacilli count. When minor complications from these treatments arose, however, physicians sent Makia to Queen's Hospital for an operation. While he was at the hospital he met a young practical nurse. He began to tell her his stories, smiling when she laughed. "To think an outside person could take an interest in me!" Makia said. "My life started to look up again."

He was back in his room at Hale Mohalu some weeks later when an orderly knocked. "Makia," the orderly announced. "Visitor." When he heard the practical nurse's familiar footsteps he stood from his chair. "She came right into my arms and kissed me," he later remembered. "We fell in love," Makia recalled, "and it made me feel good."

The following summer doctors began to prescribe a new drug to patients, called rifampin, which proved able to kill leprosy bacilli in three days. "For the first time in 100 years," the *Star-Bulletin* reported, "no one in Hawaii requires hospitalization for leprosy." Every patient at Hale Mohalu now qualified for release, including Makia. He realized he had nowhere to go.

An apartment required income, and Makia had no prospects. Unlike many patients, he had never been able to work for an extended time, and had not accrued a government pension. In Kalaupapa the eighty-one residents who were already retired got a monthly check for $195; the twenty-eight who still worked as "general laborers" earned $135. Makia did receive $90 every year to pay for his clothing, and the department paid patients an allowance of $20 a month. But because he did not reside in a cottage in Kalaupapa, he forfeited the $65 a month the department gave for food. With no money, Makia knew he could not afford an apartment.

He considered returning to his parents' home. He thought about going back to Kalaupapa, where he could live for free. But he had begun to imagine a larger life for himself. Makia wanted to become a teacher. To do so, he realized, would require going back to school. That summer he started taking classes at a community college, believing he could work his way into the University of Hawaii.

For most of the past year Makia had been dating the nurse he had met at the hospital. They were married on the Saturday before the autumn semester started. Makia had been accepted at the university, in a program for handicapped students. He spent his honeymoon in nervous anticipation, envisioning his classes, certain that he would fail. The campus spread within a valley called Manoa, dozens of buildings webbed by a network of winding paths, which climbed and twisted and dropped, depending on topography. Thickets of bicycles guarded the entrance to every building, abandoned by students rushing to class. Skateboards and scooters buzzed the walks, whirring close enough to brush Makia with waves of air. He found that merely walking to class was an act of immense faith.

Makia had been assigned a mobility guide for the first weeks. Placing a hand on his minder's arm, he categorized sound and counted steps, decoded the sequence of stairs—elevation being the enemy of the blind. In the beginning, every day offered only "morning grief and afternoon humiliations," as one newly blind writer had put it. He ate sparingly and skipped lunch to avoid the dilemma presented by a public restroom. Makia was the first person from Kalaupapa to attend the university, a distinction of which he was painfully aware. Believing that his hands were unsightly, he tried to keep them hidden. Large mirrored sunglasses concealed his shed eyebrows, and he wore his thick black hair to his collar, tumbled over his ears. Even so, "I felt so self-conscious," he admitted. "I know the young kids would stare at me." One day after class he pushed into his counselor's office quivering with embarrassment, having mistakenly guided his cane between the legs of a coed. "You could tell he was very, very anxious," recalled one of his counselors. "I'm sure he had a lot of frustration and anger." The first courses he took were religion and philosophy.

For a blind person insensitive to braille, the mechanics of education are fierce. Using a tape player modified to fit his hands, Makia recorded every lecture. "Two courses, that was the max I could handle per semester because the tapes would just pile up," he recalled. Playing the recordings at night, he would listen for five minutes, swap tapes, and record his notes on a fresh cassette. Then he traded tapes again and worked through a second stretch. Sometimes when he finished, Makia would find that he had made an hour of notes to recap a fifty-minute lecture. A reader turned his textbooks into additional cassettes, which Makia studied until he could recite them from memory. He worked at the table in the small apartment he had rented, the volume on the tape player turned low. His wife worked the early shift. When she woke, she would find Makia asleep at the table, tapes scattered, the machine still pressed to play.

During his first weeks on campus, "nobody would initiate a conversation with me," Makia recalled, "and I used to sense that people didn't want to sit near me." One afternoon another student with whom Makia had grown friendly asked if he wanted to come to the university swimming pool. Makia replied, "Heck no—with all my scars? I'm not going to have all those people stare at me." As Makia later recalled, the student then replied, "Don't let other people's hang-ups stop you from doing what you want to do." The words stunned Makia. He thought about them, turning exhilarated as their meaning took hold. "My God, I thought it was *my* hang-ups," he recalled. "Well, if I'm ugly, that's not my problem—I don't need to look at me. If somebody else no can handle, that's their problem, not mine."

As the semesters passed, Makia became a popular figure on campus, respected and well-liked. Classmates spoke of his good nature, and the comic pitch of his tales. Those who got to know him heard the melancholy in his tone, however. One remarked, "I always had the feeling that Makia had much more to tell." Sometimes Makia's classmates invited him to a concert or play. He would ask his wife to come, but she preferred to stay home. "It was such a new world for me," he later said, "a chance to leave the old one behind. I forgot she felt part of that old world." One day Makia returned to the apartment after class and found it empty. Makia moved back to Hale Mohalu. "I was trying so damn hard to be independent," he said, "I lost sight of her."

On the grounds of Hale Mohalu spread a chaulmoogra tree, transplanted from Kalihi Hospital. Workers had dug free the tree's root-ball as Kalihi was being deconstructed, wrapped it in burlap, and loaded it on a truck. The department moved the tree for symbolic reasons, a talisman of the past. A dozen other tokens also dotted the yard at Hale Mohalu: coconut palms, carried from Kalaupapa. The palms shaded the paths and ruffled softly in the breeze, towering above the buildings.

By 1977 only twenty-two patients lived at Hale Mohalu. The health department was threatening to shutter the facility to save money. It reported that the state could earn $217,800 a year leasing the site, a figure arrived at by counting 43,560 square feet and factoring in the current market rate. The report concluded: "Time did not permit a similar analysis for Kalaupapa."

The highway that curled above Hale Mohalu was now continually congested. Gasoline fumes spilled onto the grounds, at times so thick that Stephen Dawson kept a gas mask by his bed. Doors creaked and roofs leaked, and many windows did not close. When it rained the runoff channeled through the site, and nurses found frogs in the halls. Yet the patients who remained considered Hale Mohalu home, the only one many of them had. The kitchen staff knew who liked Portuguese soup, and who preferred broth; nurses had poked the patients' arms so often they could find their veins in the dark. Even the locals had turned neighborly. "The people who run the little stores around here are used to us," Bernard told the *New York Times*. "The community accepts us. We feel comfortable here with them." During a tense meeting between the department and patients, Dawson exclaimed, "This has been a home for us for so many years. The environment is beautiful and relaxing here, and we love our staff." Dawson then added politely, "If we can stay, we would be so appreciative."

But the department made its decision—Hale Mohalu would close. Patients would be moved fifteen miles away to a cramped building on the northern slope of Diamond Head, at one time a tuberculosis ward. The department said the move would save $80,000 a year. Bernard, who often spent stretches at Hale Mohalu for various health reasons, hunkered down in one of the dorms. "If the government can take Hale Mohalu away from us," he announced, "then they will be able to do the same thing at Kalaupapa." Citing the dilapidation of the buildings it had allowed to go to seed, the department had the facility condemned. On January 23, 1978, residents were asked to sign liability waivers, releasing the state from culpability if they were injured at the site. Two days later, reacting to legal moves the residents had undertaken to stop their eviction, a local judge asked, "What do the patients . . . want? Do they want someone to build them a castle?" The following morning, workers stripped the linens from beds, pulled furniture from the rooms, and tossed the residents' belongings into boxes. Health officials then began to force the patients, many of whom were in wheelchairs, from the buildings. News crews had been tipped to the event and filmed the drama, and that evening's broadcast showed officers wrestling weeping residents, who batted at them with bandaged hands. The department retreated, agreeing to provide "minimal" services at Hale Mohalu until the issue was resolved.

Throughout the summer, residents and the state battled in court. In August, the health department warned the holdouts that their water, electricity, telephone, food, and medical care would be stopped. On September 1, just before dawn, officials arrived and withdrew the lone remaining nurse. "They cut off the water—we turned it back on," Bernard later recalled. "They turned off the lights—we used kerosene lanterns." Olivia followed events from Kalaupapa. She wrote: "Authority never considers the underdog."

The remaining residents won a temporary restraining order, restoring vital services. When the order expired after three weeks, the department shut everything down again. In a letter to the *Advertiser,* one woman remarked, "There is something terrifying about a system which has moved so far from human values as to inflict this kind of persecution upon people who have suffered more than most of us can imagine." Another letter cried, "The shame of it! In the land of Damien . . ."

The standoff between the state and the holdouts lasted five years. By 1983 only three "sit-in trespassers," as one judge called them, remained at Hale Mohalu—all others had surrendered or passed away. Bernard Punikaia, Clarence Naia, and Frank Duarte lived in a corner of the Clinton Building, with a gas generator for power and a Coleman stove to warm their food. Three lawsuits filed by the patients failed in state court. Arguing against an appeal placed before the Ninth U.S. Circuit Court in San Francisco, the state insisted, "The expectations of the plaintiffs far exceed whatever duties are owed them by the state of Hawaii." The court rejected the appeals. Bernard announced, "I still believe in Santa Claus. I believe that good people will come out OK."

At 6:15 A.M. on September 21, 1983, law enforcement officers took bolt cutters to the chained front gate. Squads of officers, "some in jumpsuits and combat boots, most of them armed," according to the *Advertiser,* rushed the Clinton Building. Alongside the officers was the deputy health director for the state. If you do not vacate within ten minutes, he told the residents, you will be dragged outside and arrested. Reading from his prepared notes, Bernard answered, "All we ask is to remain on our land at Hale Mohalu where so many of our brothers and sisters lived and died in isolation, for the safety of the general public. We understood why that sacrifice was necessary. We are still waiting to understand why we must give up our home as well."

An officer announced, "Eight minutes left."

Bernard and the other holdouts began to sing. When the deadline passed, a pair of officers stepped forward and flashed their badges. "Are you ready to leave now?" one asked. Bernard said no. At 6:50 A.M. the officers "picked [Bernard] Punikaia up," one reporter wrote. "They carried him out the back, over the bridge to the field. . . . In the middle of the field, an officer leaned over Punikaia and said apologetically, 'Bernard, it's a formality, but I gotta search you.'"

Bernard replied, "But I don't have anything."

He was arrested and steered into the backseat of a waiting car. At 8:32 A.M. bulldozers began to carve away the Clinton Building, and then the other structures on the site. By nightfall, the *Advertiser* reported, "every building was destroyed." The chaulmoogra tree was spared.

Stephen Dawson was not among the residents at Hale Mohalu the day it fell. Already in his seventies, blind and with severe respiratory problems, he had agreed to move to the Diamond Head facility. Asked by a reporter if he liked his new home, Dawson replied, "I have to like it. There is no going back to Hale Mohalu. If I said I didn't like it, that would be ungrateful. Understand that?"

When it had served as a tuberculosis ward, the building in which Dawson now lived had been called Leahi Hospital at Diamond Head. The name originated from the volcanic crater on whose slope the hospital sat. In the era before European contact, the landmark had been known as Leahi, brow of the tuna—British sailors, mistaking calcite crystals glinting in lava rock for precious stone, later coined the more famous name. Both appellations were inappropriate for the new leprosy center, the department decided. It rechristened the facility Hale Mohalu.

Softer Notes

(Population 116)

Residents expected Kalaupapa to be shuttered next. What would trigger the closure remained unclear. Residents hoped to stay until the last of them died, but few believed that the health department would indulge their wish. "We've been used too many times," a resident explained. "It's going to be good only until the developers get itchy and want to move in." The department floated various figures as the minimum population that could sensibly be sustained at Kalaupapa: one hundred, then seventy-five, and then fifty. When a Honolulu newspaper suggested that the number should be zero, the governor announced: "The time frame implied in the article, 'after the present patients have died,' is not the official position of the Department of Health and far from the one I have in mind."

Residents heard constant rumors that the department had yielded to pressure and they would be evicted to make room for a resort hotel. Kalaupapa was one of the few remaining spots in the state unmarred by development. With speculators parceling every foot of oceanfront surrounding Honolulu, it seemed probable that they would turn toward Kalaupapa, the nearest coastal village to Oahu. Bernard and several others often explained in public forums that the residents had already purchased the land with a century of suffering. Yet the developers circled, as they did around other once-forbidden places. In Europe, speculators gained access to the last remaining leprosy colony on the Continent, located on a verdant delta of the Danube River; builders agreed to postpone construction until "the moment when all lepers die," the *Times* of London reported, after which the colony would be "converted into a spa for the healthy aged." A small Malaysian island that had also once held exiled leprosy victims was outfitted with twenty chalets, a luxury spa, and an adventure center where tourists took instruction in "survival skills." Similar scenarios were put forth for Kalaupapa. Describing the peninsula, a government report announced, "The area appears to have potential for future recreational [and] resort use."

As the debate bubbled into the press, the residents stated their case. "At one time this land was good enough for us, when you didn't want us out there," wrote a resident named Anita Una. "Now we realize there are bureaucrats who foresee lucrative possibilities in our lands today." Distrusting the department to protect their interests, several residents began to work with Congresswoman Patsy Mink, hoping to win National Historical Park status for Kalaupapa. The bill they submitted to Congress stated, "The Kalaupapa settlement constitutes a unique and nationally significant cultural, historical, educational, and scenic resource." Of most critical concern to the residents, however, was the provision stated in section 3(b)(6), which vowed to "prevent the dislocation or displacement of any patient or former patient presently in residence at the Kalaupapa settlement." In her statement to Congress, Mink phrased the matter in more conversational terms: "They went there first as prisoners of their disease, they are insisting that they be allowed to remain until they die."

When she introduced the bill for debate, Mink included several letters in support of the proposal, including one written by Kalaupapa's sheriff, Richard Marks. He wrote: "My grandmother (maternal), uncle, and father died there. My brother, sister, wife, and myself all live there and, like 95 percent of Kalaupapa's residents, hope to live out our lives there." As the bill advanced, one resident conducted an informal survey. "What is the worst thing that could happen to Kalaupapa in the future?" he asked. More than a third of the residents said eviction. One-fifth suggested that the presence of a hotel or an increased number of tourists would be ruinous. Most believed that the department could not be trusted "to take care of them or to preserve the area." The resident who made the survey did not state his own opinion. "It's not for [me] to decide," he told an exploratory committee. "It's for you folks and your kids. Someday I'm going to die and I don't have any children. But you and your children will still come to see this place."

On December 22, 1980, the legislation creating the Kalaupapa National Historical Park was signed into law. At the time, the National Park Service administered several of what were sometimes called dark sites, such as Alcatraz prison and the Japanese internment camp at Manzanar. Their goal, an NPS official explained, "is to [present] for understanding who we are, where we have been, and how we as a society might approach the future. This collection of special places also allows us to examine our past—the contested along with the comfortable, the complex along with the simple, the controversial along with the inspirational." The rules instituted for Kalaupapa by the NPS and the department stipulated that no more than one hundred tourists per day be admitted, and none younger than sixteen. Sightseers could not photograph residents without their permission, and all tourists had to be escorted by an official guide service. The largest such service, owned by Richard Marks, was called Damien Tours. One of his part-time guides was Henry. As he took a group through the village one day, Henry called out the local landmarks: the wharf, the general store, Mother Marianne's grave, and Rea's Store, which was in fact a bar. A tourist asked, "Where are all the lepers?"

"You're looking at one," Henry replied.

"But you don't look like a leper."

Henry said, "Looks can be deceiving."

The strange sweep of history had always interested Henry. At Carville, during his second pass through organized education, he had learned to appreciate the past's unyielding quality and take pleasure in its dark humor. Leprosy itself was a rich source of ironies, populated, as a historian of the disease wrote, with "rogues and vagabonds, saints and martyrs."

Not long after the government declared Kalaupapa a National Historical Park, Henry helped found the Kalaupapa Historical Society. The society's driving force was a young volunteer paramedic named Bruce Doneux, who hoped to generate "interest and continued resident participation" in the stewardship of settlement history, as he described it to a physician in a letter seeking items for a historical collection. When the fledgling society met for its third monthly session, the thirty residents in attendance elected Doneux president and Henry vice president. One of Henry's tasks was to help put out a monthly newsletter. He often wrote the articles himself. "In my corner of the world, I've seen 'The Good, The Bad, and The Ugly,'" Henry announced in volume 4 of the publication. "In fact, it should be quoted in reverse, starting with the ugliness of times gone into history, the bad that persisted by middle-aged resistance to improve, and the good that now prevails due to man's determination to conquer the bad and the ugly." At the conclusion of the article, Henry wrote, "Our [history], I think, ends on a softer note because it was ugly, it has been bad and, I can't say it's perfect now, and yet, it is good. As for tomorrow, it could be better. Who knows?"

When Henry had returned to Kalaupapa from Carville, he brought along the nurse with whom he had fallen in love. They married, and Henry's bride took a job in the community. In time they divorced, but the nurse decided to remain in Kalaupapa. She ended up married to Pearl Malo's ex-husband. Henry's ex-wife, who had been Makia's first wife, also still lived in Kalaupapa. Henry often ran into various pieces of this tangled history at the store, or the bar. He managed to see the comedy in it all. "It's Peyton Place," he remarked.

Henry found that the tours he gave functioned as a sort of therapy, cathartic parries with thick-headed visitors. As he learned more of the true history of the place, Henry began to shape the narrative of the colony, shifting perspective to see the reactions he elicited. Sometimes he told the story as if Damien were its centerpiece, and the patients merely colorful extras. Other times he reduced the role of saviors and spoke of survivors rescuing themselves through determination. With his own history he became playful, adding characters, changing dates, and adding a sense of drama akin to that of a film. He seemed to be trying to find a story line that was more generally pleasing—something that built to a Hollywood end.

For several years Henry and Bruce Doneux did exhaustive work in the community, unearthing forgotten documents and relics of the exiles' past. Doneux found fifty lantern slides that Jack McVeigh had produced, and old postcards Joseph Dutton had scribbled and signed and mailed. Before Hale Mohalu was razed, Doneux had swooped in and rescued thousands of glass-plate negatives that the board's photographers had made, including the entry photographs of hundreds of patients. "Behind the Bay View pool hall I found a storage closet containing the personal effects of deceased patients," Doneux reported, "and I spent two days repacking and carefully itemizing each article." By this time, Doneux was signing his letters "Project Director of the Kalaupapa Historical Collection Project." As the collection grew, Doneux wrote letters in which he described a museum for the settlement, perhaps an interactive display. "There are more inventoried items of possible historical value than initially believed," he announced excitedly. Most of the collection was stored in a room at the old hospital. A modern brick facility had been recently built, and the sagging wood-framed hospital now stood empty.

One item of historical significance never made it onto Doneux's lists. The community's lone fire engine was a half century old, its paint faded to a watery pink. Volunteer firemen kept jumper cables near because the engine's battery failed to hold a charge. One summer night a bundle of wiring in the old hospital sparked and set the building ablaze. It burned like gathered kindling, the heat warping the iron rails on the wheelchair ramps. By the time the volunteers got the fire truck started, the hospital was gone, along with everything inside.

What little remained of the collection was filed away in an unused cottage on the far side of the village. Henry kept a set of keys. No one touched the collection for years, and only rarely did Henry think about the materials, although the history itself obsessed him. He began to compose his own story of the settlement, writing on pads in graceful penmanship, casting himself in the lead role. Eventually he became curious and went to unlock the storage closet. Insects had invaded and turned the collection to dust.

* * *

As he had done with Henry, Bruce Doneux encouraged Olivia to write an account of her life in Kalaupapa. He bought several blank notebooks as gifts and gave them to her during the holidays. "There is so much I want to say about Bruce," Olivia wrote in the memoir she subsequently published. "I want to say what a wonderful friend and confidant he has been to me. It's important for you to understand how important such friendships are in Kalaupapa, at least to me. It can be very lonely and you need someone you can really talk to."

On December 19, 1982, Olivia uncapped a blue-ink pen and on an empty line of a notebook wrote, "Today is the day I have decided to put down on paper my thoughts and what has happened in my life to this date, as much as I can recall. I tell you, the reason I'm trying to do this is because I am tired of hearing the popular phrase, 'It makes me feel like a leper.' Here is how it felt and still feels to *this* leper." *Olivia: My Life of Exile in Kalaupapa* begins, "Until the year 1934, my life was ordinary and uneventful."

As the lines filled with ink, Olivia slowly began to create something resembling a genealogy. By the spring of 1984, Olivia Breitha had spent fifty years in exile. The number of residents in Kalaupapa would soon dip below one hundred for the first time since July 1866. With every death and departure, the community moved numerically closer to that initial morning of exile—history circling back toward the original colonists, twelve men and women and a single stowaway child.

Although the lineage was not by blood, every remaining resident traced his or her history to those first exiles. "They are brothers and sisters here," the Reverend James Drew, the Protestant minister in the village, explained to a visitor. "Leprosy has made sure of that." Olivia could plot the century of woven relationships on the community tree, with her own name among the branches. She remembered Bernard arriving at Kalihi; Henry as a ten-year-old complaining of hunger; the morning her girlfriend Pearl brought her little brother Makia to meet her, on one of his first days in the settlement. They were all grown men now. Olivia wrote, "Roots go deep when you live in one place for a long time."

In the autumn of 1983, Olivia and Bruce Doneux had rented an apartment together in Honolulu. Her foot had degraded since the surgery at Carville, and she needed another operation. Doneux agreed to help with the recovery, which Olivia wanted to do in the city, to test life outside. "Bruce took me to a supermarket," Olivia said. "He made me push the shopping cart." They went to the circus, and the Ice Capades, and to concerts. "It's hard, when you come from a place like [Kalaupapa], to believe that people outside can actually like you."

Bernard sometimes came to visit Olivia and Bruce at the apartment. He now divided his time between Kalaupapa and Honolulu; in the city he lived in his car. After Hale Mohalu was leveled, Bernard had launched a campaign to reclaim the land for the patients. "[He] lobbied legislators, staged small protests, talked to friendly groups, tried his hand at fund raising, and refused to let the issue die," a newspaper reported. Often he appeared on television to argue his cause. "For me to go on television, it wasn't the easiest thing in the world," he later admitted. "I have a mirror. Because I believe strongly in what we're fighting for—I make the personal sacrifice." His efforts eventually succeeded, and a senior citizen housing complex was built on the site, with a number of rooms set aside for former leprosy patients. When they christened the buildings, Bernard insisted that they be named for patients who had died during the struggle for Hale Mohalu.

He decided to run for Congress, one of six people challenging to represent the Tenth House District, which included Molokai, Lanai, and part of western Maui. A reporter asked Bernard if he had a campaign platform. Bernard replied, "Public health." When the polls closed he had finished third. He carried Kalaupapa.

Afterward Bernard joined Olivia and Doneux on a car trip they were taking across northern California. Doneux was returning to the mainland to resume his studies, and the trip was to be a long farewell. The trio began in San Francisco and made their way east toward Yosemite, then circled back along the coast. The highway rose and began to curve, air cooling as the forest thickened. When they passed a stand of ancient-growth redwoods outside Eureka, Olivia yelled to stop the car. Doneux helped her climb out, then walk into the forest. "Those redwood trees are just like a miracle," Olivia wrote. "They just stand there guarding each other." One of the redwoods was two thousand years old, thirty stories tall, as big around as her cottage. Olivia reached out her hand and stroked its dark and wrinkled skin. She spoke to the tree softly. "Remember," Olivia whispered, "I've touched you."

A Long Road

(Population 74)

At times, Makia's sight would unexpectedly return. Light flooded the room, and he could see a glowing lamp, armchairs, a vase spilling flowers. Then he would wake, terribly bewildered. Sightless people dream in different ways. Some never do so in the conventional sense, although they might experience abstract displays of shifting light, imprecise optical memory that works in the mind like a kaleidoscope. For others, usually those born blind, their dream life might be exquisitely rendered yet depict a world unrecognizable to anyone but the dreamer. A person who has become blind as an adult, however, carries a vast library of images into darkness.

In Makia's dreams he was usually in Kalaupapa. The settlement was as it had been when he was a boy. Wind swept the grass and shook the bougainvillea. The village hummed beneath a canopy of palm and algaroba and kiawe trees, and between the town and the sea was a blackboard of lava rock, the surf as white as a rush of chalk. Thrushes crested overhead, and short-eared owls and mourning doves. Winter currents moved humpback whales offshore, and he could see the orcas breach. The tides spit fat monk seals onto land near the village, including one mother that returned yearly to bear pups. "Kalaupapa was my safety net, a place I could run back to," Makia said. "In my mind, I am Kalaupapa, and Kalaupapa is me."

It took Makia seven years to earn his college degree. He spent part of every summer in Kalaupapa, living in one of the group homes or the hospital ward or any empty cottage the superintendent could find. After a month or two he would return to Honolulu. When Hale Mohalu closed, Makia had moved into a university dorm, a man in his forties among students half his age. He studied through the night in the student lounge so that his tape recorder would not wake his roommate. "We all had a lot of respect for Makia," one student later recalled. "He never made a big deal out of his disease. He told wonderful stories. People liked him." In 1979 he graduated with a bachelor's degree in Hawaiian studies. When they called Makia's name at graduation, the air filled with applause. His friends staged a party at the dorm. Pearl and her husband sent a roasted pig from Molokai to serve at the celebration luau. Makia announced, "There was a lot in between my being declared a leper and where I am today, and where I want to go with my life. But I feel good. Things have gotten much better for me. I am climbing up from the dependency of being a leprosy patient. Finally my life is leading to more independence. It's a kind of growing up. It has been a long road."

Makia began working toward a teaching certificate. He took an apartment near the center of town. Money was a constant worry. Unwilling to resort to welfare he relied on supplemental Social Security income and his small health department allowance. "I used to envy the guys working at McDonald's," Makia later said. When his tape recorder broke he applied to a government agency for funds to buy a replacement. He was turned down. Eventually the Kalaupapa Lions Club came forward with money for a new machine. After Makia earned his certification, the University of Hawaii hired him to teach a freshman Hawaiian-language class. On his first day Makia entered the room and found his place at the lectern. Thirty students crowded the classroom; a teaching assistant managed the blackboard. The students were silent; he could hear them shifting in their seats. He began to feel their gaze. "My name is Makia Malo," he announced, speaking in Hawaiian. "I grew up in a place called Kalaupapa." He thought it best to "get that out of the way," he later recalled, "so it wouldn't be so distracting."

As the weeks passed, Makia discovered that his lessons were adequate, and the students were absorbing the grammar he diagrammed out loud. But he felt like an impostor playacting a professor's role. In his mind Makia imagined the students staring, distressed by the sight of his hands. He found shadows in which to hide them, behind the lectern or in the fold of his lap. Soon he could barely hold the thread of the day's lecture, preoccupied by the idea of his disfigurement. "I had a script," he later said. "I knew I could teach. I knew that they were learning. There wasn't a problem—except for me. I could not overcome my self-consciousness. It overwhelmed everything else." When the semester ended, Makia went to the administration office. "I'm sorry," he said. "I can't teach anymore."

He hid in his tiny apartment, surviving on ramen noodles and canned salmon, "black clouds over my head," he later said. Sometimes he took the bus to where Hale Mohalu had stood, to walk the familiar grounds. Sometimes he retreated farther and returned to Kalaupapa. In the warm afternoons he would find the water's edge, wade into the surf, and start to swim. He made strong, steady strokes, timing his breaths, and when he became fatigued, he would roll onto his back and float. Makia swam until it seemed that he had gone too far, and then he would stop and scream as loudly as he could. Then the echo came off the cliff, and he knew how to find his way back.

Makia decided to fly to Carville, to have Dr. Paul Brand operate on his hands. When he arrived in Louisiana, he called Pearl at home on Molokai. "Hey, Pearl," he shouted, "guess where I am!" Over the years Brand had refined a tendon-transfer technique to open clawed grips. "Through a small incision near the wrist we pulled the tendon out, affixed a free graft from the leg," Brand wrote, "and tunneled the lengthened tendon all the way through the wrist and into the palm of the hand." The operation returned dexterity to the patient's hand and improved its appearance. Brand also pioneered cosmetic surgery at Carville. "These operations may restore courage and faith to a man who had lost all hope of being able to begin a new life," Brand wrote in the *New England Journal of Medicine.* "This is the time for the orthopedic and plastic surgeon to come forward and open the door that leads the leprosy patient from isolation back to his family life and job." After Makia's hands were fixed, doctors sliced a band of hair from the back of his scalp and remade it into bushy eyebrows. Several patients from Kalaupapa had had the operation done, including Henry, but Brand's success rate fell short of ideal. "It didn't look too nice," Makia recalled. "And then they fell out."

Makia spent seven months at Carville, while Henry also happened to be there. One afternoon they drove across Lake Pontchartrain, headed for the racetrack in New Orleans. A sister of one of Makia's college friends worked as a trainer and had secured them box seats. Afterward she took Makia and Henry on a stable tour. They paused at the stall of the horse she was training. "Here, Makia," she said, "grab this." Makia took hold of something thick. He could hear the horse snuffling, and Henry and the girl giggling.

"What is it?" Makia yelled.

"It's his tongue," she said, laughing. "I taught him to stick out his tongue." Makia held it for a few seconds more, trying to memorize the strange shape. When he let it go, the horse sneezed. They fed and petted the racehorse for a time, and then everybody went to get Chinese food. "Things don't have any substance anymore," Makia later explained. "If I'm holding a pencil, my mind knows what the pencil looks like, but it doesn't feel the same at all—it's just pressure between my forefinger and my thumb." When he had stroked the neck of the horse, Makia was able to discern a slight give. "That's how I knew his coat was soft," he said. "But I can't remember what fur actually feels like, or skin, or things like a sweater or a stone. All that's gone forever."

After he returned from Carville, Makia began to work with a service dog, a gentle black Labrador with a boxy head. Often it takes as long as a year before a guide dog and its owner are fully enmeshed. Makia's condition complicated the relationship. Lack of sensation caused a delay between his movement and the animal's, transforming walks into a series of hesitant stutters. In Kalaupapa, he would practice with the dog on the road to the airport, hiking along the row of cemeteries and pausing when he passed the grave of his brother Earl. Makia would say hello to Earl, and sing to him in a clear, high voice. Then he and his dog would continue walking, until they finally found their rhythm.

One day a community theater group in Honolulu decided to stage a play about Kakaako Hospital. The script involved Mother Marianne, Walter Murray Gibson, and a patient named Tom Burch. Someone suggested Makia for the role of Burch. At the first read-through, Makia's stomach tumbled with anxiety, and he wanted to quit. The director offered Makia some advice: imagine that you are watching from the wings, and that it is someone else onstage. Later Makia took a storytelling workshop and used the same displacement trick. "Before, when I got up in front of people, I just didn't know where to put me," he said. "I was right in front, and they could see me. I needed to put myself in a safe spot. Once I did that, then I could feel comfortable. I could be me."

He usually performed the stories while seated, his voice shifting seamlessly among a dozen characters drawn from his boyhood at Kalaupapa: Tony, Rooster, Donkey, Henry, Bernard. Makia told his tales in vernacular, comic and poignant riffs with himself as the cheerful foil. After one performance an audience member remarked, "He's like a Hawaiian Mark Twain."

One day a friend of Makia's arranged to drive him to one of his talks. In the car with her was a woman Makia did not know. "Makia," his friend announced, "this is Ann." Ann Grant was a Boston University graduate with a friendly, open face and short chestnut hair. She looked at Makia. He was wearing a pair of faded shorts, battered sneakers, and a T-shirt with speckled cows. His hair exploded as a dark cloud, framing a pair of giant sunglasses. He was smiling.

Some years earlier, Ann had visited Kalaupapa as a tourist. It gave her an appreciation of the difficulties of Makia's life. And yet, she thought, his stories and his manner seemed remarkably joyful, unhardened by his experience. "He was just so wise and elegant," she later said, recalling that first day. When Makia suggested they meet again, Ann quickly agreed. "For the first time since I was in college, my bed was piled with clothes, getting ready for a date," she recalled. "And he couldn't even *see.*" She was forty-seven and had never married. Makia was fifty-four.

In time she began to help him with the storytelling, scheduling the performances and making the short speech that preceded their start. Makia performed most often for children, usually at a school or community center. Ann would briefly explain about the disease and answer the children's questions. Afterward she would hand out a sheet with suggested activities so the children could better understand Makia's world. "Spend some time not seeing and not being able to feel with your hands," Ann's handout read. "Wear fool-proof blindfolds and potholder mittens. Have one person be your guide. Later, trade places. What was it like trusting someone to make sure you were safe?"

A few months before she met Makia, Ann had consulted a psychic and quizzed her about her prospects for love. You will marry soon, the psychic had said—a very unusual marriage. Ann did not believe her. Over the years Ann had entertained the notion that two reasons existed for marriage, and both were required. One was conventional: romantic love and physical longing. The other, as Ann described it, was "to work on your soul by marrying your opposite." In Makia, she thought she had finally found both. When Ann first began to discuss marriage, however, Makia became nervous. She told him that they did not have to legally wed; their promises to each other would suffice. But then she changed her mind and said she wanted a true marriage. Makia realized what it meant to her and agreed.

Ann decided to send a letter to her family informing them of her news. She asked her brother to read the note aloud to her parents. "Do you remember telling me that the only thing you wanted was for me to be happy?" Ann later described having written. "I am so glad to tell you that I am so happy I can't even believe it. Finally, I have met someone I want to be married to. This is the whole package. Let me tell you about him. His name is Makia Malo. He is absolutely off the charts brilliant. When he was 12 he got sick with a disease, leprosy. It's completely cured. I want you to know that he is so handsome. His hands are misshapen. And he's blind, but he's so fantastic."

When Ann's brother finished, her mother and father remained silent. Then they thanked him for reading the letter and silently left the room. "We were worried," Otto Grant later admitted, "as any parents would be. But when we finally met Makia, we could tell he was special." One day at one of Makia's performances a woman approached Ann. "I didn't know your husband was a leper," she said. Ann stared at the woman and replied, "He's not. He's a person, a man. And my husband." Later, Ann would write, "Please know that using the word leper in any way, for any reason, is inflicting pain and humiliation of a most singular kind on those who have had the disease and on their loved ones." She often quoted a speech by a person who had had leprosy: "The hell of this disease is that for the rest of your life and regardless of lab reports showing your body is cured, it is the public who will never let you heal. . . . Over and over that word reduces us to a disease we had as children and into a generic term for everything repugnant, disgusting, and unworthy of membership in the human race. And all we did, our big crime, is that years ago we caught a germ."

They found a small apartment on the eighteenth floor of a Honolulu highrise, around the corner from a bus stop. The building superintendent modified the elevator buttons so Makia could locate his floor. Once a month Makia returned to Kalaupapa for a week, in part to keep his residency, and also to give Ann a break. Marriages between patients and nonpatients often fell victim to something known as caregiver's syndrome, where the nonpatient is slowly transformed into a full-time nurse. Some patients accelerated the process and wed nurses, as both Makia and Henry had once done. Ann and Makia were mindful of the phenomenon and took care not to slide into the easy roles. While Makia was away, Ann ran errands, worked on her projects, visited friends. Makia spent his days in his cottage, writing his stories. In the late afternoon he and his dog would walk to the airport and back to stretch their legs. Then he would go to the one bar in Kalaupapa. There Makia would buy two ice cream cones and a can of soda. The bar had one large table and several small ones, and in the afternoon residents gathered to talk and watch the television until closing time, which was 8 P.M. One building down from the bar was where Katie's Store once stood. As he ate his ice cream, Makia thought about the day the lonely old man had called him into the store and bought him treats. He remembered how frightened he had been, and how he had tried not to look at the man's face. Sometimes after his performances the children would question Makia about his appearance. "The kids ask me why I don't wear glasses," Makia recalled. "I say, 'I am so ugly, why would I need dark glasses? I'm so ugly I stop traffic.'" Makia recalled one such scene that had recently occurred. During the performance, a young girl had protested when Makia turned self-deprecating. "You're not ugly," she had shouted. "You're beautiful."

When Makia was in Kalaupapa he sometimes encountered Bernard, and also Henry. Olivia had returned to live in the community but spent her evenings at home, watching television and reading. She preferred nonfiction, and anything about Father Damien. Mostly she read her Bible, kept safe on a shelf beneath a portrait of the priest. During her time outside, Olivia had found that people shied away from her when they learned she was from Kalaupapa. To evade their queries she would play guessing games. When a stranger asked where she was from, Olivia would say one of the neighbor islands. "Which island?" the person inevitably wanted to know. Olivia would reply Molokai. "What part of Molokai?" the person always asked. Finally she would just say she was from Kalaupapa. "Usually that ends the conversation." Earlier, Bernard had remarked, "If people don't know you have leprosy, you won't see prejudice, but if they know, that's when you can really tell whether it means anything or not to them, and whether they can accept you as a person or reject you because you have it."

One evening the residents of the community clicked on the news and heard the newscaster mention a disease that had officials concerned. Every evening thereafter the news had another story about the sickness. One described a San Francisco woman about Olivia's age, named Frances Borchelt, who had undergone hip-replacement surgery. Doctors had transfused three pints of blood during the operation. Six months after the surgery Borchelt was still weak, unable to put on weight or draw a full breath. On Christmas Day, more than a year and a half after her operation, Borchelt was again hospitalized. Two weeks later, the *San Francisco Chronicle* reported that an unnamed seventy-one-year-old woman had developed acquired immune deficiency syndrome from tainted blood given during surgery. Doctors sent Borchelt home to await the full onset of AIDS. Toward the end of Borchelt's life, if visitors approached and tried to embrace her, she waved away their touch. "I don't want to go out of the house," Borchelt explained to her husband. "I feel like a leper."

By the evening on which Frances Borchelt passed away, June 17, 1985, more than eleven thousand Americans had contracted AIDS. Fear of contagion prompted discussions of forced isolation of the sick. As the disease spread beyond the gay community, public panic increased. In August 1987 a California microbiologist named William O'Connor testified before the House Energy and Health Commission and recommended that all AIDS victims be exiled to Kalaupapa. O'Connor was not alone in proposing that Molokai become an AIDS colony. The U.S. surgeon general at the time, Dr. C. Everett Koop, later spoke of receiving letters from "supposedly concerned citizens suggesting that we put AIDS patients at Kalaupapa." As surgeon general, Koop had authored the government's action report on the AIDS epidemic. He had concluded, as one reporter summarized, that "any form of quarantine would be useless." The result of such an exile policy would "do little more than frighten away" the very people who would most benefit from treatment, thus deepening the epidemic. Koop had gleaned this lesson from studying historic epidemics, including leprosy in Hawaii. Later,

Koop visited Molokai. "Everything about a trip to Kalaupapa is a good lesson in reference to AIDS," he announced. "For AIDS is the modern-day leprosy."

Residents had already recognized the parallels. "Believe me," Olivia wrote, "everything I hear sends cold chills up my spine." Speaking to a documentary filmmaker, Henry remarked, "I don't want to see this again. Treat them as human beings, not like something untouchable like we were." Olivia added, "People want to get rid of the people who have AIDS. But they forget that people who have AIDS are also people, just as we were. They shouldn't banish people just because they're scared, not ever. Look what it does to a life."

A short time earlier, during a visit to topside Molokai, Olivia had met a young man named Tim, who was suffering from AIDS. When Tim grasped her hand, Olivia momentarily cringed and was immediately overwhelmed by shame. "I was so embarrassed," she confessed. "Afterwards I realized I also was scared, but that didn't make it right. I didn't know that I had it in me to feel like that." Tim and Olivia later participated in a documentary, *Olivia & Tim: Very Much Alive,* and appeared together in a scene. "People make judgments on you," Tim said in the film. "Say you're not worthy—this is a punishment for you."

"Then this is a punishment for me," Olivia had replied.

"Do you believe that?" asked Tim. "I don't."

"I wondered at first."

"I did too," Tim said. "And then I said, wait a second—that's not the way it is."

A moment later Olivia asked, "If you weren't sick, what would you feel about us?" Tim answered, "I'd probably be afraid."

In 1988, as the hundredth anniversary of Father Damien's death approached, a group of residents from the community traveled to Europe to visit his tomb. Several had also been invited to speak at the International Leprosy Congress, held that year in the Netherlands. The first congress had convened in Berlin in 1897; Dr. Eduard Arning was a featured guest, recounting his experiment on Keanu. At the Netherlands congress, the guests included Bernard, Henry, and Makia. A patients' rights advocate had arranged for their presence. "Traditionally, it was thought the social aspects of the disease and the inherent stigmatization of patients were unavoidable," she explained at the time. "With the patients attending this time, it hopefully will effect a change in the way some people view this." Several entry photographs of residents were displayed during the event, including the image of Bernard from

1937. Bernard later wrote about that picture: "Upon the face of this child I see the pain he is enduring. . . . In spirit I am able to reach out to him, to comfort him, to put my arms around him, and to reassure him that all is not lost. The pain will go away, I tell him. As I look at the photo of this six-year-old boy who was me, something happens. His pain coalesces with my spirit and that pain is no longer his alone. I want to tell him that the time will come when there will be laughter, joy, respect, and, yes, dignity. But I am unable to tell him that it will take a lifetime before this time arrives."

The group arrived in Belgium on a cool and rainy day. Damien's marble tomb occupied the basement of St. Joseph's Chapel, centered beneath a vaulted ceiling. A photograph darkened one wall, showing Damien in the late stages of the disease. Saint-makers at the Vatican were already moving Damien toward canonization. The process was complex and rigidly administered, overseen by a four-hundred-year-old body called the Congregation for the Causes of Saints. They worked from a third-floor office in a building near St. Peter's Square in Rome. Until 1983, when the system was simplified on Pope John Paul II's order, canonization was among "the longest and most complicated" juridical procedures in the world, as one church historian wrote. To be decreed a saint, a person had to first be declared Venerable, someone of "heroic virtue," in the language of the Roman Catholic Church. Damien cleared that hurdle easily. The Congregation for the Causes then investigated whether the candidate had beget an authentic miracle. If one could be proved, the person was beatified and became Blessed. Verification of a second miracle qualified the candidate for sainthood. The congregation was currently reviewing Damien's first miracle. In 1895 a critically sick French nun had prayed to Father Damien for relief and had inexplicably recovered. If investigators found no medical cause for the nun's recovery, it would be deemed a miracle.

From the main floor of St. Joseph's, Makia climbed down to Damien's crypt. He could smell fresh flowers and candles burning. "I felt detached when I first walked in," Makia later told a reporter. "But I felt enveloped. I felt a presence, something intangible, spiritual. I can't explain it. All of a sudden this overwhelming sense hit me. My only reaction was to cry. It just triggered something that was ready to blow in me, and the tears just blew." Makia began to pray as the others laid flowers on the floor of the crypt. Several people started to sing, old Hawaiian songs that Damien would have known. When they finished, they touched their hands gently to his tomb, then made their way upward. After he had emerged from the chapel, Bernard remarked, "It was like meeting a friend after a long separation."

* * *

In Kalaupapa the days peeled away unchangingly. The plane from Honolulu would land just after 8 A.M., bringing mail and newspapers. A resident drove out to collect the bundles, then dropped them at the store and the post office. Several times a week a physician flew in and spent the day seeing patients at the hospital, now called the Kalaupapa Care Home. Workers from the National Park Service arrived daily, hiking down the cliff from topside; some lived in the community for weeklong stretches, flying out on the weekends. The park service had allotted $3.5 million for refurbishments in the community. Workmen began to repair and paint the creaking buildings, level out the roads, and hack back fast-growing brush. Every few days someone would fire up a mower and expose an unknown grave, long forgotten in the weeds. The location and the name were marked and added to a long list.

Olivia seldom left her house and had her meals delivered to her. Makia also dined in his cottage, his meals usually prepared by Ann and packed into a giant plastic cooler, which he carried onto the plane. Henry ate at the hospital or in his house, or he would buy something handy at the Kalaupapa store. He spent his days driving in his truck: out to the airport to see the tourists land or the cruise ships glide by, and sometimes slowly along Damien Road, out to Kalawao. Tourists entered by plane or on the back of mules, led carefully down the cliff. The blue bus of Damien Tours picked them up and took them around the peninsula. The bus passed slowly through the picturesque town, then along the rutted dirt road to the original settlement, now grown unspeakably lovely and wild. By early afternoon the plane or the mules had taken the visitors away. "I don't want them to just come here and think this is beautiful," Olivia said of the tourists. "It came about as an ugly, ugly thing. I want them to know, and I want them to feel it."

Once each year a barge landed from Honolulu, loaded with everything the community would require for the next twelve months. Tugboats nosed the vessel toward the pier, cautious in the dangerous surf. When the boat was tied off, the crew began to off-load cases of spaghetti, peanut butter, cooking oil, lightbulbs, cookies, and cat chow. The barge brought six thousand pounds of rice, and fifty thousand gallons of gas. Boxes were stacked six feet high, slowly walling off the pier. Dishwashers, recliners, microwaves, and televisions rolled off the barge, and any new car a resident had bought. One year a shiny yellow convertible landed, and the residents took turns having their picture taken with it. On barge day people set up folding chairs and watched the supplies come ashore, clapping when something especially good appeared. Afterward everyone had a picnic.

In the summer of 1995 a plane touched down with a box in which was packed Damien's right hand, returned to Molokai as a relic. The Vatican had acknowledged his first miracle, and he was now Blessed Damien. "He became a leper among the lepers," Pope John Paul II announced. "He became a leper for the lepers." At Damien's beatification ceremony the pontiff exclaimed, "Blessed Damien . . . in your life and your missionary work, you show forth Christ's tenderness and mercy for every man, revealing the beauty of his inner self, which no illness, no deformity, no weakness can totally disfigure." Workers opened his grave in Kalawao a second time and laid the hand inside, and at the graveside Makia cried.

By the end of the 1990s the average age of the residents in Kalaupapa was seventy-four. Few residents took their sulfones anymore; bacterial counts were zero, and the possibility of reactivation low. The physicians considered the prospect of elderly patients reacting poorly to the powerful drugs, or developing a resistance to them, to be a greater danger. When the doctor came from Honolulu, he now spent his time treating the maladies of advanced age. Henry's kidneys were failing, and he would soon require dialysis. And Bernard had had a stroke. The trauma muddled his memory and speech and stole some of his movement. Doctors explained to Bernard that he would need full-time care. Workers shuttered his cottage, and he moved to Hale Mohalu, where physicians expected him to spend the remainder of his days. Not long thereafter Henry joined Bernard at Hale Mohalu, forced to live at the facility because Kalaupapa lacked a dialysis machine. Henry pleaded with the health department to buy a machine for Kalaupapa. "I want to come home," he said. "Why can't I do this back home?"

Olivia remarked, "We all make the best of our lives here. This is it for us. This is the end of our fight. You know how it is. You fight against the isolation. . . . You fight yourself, the disease, the other patients, the board of health. Then finally, you give up, and find yourself."

Leprosy could now be cured in as little as three months. The standard treatment was multidrug therapy, a combination of a sulfone-type medication, called dapsone, and clofazimine and rifampin. A single aluminum-foil blister pack, similar to a package of Sudafed, contained one month's supply of the drugs. When the regimen was completed, the disease became "a closed chapter in the life of the person," as the World Health Organization remarked. Since multidrug therapy had become common in 1985, 11 million people with the disease had been cured. Experts estimated that 2.5 million cases remained, 90 percent of them in poor South Asian and African countries without widespread access to multidrug therapy. Most new cases in the United States were recent immigrants from those areas, and their condition was often overlooked or misdiagnosed by physicians with little experience with leprosy.

In 2003, the *New York Times* reported that the number of active and inactive leprosy cases in the United States exceeded seven thousand, and increased by about one hundred cases a year. "And those are the ones we know about," said Dr. William Levis, an attending physician at Manhattan's Bellevue Hospital. "There are probably many, many more." Levis was treating about five hundred outpatients at the Bellevue clinic. "A sampling of patients, all of them wishing to remain anonymous, said they were loath to tell others about their diagnosis," the *Times* reported. One man in his sixties confessed that, forty years after becoming infected, he had still not told his wife of the past three decades that he had the disease. The World Health Organization had recently announced that "dispelling the fear of leprosy, improving awareness of its early signs, and motivating people to seek treatment" were the only means of eradicating the disease. At the Bellevue clinic, doctors referred to leprosy as Hansen's disease, in an effort to lessen the stigma. The facility, like similar outpatient clinics in the country, carried no signage—doctors discovered that if they made clear the clinic's purpose, no one would touch the door. When patients signed in, most used fictitious names. Some signed only a number.

Stay

(Population 28)

Inside Hale Mohalu, in a small square room with a railed bed and a shallow closet, Henry slowly dressed himself. It was spring 2003. On most days Henry wore a pair of shorts and a collarless cotton shirt—the uniform of a teenager—but he had a movie date this afternoon and wanted to look presentable. When he emerged from his room, he was clad in a pair of shiny black slacks, a blue button-down shirt with short sleeves, and a dark pair of scuffed sneakers, wrestled on over white cotton socks. A set of scratched aluminum crutches rode in the gaps beneath Henry's arms, but he used them reluctantly and walked cautiously down the hallway without committing his weight. The day was sticky and warm, and one of the nurses had propped open the exit door to allow in a breeze. Henry made his way outside and onto the tiny patio.

In its annual report, the department of health described Hale Mohalu as a "broad service hospital" that "accommodates patients at the end stages of life." In the years since it had opened, a gritty mélange of mixed-use development had encircled the facility. The neighborhood had a fractured, unsettled feel. A low-slung community college advanced from the south, and a series of blank multistory medical buildings crowded Hale Mohalu's eastern flank. Bordering the hospital to the north and west were rows of once-quaint homes, fallen into disrepair. Homeowners parked broken-down cars on patchy lawns, stranding them atop cinder blocks. Chain-link fencing ringed the homes, imprisoning snarling dogs.

Visitors arriving at Hale Mohalu for the first time inevitably failed to locate the entrance and blundered into the facility through an unmarked door at the end of a loading dock, which led into an area behind the nurses' station. To the front of the station ran a narrow hallway, giving access to the patients' shared rooms. At the near end of the hall was the common area, furnished with dining tables, upholstered chairs, a burst couch, and a flickering television. At the far end of the hallway was a set of doors opening onto the breezeway, a small square of poured concrete that held lawn chairs, a table, and a portable radio broadcasting Hawaiian tunes. When the weather was pleasant, patients spent the day on the patio, shaded by a magnolia tree and an overhung slab of the hospital's roof. The breezeway offered a single view: a street lined with cars, industrial fencing, and a field filled with brittle weeds. Just beyond the lot rose the backside of Diamond Head, the cone shifting colors as the day progressed. Bernard sat in a wheelchair turned toward the street and silently studied the scene.

Henry passed through the doors and onto the patio, gave a quick glance to Bernard and the other patients, then made his way to a small table set on a fringe of grass. A sketchpad and several pencils were scattered on the table, where Henry had left them. After a contemplative pause Henry took up his pencil, hunched over the pad, and began to draw. During one of his trips to Europe, Henry had visited the Louvre. "I could spend a year there and not come out," he had said. He appreciated the masters, he explained, but preferred a sparer style. On his pad a postcard view of Kalaupapa began to form, showing the lighthouse, the foamy coastline, and the cliff split by waterfalls. Every few minutes Henry stopped and closed his eyes, conjuring the scene.

After thirty minutes Henry put away the art supplies. Just then Makia also appeared at Hale Mohalu. He came to the hospital several times a week. Often Makia had no medical agenda and merely wanted to visit with his friends. Some weeks he came every day and spent the afternoon on the patio with Henry and Bernard. Ann would drop him off, or he would leave his dog at home and ride the #3 bus; it let out at the corner.

Sweeping the sidewalk with his cane, Makia crossed to a low metal gate, levered it open, and stepped onto the breezeway. He thwacked against a wheelchair.

"Hey, who's'at?" Makia asked happily. "Hey, is that Bernard? Hello, Bernard." Bernard looked at Makia through his glasses and answered, "Hey—'Kia—howz'it?"

Sometimes, if Bernard was feeling well, Ann and Makia would collect Bernard from Hale Mohalu and treat him to dinner at a restaurant. Makia would help him to the table, Bernard directing him which way to go. When one of them needed to use the restroom, they both went, to assist the other. "Don't miss!" Makia would shout, and then Bernard would begin to laugh. Makia remarked, "I guess we're pretty comfortable with each other." The stroke had imposed limits on Bernard, which at times made him irritable. "But he's just the same as always," Makia said. "If you tell him that he can't do this or can't do that—I don't care what it is—Bernard will say, 'I *can*.'"

Makia was standing on the patio talking to Bernard when Henry walked past, heading for a car parked at the curb.

"Henry?" Makia said as he sensed someone near. "Hey, Henry."

"Hi, 'Kia," Henry answered.

"Henry's heading out for the afternoon," one of the other patients announced.

"Yeah?" Makia said. "Hey, Henry, have a good time." Henry patted Makia on his broad back, then turned toward Bernard.

"So long," Henry said. "I'll see you later."

The movie theater was inside a shopping mall, crowded with children freed from school. Henry made his way through the bustling food court, which abutted the ticket office. Two girls hurried over to hold the door, and Henry smiled as he passed through. In the theater, Henry found a seat in the last row. He settled in and spread a small bag of popcorn on a napkin across his lap. The movie was called *Confidence,* and starred Dustin Hoffman. When the actor appeared onscreen, Henry quietly said, "Oh good."

Afterward, Henry went on a drive to Oahu's North Shore. The two-lane highway to the coast cut through the town where he had briefly stayed with his uncle fifty years earlier. Henry gazed at the shabby main street. "I lived here once," he quietly remarked. As the road rounded along the ocean, Henry watched the spindrift lift from the waves, and the surfers on the beach staring eagerly at the sea. Henry's dinner date was at a seafood restaurant. His table overlooked the water, and the lowering sun sliced through the window. Henry put on sunglasses to read the menu. Fish were listed by their Hawaiian names: *aku, leahi, ono, opakapaka, akule,* and *moi.* Henry selected one and his meal arrived a few minutes later, the fish roasted whole. He put a thumb on the tail and began to work his fork along its spine. Just then a father and his young son appeared at the table.

"I'm sorry to interrupt," the man said, "but we wanted to say hello." Henry looked up at them. The man explained that his son had been learning about Kalaupapa in school, and they had overheard Henry talking about the place. The boy smiled at Henry. After a moment the man said, "It's an honor to meet you."

Henry did not speak for several minutes after they left. Then he smiled and pointed to his plate. "You know," Henry said, "this fish used to be tabooed in the old days. Common people couldn't eat it. Only chiefs could have it, and the king." Henry ate a few more forkfuls, and announced happily, "This is good." It took an hour to drive back to Hale Mohalu. When Henry arrived, Bernard was still on the patio, sitting in the dark.

In the summer of 2003, the health department spent $65,000 to provide Kalaupapa with dialysis service. This was done, the *Advertiser* reported, "especially to fulfill the wish of one patient . . . to move back to Kalaupapa." Henry opened his cottage and let the breeze clear the stale air; then he started up his truck and left it idling until the engine sounded smooth. Most days Henry spent hours at the Kalaupapa hospital receiving treatment, and he often stayed the night. His room had a narrow, elevated bed with a soft cotton spread, and a television attached with brackets to the wall. Henry kept some novels and pictures in the drawer of his nightstand, a sketchpad, and the three hundred handwritten pages of his autobiography. He used a wheelchair as his sitting place and moved himself along by shuffling his feet. Henry would roll himself out to the hospital's shady porch and sit facing the cliff. In the afternoon the sheer wall grew dark, deepening from vivid green to a bluish black. An instant before the sun broke the ocean's horizon, the trail down the cliff turned brilliant in the slanting light. "It looks like a scar," Henry observed.

As a boy, Henry had stood at the rail of a steamer and spotted the Molokai cliffs for the first time. "It took forever to get here," he recalled about that day. "I thought I'd never get here." When they had put him on the boat, Henry had known nothing about Kalaupapa and imagined it might be a wasteland. Then he saw the immense curtain of rock. "That's when I knew that I'd like it here," he said. "If there were cliffs, there were streams, and if there were streams, there were beaches. It would be like home." One of Henry's friends in the community, a man named Paul, had remarked of the residents, "The more we suffer, the more strength we have. The more suffering, the closer we are to one another. Life is that way. If you haven't suffered, then you don't know what joy is. The others may know something about joy, but those who have gone through hell and high water, I think they feel the joy deeper."

About halfway between the hospital and Olivia's home, a block east of Makia's cottage, was the grave of Mother Marianne. It was one of the tourist stops, along with the lighthouse, and the massive white cross that now marked the Given Grave. A few months after Henry returned to Kalaupapa, several planeloads of visitors arrived, including a party of Franciscan nuns from Marianne's order in Syracuse. They were coming to take her home. In Rome, the Congregation for the Causes of Saints had credited Marianne with a verified miracle, the recovery of a thirteen-year-old New York girl who was dying of multiple organ failure. The girl's family had prayed to Marianne, and the girl was suddenly cured. "The woman, now a college student, does not remember anything about her brush with death," one paper reported. To prepare for Marianne's anticipated sainthood, the order was constructing a resting place for the nun's remains in New York. The Congregation for the Causes of Saints now expected to complete the canonization of both Damien and Marianne quickly, giving Kalaupapa two official saints.

Forensic scientists uncovered her casket eight feet underground. Marianne's bones had shattered over the years, and workers employed sieves to extract her skull, arm, leg, and pieces of her lower jaw. The sisters collected and carefully bagged the minor relics: 132 coffin nails, two tarnished crosses, some safety pins from Marianne's habit, and a rosary medal, smoky with age. After a day of work, the scientists managed to get about one-third of Marianne's bones from the grave—the rest had turned to powder and would have to remain in Kalaupapa. Olivia, who had followed the effort with tears in her eyes, announced, "I'm so glad they didn't get all of her."

Henry monitored the activity around Marianne's grave for almost a week. His cottage sat on a street corner, one block back from the Bishop Home, and two long blocks from the grave site. A day after the exhumation, Marianne's remains were taken to the airport and loaded into the hold of a plane; the metal box was marked "Handle with Extreme Care." A few days later a work crew drove to the gravesite, turned left, went past Henry's home, and stopped at a cottage a few doors down. They cracked open the door, raised the windows, checked the pipes and the sink, and turned on the refrigerator. The cottage belonged to Bernard: he was coming home. "He wants to try to make it on his own," a health department official said. "He thinks he's still capable of it, and there's no arguing with Bernard."

Doctors expected Bernard would spend most of his days in the Kalaupapa hospital, but if he improved enough, he could stay some of the time in his cottage. "We're hoping it works out for him," the administrator at Kalaupapa remarked. "He has plenty of people here to help him." Years earlier, Bernard had said, "Kalaupapa used to be a devil's island, a gateway to hell, worse than a prison. Today it is a gateway to heaven. There is a spirituality to the place. All the sufferings of those whose blood has touched the land—the effect is so powerful even the rain cannot wash it away."

Bernard returned to Kalaupapa on a warm Wednesday morning. Nurses had his room ready at the hospital. By the summer of 2004 the average age in the community had reached seventy-six. The youngest resident was sixty-three, and the oldest, named Sarah, was ninety-two. Sarah lived at the Kalaupapa hospital, in a room across the hall from where Henry often stayed, and several rooms down from Bernard. Sarah's maiden name was Meyer; she was Rudolph Meyer's granddaughter. On occasion Sarah's cousin—Rudolph Meyer's great-grandson, a priest named Father Henry Meyer—came to visit. He had joined the Sacred Hearts and later moved to a Trappist order, where he had selected a new religious name: Damien.

Inside the hospital, televisions softly murmured beneath the beep of medical machines. Sarah fell asleep in the early afternoons; Bernard lasted slightly longer, just into evening. Bernard was seventy-four years old and had been sent away sixty-seven years earlier. Down the hall, Henry remained awake deeper into the night. As it grew dark outside, the carbon streetlights blinked on, spilling yellow-orange light. The staff padded down the hallway, past the reception desk with its dusty jars of candy. In a few moments a nurse would come help Henry climb into bed, fuss with his blankets before leaving him alone again. A spot of light from the bedside lamp made his pillow glow; the rest of the room was in shadow. Henry was seventy-eight years old and had been sent away sixty-eight years earlier. He tried to read, but his eyes were tired, so he lay back and listened to the voices from a movie playing on the television. When Henry was asleep, the nurse crept in silently and switched off the set.

Beneath the Kalaupapa hospital ran a series of narrow drainage pipes. Mongooses used them to hide from the cats, since cats would not follow into the hole. When night arrived, the mongooses lurked at the mouth of the pipes, watching the road for movement. By 9 P.M. everyone in the community had retired and the streets were empty. A pair of mongooses crept from beneath the hospital and scurried along the drainage culvert. They had gone a hundred yards when a cat stalked out from behind a rock wall and a fight began.

Olivia heard the cats yowling, as they did every evening. Sometimes the noises woke her, the animals out among the brush and the buildings, howling through the night. When the wind was high, the flutter of the palms covered the caterwauls. Often the sea was rough enough to push swells far up the creek that ran beside her cottage, the waves making a rhythmic wash, which she used to fall asleep. Olivia was eighty-eight years old and had been sent away sixty-nine years earlier.

When she could not rest, Olivia sometimes returned to her recliner and pulled a shawl over her legs. From the vantage of her chair she could take in her entire living room. Mementos crowded every space, sent by people who had read her published memoir and wanted to make contact. Olivia kept their letters in a folder by the Bible. She liked when people took the time to write, although they occasionally phoned instead. She screened the calls on her answering machine. If Olivia did not feel like talking, she would simply listen to the voice, then watch the message light blink. Sometimes she let the light flash for days. The person would try again, Olivia knew; she wasn't going anywhere. "It seems to me that in Kalaupapa we live in a dream world," Olivia had written. "It will never be the way it was and I'm certain that it cannot remain the way it is, not for long anyway. I can almost see the end of Kalaupapa."

A few hundred yards from Olivia's cottage, Makia took his dog out to use the grass before bed. His cottage sat at the farthest edge of the village, nearer the cliff than any other except Olivia's. When animal control agents came to Kalaupapa, they employed his front yard as a staging ground, heading out each day to thin the population of spotted deer, and to hunt wild pigs. A group of veterinarians had spent a weekend in the community recently, trapping cats, which they neutered and released. The vets had counted three hundred cats in Kalaupapa. On the lawn across from Makia's cottage cages filled with cats stacked five feet high. He kept his dog inside that weekend.

A thirty-foot-long ramp climbed gradually to Makia's porch, wide enough for him and the dog. When he was inside, he felt for the telephone, on a stand against the wall to his right. Beside the phone was an ancient answering machine, which he listened to whenever he entered; there was no way to tell if someone had called without reviewing the entire tape. When the tape stopped playing, Makia phoned Ann at their apartment in Honolulu. He listened to her for a few moments, then replied, "I love you too. Good night."

By moving directly forward from the front door, he would enter the cottage's small bedroom, but Makia turned to his left and walked five steps until he was in the kitchen. He found the spigot, then felt for the dog's water bowl; after it was filled, he placed it on the floor. The dog lapped at the dish. Makia removed its harness, then his own sunglasses. Beneath the front window of the cottage was a narrow rattan couch, and beside it a small black-and-white television. Makia clicked it on, and the room filled with blue light.

Opening the refrigerator, Makia swept his hand until Styrofoam squeaked, picked up the container, and carried it to the table. Using both hands, he found the rolls of sushi inside, then ate them one by one, slowly, the dog watching for crumbs that might drop. When Makia was finished, he cleared the table, washed his hands, and went to one of the rattan chairs and sat down. The dog walked over and pushed its square head against Makia's hand, and he rubbed the fur until the dog settled and drifted into sleep, its paws twitching. Makia sat in the chair and sang songs to himself.

In the village, houselights began to go out. Soon the only glow came from the safety lamps in the halls of the hospital, and the flicker from Makia's television. He kept it playing most of the time, with the volume turned low, for the companionship of the voices. A cat screamed and the dog stirred, glancing toward the door as if something were outside. The dog sighed, looked at Makia, and laid down its head.

Makia was asleep in his chair, mouth parted slightly, breath a low whistle. Makia was sixty-nine years old. He had been sent away fifty-six years earlier. In the dreams that he sometimes had, he was swift and graceful and sighted. He scrambled along the cliff and swam naked in the warm surf; he lay on the grass, feeling the tickle of dew. When he gazed upward into the darkening sky, stars emerged. Then something broke the dream. Makia awoke. He sat up straight. He was confused. Then he remembered where he was, and relaxed against the soft cushions. Everything was the same.

Notes

On September 13, 2001, I drove west from Manhattan in a rental car, with Molokai as my ultimate destination; all airlines had been grounded in the aftermath of the terrorist attacks. Two weeks later, I scrambled down twenty-six switchbacks that score the face of an overhanging cliff and set foot for the first time on the isolated peninsula of Kalaupapa. On that day, with the television networks still electric with trepidation and unseen threats, one of the residents pointed out the irony of their situation. "Once this was considered the most dangerous place in the world," she said. "Now it's probably the safest." From the autumn of 2001 to the summer of 2003, I collected material on the history of the colony. Initially I stayed on topside Molokai and hiked into the community to speak to residents; after several months I relocated to Honolulu, to be near the archives that hold the history of the place. Thereafter, I made the twenty-five-minute flight from Honolulu to the tiny Kalaupapa airport, dropped my things in the visitors' cottage, and set out in the village. In undertaking a 140-year history of a unique community, I was incredibly naive—an ignorance matched by an almost complete lack of knowledge about leprosy. In the notes that follow, I've briefly charted the sources that helped me tell this story. Not every source is cited; doing so would result in a notes section as long as the narrative. I've narrowed the entries primarily to quotes and occasional statements of fact. Persons seeking more detail about a particular point are welcome to write to me care of my publisher, or electronically at thecolony@gmail.com.

The first half of the narrative relies almost entirely on archival material, including letters, journals, government reports, and newspaper accounts. As the story progresses toward the present, it begins to focus on four extraordinary individuals: Makia Malo, Olivia Breitha, Henry Nalaielua, and Bernard Punikaia. I've drawn on many hours of interviews to tell their stories. My interviews with Makia, Olivia, and Henry help to inform the account of their lives in these pages; Bernard's health did not allow the same personal approach, and to tell his remarkable story I have relied on previously published interviews, his published writing, and the memories and opinions of others. In some instances I have woven these and other sources into a narrative that integrates the experiences of my subjects with my own observations and interpretations, the history of Kalaupapa, and other related research. The stories of all four survivors share a common trait, beyond the obvious similarity of their circumstances. Thrust into an unjust and at times horrific situation, they fought to regain control of their fates and now live their lives with faith, humor, and dignity.

Toward the end of this project, after my interviews with them were completed, Makia Malo (and his wife, Ann) and Olivia Breitha raised objections to, among other things, certain editorial decisions connected with the book. These included the title, aspects of the book's content, and my use of select terms and details specific to the disease and its victims. To my regret, both declined to participate further in the project, and asked to be left out of the book. While I've attempted to be responsive to their concerns, I recognize that they do not agree with the editorial decisions I have made and they do not endorse the book.

Anyone writing about leprosy confronts a basic dilemma: should the words *leper* and *colony*, which certain people find offensive, be employed? Some have opted for historical revisionism and excised the terms from their accounts. Others have embraced the words and deployed them for maximum sensational effect. In writing this book I tried to navigate a different path—use the words carefully and only in their proper historical context, or within direct quotations. Similarly, I have attempted to render the physical effects of leprosy as sensitively as possible. Readers will judge whether I've succeeded on these counts.

ABBREVIATIONS

AH	State Archives of Hawaii
BE	*The Brooklyn Eagle*
BH	Board of Health, AH
BHL	Board of Health Letters, AH
BHM	Board of Health Minutes, AH
BPBM	Bernice Pauahi Bishop Museum
DHR	Department of Health Report, AH
HA	*Honolulu Advertiser*
HAA	*Hawaiian Almanac and Annual*
HG	*Hawaiian Gazette*
HHS	Hawaiian Historical Society
HJH	*Hawaiian Journal of History*
HL	Hamilton Library, University of Hawaii, Manoa
HMJ	*Hawaii Medical Journal*
MML	Mamiya Medical Heritage Center, Hawaii Medical Library
NYT	*The New York Times*
PCA	*Pacific Commercial Advertiser*
RBH	Report of the President of the Board of Health, AH
RBHS	Report of the Board of Hospitals and Settlement, AH
SB	*Honolulu Star-Bulletin*
SFC	*San Francisco Chronicle*
SFE	*San Francisco Examiner*
WP	*The Washington Post*

RUN

Multiple accounts of Koolau's rebellion and the murder of Louis Stolz exist, and vary dramatically. When possible, I've used details recorded by actual participants. In 1906, Koolau's widow dictated her recollections to John G. Sheldon; the story was later translated from Hawaiian to English by Frances Frazier and published as *The True Story of Kaluaikoolau, As Told by His Wife, Piilani.* Dr. Charles B. Cooper's field autopsies of the dead soldiers, and his observations of the manhunt, are held in his unprocessed file at the Mamiya Medical Heritage Center, Hawaii Medical Library. Charles B. Reynolds and Captain William Larsen filed several reports concerning their actions in Kalalau Valley to William O. Smith, attorney general of the Provisional Government and president of the board of health, and these reside at the State Archives of Hawaii. Several of the men and women with leprosy who joined Koolau during various periods of his resistance gave details to the Hawaiian-language newspaper *Kuokoa,* and the *Pacific Commercial Advertiser,* June 30; July 3, 5, 6, 10, 11, 12, 14, 15, 17, 19, 22, 24; August 5, 8, 1893.

The story of Koolau has been woven into fiction many times. Two attempts merit special attention. Jack London's short story "Koolau the Leper," while veering greatly from the facts, is both sensationalistic and engaging. W. S. Merwin's book-length poem, *The Folding Cliffs,* is the most beautiful and sensitive telling of the story; it is also one of the most accurate.

* * *

7 *By nine-thirty in the evening:* Kaluaikoolau, *True Story,* 20.

7 *"I hear something":* All dialogue in this scene is as recounted by Piilani. Kaluaikoolau, 20–21.

7 *As he fell:* Piilani does not detail the precise sequence of the shooting. Koolau told his version to several valley residents in the hours after the killing. PCA, August 8, 1893.

8 *One more decision to make:* After Stolz was shot, "in order to save himself, and, as [Koolau] says, to put Stolz out of his misery [he] deliberately fired to pierce his heart." Ibid.

8 *Piilani had been the first to notice:* Kaluaikoolau, 8.

8 *"the sickness that is a crime":* As O. A. Bushnell explains in *The Gifts of Civilization: Germs and Genocide in Hawai'i,* when Hawaiians began to encounter specific infectious diseases, they supplied them with startlingly literal names. Thus, for instance, an intestinal infection with a symptom of severe dysentery was called *mai okuu,* or "the squatting sickness," and smallpox was known as *mai puupuu liilii,* the "the sickness of small bumps." Bushnell, *Gifts,* 37.

8 *Officially, Koolau would be dead:* In the board president's 1882 report to the legislature,

Koolau; his wife, Piilani; and their son, Kaleimanu, shortly before their escape into Kalalau Valley. Koolau's mother is seated in the foreground.

a government physician named George Fitch summed up the fate awaiting Koolau: "Once declared a Leper the person is civilly dead, incapable of suing or being sued, divorced from wife, separated from family, the mother torn from her nursing babe, children of tender age taken from their parents, and all hurried off to a living tomb. . . . Criminals have far more consideration shown them. The greatest scoundrel who walks has the privilege of trial by jury, with a lawyer to defend and a judge to see a fair and impartial trial is had. But woe betide the unfortunate sick person, if upon dictum of one man and he not infallible, be the sick one unfortunate enough to be declared a Leper. No hope: no appeal." Extracts from the biennial reports were routinely published in the Honolulu press, in both English and Hawaiian. The legal status of exiles was initially raised in the board president's report to the legislature in 1868.

8 *Leprosy works with a tortuous deliberateness:* Average incubation time is three to five years, "and not uncommonly it is 10 to 25 years from the last known contact to apparent onset," Joseph C. Hathaway, *Hawaii Medical Journal,* July–August 1970.

8 *a government agent appeared:* Kaluaikoolau, 10.

8 *The physician examined the blemishes:* I've used the exam procedures set down by the board of health at the time as the basis for this scene. In its most recent instructions to government physicians in the twenty-six districts on the various islands, the board stressed that their primary duty was "inspection of Lepers, and delivery of names of same to the Sheriff or his Deputy for apprehension." The instructions were adopted at a board meeting on June 17, 1891.

8 *Leper, Suspect, Not a Leper:* The board maintained a "Leper Index Book," in which the person's status was noted under the heading "Condition." Several volumes, in various states of decay, are in the State Archives of Hawaii. Apparently, maintaining these logs

Members of Company F, ranked behind the temporary graves of Privates John Anderson, John McCabe, and John Herschberg.

could grow tiresome: in the volume covering 1881–85, a nineteenth-century secretary had passed the time by doodling in the wide margins.

8 *He would be taken to Kalihi Hospital:* By 1893 the board's leprosy facility at Kalihi was in its second incarnation and officially named Kalihi Receiving Station; its predecessor was called Kalihi Hospital and Detention Center. However, both facilities were commonly referred to as Kalihi Hospital. BHL.

9 *Awaiting him there:* Kaluaikoolau, 10. English-language and Hawaiian-language newspapers on the islands printed hundreds of stories each year about conditions in the colony, including accounts from the exiles themselves. Negative press from the settlement was widely disseminated even in Kalalau. According to a report filed by Lieutenant G. W. R. King, soldiers found a recent copy of *Hawaii Holomua,* an English-Hawaiian newspaper, in the fugitive Paoa's home; the copy had Koolau's name written in pencil on it and had been lent to Paoa by Koolau. In a letter he wrote to the board on July 8, 1887, Charles B. Reynolds remarked that his job of apprehending suspects would be easier if people learned that the colony "is not such a Hell upon earth as it has been represented." BHL.

9 *Over the years other Hawaiians:* On September 5, 1887, the board had debated establishing Kalalau Valley as a satellite leprosy settlement. "Should Kalalau be used as a leper station, perfect segregation could be insured, and people would go willingly," its board minutes record. Board members discussed the issue over two meetings and even undertook an excursion to Kalalau to judge its suitability. At the time "11 or 12 lepers" resided in the valley, and healthy residents "expressed their willingness to give up the valley for the purpose of establishing a Branch Leper Settlement." However, the board president at the time, Dr. Georges Trousseau, forcefully expressed his opinion that "not one [leper] should remain at large in the land" and moved that the project be aban-

Dr. Charles B. Cooper *(left)* and *Advertiser* reporter Frank L. Hoogs *(right)* in Camp Dole, the soldiers' staging area in Kalalau Valley.

doned. The motion drew a tie vote, 2–2. In such cases the board president broke the tie, and Trousseau killed the idea of a Kalalau sanctuary. BHM.

10 *A revered Hawaiian jurist, Judge Kauai:* The judge's political efforts and Hawaiians' regard for him are detailed in Alfons L. Korn, *News from Molokai: Letters between Peter Kaeo & Queen Emma, 1873–1876,* 301–2. On June 28, 1893, the *Pacific Commercial Advertiser* reported, "Most of the resistance which has heretofore been offered to removal has come from ex-Judge Kauai." Also see Edward Joesting, *Kauai: The Separate Kingdom,* 235–36.

10 *Stolz who had reported him:* PCA, July 10, 1893.

10 *a fast-eyed man:* For his book *The Olowalu Massacre, and Other Hawaiian Tales,* Aubrey P. Janion solicited a description of Stolz from his daughter-in-law, Dr. Lois M. Stolz.

10 *"a cheerful voice":* Kaluaikoolau, 12.

10 *related by marriage to the man:* Nineteenth-century Hawaii was a small place. Both Mary and Clara Rowell were daughters of the Reverend George B. Rowell, a Protestant missionary from New Hampshire who settled in Waimea in 1842 and founded a church and a school—Koolau had been a student of Rowell's. Kauai was also home to two other prominent missionary families, the Doles and the Smiths. Sanford and George Dole were classmates and friends of the Reverend Rowell's children as well as the children of Dr. James W. Smith, including William O. Smith, known as Willie. The closest friend of Anna Dole, Sanford's wife, was Clara Rowell Dole; the two met often on Kauai, presumably at times in the company of Clara's sister, Mary Rowell Stolz. Thus the three men most directly responsible for Koolau's fate—Louis H. Stolz, Sanford B. Dole, and William O. Smith—were intimately connected. See Ethel M. Damon, *Sanford Ballard Dole and His Hawaii.*

The negative effects of the exile policy plagued William O. Smith in later years. Four years after the killing of Louis Stolz, Smith's brother, Dr. Jared K. Smith, was murdered by a Hawaiian whose mother and sister had been ordered to the colony. Upon hearing Dr. Smith's diagnosis of leprosy, the man, named Kapea, declared that he "would not rest until he had killed that white man," according to witnesses at his trial. "My gun has feasted on a man and is now satisfied," he reportedly announced after the murder, which occurred September 24, 1897. Nine of the twelve members of the jury voted to convict. "There were tiny drops of rain sifting through the sunshine when Kapea was brought out to be hanged," the *Advertiser* reported. "The party appeared from within the prison just as four bells (ten o'clock) had been struck. In two minutes, the fine form of the young man was dangling from the rope end."

11 *"The amount and kind of intimacy":* Stolz to W. O. Smith, June 8, 1893, BHL.

11 *"I am not hankering":* Stolz to board of health, May 12, 1893, BHL.

11 *"I was overwhelmed with grief":* Kaluaikoolau, 13.

11 *"I first ask whether my wife will be allowed":* Ibid., 15.

11 *"should the obstinate ones be removed":* Stolz to W. O. Smith, June 8, 1893, BHL.

12 *"I will hurry up things":* Stolz to W. O. Smith, June 26, 1893, BHL.

12 *the deputy's polished metal badge:* PCA, July 10, 1893.

12 *Details of Stolz's death arrived:* For my account of the government reaction to Stolz's killing, and a narrative of the military's actions, I've relied mainly on reporting contained in the *Pacific Commercial Advertiser,* July 3, 5, 6, 10, 11, 12, 14, 15, 17, 19, 22, 24; and August 5, 1893. Two of the most exhaustive reports were filed by a correspondent

named Frank L. Hoogs and fill the better part of a broadsheet page in the July 5 and July 10 editions. A somewhat more sympathetic account of Koolau and his flight occupies the August 8, 1893, issue. Reports filed by military members of the expedition are contained at the State Archives of Hawaii, filed in incoming letters to the adjutant general, 1893.

13 *and Dr. Charles B. Cooper:* Physician's File, MML.

13 *"to give us a fair mark":* Reynolds recounted the episode in his June 1888 "Report of Expedition to Kauai to Arrest Lepers," BHL.

14 *dragged his damaged body:* When Judge Kauai arrived at Honolulu on July 9, 1893, "he had to be carried ashore . . . by four men." Joesting, *Kauai: The Separate Kingdom,* 238.

16 *Cooper performed field autopsies:* Cooper to E. G. Hitchcock, July 7, 1893, MML.

16 *"In the midst of this trouble":* Kaluaikoolau, 27.

17 *editorials that pondered:* Responding to an editorial in the *Hawaiian Gazette,* the *Pacific Commercial Advertiser* declared, "It is doubly unfortunate that . . . partisan zeal has misled [the paper] to throw the blame of Sheriff Stolz's death upon the president of the board of health." Though it defended Smith against attacks from the rival newspaper, the *Advertiser* freely mocked the official effort to capture Koolau. On July 24, 1893, it published the story of a teenager named A. R. Bindt who was offering to assist the government. Bindt's scheme was to trick Koolau into drinking too much bootleg whiskey; when Koolau passed out, the boy would arrest him. All he needed to get started on this plan, Bindt told a reporter, was a whiskey still and a good amount of mash, which he hoped the government would provide. The paper dryly noted that if "Young Bindt" succeeded, "he will make the members of the Larsen expedition grow green with envy."

18 *Koolau stood on a distant ridge:* PCA, July 17, 1893.

18 *"wandering life in the wild valleys":* Kaluaikoolau, 32.

19 *Placing Koolau's rifle:* Some confusion exists about the fate of the rifle. In 1934 a newspaper reported that Koolau's grave and rifle had been discovered in 1897, and that the weapon subsequently ended up in the gun collection of the Honolulu Police Department. In 1981 a police sergeant combed the collection and found an 1870 Remington buffalo rifle, identical to one Piilani holds in a photograph published in her book. However, Piilani insisted that her husband's grave had never been found; the rifle she wields in the book, Piilani said, was a prop for the photograph.

19 *more than a thousand men and women and children:* According to board records, in 1895 the patient population in the colony totaled 1,090. Nineteen people were removed from Kalalau to Kalihi Hospital in the weeks after Stolz's murder, including three girls, aged seven, eleven, and twelve, and Paoa, the man Louis Stolz originally arrested. "The leper Paoa was among the first to land [at Kalihi]," the *Advertiser* reported. On July 25, 1893, most of the patients were exiled to Molokai. BHM.

SCATTERED SEEDS

The most comprehensive source for details on the creation and management of the settlement are the biennial reports of the presidents of the board of health to the king and the legislature (RBH, RBHS). Typically written by the head of the board, the reports offer data and open a window into the mind-set of the president and the board itself. During the first half-century of exile, the board of health shifted between an approach in which it made treatment of the disease the highest priority, and one in which eradication of the disease took precedence. The prevailing political climate dictated the approach, but the board president supplied the tenor, either sympathetic or harsh. A livelier and unvarnished account of the board's workings unfolds in the minutes of the board meetings (BHM), although several ledgers have been rendered partly illegible by insects and rodents. The reports and minutes supply only the government's version of exile; the perspective of the exiles themselves is available through their letters, lawsuits, and journals.

20 *Suspect cases appeared as early as May 1786:* Bushnell, *Gifts,* 42.

20 *"the beauty of the climate":* Ibid.

20 *Possibly Rollin was mistaken:* In "The Diagnosis of Leprosy," a 1949 supplement published by the American Society of Tropical Medicine, Dr. Frederick A. Johansen offers a list of the conditions most commonly mistaken for leprosy, including syphilis, sarcoid, ringworm, acne vulgaris, lupus vulgaris, and Raynaud's disease, among others. The paper notes that determining the true cause of some leprosy symptoms "is exceedingly difficult and sometimes impossible."

20 *A Spanish explorer, John Gaetano:* Alexander, *Brief History,* 99. See also Bushnell, *Gifts,* 19.

20 *By 1810 the sixty-person white population:* Bushnell, *Gifts,* 200.

21 *"We seldom walk out without":* Mouritz, *Path of the Destroyer,* 29.

21 *Naea had purportedly contracted:* D. Baldwin to board, May 26, 1864, BHL.

22 *Dr. Wilhelm Hillebrand had journeyed:* Biographical details on Wilhelm Hillebrand come from his Physician's File, MML, and "Wilhelm Hillebrand: 1821–1886," published first in *Hawaiian Almanac and Annual* (1919): 53–60, and in slightly different form in *The Asa Gray Bulletin* (Spring 1957). One of Hillebrand's biographers, Ursula H. Meier, also provided valuable details from *Hawaii's Pioneer Botanist: Dr. William Hillebrand, His Life & Letters,* Honolulu, Bishop Museum Press, 2005.

Dr. William Hillebrand, who raised the initial alarm about leprosy in Hawaii. He is pictured circa 1866, at about age forty-five.

22 *drawing a salary of $1,500:* PCA, July 28, 1859.

23 *"all was perfectly clean":* Korn, *Victorian Visitors,* 109–10.

24 *letters in the winter of 1861:* See Smith to board, January 8, 1862, BHL.

24 *"No doubt there are others":* John H. Brown to board, December 2, 1861, BHL.

24 *submitted a list of thirty-two:* Pease to board, March 24, 1864, BHL.

25 *the merchant vessel* Charles Mallory *had drifted:* Parke, *Marshall,* 50.

25 *Estimates of the dead ranged:* Halford, *9 Doctors,* 212.

26 *"The decrease of our population":* As the first census in Hawaii didn't occur until 1823, it's impossible to know exactly how many persons inhabited the islands before contact by outsiders. Various officers who landed with Captain Cook—including his sailing master, a twenty-two-year-old martinet named William Bligh—offered their opinions, ranging from 242,000 to 400,000. Later estimates place it anywhere between 100,000 and 1 million, although a consensus has settled the figure at 350,000. No matter what the precise starting point, people began perishing almost immediately after Cook's arrival, and with such terrible consistency that depopulation came to be called "the sliding way of death." When missionaries assembled the 1823 census, they recorded 142,050 Hawaiians—about half of what they had numbered just forty-four years earlier.

27 *Divided with tall, sturdy fences:* August 10, 1864, BHM.

27 *"An Act to Prevent the Spread of Leprosy":* RBH, 1868. The act was signed into law on January 3, 1865.

ALMOST-ISLAND

29 *He had been preparing for this day:* The board issued the first notice on October 25, 1865.

29 *his bounty began to land: The Friend,* October 2, 1865. See also PCA, April 4, 1865.

30 *Within an hour sixty-two persons:* HG, November 18, 1865.

30 *"It is gratifying indeed to observe":* HG, November 18, 1865.

30 *"Dr. Hoffmann . . . comes in early and attends":* HG, December 2, 1865.

31 *Ferdinand Hutchison had suggested:* June 10, 1865, BHM. Also see RBH, 1866.

31 *"The lands are ready":* R. W. Meyer to board, November 28, 1865, BHL.

31 *"Their places at the Kalihi Hospital":* Board to Treadway, March 5, 1866, BHL.

31 *The vessel had arrived in Hawaii:* Thomas Mifflin, *Hawaiian Interisland Vessels and Hawaiian Registered Vessels* (Santa Barbara, Calif.: Seacoast Press, 1982), 47.

32 *She belonged to Edwin Jones:* See BHM for April 18, 27, 1866. On April 22, 1871, an Edwin Jones took out a display ad in the *Advertiser* offering himself as a ship chandler. The board's records variously record Jones's name as Ed., Edwin, and Edward.

32 *In the board's logs, Kahauliko was recorded:* Hawaiians did not create a written version of their language. In the 1820s missionaries invented a system of transcribing Hawaiian into Roman characters and on January 7, 1822, published a pamphlet with this Hawaiian alphabet and some simple lessons in spelling and reading. (The alphabet they standardized has only twelve letters: *a, e, i, o, u, h, k, l, m, n, p,* and *w.*) Missionaries then began to print a never-ending stream of religious tracts and Hawaiian-language Bibles, from which most Hawaiians in the early nineteenth century learned to read. This sequence—creation of a simple yet often confusing written language, and the use of religious material to teach it—had two significant consequences. First, the biblical stigma against leprosy, previously unknown to Hawaiians, began to filter out

among the people. And second, the records kept by the board became rife with errors, since Europeans and Americans invariably mangled the spelling of Hawaiian names. Often in the board's records an exile's name will be spelled four or five different ways; I've simply used the most consistent or logical spelling. Similarly, when the board assigned numbers to each exile, these numbers often became tangled in misspellings and the same person marked down several different times. Logs were kept in the board's offices, in the settlement, and at branch hospitals such as Kalihi; on occasion a person was assigned a different number when being transferred among facilities and may thus be referred to by several different numbers. In the case of conflicts I've used the most consistent or logical patient number.

The Hawaiian language employs a variety of glottal stops and macrons. Hawaii is, properly, Hawai'i, and the island that contains the settlement is Moloka'i. For readability I've chosen to use standard spellings. Grammarians should refer to the *Hawaiian Dictionary,* compiled by Mary Kawena Pukui and Samuel H. Elbert. To approximate pronunciation of Hawaiian words and names, try sounding out each vowel individually, including double vowels. All syllables end in a vowel, and the accent usually lands on the next-to-last syllable. Thus: Mo-lo-*ka*-i.

33 *"Never, should I live":* Charmian K. London, *Jack London,* 105.

33 *Under the best circumstances:* Kuykendall, *Hawaiian Kingdom: 1854–1874,* 6–7. Most nineteenth-century visitors to Hawaii commented on the rough passages between the

Dr. Edward Hoffmann, medical director of Kalihi Hospital, in 1866.

various islands. One of the most vivid accounts of a crossing was written in early 1866 by Mark Twain, who traveled on the schooner *Boomerang*: "The first night, as I lay in my coffin, idly watching the dim lamp swinging to the rolling of the ship, and snuffing the nauseous odor of bilge water, I felt something gallop over me . . . presently something galloped over me once more. I knew it was not a rat this time, and I thought it might be a centipede, because the captain had killed one on deck in the afternoon. I turned out. The first glance at the pillow showed me a repulsive sentinel perched upon each end of it—cockroaches as large as peach leaves—fellows with long, quivering antennae and fiery, malignant eyes. They were grating their teeth like tobacco worms, and appeared to be dissatisfied about something. I had often heard that these reptiles were in the habit of eating off sleeping sailors' toenails down to the quick, and I would not get in the bunk anymore."

34 *In his first weeks of practice:* Hoffman to board, March 2, 1866, BHL.

35 *the waiting crops began to rot:* Meyer warned about the spoilage of crops in several letters. See Meyer to board, November 7, 20, 28, 1865; December 5, 1865. The most comprehensive weather data for Kalawao covers a thirteen-year period from 1905 to 1918 and provides a fair estimate of the seasonal changes colonists would have experienced. Mean maximum/minimum temperatures: January 76.9/64.4; February 77.5/63.8; March 76.9/64.3; April 78.1/65.7; May 80.2/67.5; June 81.3/69.6; July 82.4/70.7; August 83.1/71.2; September 83.5/70.9; October 82.4/69.5; November 79.9/68.1; December 77.5/66.1. The annual range is 80.0/67.6, and November, December, and January tend to be the rainy period, with about eighteen inches of rain each month.

The Honolulu waterfront circa 1870.

35 *onto the* Warwick *as a stowaway:* Meyer to Hutchison, January 22, 1866, BHL. Meyer reported that the exiles "even managed to keep the boy secreted during the daytime in the asylum for some days." This was not the only healthy child to sneak aboard the schooner with an exiled parent; a young girl named Manaole stowed away in one of the first shipments and remained undiscovered until February 1867. HG, February 13, 1867.

35 *Rudolph Meyer was thirty-nine years old:* Meyer, *Meyer and Molokai.* See also Rhoda E. A. Hackler, *R. W. Sugar Mill.*

36 *"sunburnt and dust-covered":* Stoddard, *Lepers*, 19–20.

36 *evenings arrived in Kalawao:* Gibson, *Under the Cliffs*, 58.

36 *Meyer tried upping the price:* See Meyer to Charles de Varigny, July 24, 1865.

36 *"to live among the lepers":* September 20, 1865, BHM.

37 *One island skipper named William Sumner:* Gibbs, *Shipwrecks in Paradise*, 74. Sumner's son, William Sumner II, became infected with leprosy and was exiled; in 1878 he served briefly as assistant resident superintendent.

37 *the* Warwick *brought the first:* Lepart to Heuck, January 8, 1866, BHL. A common misconception is that the initial group of exiles were dumped in the water on the Kalawao side, and that the board had arranged for no one to meet them. Lepart's report contradicts that myth.

38 *Men received a shovel:* Lepart to board, January 1, 8, 1866, BHL. Lepart kept a concise inventory of the items he distributed. On January 7, 1866, Kahauliko received "1 Blanket, 1 axe, 1 shovel, 1 hoe." On April 10, Lepart gave Kahauliko "1 tin cup, 1 dish, 1 tea pot."

38 *It took an hour to reach their destination:* A portion of the original trail between the villages cuts close to the base of the cliffs, on the southern side of a creek that empties on the western shore; an improved path between the villages was later carved and became known as Damien Road. The estimate of travel time between the villages is based on a hike I made along the original road.

Rudolph W. Meyer, superintendent of the colony.

"A KIND OF COLONY"

40 *Lepart had left a few bags:* Lepart to Heuck, January 8, 1866, BHL.

40 *took command:* Kahauliko to board, February 19, 1866, BHL. Responding to charges that he was mistreating members of the second party of exiles, Kahauliko detailed the efforts he had made with the first group and claimed that he, not Lepart, was the only one to give aid to the second group: "I alone accommodated them on their arrival." He signed the letter, "Your leprous servant."

40 *Kalawao was stripped bare of timber:* Lepart to Heuck, February 4, 1866, BHL. For three decades, the area surrounding Kalawao remained mostly barren of trees, although patients began to plant shrubs and flowers immediately after arriving. The explosive growth of forest now in evidence in Kalawao and parts of Kalaupapa is mainly the result of two tree-planting contests staged after the completion of a water pipeline. The first, initiated by board president William O. Smith in July 1899, offered a first prize of fifty dollars to the resident who planted the most trees within a set period; second prize brought forty dollars, and so on. The board hoped the contest would beautify the settlement and "awaken emotion" in the residents. "There is nothing worse for any set of people than to sink into dull apathy," the board commented. A similar contest was staged several years later by superintendent Jack McVeigh.

41 *five patients became incapacitated:* Lepart to Heuck, March 27, 1866, BHL.

41 *Or so the board believed:* RBH, 1866.

41 *Three helpers, including Kahauliko's:* January 21, 1866, BHM.

41 *farmers living in a nearby valley:* RBH, 1866, 1868.

41 *Forty square feet of well-planted:* Nordhoff, *Nordhoff's West Coast,* 35.

42 *They were the first to die:* According to the board's records, the first exiles were nine

Dr. Ferdinand W. Hutchison, who proposed the site for the colony, and whose son would spend fifty-three years in exile.

men: J. D. Kahauliko (d. November 4, 1870), J. W. Lae (d. July 20, 1866), Liilii (d. September 30, 1869), Puha (d. July 13, 1868), Kini (d. January 1, 1869), Lono (d. January 1, 1867), Waipo (d. August 7, 1867), Kainaina (d. November 27, 1866), Kaaumoana (d. April 25, 1875); and three women: Nauhina (d. August 5, 1866), Lakupu (d. August 5, 1866), Kepihe (d. October 3, 1869). BH.

42 *"make these poor people as comfortable":* Board to Lepart, January 29, 1866, BHL.

42 *"It is not so, is it?":* Lae to Heuck, February 7, 1866, BHL. Lae details the efforts he and Kahauliko were making to keep the others alive and explains how they were dividing food and labor. The next day Lae wrote a second letter, asking the board to send a newspaper for the exiles: "We are living in total darkness here, and have not heard of the news of A.D. 1866."

43 *One afternoon Kahauliko went:* Kahauliko to Heuck, February 1, 1866, BHL.

43 *"they are strangers there":* Board to Lepart, February 12, 1866, BHL.

43 *"It had been anticipated":* RBH, 1866.

43 *led eleven more people into Kalawao:* On average, the second party of exiles lived for twenty-four months. Three women from this group, Kuapuu, Pahu, and Mahae, as well as a man named Kolikoli, who arrived on the third boat, all died on August 29, 1868.

43 *the crew had pilfered much of it:* Lepart to Heuck, March 25, 1866, BHL.

43 *enjoy the fruits of the labors of the exiles:* RBH, 1868.

44 *"organize a kind of Colony":* Board to Lepart, March 18, 1866, BHL.

44 *"Be kind, considerate, just, but firm":* Ibid.

44 *Lepart called a meeting:* Lepart to Heuck, March 26, 1866, BHL.

44 *A day earlier the* Warwick *had delivered:* The *Warwick* carried patients number 52 to 63, including two women. The exiles continued to die in groups, typically as a result of cold snaps. Five members of the fourth party to land expired together on February 24, 1869.

44 *the crew was stealing:* Lepart to Heuck, July 30, 1866, BHL. In one of many such incidents, Lepart reported that the crew had apparently taken a trunk belonging to a patient named Kaolelo.

44 *"much grumbling":* Lepart to Heuck, March 25, 1866, BHL. "It is entirely useless . . . to separate the lepers if the healthy ones can communicate night and day with the patients," Lepart complained. He suggested he be made magistrate and authorized to arrest and fine the healthy residents of Kalaupapa, a desire that the board accommodated.

44 *"the idle ones will have no":* Lepart to Heuck, March 26, 1866, BHL.

45 *"There is a basic point I ask":* Lepart to Heuck, March 27, 1866, BHL.

45 *"Five or six of the patients":* Ibid. Many exiles arrived already close to death. On March 28, Peter Treadway wrote the board from Lahaina asking how persons crippled by leprosy should be loaded aboard the *Warwick;* he thought they could be carried onto the boat with a litter, but believed off-loading them at their destination might prove a problem.

45 *"We are receiving great":* Kahaupau, Pu, and Kaleo to board, date illegible, 1866.

46 *bewildering array of terms:* See BHL for 1866, 1867, 1868, 1869, 1870; RBH 1866, 1868, 1870. For one of the first usages of *colony,* see March 16, 1865, BHM.

46 *tested an original coinage:* Meyer was the most persistent employer of this term. See Meyer to board, November 21, 1870, among others, BHL.

46 *In a typical account:* G. W. Smith to Heuck, March 31, 1866, BHL.

46 *For the two-year period:* RBH, 1866. Also, in the minutes from the September 12, 1866, meeting the board laments that its biennial appropriation "was already heavily drained upon."

47 *"We will try to keep the ball in motion":* Board to Treadway, March 5, 1866, BHL.

47 *"If the sick won't come to us":* Ibid.

47 *Neither man filed entirely accurate accounts:* Often when Lepart's reports were translated and recorded in the board minutes, details became garbled or incorrectly stressed, underplaying the growing crisis; whether this resulted from error or intent is unclear. Rudolph Meyer tended to purposely downplay bad news from the colony, perhaps because he felt responsible for the local operation. In a letter dated January 22, 1866, Meyer reported to the board that the exiles' new home "seems like a paradise to them." On September 19, 1866, Lepart wrote to T. C. Heuck, "I am very distressed by not being able to write in English, but that is impossible for me, if I were able to do so I would never wait for your request. For any significant communication I will continue, as today, to have recourse to Mr. Meyer." BHL.

48 *Lepart had been told to expect:* Lepart to Heuck, April 30, 1866, BHL. Occasionally, Lepart found that the number of exiles in a shipment was reduced by more understandable reasons. In the board's account of the seventh shipment of patients, a man named Waiwaiole is recorded as having "died at sea, May 30, 1866." BH.

48 *Earlier in the month the schooner:* Treadway to board, June 21, 1866, BHL. The sheriff listed a variety of complaints against the *Warwick* and its crew, and ascribed this most recent failing to "Capt Henry being off on a potatoe drunk."

48 *the* Warwick *was gone again:* Lepart to board, April 14, 1866, BHL.

48 *decided to purchase the* Warwick: April 18, 1866, BHM.

49 *"they are not satisfied":* Lepart to Heuck, June 12, 1866, BHL.

49 *"Alone as I am among":* Ibid.

49 *shipped to the colony to use as a jail:* Board to Lepart, June 27, 1866, BHL. "It is the earnest wish of this board that you are to thoroughly control these people," the board instructed Lepart. "While being kind and just and fair to all do as absolutely necessary that vagabonds and dissenters should be made to fear the consequences."

49 *"the most quiet and laborious lepers":* Lepart to Heuck, July 19, 1866, BHL.

49 *"I have no doubt that one or two months":* Lepart to board, August 9, 1866, BHL.

50 *were mostly destitute:* February 2, 1866, BHM.

50 *diagnosed John Boehle:* A married merchant living in Lahaina, Boehle was friendly with Sheriff Peter Treadway. On December 14, 1865, the board had notified Boehle of the results of his most recent exam. His disease was "a very doubtful case of leprosy," they reported, and likely "of a syphilitic character." The board cautioned Boehle to be careful in his "intercourse" with others.

51 *"might be avoided if the Board":* Lepart to Hutchison, February 13, 1867, BHL.

51 *Heuck took his pen and slashed a line:* Lepart's translated letters often bear evidence of the board's reactions, usually in the form of marginalia presumably scrawled by Heuck, the board secretary. If something displeased Heuck, he tended to underline or circle the offending word or sentence; if amused, he marked the page with an exclamation point.

51 *"Do you mean we will have to feed":* Heuck to Lepart, August 7, 1866, BHL. See also September 12, 1866, BHM.

52 *his résumé included:* Physician's File, Ferdinand William Hutchison, MML. Hutchison's name was often incorrectly recorded as Hutchinson, even in official board documents.

52 *"He has sandy hair":* Day, *Mark Twain's Letters,* 119.

52 *"supply absolutely for the future wants":* RBH, 1868.

52 *"was already heavily drained":* September 12, 1866, BHM. As of January 1, 1867, the board had spent $1,218 to purchase the land on Kalaupapa. By that same date, they had paid $1,822 to secure the *Warwick* and keep it afloat. The total bill to date for coffins for the colony was $54.25.

52 *"Insufficiency of means can never be a just reason":* Ibid.

53 *Ambrose was already infected:* Mouritz, *Destroyer,* 204. Ambrose Hutchison responded to a request by Dr. Mouritz that he detail his infection with leprosy. On November 16, 1914, Hutchison sent Mouritz a chronology of his illness; he later incorporated the same material in an uncompleted memoir.

ORDER

54 *"I forward you six":* Neville to Heuck, undated, BHL. The deputy sheriff added a footnote: "I think I shall send another as soon as I can get him; the police are after him."

54 *"I send this day":* Dozens of letters from the board's agents arrived each month and were reconciled into a master list. See BHL, 1865, 1866, 1867.

54 *"becomes emaciated":* Nordhoff, 255. Mark Twain also noted the similarity between the presumed symptoms of leprosy and those of the awa drinker: "It turns a man's skin to white fish-scales that are so tough a dog might bite him, and he would not know it till he read about it in the papers." New York *Daily Tribune,* January 9, 1873.

54 *Lee spotted:* Name illegible, deputy sheriff of Maui, to board, March 5, 1869, BHL.

55 *"I have seen two persons today":* Treadway to board of health, March 5, 1866, BHL. For all his fretting over false reports, Sheriff Treadway was not immune to using the menace of the system to his own end. In 1868 Treadway summoned Dr. David Lee to examine his wife, whom he claimed he suspected of having the disease. Lee arrived to find Mrs. Treadway sobbing fearfully. His report notes that she was a heavy awa drinker, had vertigo, and "is of corpulent dropsical habit"—but she did not have leprosy. Dr. Lee reported that the right side of Mrs. Treadway's face was heavily bruised and swollen, the consequence of her husband having "cuffed" her. Apparently this was a domestic dispute, Lee decided; the sheriff was wielding the threat of Molokai to keep his spouse in line. See Lee to board, September 24, 1868, BHL.

55 *"Had the present number":* Meyer to Heuck, September 21, 1866, BHL. Meyer supplied the board with his breakdown of which exiles were industrious and which were not. At present, the colony included 87 men, 35 women, and 2 children. Meyer reported that 12 settlers were unable to work, 56 were planting, fishing, and generally working, and 9 exiles were refusing to work "or are too lazy."

56 *Another petition followed:* various to board, October 12, 1866, BHL.

56 *"beseech forgiveness":* Lepart to board, December 1, 1866, BHL. Lepart's original letter reads, "I don't think I will be able to keep them chained two more weeks, because, as I had the honor to inform His Excellency, the poor wretches greatly swell on the arms and legs, which makes the skin very tender, and as a result after a few days clapped in irons, the prisoners have their wrists flayed alive, and suffer from very acute, unbearable pain. But this leads to the undeniable conclusion that irons make them very humble."

56 *considered themselves Protestant Congregational:* Damon, "Siloama," 10.

56 *burned down their chapel:* HG, February 6, 1867.
57 *photographer named King:* PCA, December 29, 1866.
57 *Lepart also noticed:* Lepart to Hutchison, January 23, 1867, BHL. Lepart explained that Dr. Bechtinger "wanted to discover errors in the running of the camp of lepers and to criticize the Board and his members."
57 *"There they are":* PCA, January 12, 1867.
57 *"human infamy":* PCA, December 29, 1866. Forbes's letter to the editor containing this quote is signed "Anonymous." Lepart exposed the author's identity, however, as did Rudolph Meyer, when he wrote to the *Advertiser* on January 31, 1867: "[I] feel it my duty to correct some statements which lately appeared in the columns of your paper," Meyer explained.
57 *"Here is a clear impartial":* PCA, January 12, 1867.
57 *"There is no doubt":* PCA, January 31, 1867.
57 *"to keep the children":* D. Walsh to board, September 8, 1867. By March 31, 1868, Walsh's school held seventeen students: a dozen boys and five girls. BHL.
58 *"I remember the charity":* Stoddard, *Lepers*, 49.
58 *"working like a slave":* Lepart to Hutchison, May 6, 1867, BHL.
58 *"I have hardly time":* Lepart to Hutchison, June 22, 1867, BHL.
59 *"Civilization leaves me bit":* Simpson, *Oxford Book of Exile*, 254.
59 *"I am sorry to acquaint":* D. Walsh to Hutchison, November 25, 1867, BHL.
59 *"drum her out":* D. Walsh to board, December 3, 1867, BHL.
60 *"fearful to contemplate":* Ibid.
60 *of the 179 persons exiled:* RBH, 1870. See also Hoffman to board, January 20, 1868.
60 *"This house is cold":* D. Walsh to board, May 30, 1867, BHL.
61 *"It appears to have":* D. Walsh to board, December 3, 1867, BHL. See also D. Walsh to board, June 22, 1867, BHL.
61 *October 15, 1867:* BH. Boehle is listed in the board's records as patient number 175.

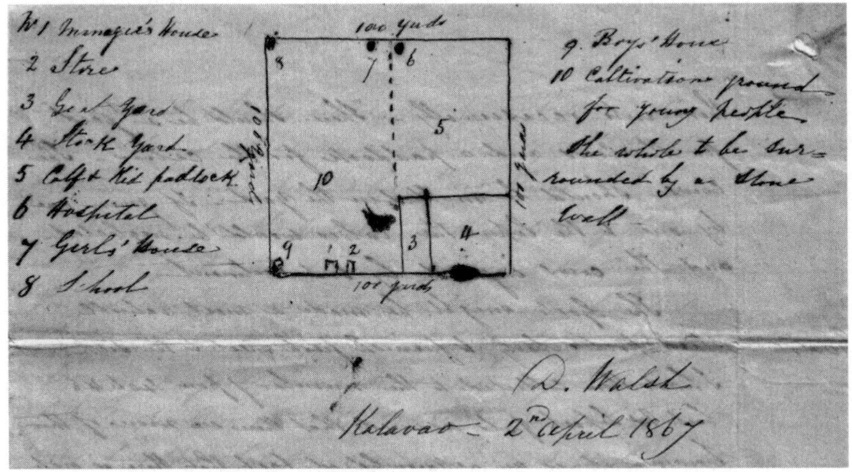

Donald Walsh's original blueprint for the village center in Kalawao.

62 *"In this place there is no law":* The phrase (*A ole kanawai ma keia wahi,* in Hawaiian) is perhaps the most famous utterance to emerge from the colony and was widely spread by the accounts written by Robert Louis Stevenson after his visit. Stevenson would have initially found the quote in a history of Kalawao's early period, written for the board by Father Damien de Veuster and published in its biennial report for 1886. See "Special Report from the Rev. J. Damien," March 1886.

62 *"a man with whom":* D. Walsh to board, October 3, 1867, BHL.

62 *Epsom salts and citrine ointment:* D. Walsh to board, November 14, 1867, BHL.

62 *63 had expired:* Lepart to Hutchison, June 22, 1867, BHL.

63 *"If they must have pets":* David Lee to board, March 1, 1869, BHL.

63 *"Mr. Boehle and myself":* D. Walsh to Hutchison, November 21, 1867, BHL.

63 *"If I were to handcuff":* D. Walsh to board, December 3, 1867, BHL. Walsh wrote, "There is not an orphan here that has not 4 or 5 fathers ready to question all my acts connected with *their* children."

63 *"They are probably the most depraved":* D. Walsh to board, March 27, 1868, BHL.

63 *"a hundred times a day":* Stoddard, *Lepers,* 50.

64 *In September the* Warwick *had wrecked:* Though the board never noted the distinction, the schooner actually had two incarnations, as its entry in Mifflin, *Hawaiian Interisland Vessels* details: "Warwick, schooner, 18 tons. Hawaiian register number 156-O. Imported to Hawaii on the deck of the ship Eliza Warwick in July 1850. Served as coaster under a number of owners until she went ashore on the southeast point of Kauai on September 3, 1867. Warwick II, schooner, 23 tons. Haw Reg. No 115-N. Completed April 11, 1868 . . . to replace the original Warwick. Operated as a coaster to Molokai, Maui and Lanai until she left Honolulu on Dec 21, 1881 for Kalaupapa, Molokai and was never afterwards heard from." In fact, the vessel was wrecked multiple times, once on the Lanai coast, and then repaired and put back in service. During her absences the board sent other charters on the Molokai run.

64 *"of fresh armies of lepers":* August 29, 1867, BHM.

64 *"seem to have a holy horror":* Illegible to board, April 27, 1868, BHL.

64 *"several lepers at large":* PCA, September 19, 1868. By the end of 1867, four patients had escaped from Kalihi Hospital. See Hoffman to board, January 1868.

64 *"It would seem that the whole system":* Ibid.

64 *"As may easily be imagined":* RBH, 1868.

64 *"Their poor weak heads are quite turned":* D. Walsh to board, June 1, 1868, BHL.

65 *"Don't let him away!":* D. Walsh to board, June 28, 1868, BHL. In a letter he sent one week earlier, Walsh listed the ringleaders of the mob: Hao, Puhaula, and Paiaina.

65 *"I know your evil intentions":* Ibid. To punish the exiles, Walsh served out spoiled meat for their rations.

65 *"henceforth their revolts":* July 21, 1868, BHM.

65 *the half-Hawaiian William Humphreys:* Humphreys was the son of a New Hampshire man who had settled on Maui and married a Hawaiian. Though bilingual, Humphreys wrote mainly in Hawaiian; he had been a member of the 1864 legislature. On May 2, 1866, a Maui sheriff reported to the board that a district physician had declared Humphreys a leper; at Kalihi, however, Humphreys was examined and discharged. He was finally exiled on August 24, 1868, and lived to March 29, 1873. In board records he is listed as patient number 180, and also number 599. See BHL, BHM.

65 *"You must not think that all":* Damon, "Siloama," 12.

66 *"skilled at flattery and defense":* Hao to Hutchison, September, date illegible, 1870, BHL. There were two patients named Hao in Kalawao at the time; J. H. Hao was often referred to as Hao 1.

66 *"Last night Humphries [*sic*] woman":* C. Walsh to Hutchison, March 25, 1870, BHL.

66 *"has been quite deranged":* Meyer to board, November 9, 1869, BHL. Rudolph Meyer, ever exacting, reported that William Walsh had caused $159.12 worth of damage during his last "fit." Meyer wrote, "He has really done a good deal of tearing and breaking."

66 *"With what tenderness they spoke":* Stoddard, *Lepers,* 49.

67 *"in the event":* D. Walsh to board, October 30, 1869, BHL.

67 *"It is the peoples wish":* W. Humphreys to Hutchison, November 9, 1869, BHL.

67 *The crew had to tie:* Stoddard, *Lepers,* 53. The William Walsh episode has a curious footnote, which caused problems with the board's records. Donald Walsh had suggested that after he died the board hire his brother-in-law as an assistant to Caroline Walsh. Instead, the board hired a man named William Welsh. Thereafter, records constantly confused William Welsh and William Walsh. The hire was not successful. In a letter she wrote on December 29, 1870, Caroline Walsh reported that because Welsh did not speak Hawaiian he was wholly dependent on William Humphreys. That, she warned, "together with his overbearing temper will be the cause of serious trouble." Welsh subsequently got into a fight with an exile; when the patient threw a sheep bone at him, Welsh threatened to shoot him, causing patients to stream from the hospital on a mission to "kill that white man." The board soon dismissed Welsh.

67 *"not fit to write":* C. Walsh to board, April 14, 1870, BHL.

68 *"stronger than brandy":* Ibid.

68 *According to a letter Dr. David Lee:* Lee to board, August 25, 1868, BHL.

68 *"committing adultery":* Hao to Hutchison, September, date illegible, 1870, BHL.

68 *"Oh dismiss him!":* Ibid.

READY TO BELIEVE

69 *"We were dropping":* Stoddard, *Lepers,* 33.

69 *do some "botanizing":* Hillebrand to Hutchison, undated, June 1870, BHL. This long letter describes in detail Hillebrand's tour of the colony and serves as the basis for his scenes in this chapter.

69 *"Molokai is a more isolated place":* Ibid.

69 *schoolboy named Lydgate:* J. M. Lydgate published an account of his visit as "Reminiscences of an Amateur Collector," in HAA, 1920.

70 *"struck by a falling stone":* Ibid., 123.

71 *"the swollen nerve squeezes":* Yancey and Brand, *Gift of Pain,* 153. For layman's knowledge of the disease I relied on multiple sources. Yancey and Brand's *The Gift of Pain* is a compendium of pieces Brand wrote for various medical journals, recast in accessible form. Another fine resource is Patrick Feeny's *The Fight Against Leprosy.* I found *Essentials of Leprosy,* by Leo J. Yoder and J. M. H. Pearson, invaluable. Persons seeking current information on the disease should look online at the World Heath Organization's Leprosy Elimination Group (www.who.int/lep). The International Federation of Anti-Leprosy Associations (www.ilep.org.uk) is a good source for news about the disease and the global effort to eradicate it.

73 *"little rebellion":* Hillebrand to Hutchison, undated, June 1870, BHL.

73 *"private interests are of greater importance":* Ibid.
73 *"The view is generally picturesque":* RBH, 1872.
73 *"the ordinary school instruction of the islands":* Ibid.
74 *providing regular medical attention:* Budget constraints were the most common reason the board failed to secure competent doctors. Occasionally other issues arose, however. In the summer of 1870 the board hired Dr. Edward Storer to make calls on the colony, a duty he performed competently. But on July 12, 1870, a Reverend Green filed a complaint against the doctor, as "a man wholly unfit, morally, to sustain this office." In his letter to the board, Green accused Storer of adultery with one of his parishioners. The affair was exposed after the cuckold discovered a love letter from Storer, written in invisible ink, among his wife's belongings. The husband held the note over a candle, revealing a "letter of offensive and criminal character," as the reverend put it. Green demanded that the exiles be protected from the wanton doctor. "Let [them] fall into the hands of God not into the power of an adulterer," he wrote. "Better that the people die from disease natural than wickedness."
74 *"pleasure trip":* Lee to board, September 24, 1868, BHL. Dr. Lee was among those who subscribed to a theory that leprosy was spread through intercourse, and he referred to women in the colony as "this class of leper breeders." He pleaded with the board to do something about the prostitutes on the Lahaina waterfront, having decided that most had the disease: "Whale ships are coming here and I see every evening Leprous women on the street enticing the sailors to ruin." See Lee to board, November 5, 16, 1868, BHL.
75 *Yet the public assumed:* A typical point of view is expressed in the *San Francisco Chronicle,* July 3, 1873, in "A KINGDOM INFECTED WITH LEPROSY." The reporter remarked, "Of course, when a leper began to drop his joints about in the streets, the authorities arrested him . . . and shipped him to Molokai."
75 *"roasting fish or meat":* Meyer to board, August 13, 1886, BHL.
76 *One man took a butcher's blade:* This was a Maui man named Kahoomana, sent away at twenty years old as patient number 2947. The board's records indicate he "stabbed himself with butcher knives." The suicide came in the aftermath of Kahoomana's murder of another patient, Kaaimaku.
76 *the simplest exit route:* In March 1890 Meyer reported to the board that a new trail into the settlement was complete and suggested that it be closed with a locked fence and guard. The board authorized the move on April 16, 1890. That same year, Robert Louis Stevenson learned the story of a successful escape from Molokai by sea. The writer was sailing near a South Pacific atoll called Penryhn when another passenger approached him with a tale about a patient who had escaped by small boat from the settlement and come aground more than two thousand miles away at Penryhn. Stevenson wrote, "He landed . . . enjoyed for a while simple pleasures, died, and bequeathed to his entertainers a legacy of doom." Within a few years, Stevenson reported, "the island was dotted with lepers" and whole families were "entirely contaminated." Through the efforts of some passing missionaries the diseased were banished to a tiny islet, three miles over water from their former village—they called the island prison Molokai.
77 *when Kahoohuli mustered a posse:* Parke, *Marshall,* 94.
77 *islanders' religious faith:* See Kuykendall, *Hawaiian Kingdom: 1778–1854;* Daws, *Shoal of Time;* and Alexander, *Brief History.*
78 *"until the skin came off":* PCA, May 13, 1871.

78 *One such assassin: Nupepa Kuokoa,* October 20, 1866. Wailiilii, the paper reported, had "a plump body but red eyes that do not see well. . . . He is a bad hearted kahuna, selfish, given to grumbling, a sorcerer (literally eater-of-filth) and so on. . . . Strange are the deeds of this mischievous kahuna, he murders at once."

78 *A notorious female kahuna:* Korn, *News,* xxii, 46.

78 *prophet named J. Kaona:* Parke, *Marshall,* 99.

78 *"utter extermination of any":* Ibid., 100.

79 *"Pedestrians and riders":* Varigny, *Fourteen Years,* 211. The eruption was attributed to an angry Pele, goddess of volcanoes. She, like many other Hawaiian gods, was alleged to be an immigrant to the Hawaiian Islands, having arrived in ancient times from near Samoa. According to legend, Pele lived first on the island of Oahu, then moved to a site she found more agreeable: Kalaupapa.

80 *"Kaona, understanding the superstitious character":* Ibid., 216.

80 *"by a shower of stones":* Parke, *Marshall,* 102.

80 *his leprosy was supernatural retribution:* This characterization comes from several residents who recounted Kahoohuli's history to Robert Louis Stevenson. See Day, *Robert Louis Stevenson's Travels in Hawaii,* 57, and Stevenson, "Historical Sketches."

80 *"must either rule or rebel":* Stevenson, "Historical Sketches."

A FAR DIFFERENT POSITION

81 *"a Knight of the Imperial Order":* PCA, May 11, 1872. For biographical material on Trousseau I have relied on his Physician's File, MML, and "Doctor Georges Phillipe Trousseau, Royal Physician," by Jean Greenwell, published in HJH, vol. 25, 1991.

82 *"He had an only son":* HJH, vol. 25, p. 131.

82 *"Sir, I hear from various":* Ibid.

83 *The crude outlines of the theory:* A fine history of the rise of germ theory appears in Nancy Tomes's *The Gospel of Germs: Men, Women, and the Microbe in American Life.*

Dr. Georges Trousseau, pictured circa 1873, at about forty years old.

The American public first became aware of germ theory through magazines such as *Popular Science Monthly,* founded in 1872, which devoted page after page to the news that invisible "bugs" were conspiring to kill its readers. To combat this cloud of unseen menace, a British surgeon named Joseph Lister created a mixture of carbolic acid, which he would spray in his operating room, an innovation hijacked by entrepreneurs and pitched to the public under such names as Germ-a-thol, Listerine, and Pasteur's Marvellous Disinfectant. Hygiene manuals of the era cautioned that germs could attach themselves to innocent objects, turning them into "fomites." One pamphlet issued by the Massachusetts Board of Health insisted that contagion was spread by "air, food, clothing, sheets, blankets, whiskers, hair, furniture, toys, library-books, wallpaper, curtains, cats [and] dogs." As this idea seeped into the public imagination, men sacrificed their beards and mustaches, and hemlines rose off the floor so as not to trap deadly dust. Homes changed as well: the wood cabinetry of the commode gave way to the china toilet, and bedsheets grew in length—the resulting "long sheet movement," the *New York Times* reported, allowed the clean top sheet to be folded deeply back over infrequently washed quilts, "so that the inhalation by the occupant of bacteria &c, may be prevented and minimized."

83 *"the immediate, energetic":* March 1, 1873, BHM.

83 *"the seeds of death": Ka Nuhou,* March 14, 1873. This is Walter Murray Gibson writing, in the first newspaper he published after coming to the islands, a Hawaiian-language weekly that carried the slogan "A Friend and Champion of the Hawaiian People." Gibson used the paper as a springboard for his political career. The history of newspapers in Hawaii during the early period of exile is complicated and fascinating; by 1900 the islands had ninety newspapers, publishing in five languages. The historian Helen Geracimos Chapin wrote a fine account of the era's papers in HJH, vol. 18, 1984.

83 *"Let us think for a moment":* RBH, 1872.

84 *"The infected ones are":* PCA, May 13, 1871.

84 *Removing a pistol:* NYT, April 30, 1873. See also *Ka Nuhou,* April 4, 18, 1873.

84 *"As Mr. Parke":* Ibid.

84 *"emotional insanity":* PCA, April 19, 1873. On April 18, 1873, the *Ka Nuhou* remarked that "leprosy is enough to turn any man crazy." Jim Kamai subsequently escaped from custody twice, once before being exiled to Molokai, and once when he slipped away by canoe from Kalawao and landed on Oahu, where he was arrested and returned to the colony.

85 *"Alas, we dare not think": Ka Nuhou,* April 22, 1873.

85 *"They smashed the Bottles":* Korn, *News,* 66.

RUSH SLOWLY

By a large measure, the best-known figure from the colony's history is Joseph de Veuster, Father Damien. He has been the subject of a dozen major biographies, beginning with Charles Warren Stoddard's *The Lepers of Molokai*—Stoddard had originally hoped to call the work *The Martyrs of Molokai,* but after Damien professed embarrassment, the writer edited the title. In 1901 Stoddard's book was rereleased as *Father Damien: The Martyr of Molokai.* Of the many biographies, I found Stoddard's book and his diaries to be most useful, as well as Gavan Daws's *Holy Man,* and Vital Jourdain's somewhat less judgmental *The Heart of Father Damien.* For a more piercing examination of Damien's tenure in the settlement, see Pennie Moblo, "Blessed Damien of Molokai: The Critical Analysis of Contemporary Myth," *Ethnohistory* 44. Moblo has written two other papers stressing the political and ethnic contexts of the settlement's early history. See "Ethnic Intercession: Leadership at Kalaupapa Leprosy Colony, 1871–1887," *Pacific Studies,* June 1999, and "Institutionalizing the Leper: Partisan Politics and the Evolution of Stigma in Post-Monarchy Hawaii," *Journal of the Polynesian Society,* September 1998. Both are worth the effort required to find them.

89 *The eight missionary priests knelt before:* Jourdain, *Heart of Father Damien,* 96.
89 *"They ask me for a priest":* Yzendoorn, *Catholic Mission,* 200.
90 *"Are you not afraid of making":* Daws, *Holy Man,* 22.
91 *"I am to go instead of you!":* Ibid., 31.
91 *"I find sheep everywhere":* Yzendoorn, 204.
91 *"Here I am a priest, dear parents":* Daws, *Holy Man,* 34.
91 *"Many of our Christians here":* Jourdain, 98.
92 *"passed their time with playing cards":* RBH, 1886. See also Jourdain, 91.
93 *"Send me some wine":* Jourdain, 99.
93 *"They are talking about me":* Ibid., 101.
93 *"a subscription for the benefit":* PCA, May 24, 1873.
93 *"one could only hear of the devotion":* See HG, May 21, 1873; *Ka Nuhou,* May 23, 1873.
93 *"Considering the circumstances":* Daws, *Holy Man,* 63.
94 *exiled William Williamson:* PCA, April 18, 1873. See also RBH, 1874. William Williamson was sent to the colony on July 5, 1873, as patient number 1145.
95 *"acts as though he were director":* Jourdain, 105.

Father Damien de Veuster in 1873;
he landed in the colony on May 10 of that year.

95 *"Picture to yourself a collection":* Damien to Pamphile, November 1873; quoted in Jourdain, 121. Damien pointedly teased his brother in his letters, which often left the settlement grimed with dirt. "As I have had to work all week and cook on Sunday," he wrote, "you will excuse me if my hands are not as clean as yours, which do nothing, I suppose, but turn the pages of books."

95 *"The earth is only a place":* Jourdain, 179.

95 *"Almost from one house to the next":* Daws, *Holy Man,* 85. Ambrose Hutchison later described Damien's "lone drive to dry up and stop the drinking orgies," which he did with the help of his heavy wooden cane. If Damien heard suspicious noises, he would hurry toward the hut. "The alarm is given by some one person 'here comes Father Damien,'" Hutchison wrote, "the hula ceased and the hilarious feasters make a hasty retreat through the backdoor exit to escape Father Damien's big stick." Damien would shatter the jars of liquor, then dash out the back door "frantically shaking his big stick and shouting at the fleeing people 'naughty children.'" Hutchison wrote that it was "a dramatic sight to see a Catholic priest in action."

96 *laid the foundation of lepraphobia:* For an abbreviated but engaging history of lepraphobia, see Berton Roueche's "A Lonely Road," in *The New Yorker,* October 17, 1955. I relied also on Sheldon Watts's *Epidemics and History: Disease, Power and Imperialism;* Mary Douglas's "Witchcraft and Leprosy: Two Strategies of Exclusion"; and S. N. Brody's *The Disease of the Soul: Leprosy in Medieval Literature.*

98 *"this loathsome, incurable":* PCA, June 14, 1873. One of the signers of the statement was Louis Lepart's former nemesis, the Reverend A. O. Forbes.

99 *"I have had great difficulty":* Jourdain, 121.

Damien with the members of the St. Philomena choir circa 1875.

"BE AMBITIOUS AND BOLD"

100 *Isabella Bird, of Yorkshire:* For a description of Bird's journey, and her impressions of William Ragsdale, I relied on Bird's *Six Months in the Sandwich Islands.* The author also published a short chapter about the colony itself, relying on the board's biennial reports for her information. The interisland steamer *Kilauea*, on which Bird toured the islands, was also involved in one of the more storied episodes from Damien's early tenure in the colony. During a period when the board had tightened access to the settlement, no Sacred Hearts priest was allowed to enter and confess Damien, a dire situation for the priest. Thus one day when Damien learned that Father Modeste Favens was aboard the *Kilauea,* anchored briefly off Kalaupapa, he commandeered a small boat and rowed out to the vessel. Damien yelled to Father Modeste that he must be confessed. The provincial reluctantly agreed, and Damien knelt in the boat and shouted up his sins as the steamer's passengers eavesdropped.

100 *"The mental caliber": Sacramento Weekly Union,* June 23, 1866.

100 *"with a readiness and facility":* Ibid.

101 *Ragsdale was the son:* Author interview with Cari Castro, a Ragsdale descendant. William Ragsdale's father, Alexander Ragsdale, arrived in Hawaii in 1819 and married a Hawaiian woman of minor royal birth. The couple had three children: Annie, William, and Edward. One of Annie Ragsdale Dowsett's grandchildren, William Dowsett, later adopted her maiden name, to continue the Ragsdale line after William died in the colony.

101 *Twain began to jot an outline:* In *Mark Twain and Hawaii* (Chicago: Lakeside Press, 1947), Walter Francis Frear details Twain's undertaking of a Ragsdale novel. See pp. 104–5.

William P. Ragsdale, shortly before he was diagnosed with leprosy and exiled.

101 *Ragsdale later explained:* NYT, January 27, 1878. Ragsdale offered different versions of this story over the years. I have relied on the account published in the *Times,* which is similar to one Ragsdale told Dr. George Woods and described in "Reminiscences of a Visit in July 1876 to the Leper Settlement of Molokai," *Damien Institute Monthly Magazine,* August 1895. A government physician named Frank H. Enders reported a less dramatic version in *Leprosy as Observed in the Sandwich Islands.* Enders wrote that Ragsdale "says that the first indication of leprosy apparent in his case was an ulcer on the bottom of his foot which could not heal. He supposed this to be the result of syphilis, and so believed until the contraction of the flexor muscles, and the thickening of the skin on his forehead and cheeks, occurred, when he recognized himself to be a leper."

101 *a beautiful half-white girl:* Twain, *Following,* 56.

101 *"I therefore surrender":* HG, June 18, 1873.

101 *"The relations of those":* Bird, *Six Months,* 245.

102 *Landing with Ragsdale:* Peter Kaeo's letters are collected in Korn's *News from Molokai: Letters between Peter Kaeo & Queen Emma, 1873–1876.* Unless otherwise indicated, all quotes from Kaeo and Emma come from this collection.

102 *"Peter Kaeo ought":* Korn, *News,* 7.

104 *he was actively campaigning:* Ragsdale to board, July 12, 1873, BHL.

104 *"I will carefully post":* Ibid.

104 *"try to the* best of my ability": Ragsdale to board, October 23, 1873, BHL.

104 *"I mean to make the balance":* Ragsdale to board, July 7, 1873, BHL.

104 *"The superior mind of Ragsdale":* PCA, April 18, 1874.

Peter Kaeo, who arrived in the settlement on the same boat as William P. Ragsdale, landing June 29, 1873.

105 *"a few short lines from this place":* *Hawaii Ponoi,* July 9, 1873.
105 *all but "real lepers":* November 1873, BHM.
105 *"A heavy south wind blew":* RBH, 1886.
105 *"did the work of erecting":* Ibid.
105 *"I lend them my arms":* Englebert, *Damien,* 114.
106 *broken by the elaborate royal funeral:* The monarchy was rarely frugal in matters of its members' deaths. The bill to bury Kamehameha III in 1855 amounted to $28,000, one-tenth of the government's total revenue at the time. Two thousand of the monarch's retainers were provided with black mourning suits and an awesome cortege assembled. The coffin itself was "covered with crimson velvet and decorated with armorial paintings," as the *Polynesian* reported. Marshall William Cooper Parke had to deal with the many bills. He divided a towering pile of government gold coins "into two sums of $14,000 each, and placing one-half in a wheelbarrow, wheeled by a soldier and strongly guarded by other soldiers, I went from store to store settling up accounts," he wrote. It took two weeks to distribute the money. Parke, *Marshall,* 78.
106 *"Mr. Ragsdale is well known":* PCA, April 18, 1874.

ESCAPE

108 *"are not prepared to advance":* RBH, March 1876.
109 *"are trying to do all they":* Ragsdale to Gulick, January 16, 1874, BHL.
110 *"leprosy had only":* Dr. G. W. Woods, "Reminiscences of a Visit in July 1876 to the Leper Settlement of Molokai," *Damien Institute Monthly Magazine,* August 1895.
110 *named William Powell:* Another who believed he could cure Peter Kaeo was Father Andre Burgerman, a quick-tempered Sacred Hearts priest who served topside Molokai and spent several brief stretches in Kalaupapa. Burgerman had come to Hawaii from the Sacred Hearts mission in Tahiti, where he had contracted a skin disease thought to be elephantiasis. He had taught himself medicine and held a special interest in leprosy. "The new Catholic Priest came in to see me," Kaeo wrote on June 20, 1874. "He . . . looked at my sore foot . . . and said that he could cure it." A few days later Burgerman visited again and told Kaeo not to use the board's medicine, "which is very bad." Burgerman wanted Kaeo to try a concoction of the priest's own making; he told Kaeo that he had worked with lepers in Tahiti and in so doing "he also caught [leprosy] but was fortunate enough to get well."
110 *"This ended Dr. Akana's":* RBH, 1876.
110 *named David Ostrom in charge:* August 13, 1875, BHM. Ostrom is listed as patient number 1431 and came to the settlement with his wife, Nawahine Ostrom, aged forty-six. He is often mistakenly listed in the board's records as Tom Ostrom. See also Meyer to Gulick, September 13, 1875, BHL.
110 *"He feels satisfied that his":* J. H. Bemiss, M.D., "A Few Cases of Leprosy," *New Orleans Medical and Surgical Journal,* April 1880.
111 *It closed Kalihi Hospital:* RBH, 1876.
111 *"the sick are retained":* Ibid.
111 *"that he should remain":* June 27, 1876, BHM.
112 *"Righteous Indignation":* PCA, May 4, 1878.
112 *"the Hon. P.Y. Kaeo died":* HG, December 1, 1880.
112 *"appropriate honors":* PCA, December 4, 1880.

112 *"his contracted claw-like gloved hand":* Dr. G. W. Woods, "Reminiscences of a Visit in July 1876 to the Leper Settlement of Molokai," *Damien Institute Monthly Magazine,* August 1895.

113 *"Our beloved Bill Ragsdale is nearly":* Daws, *Holy Man,* 90.

113 *"for the very efficient":* November 13, 1877, BHM.

113 *"DEATH OF THE KING":* NYT, January 27, 1878.

113 *"Who will supply his place?":* PCA, December 8, 1877.

113 *"the loathsome and lingering death":* Twain, *Following,* 63.

114 *his friend William Dean Howells:* Twain to Howells, January 7, 1884. The letter reads in part, "My billiards table is stacked up with books relating to the Sandwich Islands: the walls are upholstered with scraps of paper penciled with notes from them. I have saturated myself with knowledge of that unimaginably beautiful land and that most strange and fascinating people."

114 *informed another acquaintance:* Twain to Mary Mason Fairbanks, January 24, 30, 1884.

114 *seventeen typewritten pages:* The manuscript pages are in the Bancroft Library, University of California at Berkeley: The Mark Twain Papers, DV 111. The opening lines begin with the islands themselves: "Away out there in the mid-solitudes of the vast Pacific, and far down in the edge of the tropics, they lie asleep on the waves, perpetually green and beautiful, remote from the work-day world and its frets and worries, a bloomy, fragrant paradise, where the troubled may go to find peace, and the sick and tired find strength and rest."

114 *a Twain scholar realized:* See Fred W. Lorch, "Hawaiian Feudalism and Mark Twain's *A Connecticut Yankee in King Arthur's Court,*" *American Literature* (1958). While not draw-

A group of visiting legislators on an inspection tour in Kalawao.

ing as pure a connective line between the characters as Lorch, Twain scholar Stephen H. Sumida remarks, "Ragsdale . . . in himself was symbolic of the conjunction and conflict of cultures that Twain planned to dramatize" in both *Yankee* and the unfinished Hawaiian novel. See "Reevaluating Mark Twain's Novel of Hawaii," *American Literature.*

Twain never did set foot on Hawaii again. As Frear describes in *Mark Twain and Hawaii,* in September 1895 the steamer *Warrimoo,* on which Twain was traveling, dropped anchor one mile from Oahu's shore. Honolulu was still dark. "Through my port I could see the twinkling lights of Honolulu and the dark bulk of the mountain-range that stretched away right and left," Twain wrote. When day broke, a small lighter used by the quarantine officer glided across the water. Cholera had broken out in Honolulu, the officer then explained, and no one could land. Twain was crestfallen. He offered the customs officer, a man named Clarence Crabbe, a thousand dollars if he would look the other way while Twain snuck ashore, but Crabbe refused the bribe. "There was nothing . . . to do," Twain wrote in his diary, "but sit about the decks in the shade of the awnings and look at the distant shore." He added, "Thus did my dream of twenty-nine years go to ruin." *Following,* 25.

THE LIKES OF US

115 *"will grumble him":* Damien to Rose, November 20, 1877. Quoted in Jourdain, *Heart of Father Damien,* 155.

115 *"he was easily excited":* Mouritz, *Path of the Destroyer,* 231.

115 *"I would caution you":* Meyer to Damien, December 19, 1877. Quoted in Jourdain, 156.

115 *"And now I'm free again!":* Beevers, *Man for Now,* 84.

115 *"order and quiet":* RBH, 1878.

115 *"with first rate executive ability":* PCA, July 13, 1878.

116 *Strawn was the child:* Biographical details for Clayton Strawn come from two privately published family histories: Clarence V. Roberts's *Early Friends Families of Upper Bucks,* and Lily Strawn Painter's *History of the Strawn Families: Book IV.* The 1860 U.S. Federal Census lists Strawn as residing in Doylestown, Pennsylvania, and gives his year of birth as 1839; family historians suggest the actual year was 1836. In the board's records, Strawn was assigned two patient numbers, 1836 and 3410, which reflect his transfer from Kalaupapa to Kakaako. Robert Louis Stevenson also described Strawn's lawless past in "Historical Sketches of the Lazaretto," although he misspelled the name as Strahan.

116 *Strawn had been a slave trader:* The South Seas slave trade reportedly began in 1805, when a New London captain grabbed twelve men and ten women from Easter Island. After the ship was several days out to sea, the captain cut the ropes that bound the prisoners, only to watch in shock as they leapt overboard and began to furiously swim toward the empty horizon. The slave trade took a heavy toll in the region—of the two hundred persons abducted from one South Pacific island in what is now Kiribati, only two returned alive. Sailors overseeing these kidnappings were often reprobate American seamen, at large from other crimes. By the mid-nineteenth century, abductions were so common that the sight of a blackbirder's boat incited terror. Captains devised ways to disguise their intent, often camouflaging their boats as missionary ships. The deception rarely worked. Vessels such as the one Clayton Strawn had allegedly manned were easily identified—locals called them *snatch-snatch.*

116 *"Good God, Strawn!":* Stevenson, "Historical Sketches."

116 *"This place can be made":* Strawn to board, September 1, 1878. I have gleaned additional material from Strawn's letters to the board on August 28, 1878; September 1, 9, 16, 22, 1878; April 9, 1878; May 7, 1879; August 9, 1879. Also see "The Journals of Sister M. Leopoldina Burns," held at the Archives of the Sisters of St. Francis, Syracuse, New York.

117 *"Father Damien's bitter slanderers":* Ambrose Hutchison, "In Memory of Reverend Father Damien J. De Veuster," 22. This is the eighty-six-page unpublished and incomplete memoir written by Hutchison and discovered after his death in 1932. Hutchison undertook the effort at the request of people who wanted his firsthand memories of Father Damien; he then began to expand it into a personal narrative. Partial drafts of the document are held at the State Archives of Hawaii (BHL, box 34); the early pages are written by Hutchison, but as his health declined, he apparently received help either in transcribing material or in taking down his dictation. Judging from handwriting samples available in letters to the board, it is likely that his secretary was Jose de Souza Jr., exiled from Kohala, Hawaii, in February 1907. De Souza was paroled in November 1922 but remained in the settlement as a kokua. Unless otherwise indicated, all quotes attributed to Ambrose Hutchison come from this memoir.

117 *"Damien was a good fighter:* Mouritz, *Path,* 231.

117 *"The good Father Damien":* A. Hutchison, 23.

117 *"To do good to souls I must":* Jourdain, 235.

117 *"Why don't you do it?":* Stevenson, "Historical Sketches."

118 *"entirely too small, badly":* Report of the Special Sanitary Committee, 1878. The chair of the committee—and author of the report—was Walter Murray Gibson.

118 *"a spectacle of terrible human woe":* Ibid.

118 *"Every leper is a possible source of infection":* Report of N. B. Emerson to board, January 1880. See also Emerson to Wilder, October 4, 15, 21, 1879, BHL.

119 *A German named Christian Bertelmann:* Joesting, *Kauai,* 238.

119 *named Charles Derby: Boston Globe Supplement,* December 18, 1882; *Boston Globe,*

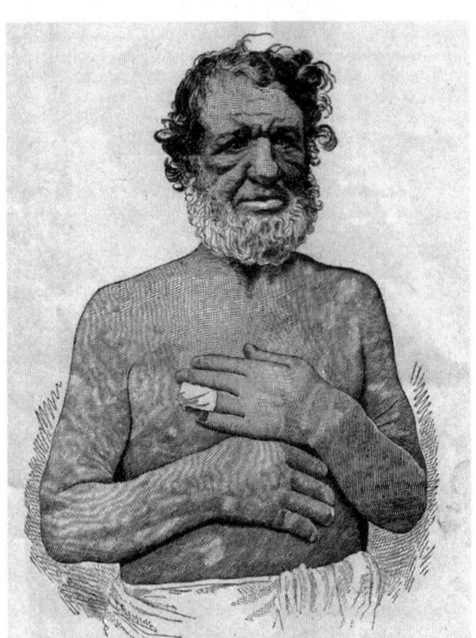

The patient David Ostrom, a New Yorker who arrived in the settlement on August 13, 1875.

December 19, 21, 1882; *Salem Observer,* January 6, 27, 1883. Charles Warren Stoddard maintained a poignant friendship with Derby, which he describes in "The Drama in Dreamland," *Overland Monthly,* August 1883.

119 *"he did not mingle":* August 16, 1878, BHM.

119 *woman named Malie Moa:* F. W. Hutchison's Physician's File, MML. Ambrose Hutchison on occasion wrote his mother's name as Maria Moa.

120 *on official records:* U.S. Federal Census, Kalawao, 1900, 1910, 1920.

120 *"The first symptoms I noticed":* Mouritz, *Path,* 204.

122 *"He was active and vigorous":* Ibid., 229.

123 *"Thus at night I am the sole keeper":* Jourdain, 231.

123 *made a list of his daily routine:* Hilde Eynikel, "Father Damien, A Progressive Priest," unpublished 1996 doctoral dissertation, 175. Damien's daily schedule had been printed in multiple biographies, and these vary. As is the case with letters and reports written by Damien, various translations exist. (Damien wrote in French, Flemish, and, poorly, in English.) In the absence of an original document, I have chosen the most likely translation.

124 *"Dr. F.H. Enders: I have taken":* J. H. Bemiss, M.D., "A Few Cases of Leprosy," *New Orleans Medical and Surgical Journal,* April 1880.

124 *"Be careful not to expose":* Daws, *Holy Man,* 84.

125 *"Fr. Damien took no precautions":* Mouritz, *Path,* 236.

125 *"genetic quirk": National Post* (Canada), January 26, 2004.

125 *"Sad news from Dr Brodie":* Adler and Barrett, *Diaries,* 48.

STRANGE OBJECTS

126 *first encountered leprosy in 1869:* Stoddard, *Lepers,* 11. For biographical material on Stoddard, I relied on Robert Gale's *Charles Warren Stoddard* and "A Life of Charles Warren Stoddard," an unpublished 1939 doctoral dissertation by Carl Stroven. Stoddard mined his own life for both his fiction and nonfiction, and I found additional personal details in these works: *A Troubled Heart and How It Was Comforted at Last* (Notre Dame: 1896); *Hawaiian Life: Being Lazy Letters from Low Latitudes* (Chicago: 1904); *A Trip to Hawaii* (San Francisco: 1897); and *South-Sea Idyls.* The diary Stoddard kept during his second visit to the settlement was published as *Charles Warren Stoddard's Diary of a Visit to Molokai in 1884* (San Francisco: 1933).

126 *"the doctor looked very grave":* Stoddard, *Idyls,* 23.

127 *"What a background for a novel!":* Stroven, 215.

127 *"where I sat presently":* See Stevenson and Osbourne, "The Wrecker" (London: Cassell, 1892).

127 *Stevenson learned that Stoddard's dream:* Stevenson was not the only person to get a note about Stoddard's impending trip. "Charles Warren Stoddard has gone to the Sandwich Islands . . . Lucky devil," Mark Twain wrote to William Dean Howells. "This fellow's postal card has set the vision of those gracious islands before my mind again, with not a leaf withered, nor a rainbow vanished, nor a sun-flash missing from the waves, & now it will be months, I reckon, before I can drive it away again." Twain added, "It is beautiful company, but it makes one restless & dissatisfied."

128 *Testimony at the trial soon revealed:* Transcripts of the trial were published in 1883 as *Leprosy and Libel: The Suit of George F. Fitch Against The Saturday Press,* by the defen-

The writer Charles Warren Stoddard, who visited the settlement twice, in 1869 and 1884.

Ira B. Dutton, as a twenty-year-old Civil War lieutenant. Dutton arrived in the settlement on July 29, 1886.

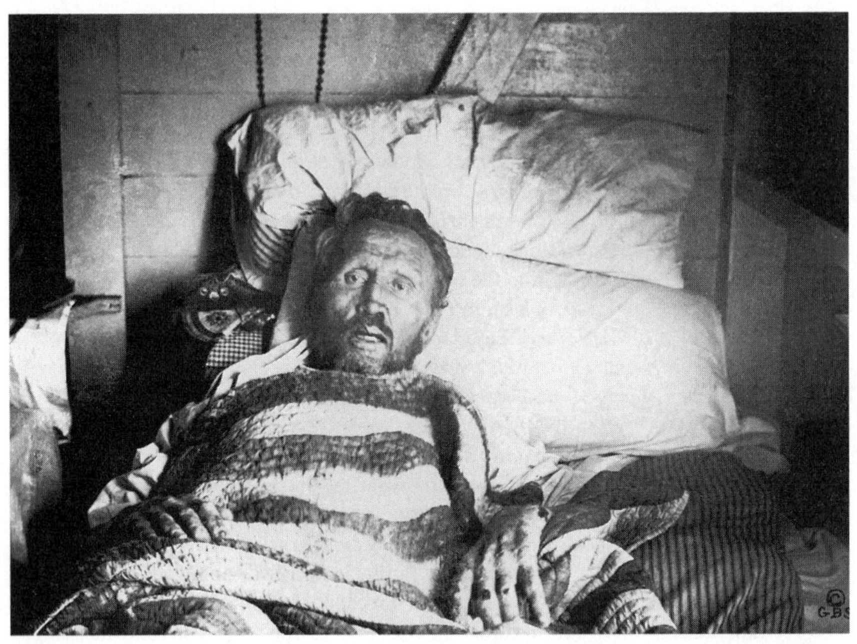

Dr. Sydney Bourne Swift's deathbed photo of Father Damien, taken two days before the priest passed away on April 15, 1889.

dant newspaper. During the proceedings, defense lawyers described Dr. Fitch's typical diagnostic method: having the patient stick out his or her tongue so that he could look for "fissures," which Fitch believed indicated leprosy. Such exams lasted only seconds. In one six-hour stretch at Kakaako, Fitch examined 323 persons and claimed that every one of them had leprosy.

129 *named Arthur Albert Mouritz:* Physician's File, MML.

129 *"concession to feelings":* August 14, 1880, BHM.

129 *"essentially a neurosis":* Neilson to board, July 1881, AH. Dr. Neilson's name is spelled a variety of ways in the board's records; I've used the most common spelling.

130 *"The place was dingy and dirty":* Stoddard, *Diary,* 15.

130 *"Him I might easily learn to like":* Ibid., 19.

131 *"A corner of the blanket":* Stoddard, *Lepers,* 99.

132 *"The first meeting I had":* Mouritz, *Path,* 231.

HUMAN SOIL

133 *dead Japanese carpenter:* This scene is based on court testimony, and accounts of the crime and Keanu's trial in PCA, February 25, 1884; May 12, 1884; July 12, 14, 18, 19, 30, 1884; August 4, 1884.

134 *"With the prisoner's permission":* Arning recounted the experiment in several reports to the board, which were published in the board's biennial report to the legislature. See RBH, 1886, Supplement, 154–57, and Appendix, xliii. For biographical details on Arning, I've relied on "Eduard Arning," an unpublished biography by Omer P. Steeno, and O. A. Bushnell's "Dr. Edward Arning: The First Microbiologist in Hawaii," HJH, vol. 1 (1967). The late Dr. Bushnell was a professor of microbiology at the University of Hawaii, and an accomplished historian and novelist. He wove the story of Arning and Keanu into *Molokai,* an engaging and moving novel about the colony. Though based on fact and steeped in medical detail, Bushnell's depiction of Keanu's inoculation in the novel differs from the actual experiment in several aspects, which Bushnell readily admitted.

134 *"bacteriomania":* Markel, *Quarantine!* 29.

135 *man named Johannes Gül:* Feeny, *Fight Against Leprosy,* 65.

136 *"Probably you have read":* See RBH, 1886.

136 *"It gives me great pleasure":* Ibid.

137 *"Walter Murray Gibson is a tall, thin":* In a movie of Gibson's life, the lead would go to Donald Sutherland. Such a film would not lack for material; Gibson is perhaps the most intriguing figure in Hawaiian history, and among the most colorful men of the nineteenth century. For my account, I've relied on *The Fantastic Life of Walter Murray Gibson,* by Jacob Adler and Robert M. Kamins, and *The Diaries of Walter Murray Gibson,* by Jacob Adler and Gwynn Barrett. Unless otherwise noted, all of Gibson's diary quotes come from these two sources. I also found Paul Bailey's *Hawaii's Royal Prime Minister* (New York: Hastings House, 1980) useful, as well as "Gibson, the King's Evil Angel," by James A. Michener and A. Grove Day, published in *Rascals in Paradise* (New York: Random House, 1957). A unique perspective on Gibson is supplied in *A Song of Pilgrimage and Exile,* a fine biography of Mother Marianne Cope written by Sister Mary Laurence Hanley and O. A. Bushnell.

138 *"The vicissitudes of his life":* Nathaniel Hawthorne, *The English Notebooks,* 94.

138 *"This is the nucleus":* Adler and Kamins, *Fantastic Life,* 66.
139 *"How can we vote":* PCA, July 13, 1878.
139 *"Gibson's persevering":* Damon, *Sanford Ballard Dole,* 157.
140 *"It is months since we thought":* Ibid., 172.
140 *"the treatment and understanding":* RBH, 1886.
141 *"The site is most wretchedly":* Fitch to board, April 12, 1884. RBH, 1886.
142 *"leper manufactory":* Ibid.
142 *"THE LAND OF THE LEPERS":* SFC, March 1, 1883.
142 *"It will not do to trifle": San Francisco Bulletin,* August 17, 1878.
142 *"thick with filth and flies":* Hanley and Bushnell, *Song of Pilgrimage,* 125.
144 *"I had no idea that the sick":* Ibid., 127.
146 *"a variety of animals":* Arning to board, November 14, 1885, RBH, 1886.
146 *"I was able to prove the presence":* Ibid.
147 *"splendid field for experimental work":* Mouritz, *Path,* 141. For the scenes involving Dr. Mouritz's experiments, I've relied on his *Path of the Destroyer,* 141–53 and 190–93. Additional material can be found in his handwritten diary pages, AH, and in letters he wrote to the board, particularly BHL, 1885, 1886.
150 *"broke open the door of Van Giesen's":* PCA, March 8, 1884.
150 *"I am telling you unofficially":* A. Hutchison, 34.
151 *"Here is a nonleper child":* Ibid., 41.
152 *"We were as much prisoners":* Ibid., 57.

Dr. Eduard Arning in 1884, about the time he began his experiment on Keanu.

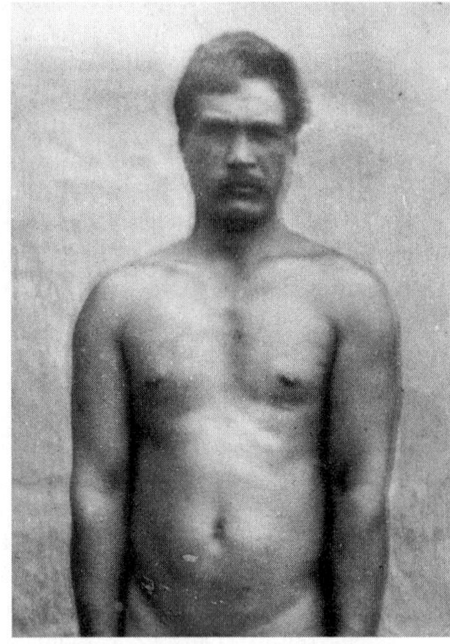

Keanu following his arrest; he was inoculated by Dr. Arning in September 1884.

153 *"Leprosy in Hawaii":* RBH, 1886.
153 *"I do not consider my experiment":* Arning to board, November 14, 1885, RBH, 1886.
153 *"Twenty-five months after [his] operation":* Mouritz, *Path,* 154.
154 *"Of course I do not know":* Arning to board, May 10, 1886, BHL.
154 *"I consider it my duty":* Ibid.
154 *"Will it not stand as having been done":* Steeno, 39.
154 *"For 6 weeks":* Ibid., 70.
156 *"from each and every office":* Quoted in Adler and Kamins, 184.
157 *a note from Marianne:* Ibid., 184.
157 *"A LIFE FULL":* NYT, February 21, 1888.
157 *"W.M. Gibson. One Corpse. No Value":* HG, February 21, 1888.

"A STRANGE PLACE TO BE IN"

158 *Yellow blemishes bloomed:* Joseph Dutton recorded Damien's medical history in a report dated March 10, 1889, HHS.
158 *"Soon I will be disfigured entirely":* Jourdain, *Heart of Father Damien,* 253.
158 *"deeply into the flesh":* Mouritz, *A Brief World History of Leprosy* (Honolulu: A. Mouritz, 1943), 85.

Walter Murray Gibson, Hawaiian prime minister and president of the board of health, pictured circa 1884.

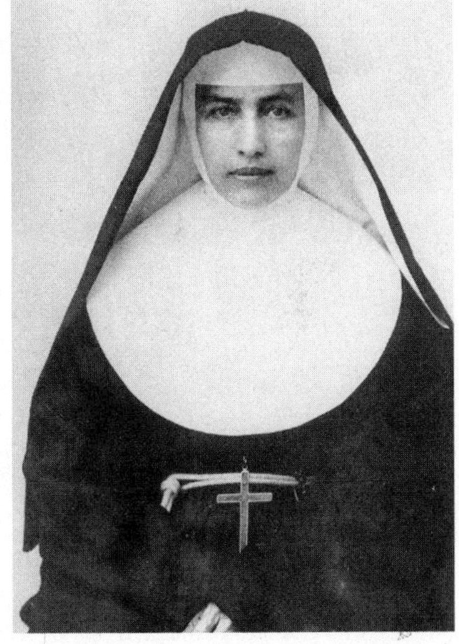

Mother Marianne Cope shortly before she landed in Honolulu, on November 8, 1883. She arrived in the settlement almost exactly five years later.

159 *"I was sorry to hear of your illness":* Jourdain, 256.
159 *"I have never been so isolated":* Stewart, *Leper Priest,* 272.
160 *"Belgian papers announced the leprosy":* quoted in Stewart, 298.
160 *Damien was now patient 2886:* Damien was actually listed in several board ledgers, each time with a different patient number. I've chosen the number from the most complete and accurate of the patient rolls. Over the years, logs of patients were frequently damaged or lost, and the board attempted to reconstruct or reconcile the ledgers. Thus patient numbers should not be interpreted as strictly chronological. Though Damien was listed as patient number 2886, he was not the 2,886th person sent into exile. By one board accounting, as of the spring of 1886 exactly 2,864 people had been sent into exile, and 2,254 of them had died.
160 *"I had never heard of him":* Joseph Dutton wrote letters indefatigably, and I have relied on his collected letters to tell his story. The most useful collections are held in the University of Notre Dame Archives: Joseph Dutton Papers. A smaller number of original letters are at the Hawaiian Historical Society. Military records are culled from Civil War Compiled Military Service Records, at the United States National Archives. During the forty-four years he spent in Kalawao, Dutton was the subject of hundreds of news articles; following are several of the most sweeping and useful: *L. & N. Employees' Magazine,* September 1925; SB, December 9, 1916; SB, April 28, 1923; HA, July 31, 1926; *National Tribune* (Washington), January 10, 1929; HA, July 13, 1930; SB, March 26, 1931; HA, March 26, 1931; NYT, March 27, 1931. The best single source on Dutton's life is *Joseph Dutton: His Memoirs,* edited by Howard Case. Unless

Robert Louis Stevenson with King David Kalakaua, who arranged permission for the writer to visit the settlement despite the board's apprehensions. Stevenson landed in Kalaupapa on May 14, 1889.

otherwise noted, all quotes attributed to Dutton and all biographical details arise from his memoirs or letters.

161 *"the gathering of the dead":* Gibson, *Under the Cliffs,* 170.

162 *"The rider, a young girl":* Thomas Merton, *The Waters of Siloe* (New York: Harcourt Brace Jovanovich, 1979), 136.

162 *"When he left the monastery":* Ibid.

163 *"Capt Ira B. Dutton called":* Adler and Barrett, *Diaries,* 60.

163 *"He wore a blue denim suit":* Mouritz, *Path,* 285.

164 *"Brother Dutton soon demonstrated":* Ibid. See also A. Hutchison, 70.

165 *"dearest and best friend":* "The Journals of Sister M. Leopoldina Burns," Archives of the Sisters of St. Francis, Syracuse, New York.

165 *"he tottered in his walk":* Jourdain, *Heart of Father Damien,* 270.

165 *"You must eat this":* Beevers, *Man for Now,* 99.

166 *started hiking up the cliff:* PCA, August 9, 1906.

167 *"Now, since the disease":* Dutton typescript, March 10, 1889, HHS.

167 *"Even Saints and Martyrs":* Meyer to Ashley, April 11, 1889, BHL.

167 *"if I have any credit":* Jourdain offers two versions of this scene on pp. 374, 421. Several more exist, differing only slightly in actual language. Also see Beevers, 138.

167 *Dr. Swift entered the room:* Dutton described the deathbed scene. See also Meyer to Ashley, April 6, 1889, BH; Emerson to Swift, October 25, 1889, BHL; Jourdain, 369.

A typical landing at the Kalaupapa waterfront, pictured here circa 1902. The interisland steamer *Likelike* is in the distance.

168 *"On the day of his burial":* Jourdain, 240.

169 *"Please spare a moment":* Swift retained the original note, which his family later attempted to sell along with other Damien relics. A copy is contained in the Kalaupapa Historical Society collection.

170 *"But this time I had seen her face":* Stevenson, *Travels in Hawaii,* 45.

171 *"My horror of the horrible":* See Stevenson to Mrs. R. L. Stevenson, May 1889, *Letters of Robert Louis Stevenson,* 2:83.

172 *"It's doggerel":* Stevenson, "Historical Sketches."

172 *"There are Molokais everywhere":* This quote is often misattributed to Stevenson.

173 *"It was interesting to watch them":* O. A. Bushnell, "Stevenson and Molokai," *Biography* 5, no. 2:23

173 *"waved the sheets until the boat":* "Notes of Sr. M. Antonia Brown," Archives of the Sisters of St. Francis, Syracuse, New York.

174 *writing on a lined journal:* Stevenson's journal and manuscript copy of "Historical Sketches of the Lazaretto" are held at Harvard University's Houghton Library. The pages show Stevenson's edits of his material, as he sharpened his criticism of the board and its actions.

174 *"I have seen sights that cannot be told":* Robert Louis Stevenson's visit has an infamous epilogue. Two months after Stevenson sailed from Molokai, a Protestant minister on the mainland sent a letter to a Honolulu clergyman named C. M. Hyde. Aware that Reverend Hyde had known Damien, he was curious if the growing testimonials to the priest were excessive. Hyde replied, "In answer to your inquiries about Father Damien, I can only reply that we who knew the man are surprised at the extravagant newspaper laudations, as if he were the most saintly philanthropist. The simple truth is, he was a coarse, dirty man, headstrong and bigoted.... Others have done much for the lepers, our own ministers, the government physicians, and so forth, but never with the Catholic idea of meriting eternal life." Although Hyde's letter leaked to the mainstream press, he believed his criticisms of Damien would go unnoticed. They might have, had Stevenson never seen a published copy of Hyde's letter. Infuriated, Stevenson responded with a blistering thirty-two-page defense of Damien, in the form of a public letter to Hyde: "I conceive you as a man quite beyond and below the reticences of civility," he wrote. "I rejoice to feel the button off the foil and to plunge home." Stevenson had the evisceration published as a book and sent around the world, a tactic that further elevated Damien's fame while simultaneously destroying Hyde's reputation. Stevenson's attack hit Honolulu "like a fierce slap from the back of a hand," a granddaughter of one of Hyde's colleagues wrote. Reverend Hyde collapsed in his study. "That afternoon, he seemed to be an extinguished candle with the last remnants of life ebbing out of the light that had been," the young woman reported. "He was crushed, distracted and himself on the verge of tears." Suddenly rising from the couch, he cried, "Oh ... what have I done?" Hyde then turned to the girl and said, "I have just suffered the greatest undoing of my entire life. I am now being crucified by the most widely read author of our day and on the charges of telling the truth about that sanctimonious bigot on Molokai."

KINDRED DUST

177 *"arranged in reference to streets": The Friend,* September 1895.

178 *"They are comfortable, well-housed":* HAA, 1892.

178 *"He laid aside his cherished books": Brooklyn Eagle,* December 8, 1895.

178 *recording a census:* For specific details about housing arrangements and the makeup of the settlement's population, I have relied on the 1900, 1910, 1920, and 1930 U.S. Census for Kalawao County. The board continued to maintain a patient log, marked as the "Register of Lepers at the Leper Settlement, Molokai." Held at the State Archives of Hawaii, the register is a leather-bound book approximately three feet by two feet. Beginning in 1895, the ledger includes entry fields for "Locality of first lesion," "History of case," "Leprous relations," and "Remarks." Often these fields are left blank, but some columns contain personal ephemera, such as "husband has deserted her," "very bad case," "dangerous to society," "surrounded by children and very liable to spread disease." Fragments of diagnosis also dot the pages: "all over body," "on forehead," "father a leper," and "both hands contracted and flesh falling away."

179 *"on a secular basis":* January 12, 1898, BHM.

179 *"to instruct Mr. Hutchison":* September 1, 1897, BHM.

180 *He carved a family plot:* Meyer, *Meyer and Molokai,* 25.

181 *"had lived in the same house":* Mouritz, *Path,* 154.

181 *No successful inoculation of a human subject:* Despite the failure to clinically prove transmission of leprosy by inoculation, some intriguing anecdotal instances have occurred. One of the most bizarre took place in June 1943 and involved two U.S. Marines in their early twenties. The men served in the same unit and were "friends and residents of the same [home] town," reported the *American Journal of Pathology,* in 1947. While on leave in Melbourne, Australia, they were each tattooed on the lower left forearm. "Both the Marines and the tattooer were inebriated," the *Journal* reported, "and a number of needles were broken during the process." Two years later, one of the marines noticed that the area surrounding the tattoo had become insensitive, and "while at a party, he deliberately burned himself . . . with a lighted cigarette to prove the loss of sensation." His friend also soon noticed symptoms of the disease, which developed at the site of his tattoo. Both men were diagnosed with tuberculoid leprosy in November 1946.

181 *"Accompanying his resignation":* Greenwell, HJH, vol. 25.

181 *Anna Dole wore her gloves indoors:* Allen, *Sanford Ballard Dole,* 161.

182 *"Shall We Annex Leprosy?":* See also "Leprosy and the Hawaiian Annexation," *North American Review,* September 1898.

183 *but would not allow them to perform:* This detail comes from the May 5, 1938, issue of *Ken: The Insider's World,* a short-lived adventure magazine whose managing editor was Arnold Gingrich, soon to become a legendary editor at *Esquire.* "Where Leprosy Breeds" was unsigned and ran alongside typical *Ken* fare such as "Blindman's Bluff with Bullets," "Cheating Death on Highways," and "How Hitler Conquered England." Ernest Hemingway is listed among the magazine's contributors. "The Hawaiian lepers' island of Molokai is an unsanitary pesthole of infection," *Ken* reported. The sensational article warned that "each leper infects at least one well person" and that "perhaps some letter you received today rode in a mail bag along with an unfumigated letter from a leper on Molokai, destined for some movie star or even to the offices of

(1)

In Memoria
of
Reverend Father Damien Joseph
De Veuster

An
Introductory Apology

The writer of this Memoir an exiled from all a man hold dear in life and by forced of law, like many other unfortunate outcasts sufferers held a prisoner for no Crime other than of having Contracted a loathesome disease has at different times asked by friends to write about Father Damien but hesitated I felt unequal to do the subject matter justice, knowing that other good friends more Competent wielding abler pen than mine hast written about Father Damien and his life work among the lepers of Molokai has at last accepted to undertake the task to please these good friends.

Father Damien

I was taken from my home at Honomaele Hana Island of Maui by a squad of native Police headed by the Sheriff of the District and locked in a prison cell like a felon without food and drink and sent to Honolulu and from there after

The opening page of Ambrose Hutchison's autobiography, begun as a reminiscence of Father Damien.

the chief executive of the United States." The article received so much notice in Hawaii that the board of health asked the superintendent to make a formal report "on the handling of mail at the institution by inmates." On May 13, 1938, the *Star-Bulletin* wrote, "What is the circulation of the magazine *Ken* or how long it will last we don't know. . . . But to whatever number of people the issue goes, a false, a harmful and unfair impression of the island and the settlement will go."

183 *St. Catharine's Industrial School:* Gibson, *Under the Cliffs,* 153.

183 *"Hawaii's Future":* PCA, December 13, 1900.

184 *"Paradise of the Pacific":* See *Writings of Lorrin A. Thurston,* ed. Andrew Farrell (Honolulu: 1936), 81.

185 *required only six crew members:* In the weeks before his departure thousands of people wrote to Jack London, begging him to include them in the *Snark*'s crew. Young boys scribbled plaintive notes in colored pencil; eager women volunteered to be cabin maid or cook or secretary. "Write immediately if you need me," one woman insisted. "I shall bring my typewriter on the first train." Another applicant informed London, "I have a father, a mother, brothers and sisters, dear friends and a lucrative position, and yet I will sacrifice all to become one of your crew."

185 *"is a young fellow your own age":* Jack London to Martin Johnson, November 17, 1906, *Letters of Jack London,* 2:632.

185 *He was Deputy Sheriff Louis Stolz's son:* PCA, December 21, 1932. Mary Powell Stolz, the widow of Louis Stolz, had moved with her two children to Redlands, California, following her husband's murder. She later earned a medical degree and became one of the first female homeopathic physicians in the state.

The Baldwin Home for Boys in Kalawao circa 1898.

CIVIC DUTY

The life of John Early would make a fine book. In the absence of a biography, I have relied mainly on newspaper accounts spanning two decades. Details of Early's discovery and his subsequent escapes come from the *Washington Post* (WP), September 3, 7, 8, 11, 12, 16, 24, 29, 30, 1908; October 7, 24, 30, 1908; November 9, 1908; December 1, 24, 26, 1908; March 18, 1909; April 1, 1909; May 20, 31, 1909; June 3, 29, 1909; August 4, 7, 9, 1909; November 8, 1910; May 8, 1911; June 29, 1911; August 25, 1911; July 10, 20, 1913; June 5, 9, 1914; July 11, 15, 1914; December 11, 1914; June 20, 1915; December 20, 1915; May 2, 1916; April 8, 1917; October 8, 1918; March 28, 1920; May 4, 1920; July 17, 22, 1923; April 12, 21, 24, 25, 28, 30, 1927; May 3, 1927; July 12, 24, 1927; August 15, 19, 1927; November 25, 1928; March 10, 1929. The *Evening Star* (Washington, D.C.) duplicated or expanded on much of the *Post*'s material, and the following issues hold particularly rich detail: August 23, 24, 25, 1908; December 26, 1928. Also, NYT, August 8, December 4, and October 15, 1909, published interesting accounts of Early's always colorful exploits. Unless otherwise noted, all quotes in this chapter have been culled from these articles.

186 *"stimulated the appetite":* WP, August 31, 1908. Also see the *Evening Star,* August 24, 1908, for details on the "morbid crowd [that] visits his lonely tent."

186 *Chinese student named Mock Sen:* Stein and Blochman, *Alone No Longer,* 97. Such episodes occurred no matter the nationality of the patient, and the consequences could be horrifying. In one notorious case, a former Civil War general named Wardwell died from a heart attack while trying to sneak his leprosy-stricken wife across Arizona and into Mexico. The trauma tipped her into insanity, as the *Evening Star* reported on August 23, 1908: "The leper maniac was placed in isolated confinement, but escaped, and whole communities were paralyzed with fear that she might bring this scourge of the Orient into their midst." See also NYT, August 10, 1908.

187 *"came as a shock to Mrs. Early":* WP, September 4, 1908.

187 *"Our lives are linked": Munsey's Magazine,* September 1909.

187 *"Go away, Manly!":* Ibid. While detained in the abandoned farmhouse Lottie Early gave birth to her second child, attended only by her mother. They delivered the boy themselves, by candlelight—Lottie later described how rats crept to the edge of the light to watch. "I like to forget that time," she recalled.

187 *"I could hear his voice":* The city took extraordinary measures to prevent John Early from touching anyone or anything. On September 11, 1908, the *Post* described the maneuvers Early made to endorse a $165 pension check. The check was placed in a slitted envelope, impaled on a stick, then passed into the tent while a notary public watched from a safe distance. Early signed the check through the slit. "Without touching the slip of paper, save with the point of a pen, the diseased man [then] endorsed it over to his wife." One reporter remarked that this was "a rather spectacular display out at the tent."

187 *"Can you care for leper there?":* A copy of the cable is held at the Mamiya Medical Heritage Library.

187 *"Though virtually a part of the United States":* NYT, August 10, 1908. On November 2, 1908, the *Times* announced, "A published story yesterday that John Early, the leper,

would be disposed of by the Federal Government by transporting him to the leper colony at Molokai, in the Hawaiian Islands, was denied on all sides to-day."

187 *"is not wanted at the Molokai home"*: SB, date illegible, 1913, Clipping File, AH.

188 *Early's plight received wide publication: Evening Star,* August 25, 1908.

188 *"subluxations"*: WP, September 15, 1908. Palmer, the paper reported, was "the discoverer, developer, and founder of the science of chiropractic."

188 *allow a New York dermatologist:* WP, October 15, 1909. The physician's name was L. Duncan Bulkley, head of the New York Skin and Cancer Hospital.

188 *"[An] ultra red ray"*: WP, August 9, 1909.

188 *use the name John Western:* NYT, July 29, 1923. This is one of the better summaries of Early's multiple flights, despite the headline it carries: "EARLY, THE SUPPOSED LEPER, A MODERN 'WANDERING JEW.'" Also see WP, August 7, 1909.

188 *Second International Leprosy Congress:* Ibid. Also see WP, August 19, 1909.

188 *"serious blunder"*: WP, August 19, 1909.

188 *"a complete report on leprosy"*: "Report of the Sanitary Board on the prevalence of leprosy in the United States," Senate Document no. 269, 57th Congress, 1st sess.

189 *"Is Hawaii to be the dumping ground"*: SB, date illegible, 1909, Clipping File, AH.

189 *larger than any complex:* Bushnell, "United States Leprosy," 84.

190 *"The [station] grounds"*: Gibson, *Under the Cliffs,* 13. The Gibsons had been married only a few weeks when the offer came to go to Molokai. "Our friends and other offi-

THE LEPER OF WASHINGTON.

JOHN R. EARLY.

From photo taken by a Star photographer this morning.

John Early in his prison tent on the banks of the Potomac River, in Washington, D.C. He was photographed on the morning after his arrest, August 23, 1908.

cers fairly begged us not to go," Emma wrote. "But we were young and full of Romance." They were to leave from San Francisco and were preparing to depart when on April 18, 1906, the great earthquake struck. "Eventful days!" Gibson later wrote. "Dramatic and terrifying days!" In the chaotic aftermath, the couple gave away most of their belongings to earthquake victims and boarded the transport ship *Logan* with only a few bags. The captain assigned them the "honeymoon suite."

190 *"Young, modest, patient, persistent":* PCA, January 22, 1906.

190 *"His precautions became offensive":* Bushnell, "United States Leprosy," 83.

190 *multimillionaire Nelson White:* HA, July 7, 1906.

190 *battle with a salivating dragon:* Gibson, 22.

190 *"experiments with serum":* Bushnell, "United States Leprosy"; Gibson, 14; HA, April 4, 1907.

191 *Boston papers initially cited: Boston Globe,* March 3, 1911.

191 *"the note began":* Gibson, 52.

191 *"They are nice":* Ibid., 53.

191 *typical six-month period:* McVeigh to board, 1913 Leper Settlement Report, BH.

192 *performed 267 major:* Ibid., BH.

192 *"Swollen Head Fever":* Goodhue to board, illegible, 1916, BH. Swollen Head Fever struck in 1890 and again in 1904—Goodhue also reported that Mother Marianne claimed to have seen an outbreak in 1900. Described by the doctor as "an acute, epi-

The ill-fated U.S. Leprosy Investigation Center, built on the Kalawao shoreline, just beyond the Baldwin Home for Boys. Emma Gibson's home is the second building from the far right.

demic painful inflammatory leprous fever," its symptoms seem to resemble the attack known as erythema nodosum leprosum, although Dr. Goodhue insisted that Swollen Head Fever was "very infectious, but only among lepers." Whatever its origin, the episode was terrifying, beginning with a severe chill, chattering teeth, and then a rapid spike in temperature. One half of the face swelled tremendously; after three days, the other half also ballooned. The enlargement—which could double the size of the person's head—lasted two weeks. The victim's hair then fell out, and the skin on the face, neck, and ears sloughed off. Goodhue reported that elderly and sick patients inevitably died; younger ones survived.

192 *"the greatest institution on the islands":* SB, December 9, 1916.

192 *"dry-rotting from lack of use":* This is Jack London writing, following his second visit to the settlement. Gibson, 151.

193 *New York City segregated:* Markel, *Quarantine!* 55. See also the *Brooklyn Eagle*, November 2, 1897.

193 *its sick to Penikese Island:* McCoy, "History of Leprosy."

193 *"could be put to gardening":* SB, June 22, 1914.

193 *"Hello, John":* WP, November 28, 1928.

194 *"we were properly disinfected":* WP, November 25, 1928.

194 *Diamond Point leprosy camp:* Many reporters confused the name Diamond Point with the volcanic headland on Oahu known as Diamond Head; thus, they reported incorrectly that Early had escaped from Hawaii and the colony on Molokai.

194 *turned Early "insane":* WP, July 11, 1913. The *Post* reporter recalled that in 1908 he had

Sanford B. Dole *(left)* and his colleague Lorrin A. Thurston, pictured in Dole's private office in 1898.

interviewed Early, who at the time remarked that his exile "is enough to drive a man insane, but I will not go insane. I will keep up my courage." The news of Early's apparent madness, the reporter remarked, "throws a deep pathos" on the quote.

194 *"prostrated from fright":* WP, July 20, 1913.

194 *"He seemed to detest":* Ibid.

195 *Lottie clipped a piece of his skin:* WP, July 20, 1913; September 25, 1909. On several occasions John Early claimed to have cut the sample and mailed it himself: WP, November 25, 1928; August 19, 1909. This seems less likely than Lottie's version.

195 *"He was compelled to admit":* WP, July 20, 1913.

195 *"serve as a great national example":* WP, November 28, 1928.

195 *"deluxe tour":* NYT, June 3, 1914.

196 *Early had passed a $2 bill:* WP, March 1, 1938.

196 *largest manhunt since: Washington Times,* July 21, 1989.

196 *"I am John Early":* WP, March 1, 1938. As the *Post* reported on February 20, 1916, Early's physical presence was not required to make his point. During one debate concerning a national leprosarium, Early mailed the presiding senator a letter advocating the bill, "which the senator handled gingerly, even though it had been well disinfected."

196 *"I remember the first time":* Stein and Blochman, *Alone No Longer,* 183.

196 *"Haven't they kept me cooped up":* WP, August 30, 1927. On April 24 the *Post* had interviewed Hugh Banks, the North Carolina sheriff dispatched to arrest Early. "I have

Memorial Day in Kalawao. Joseph Dutton is visible raising the flag.

routed stern moonshiners and captured clever criminals," Banks said, "but I surely don't relish the job of tackling a leper in his lair."

196 *"His eccentricities have":* WP, November 19, 1928. Also see WP, March 1, 1938: "LEPER CRUSADER DIES; WON LAW BY SCARING D.C."

GOOD BREEZE

"I'm the rottenest letter-writer that ever come down the pike," Jack London complained to Sinclair Lewis, in November 1910. "I hate letter-writing." In truth, London was a prolific and gifted correspondent, and his letters serve as the basis for much of this chapter. These are taken from *The Letters of Jack London,* vols. 1–3 (Stanford, Calif.: Stanford University Press, 1988). London describes his first visit to Kalaupapa in "The Lepers of Molokai," *Woman's Home Companion,* January 1908; Charmian Kittredge London later published her reminiscences of the visit in *Jack London in Aloha-Land,* also published in a slightly different edition as *Our Hawaii.*

197 *Jack London's boat* Snark *finally:* Day, *Jack London,* 16.

197 *"He was incompetent":* London to N. Eames, May 28, 1907.

198 *"Never mind, Martin":* Day, *Jack London,* 40.

198 *"We had a beautiful voyage":* London to F. Bamford, undated, June 1907.

198 *return to Stanford: Letters,* 2:692. Herbert Stolz became a Rhodes Scholar and later earned a medical degree. From 1926 to 1934 he was director of the Institute of Child Welfare at the University of California, Berkeley. Later, he became director of special

Jack London and his wife, Charmian, aboard London's unfinished yacht *Snark.* The Londons arrived in the settlement on July 2, 1907.

schools and services for the state of California. Interestingly, when he returned to Hawaii in November 1958, he told reporters it was his first visit back since he'd left the islands at age six. For details of Stolz's ineptness at sea, see London's letter to N. Eames, July 25, 1907.

198 *"It is time to cease crying":* "The Molokai Settlement," January 1, 1907.

198 *"the Leper Settlement into up to date":* Pinkham to Buchanan, October 27, 1906, BPBM. Pinkham was corresponding with his friend James L. Buchanan, who was working as an engineer in Pretoria, South Africa. Pinkham begins his letter of July 22, 1906, "I am writing you from one of the strangest places on earth, the Leper Settlement on Molokai." The unmarried Pinkham also sent gossip about his usually uneventful love life. "I came out of my shell . . . long enough to head a reception [for] Miss Alice Roosevelt," Pinkham wrote. Having apparently become smitten with the president's daughter, who was visiting Honolulu, he remarked to Buchanan, "As she is now hobnobbing with King Edward VII and William III she has forgotten me."

199 *"beer makers, drunkards and law breakers":* McVeigh to board, 1902 Leper Settlement Report, BH.

199 *burned the wound out with acid:* HA, June 21, 1925. For biographical material on Jack Devine McVeigh, I have relied on HA, June 21, 1925; February 8, 1927; January 31, 1930; February 2, 1930; June 10, 1964; August 31, 1983. His voluminous correspondence with the board also offers insights into his character.

199 *"He made himself respected":* HA, February 2, 1930.

199 *"When Mr. McVeigh took charge":* HA, August 31, 1983.

199 *"He who seeks sunshine":* "The Molokai Settlement," January 1, 1907.

Jack D. McVeigh, the superintendent at the time of London's visit, pictured outside his cottage in Kalaupapa.

Dr. William J. Goodhue, who pioneered surgical treatment of leprosy while serving as resident physician.

200 *"We are not merry":* C. London, *Jack London in Aloha-Land,* 105.

200 *Kalaupapa Rifle Club just happened to be:* Ibid., 111.

201 *piano that Robert Louis Stevenson:* Hanley and Bushnell, *Song of Pilgrimage,* 328. Stevenson also composed a poem about the settlement as a gift for Mother Marianne: "To see the infinite pity of this place, / The mangled limb, the devastated face, / The innocent sufferers smiling at God, / A fool were tempted to deny his God. / He sees, and shrinks; but if he look again, / Lo, beauty springing from the breast of pain!— / He marks the sisters on the painful shores, / And even a fool is silent and adores." Stevenson dated the poem "Kalawao, May 22, 1889."

202 *"Antiques and Horribles":* Charmian London describes this annual parade in *Jack London in Aloha-Land,* 122. For a similar account, see PCA, July 16, 1904.

202 *with his Kodak:* London brought three cameras with him to the settlement, two folding pocket Kodaks and a panoramic camera. He shot nine rolls of film. J. London to N. Eames, July 11, 1907.

202 *"The Lepers of Molokai":* When he sent the piece to editor F. Hayden Carruth, London wrote, "While leprosy is a distasteful subject, I think I have handled it fairly decently for your readers; and that have given a side of it that has not hitherto been given to it—namely, the happier, brighter side." London to Carruth, July 11, 1907.

203 *"of a value to Hawaii":* C. London, *Our Hawaii,* 296.

203 *"throw down his pencil":* Farrell, *Writings,* 105.

203 *"a sneak of the first water":* Ibid., 117.

204 *"Dear friend":* PCA, May 22, 1910. The fierce epistolary battle between London and Thurston is comically entertaining. Thurston, as the *Advertiser's* editor, was printing every letter between them in the paper in an attempt to drive circulation. London soon remarked to Thurston, "If I get 25¢ a word, think of all the words the *Advertiser* is getting for nothing!" London to Thurston, February 1, 1910. See also London to *Advertiser,* January 7, 1910; London to Thurston, June 11, 1910.

A TERRIBLE MISTAKE

205 *"Death of Mikala Kaipu":* Supreme Court Case no. 172, May 13, 1907.

205 *"the result of a wound":* BHM, September 6, 1904.

205 *"It was decided that both Mrs. Mikala Kaipu":* Ibid.

206 *"How many more unfortunate victims": Honolulu Evening Bulletin,* June 3, 1909.

207 *under the name Antileprol:* Feeny, *Fight Against Leprosy,* 108.

207 *"The women fainted, and the men trembled":* Gugelyk and Bloombaum, *Separating Sickness,* 103.

208 *beset by insomnia:* Gibson, *Under the Cliffs,* 154.

209 *steaming across the Pacific:* NYT, July 14, 1908.

209 *before sunset on September 1, 1909:* Dean, *Lighthouses of Hawaii,* 101.

210 *Goodhue wed one of Rudolph Meyer's:* Meyer, *Meyer and Molokai,* 85.

210 *"specially constructed hermetically sealed":* RBH, 1908, AH.

210 *"in her little parlor":* See Hanley and Bushnell, *Song of Pilgrimage,* 392.

211 *the sad theft of his wallet:* Father Maxime wrote, "He stole my wallet which contained maybe 90 cents and the key of the church trunk." In his diary, the priest was often a keen critic of the government. On March 26, 1921, he wrote, "Some members of the legislature arrived and they have promised a lot. But will they come through? They

The research laboratory at Kalihi Hospital. After the board revised exam procedures, inmates were brought to Kalihi for reexamination. Of the first eleven patients tested, none were found to have leprosy.

Martin Jensen with his plane the *Aloha*. Jensen took second place in the Dole Derby, a contest that claimed twelve lives.

Mother Marianne in Kalaupapa, shortly before her death on August 9, 1918.

announced that soon all leper patients will be cured by the use of the Chaulmoogra oil and there will not be any leprosarium on Kalaupapa."

211 *"have hoarded their savings":* Ibid.

212 *"During those sleepless nights":* Hanley and Bushnell, 406.

213 *"The gift of nearly $250": Maui News,* March 1, 8, 1918.

213 *"The other day a friend of mine":* Dutton and Case, *Memoirs,* 146.

213 *had fallen to 546:* RBH, 1920.

214 *"In no equal in the whole history of the segregation":* Ibid.

215 *would again become "quasi-penal":* HA, June 28, 1929.

216 *"deportation of Dawson":* SB, June 11, 1926.

216 *"I like the place": Leslie's Illustrated Weekly,* July 30, 1921. NYT, February 10, 1929.

216 *The elderly Thurston was now:* Thurston purchased the paper in 1895 and remained publisher until his death on May 11, 1931. In 1921, he changed the paper's name from the *Pacific Commercial Advertiser* to *The Honolulu Advertiser.* Thurston's son, also Lorrin Thurston, succeeded him as publisher; documents frequently confuse the two Lorrins. For further insight into the father's many promotional campaigns, see Thurston, *Writings.*

216 *"From angle advertising islands and yourself":* Gwynn-Jones, *Wings Across Pacific,* 65.

217 *handed each pilot a Bible:* Ibid., 74. Details on the Dole Derby are drawn from Lesley Forden, *Glory Gamblers;* Gwynn-Jones, 65–88; SFE, August 14, 15, 16, 17, 18, 19, 1927; PCA, August 14, 15, 16, 17, 18, 1927; *San Francisco Call-Bulletin,* October 10, 1955; HA, August 5, 1982, January 20, 1985; and the *Maui News,* December 2, 1950.

218 *"DOLE'S RACE TO DEATH":* Gwynn-Jones, 89.

219 *"publicity-mad promoter":* Ibid., 81.

ALL A MAN HOLDS DEAR

220 *"A wail":* Judd, *Autobiography,* 23.

221 *"Almost my first thought":* Ibid., 141.

221 *"in all its phases":* NYT, February 9, 1930.

221 *"Your committee has studied the subject":* "Report of the Governor's Advisory Committee on Leprosy in Hawaii," October 1930, MML.

222 *after twenty-three years in the settlement:* HA, June 18, 1925. Jack McVeigh died January 30, 1930, at age seventy-one; for the last several years of his life he had served on the board of health. McVeigh's tenure at the settlement, the *Advertiser* noted in his obituary, "bridged the period of slow change and readjustment during which Kalaupapa Settlement was thought and spoken of as a place of hopeless exile, and the present period of dissatisfaction, inquiry, active discussion and hope." McVeigh's Kalaupapa colleague Dr. William J. Goodhue died in Shanghai, China, in 1941, amid unconfirmed rumors that he had contracted the disease.

222 *"Could you spend three hundred thousand":* R. L. Cooke to illegible, January 14, 1932.

222 *"Your problem is one":* SB, date illegible, 1932, MML.

222 *"serve a dessert":* Caroline Edwards to Judd, January 27, 1931, HL. Oatmeal cookies were an apparent favorite.

222 *"The pall of hopeless tragedy":* SB, July 7, 1932.

223 *steamer* Kaala *sounded a distress signal:* HA, January 6, 1932. The *Kaala* was only one of many vessels to become shipwrecked at Kalaupapa. On the evening of October 25,

Joseph Dutton in his office.
On the photograph he indicates his age, writing, "79 yrs (on the home stretch). Yours Cheerfully, Joseph Dutton."

Lawrence M. Judd, governor of the territory of Hawaii, and later superintendent of the settlement, pictured circa 1930.

A view of Kalaupapa in 1931.

1935, a forty-foot Chinese junk wrecked several hundred yards out from the landing, with two starving and delirious crewmen aboard. According to a memoir later written by the captain, Eric de Bisschop, and held at BPBM, the men were members of the French Geographic Society, sailing across the Pacific in a somewhat confused attempt to prove that Pacific Islanders had originally come from Central America. They had run out of food fifteen days before reaching Molokai; when a cruise ship steaming from Honolulu to Sydney passed, Bisschop had waved his arms and croaked, "We're starving! We're starving!" The passengers merely waved back.

224 *"It was grand!":* Gibson, *Under the Cliffs,* 167.

224 *"a bit tired, and suddenly cold":* Ibid., 164.

224 *"Honolulu!":* HA, July 5, 6, 1930.

224 *"One of the sisters here has answered":* See Gibson, 110.

224 *"I forget so many things now":* HA, July 6, 13, 1930.

226 *"I was astonished to see": Hawaii Catholic Herald,* April 14, 1989.

227 *"It was not suicide":* NYT, February 12, 1936.

OLIVIA

228 *Olivia Robello put the record:* This scene is based in part on details recounted by Olivia in her memoir, *Olivia: My Life of Exile in Kalaupapa,* published in 1988. All instances that refer to Olivia's writing arise from that work. In addition to her memoir, I've relied on previously published interviews, documentary footage, and personal interviews with Olivia to tell her story. Of particular value was a series of interviews conducted by sociologists Ted Gugelyk and Milton Bloombaum as part of the Social Aspects of Leprosy Research Project and published in HA, October 22, 1980; SB, January 15, 1980; and in book form as *The Separating Sickness.* Olivia is quoted anonymously, but revealed herself to me as the source of her quotes. In some instances wording differs slightly from the published sources. In these cases, Olivia has retold a version of the story to me, and I've combined accounts.

228 *"So many dreams":* Breitha, *Olivia,* 4.

228 *"Then he told me it was a leprosy hospital":* Author interview, Olivia Breitha.

229 *"See, I already felt like":* Breitha, *Olivia,* 7.

229 *"I knew already":* Ibid., 8. Also see Gugelyk and Bloombaum, 57–59.

229 *"My heart felt":* Breitha, *Olivia,* 10.

230 *"You stupid man":* Author interview, Olivia Breitha.

230 *"I felt so sure":* Breitha, *Olivia,* 10.

230 *"humanized" the language:* RBHS, 1931, HL.

231 *named Robert Purdy:* September 14, 1933, Report of Parole Officer C. Kiilehua to Superintendent of BOHS, MML. Purdy was exiled for helping two other patients, S. Kaanana and W. Kihe, avoid transfer to Molokai. The two escaped from Kalihi on their original transfer day, but were quickly captured and returned. On the day of their next scheduled transfer to Molokai, the men hid in an attic in one of the Kalihi buildings. When guards attempted to remove them a brawl erupted, and Purdy joined in on the patients' side. Afterward the attorney general gave authorization to take all three men "by force" at the next opportunity and put them on the boat to Kalaupapa.

231 *"Hawaii's physicians, as a group":* "Report of the Governor's Advisory Committee on Leprosy in Hawaii," October 1930, MML.

232 *"I think she disowned":* Breitha, *Olivia,* 15. Being abandoned by families was not rare. In June 1920 a truck driver named Moichi Takenaka was diagnosed with leprosy and placed in Kalihi Hospital; four years later he was sent to Kalaupapa, where he died in 1935, at age fifty-two. Sixty-two years later, one of Takenaka's grandchildren, Rodney R. Shinkawa, learned about his grandfather's fate for the first time. Shinkawa wrote, "Now that the story was out, our older relatives . . . all admitted to the leprosy that afflicted Grandfather Takenaka. Prior to that . . . nothing was mentioned about relatives with the disease." On April 10, 1997, Shinkawa and his sister visited Kalaupapa, found their grandfather's grave, and placed flowers and traditional Japanese offerings on the site.

232 *"Special Incidents":* "Report of Matron," 1937, MML.

232 *"those men will lasso you":* Author interview, Olivia Breitha.

233 *"Suddenly I loved:* Breitha, *Olivia,* 19.

234 *They would claim to be a couple:* Author interview, Olivia Breitha.

234 *"Many of the things":* Ernie Pyle, December 27, 1927, typescript, HL. At the end of his visit, Pyle experienced a bizarre reluctance to leave. "It wasn't romantic, it wasn't drama," he wrote of this desire to remain in Kalaupapa, "it was something akin to that urge that lures people standing on high places to leap downward."

234 *patients took turns as mourners:* "The Final Stage of Mai Pake," *Honolulu Magazine,* April 1979. A patient named Jacob recalled that funerals occurred so frequently that he would become weary walking back and forth to the graveyard. After one service Jacob sat down next to the fresh grave to rest. Five minutes later, gravediggers arrived and told him to move—they had another grave to dig.

236 *"so if I make a mistake": Quest for Dignity: Personal Victories Over Leprosy/Hansen's Disease,* 97.

236 *"I asked Ernie Pyle ONE favor":* Fennel to Raymond Coll, August 17, 1944. Fennel annotated Pyle's columns with his own observations and experiences in the settlement. HL.

237 *"I went down to the Store":* Ibid.

The visitor's area at Kalaupapa. Patients remained on one side of the chain-link screen, visitors on the other.

237 *"Even voices had changed":* Breitha, *Olivia,* 26.

237 *"just a few years ago":* Ibid.

238 *"There, in the open air":* Judd, *Autobiography,* 257. See also HA, June 8, 10, 15, 1948.

239 *identified in records only as D:* "A Study of the Care of Children Under the Jurisdiction of the Territorial Board of Hospitals and Settlement," unpublished 1950 master's thesis by Hazel M. Ikenaga, HL.

239 *"In permitting the physically":* April 22, 1919, "Report of Special Subcommittee on Leprosy Investigations," Appendix B. Originals of the report are held at the National Archives, in Washington, D.C.

239 *by 1933 twenty-seven states:* A California-based organization, the Human Betterment Foundation, maintained a running tally of the operations in the various states. As of January 1, 1933, California had sterilized 8,504 men and women. New York meanwhile had sterilized forty men and one woman before the state's eugenics statute was declared unconstitutional.

239 *"Isn't the time now ripe":* SB, January 16, 1932.

239 *"morons":* Ibid.

239 *"The 140 [children] that are now":* Ibid., April 7, 1932.

239 *"HAWAII PAYING HIGH PRICE":* Ibid., February 20, 1933.

240 *establish a eugenics:* Ibid., April 22, 1932.

240 *"You had no choice":* Gugelyk and Bloombaum, 40. See also the *Hawaii Sentinel,* January 23, 1941, under a heading "Sterilization Cuts Birth Rate."

240 *"I am of the opinion":* Breitha, *Olivia,* 100.

240 *Among the men:* Author interview, Olivia Breitha.

ATTACK

243 *The disease struck Bernard Punikaia:* When possible, I've relied on Bernard's own words to tell his story. The series of interviews he gave to Milton Bloombaum and Ted Gugelyk proved valuable, as did more than a hundred newspaper articles in which Bernard is quoted. These were the most helpful: SB, October 12, 1968; November 18, 1968; March 21, 1969; July 19, 1969; February 26, 1978; January 15, 1980; May 28, 1988; September 5, 1988. HA, October 22, 1980; April 15, 1983; August 21, 1988; August 29, 30, 2002. NYT, June 12, 1981; October 11, 1983. *Ka Haliau,* October/November 1983. I also mined Bernard's own writing, the minutes of the Patient's Advisory Committee meetings, board of health and department of health correspondence, and the memories of other Kalaupapa residents.

244 *made his rabbit sick:* Bernard Punikaia, "Leprosy in Hawaii—A Hundred Years of Separation: Its Meaning for Us," November 1987.

244 *"They lived and they died":* Ibid.

244 *"in the shadows of the bomb-release":* RBHS, 1940.

244 *Just before dawn on Sunday, December 7:* For the chronology of the Pearl Harbor attack, I've relied on Walter Lord's *Day of Infamy,* as well as HA, December 8, 9, 1941; NYT, December 8, 9, 10, 11, 1941.

245 *Patients ran for the chapel:* Gugelyk and Bloombaum, *Separating Sickness,* 104.

245 *"The plane was very low":* Ibid.

245 *Elroy Malo was shooting marbles:* Author interview, Makia Malo.

246 *"A noise caught my attention":* Ibid.

246 *Olivia had just returned:* Author interview, Olivia Breitha.
246 *It decided to transfer:* RBHS, 1941–44, HL.
247 *"Those kids turned and ran":* Author interview, Olivia Breitha.
247 *"I sterilized a needle":* SFE, December 11, 1960.
247 *"THEY SCOUT ALONE":* Hal Stein, *Scouting Magazine,* April 1947.
247 *Residents carried quota cards:* Samples of the cards are held in the Kalaupapa Historical Society collection.
248 *"with the exception of eight patients":* RBHS, 1942.
248 *shells thumped in the yard:* Author interview, Henry Nalaielua. See also RBHS, 1942. Also of interest is the SB series "War-Time Life in Kalaupapa," March 11, 13, 14, 15, 16, 17, 18, 20, 21, 22, 23, 1944.
248 *including 175 of Japanese descent:* Dennis M. Ogawa and Evarts C. Fox Jr., "Japanese Internment and Relocation: The Hawaii Experience," 1983, HL.
249 *"RATS IN ATTIC":* Mouritz's stained and battered diary is held in his file at the State Archives of Hawaii.
249 *favorites was Henry Nalaielua:* SB, May 7, 1985. My account of Henry's life is based on personal and published interviews, news articles, and his published work, primarily undertaken for the Kalaupapa Historical Society newsletters.
249 *"If people were going out fishing":* Author interview, Henry Nalaielua.
250 *"I remember getting experimented on":* Gugelyk and Bloombaum, 103.
250 *"lepra reactions":* Sloan, "Early Diagnosis."

Pearl Harbor on the morning of December 7, 1941, with the Japanese attack in progress. Kalihi Hospital is just beyond the frame, to the upper left.

LIKE A PEBBLE THROWN

251 *"heaved sighs of relief"*: WP, November 19, 1928.

251 *"goes forth now to mingle"*: HA, January 2, 1929.

251 *scribbling political pamphlets:* John Early wrote poetry as well. "I wonder is His blessing for me . . ." one poem reads, "Is Thy blessing meant for me— / To cleanse me through Thy faith and word / 'Till spotless all and free." WP, November 25, 1928.

252 *"Pogge cure-all cocktail"*: Stein and Blochman, *Alone No Longer,* 222. See also *Colliers,* January 22, 1954; *Newsweek,* October 23, 1950.

252 *"even the most hopeless cases"*: *Time,* December 30, 1946. See also NYT, February 23, 1947.

253 *"Our patients were naturally eager to try it"*: Sloan, "Promin."

254 *"We thought it was the end of the world"*: Henry Nalaielua, "Tidal Wave!" Kalaupapa Historical Society Newsletter, May 1985.

254 *"Tidal wave!"*: Author interview, Olivia Breitha. For a good account of the tsunami's fury, see HA, April 2, 3, 4, 5, 1946; SB, April 1, 3, 1946.

254 *"The long line of cemeteries was left a shambles"*: RBHS, 1946.

254 *"I have never been satisfied"*: Sloan, "Promin."

255 *"Nausea is common"*: Sloan et al., "Sulfone Therapy."

255 *"Oh joy, for most of us"*: Breitha, *Olivia,* 38.

255 *"He was heavily nodular"*: E. A. Fennel, appendix to Sloan, "Promin."

256 *"My early days at Kalaupapa were mostly"*: Gugelyk and Bloombaum, 106.

256 *"After I got well, I did all"*: Bernard Punikaia, "Leprosy in Hawaii—A Hundred Years of Separation: Its Meaning for Us," November 1987.

The U.S. Public Health Services Hospital at Carville, Louisiana.
The row of buildings are patient dormitories.

MAKIA

257 *Makia Malo was walking home:* Author interview, Makia Malo. My account of Makia's life is drawn from personal and published interviews, interviews of others, news articles, and his published work.

257 *"Why is your eye so red?":* Ibid.

257 *offices of Dr. Edwin Chung-Hoon:* Biographical details of Chung-Hoon are contained in his physician's file, MML. In April 1963 a twin-engine Beechcraft carrying the doctor crashed while attempting to land at Kalaupapa. The plane slammed into the rocks at the leading edge of the airfield, just at the waterline, and burst into flame. One survivor exclaimed that the passengers "would have burned alive in another minute." The pilot, a social worker, and the three doctors on board were treated at Kalaupapa Hospital. Dr. Chung-Hoon suffered a compression fracture of the spine, and multiple cuts and burns. He retired due to the injuries a short time later.

257 *"The entire skin surface":* Sloan, "Early Diagnosis."

258 *"Chung-Hoon announced":* Author interview, Makia Malo.

259 *"Mama's tears were falling":* Ibid.

260 *"Then I started to cry":* Ibid.

260 *"I thought, what a town":* Gugelyk and Bloombaum, *Separating Sickness,* 93.

260 *"I wasn't frightened by what I learned":* Ibid.

260 *"I wouldn't say":* Makia Malo recounts the episode in his Audiobook, *Tales of a Hawaiian Boyhood.*

Dr. Norman R. Sloan,
resident physician in Kalaupapa at the time
of the sulfone treatment breakthrough.

Former governor Lawrence M. Judd,
who arrived as superintendent
of Kalaupapa in June 1947.

260 *"Never will I forget":* Judd, *Autobiography,* 247.
261 *"Wherever we went":* Breitha, *Olivia,* 25.
261 *prohibited from mailing money:* SB, March 17, 1944. The board had been concerned about contamination of money since the 1890s, when it opened a money order office in the settlement. In a board meeting on May 3, 1893, members discussed disinfecting all coins sent out of the settlement. The matter soon spilled over into a larger debate about mail—and specifically stamps—leaving Kalaupapa. Rudolph Meyer suggested to the board that "germs of leprosy are apt to be conveyed" by licked stamps. On March 14, 1894, the board issued guidelines on perforating and fumigating all settlement mail; such measures remained in effect until 1969. For an interesting history of leprosy colony money and mail, see *The Numismatic Aspects of Leprosy: Money, Medals, and Miscellanea,* by Roger R. McFadden, John Grost, and Dennis F. Marr.
261 *The board banned photography:* SB, February 25, 1949. The legislature was considering a bill to allow some photographs to be taken in the settlement, so residents could send personal snapshots to their families, "thereby brightening up the patients' lives."
261 *"This place isn't like a jail anymore!": Maui News,* November 17, 1948.
261 *"You cannot imagine":* Breitha, *Olivia,* 41.
261 *He invited the Lions Club:* Judd, 252; HA, April 26, 1948.
262 *"instruction in cosmetology": Maui News,* February 26, 1949.
262 *"Blow, boy.* Blow!*":* Malo, *Tales of a Hawaiian Boyhood.*
262 *"Mr. Judd was a man":* Breitha, *Olivia,* 40.
262 *"Perhaps the only difference between":* HA, June 14, 1950.
262 *"For Mama taught me": Chicken Soup from the Soul of Hawaii,* Jack Caufield and Mark Victor Hansen (Deerfield Beach, FL) 144.
263 *"We seek the organisms":* Sloan, "Early Diagnosis."
263 *"I packed my clothes":* Breitha, *Olivia,* 48.
264 *"tickets of leave":* Judd, 259.
264 *"dangerously diseased patients":* HA, May 25, 1949. See also HA, May 28, 29, 1949; SB, May 25, 30, 1949.
265 *"That would be one of the worst":* HA, May 29, 1949.
265 *"If I am not wanted here":* SB, May 28, 1949.
265 *"pleaded to be allowed":* Judd, 282.

WHEN YOU START TO MAKE A FIST

266 *"I was like a hobo from some movie":* Author interview, Henry Nalaielua.
266 *"I was scared as hell":* "Remembering the Time of Separation," *National Parks,* November 1995.
266 *"There are many reasons":* HA, March 13, 1949.
266 *"crowded movie house":* HA, June 27, 1949. The letter was written by Mrs. G. P. Weltmir. On July 2, 1949, a patient who signed his name as J. J. wrote, "Mrs. Weltmir it is your hysterical fear upon a subject of which apparently you know very little that is dangerous."
266 *"It is in this stage":* P. W. Brand, "Surgical Aspects of the Rehabilitation of Leprosy Patients," date illegible.
267 *"know that the success or failure of her return to society":* SB, May 4, 1955.

267 *Henry discovered that his:* Author interview, Henry Nalaielua. "Remembering the Time of Separation," *National Parks,* November 1995.
267 *"what are you doing with your life?":* Author interview, Henry Nalaielua.
267 *"That's where I started meeting other people":* Ibid.
268 *"When you went out in public," one woman wearily admitted:* "Leprosy in Hawaii—A Hundred Years of Separation: Its Meaning for Us," November 1987.
268 *"It was heartbreaking," one resident recalled:* Gugelyk and Bloombaum, *Separating Sickness,* 94.
268 *"I used to feel the leprosy germs inside me":* Ibid., 71.
268 *job was gone, car repossessed:* Chiyeko Evelyn Nakasora, "A Descriptive Analysis of the Socio-Cultural Characteristics of 39 Hansen's Disease Patients Immediately Released as Non-Communicable," unpublished 1962 master's thesis.
268 *"never let me see my daughter":* Gugelyk and Bloombaum, 40.
268 *"A friend was leaving and I went to the airport":* Author interview, Makia Malo.
269 *"It is believed the couple":* HA, January 9, 1950.
269 *"This causes leprosy to bear greater":* RBHS, 1940, HL.
269 *"when the government offered":* Hawaii State Department of Health, "The Inpatient Leprosy Program in Hawaii: An Analysis," February 1975.
270 *"We can all go around nonchalantly not even realizing":* Gugelyk and Bloombaum, 108.
270 *"That we are zombies, incapable of thinking":* Ibid., 109.
270 *"We aren't drop-outs," he exclaimed:* SB, October 12, 1968.
270 *"I chose to remain":* Gugelyk and Bloombaum, 95.
271 *"The windows were all curtained":* Breitha, *Olivia,* 27.
271 *"a small sleeping town":* Gugelyk and Bloombaum, 93.
271 *"I need my space," she said:* Author interview, Olivia Breitha.
271 *"Thirteen pieces of furniture ordered by":* HA, September 17, 1956.
272 *"Life Beat But Never Bested Him":* SB, August 15, 1957.
272 *"You never really dated":* Author interview, Makia Malo.
272 *"We just never learned to do that":* Ibid.

Kalaupapa residents fishing on the western shore, in March 1955.

272 *"About two-thirds of the town is laughing":* Ibid.
273 *"I felt pain":* Ibid.
273 *"The fingers and thumbs account for 95 percent":* Yancey and Brand, *Pain,* 170.
273 *"Insensitive persons tend to lie on the same spot":* Ibid., 172.
273 *During one twelve-month span: Maui News,* May 19, 1934.
273 *"the way they do when you start to make a fist":* Author interview, Makia Malo.
273 *"It is definitely toxic":* Sloan, "Promin," HMJ, September–October 1947.
273 *"I kept going," Makia later:* Gugelyk and Bloombaum, 95.
273 *"There was nothing left to feel but despair":* Author interview, Makia Malo.

STAND UP STRAIGHT

274 *"No pain sensors are more sensitive":* Yancey and Brand, *Pain,* 145.
274 *"one of the most agonizing afflictions":* Stein and Blochman, *Alone No Longer,* 186.
274 *"would lie awake":* Ibid.
275 *"like looking through smoke":* Author interview, Makia Malo.
275 *"a separate people even among the leprosy":* Gugelyk and Bloombaum, *Separating Sickness,* 96.
275 *"I would eat alone in my room and try to feed":* Ibid., 95.
275 *"I was shocked she used the word* blind*":* Author interview, Makia Malo.
276 *"Without a doubt":* Yancey and Brand, *Pain,* 144.
276 *"I closed myself off completely":* Gugelyk and Bloombaum, 96.
277 *"Miss Meheula [has] never heard":* SB, December 3, 1957.
277 *"argument that Hawaii was too far away":* Kuykendall and Day, *Hawaii: A History,* 291.
277 *"Evidence shows . . . the people of Hawaii:* Ibid., 297.
278 *"He sounded exactly like he did onscreen":* Author interview, Henry Nalaielua.
278 *"They thought if I went over":* Author interview, Shirley Temple Black.
278 *"Now we were to meet them face to face":* Trapp and Murdoch, 154.
279 *hired Booz, Allen & Hamilton:* HA, March 16, 1961.
279 *"They might have talked to us":* Ibid. See also Milton Bloombaum and Ted Gugelyk, "Voluntary Confinement Among Lepers," *Journal of Heath and Social Behavior.*
279 *"Where the problem once":* HA, June 17, 1963. Though many residents of the community were now loath to leave Kalaupapa, exile was still feared. In February 1957 health officials were called to the Honolulu home of twenty-eight-year-old Edith Clark. She was dead when they arrived. Clark's body, reported the *Honolulu Star-Bulletin,* "show[ed] visible signs of the advanced stage of" leprosy. She had become infected as a teenager, her mother explained. Unwilling to have her daughter sent away, Mrs. William Clark had locked Edith in the house for more than a decade, and never "allowed [her] outside." A board spokesman noted that "harboring a person afflicted with a disease is a violation of territorial law," but no charges were filed. After Edith Clark's funeral, one board physician stated that had she submitted to Kalaupapa, Edith might have "lived a normal life." SB, March 1, 1957.
279 *"It's too late to start all over again":* HA, June 17, 1963.
279 *"I wish the powers-that-be would stop begrudging":* HA, January 23, 1964.
279 *"became a watchdog for patients' rights":* HA, November 2, 1973.
279 *"If I don't speak out for my people":* Gugelyk and Bloombaum, 118.

279 *"Sometime, I hope that the Health Department":* Bernard Punikaia, "Leprosy in Hawaii—A Hundred Years of Separation: Its Meaning For Us," November 1987.
279 *"abide by rules that could be called ancient":* SB, July 19, 1969.
280 *"a system of informers":* Ibid.
280 *"If a 16-year-old girl were recognized":* SB, August 19, 1968.
280 *"I think leprosy patients are frightened to stand":* Gugelyk and Bloombaum, 109.
280 *"as is the case with other diseases":* SB, March 21, 1969.
281 *"They just change the words":* SB, September 18, 1969.
281 *"People got a little drunk," Henry recalled:* Author interview, Henry Nalaielua.
281 *"by a biological isolation suit":* SB, July 18, 1969.
281 *"quarantined like lepers":* Alex Shoumatoff, "The Carville Hansenarium," *Saturday Review,* October 28, 1972.
282 *"After three or four days on leave with family":* Hawaii State Department of Health, "The Inpatient Leprosy Program in Hawaii: An Analysis," February 1975.
282 *"As you must know":* Breitha, *Olivia,* 60.
282 *Brand was a quiet, intensely religious man:* Yancey and Brand, *Pain.* See also Dorothy Clarke Wilson's biography of Paul Brand, *Ten Fingers for God.*
282 *"Dear Right Foot: This letter is to you":* Breitha, 76.
282 *"We don't tell them where to go":* SB, April 28, 1971.
283 *titled* Red Blanket: SB, February 23, 2003.
283 *"A visit to see Stanley during the last":* Yancey and Brand, *Pain,* 164.
283 *primarily a place to read magazines:* The magazines listed are from an inventory of the Kalaupapa library's current subscriptions as of February 20, 1973.
283 *"It is the leper's fate that he is never the hero of a story":* Weymouth, *Through the Leper-Squint,* 118.
284 *"He took one deep breath":* Breitha, 68.
284 *"I knew that my aloneness":* Ibid., 69.

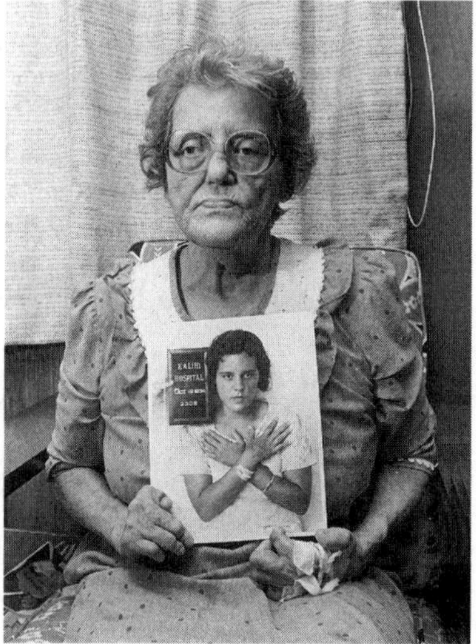

Olivia Breitha pictured in her Kalaupapa cottage; she holds a copy of her entry photograph, taken almost a half-century earlier.

ORIENTATION

285 *"Of course, I had to fight off the panic":* Gugelyk and Bloombaum, *Separating Sickness,* 97.

286 *"Just tell me which way," Makia said:* Ibid., 96.

286 *entry beside Hale Mohalu read: "None, ever":* Hawaii State Department of Health, "The Inpatient Leprosy Program in Hawaii: An Analysis," February 1975.

286 *"Reportedly, the 3 have not cooperated":* Ibid.

286 *Persons who "react unfavorably to anti-leprosy drugs":* Ibid.

287 *"Mama was comfortable in there":* Author interview, Makia Malo.

287 *where patients took lessons in sewing, auto mechanics:* HA, June 16, 1968.

287 *"This is for real?" Makia cried":* HA, May 13, 1970.

287 *"To think an outside person could":* Gugelyk and Bloombaum, 97.

287 *"For the first time in 100 years":* SB, December 19, 1974.

288 *program for handicapped students:* In a nicely resonant touch, the University of Hawaii's program for students with disabilities is called KOKUA.

288 *"morning grief and afternoon humiliations":* Hoagland, *Compass Points,* 26.

288 *"I felt so self-conscious":* Gugelyk and Bloombaum, 98.

288 *"You could tell he was very, very anxious":* Author interview, Ann Ito.

289 *"Two courses, that was the max":* "Triumph of Laughter," Hana Hou, August/September 2002.

289 *"nobody would initiate a conversation":* HA, April 1, 1979.

289 *"Heck no with all my scars":* "Triumph of Laughter," Hana Hou, August/September 2002.

289 *"It was such a new world for me":* Author interview, Makia Malo.

289 *"I always had the feeling that Makia had much more to tell":* Author interview, William Astman.

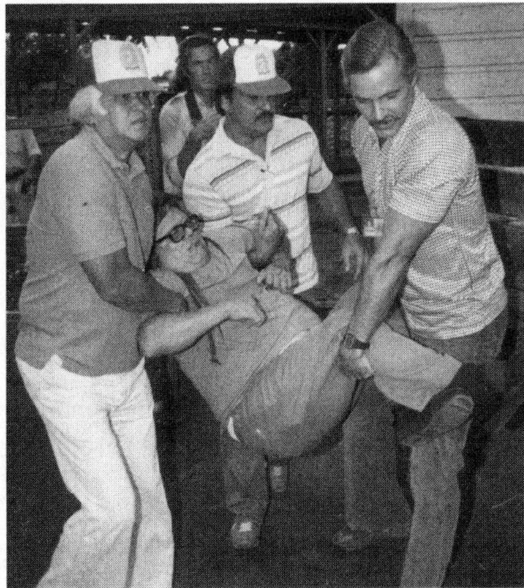

Bernard Punikaia being removed from Hale Mohalu on September 21, 1983.

290 *"Time did not permit a similar analysis for Kalaupapa":* Hawaii State Department of Health, "The Inpatient Leprosy Program in Hawaii: An Analysis," February 1975.

290 *"The people who run the little stores around here are used to us":* NYT, June 28, 1978.

290 *"This has been a home for us for so many years":* HA, November 2, 1973.

290 *On January 23, 1978, residents were asked to sign liability waivers:* The account and quotes from the Hale Mohalu protest are drawn from SB, March 11, 1968; August 3, 1978; March 6, 1982; September 5, 1983; October 1, 1984. HA, December 27, 1982; May 11, 1983; September 8, 22, 1983; October 2, 1983; January 20, 25, 26, 1984; February 4, 1984. For insight into the participants, I relied on the series of interviews assembled for a 1987 forum, "Leprosy in Hawaii—a Hundred Years of Separation: Its Meaning for Us," and "Save Hale Mohalu," a collection of fund-raising calendars that contain brief quotations from the facility's residents. See also Skinsnes, "Hale Mohalu: A Historical Perspective."

291 *"They cut off the water":* Bernard Punikaia, "Leprosy in Hawaii—A Hundred Years of Separation: Its Meaning for Us," November 1987.

291 *"Authority never considers the underdog":* Breitha, *Olivia,* 81.

291 *"I still believe in Santa Claus":* HA, December 27, 1982.

291 *"some in jumpsuits and combat boots":* HA, September 22, 1983.

291 *"All we ask is to remain on our land":* Ibid.

292 *"Are you ready to leave now?":* Ibid. Bernard was later cleared of all charges.

292 *"I have to like it. There is no going back to Hale Mohalu":* SB, February 23, 1978.

SOFTER NOTES

293 *"We've been used too many times," a resident explained:* HA, May 16, 1979.

293 *"the moment when all lepers die":* *Times* (London), November 1, 2003. The colony in Tichilesti, Romania, was first opened in 1877, but most patients perished during the First World War; the facility reopened in the 1920s. Carville also became subject to frequent discussions about alternative use, most notably in December 1990, when the Federal Bureau of Prisons announced that two hundred inmates from its overcrowded system would be moved to the facility. "Obviously we're not going to mix civilians in with convicted felons," a spokesman told the *New York Times* on December 2, 1990. The prisoners were to be culled from federal prisons in Texas and Missouri, and a portion of Carville was to be turned into "a federal prison hospital." The fate of Carville typically received much press, in part because of the facility's connection to political consultant and media personality James Carville, whose family supplied the name for the town in which the hospital is located. As a child in the 1950s, James Carville played softball with patients, and was a featured speaker at the hospital's centennial celebration.

293 *"The area appears to have potential for future recreational":* Hawaii State Department of Health, "The Inpatient Leprosy Program in Hawaii: An Analysis," February 1975.

293 *"At one time this land was good enough for us":* SB, March 19, 1975.

294 *"The Kalaupapa settlement constitutes a unique and nationally":* "Committee on Interior and Insular Affairs on H.R. 11180," U.S. Government Printing Office, Washington, D.C., 1976.

294 *"They went there first as prisoners of their disease":* Ibid.

294 *"My grandmother (maternal), uncle, and father died there":* Richard Marks to Patsy Mink, April 22, 1976. Marks, one of the best-known Kalaupapa residents, is famously

contrarian when it comes to terminology for the disease and its victims. "That Hansen's Disease is a bunch of crap," the *San Francisco Examiner* quoted him as saying on September 8, 1996. "I'm a leper. They treated me like a leper all my life. They tore us away from our families and homes, segregated us here and treated us like untouchables. They only use that other word because 'leper' now makes them feel uncomfortable."

294 *"What is the worst thing that could happen":* HA, August 19, 1979

294 *were sometimes called dark sites:* See Carolyn Strange, "Symbiotic Commemoration: The Stories of Kalaupapa," *History & Memory* 16, June 2004.

294 *NPS official explained, "is to [present] for understanding":* Rolf Diamant, "From Management to Stewardship: The Making and Remaking of the U.S. National Park System," *The George Wright Forum* 17, 2000.

295 *"Where are all the lepers?":* Author interview, Henry Nalaielua.

295 *"rogues and vagabonds, saints and martyrs":* Feeny, *Fight Against Leprosy,* 28.

295 *generate "interest and continued resident participation":* Bruce Doneux to Dr. Elizabeth Li, December 5, 1982.

295 *"It's Peyton Place," he remarked:* Author interview, Henry Nalaielua.

297 *"There is so much I want to say":* Breitha, *Olivia,* 72.

297 *"Today is the day I have decided to put down":* Ibid., viii.

297 *"They are brothers and sisters here":* "The Final Stage of Mai Pake," *Honolulu Magazine,* April 1979.

297 *"Roots go deep":* Breitha, *Olivia,* 100.

297 *"Bruce took me to a supermarket":* HA, June 11, 1984.

298 *"lobbied legislators, staged small protests":* HA, September 21, 2003.

298 *"For me to go on television":* Bernard Punikaia, "Leprosy in Hawaii—A Hundred Years of Separation: Its Meaning for Us," November 1987.

298 *one of six people challenging to represent:* HA, September 12, 1986.

298 *"Those redwood trees are just like a miracle":* Breitha, 93.

A LONG ROAD

299 *Sightless people dream in different ways:* For insight into adult-onset blindness and its effect on dreams, I've relied on *Touching the Rock: An Experience of Blindness,* by John M. Hull.

Kalaupapa resident Henry Nalaielua, pictured in 2002, sixty-six years after being sent away.

299 *"Kalaupapa was my safety net":* Author interview, Makia Malo. Makia's early days at Kalaupapa are also recounted in his Audiobook, *Tales of a Hawaiian Boyhood: The Kalaupapa Years,* which can be purchased by writing Makia Malo, 581 Kamoku Street, Suite 1804, Honolulu, Hawaii 96826.

299 *It took Makia seven years to earn his college degree:* In 2000 Makia and Ann Malo created a scholarship fund to help underwrite the education of native Hawaiian students pursuing careers in medicine, dentistry, and law. The scholarship is offered in the name of Makia's late brother, Earl Darcey Pilipili Malo, who was exiled in 1943, at age seven. Persons interested in learning about or contributing to the scholarship fund should write to the Hawaii Community Foundation, 1164 Bishop Street, Suite 800, Honolulu, Hawaii, 96813. Additional information may also be obtained by writing directly to Makia and Ann Malo, at 581 Kamoku Street, Suite 1804, Honolulu, Hawaii 96826.

299 *"We all had a lot of respect for Makia":* Author interview, William Astman.

300 *"There was a lot in between my being declared a leper":* Gugelyk and Bloombaum, *Separating Sickness,* 91.

300 *"I used to envy the guys working at McDonald's": Asheville Citizen-Times* [North Carolina], August 31, 1993.

300 *"My name is Makia Malo," he announced:* Author interview, Makia Malo.

300 *"I had a script," he later said:* Ibid.

301 *"Hey, Pearl," he shouted:* Ibid.

301 *"Through a small incision near the wrist":* Yancey and Brand, *Pain,* 112.

301 *"These operations may restore courage and faith":* Paul Brand, "Treatment of Leprosy: The Role of Surgery," *New England Journal of Medicine,* January 1956.

301 *"It didn't look too nice":* Author interview, Makia Malo.

301 *"Here, Makia," she said, "grab this":* Author interviews, Makia Malo, Henry Nalaielua.

302 *The script involved Mother Marianne:* SB, October 23, 1985.

302 *"Before, when I got up in front of people":* Author interview, Makia Malo.

302 *"Makia," his friend announced:* Author interviews, Makia Malo, Ann Malo.

Makia Malo pictured in Kalaupapa, fifty-five years after being sent away.

302 *"He was just so wise and elegant":* Author interview, Ann Malo.
303 *"to work on your soul by marrying":* Author interview, Ann Malo.
303 *"Do you remember":* Ibid.
303 *"We were worried," Otto Grant:* Author interview, Otto Grant.
303 *"Please know that using the word": Quest for Dignity: Personal Victories Over Leprosy/Hansen's Disease,* 91.
304 *"The kids ask me why I don't":* Author interview, Makia Malo.
305 *"Which island?" the person inevitably:* Gugelyk and Bloombaum, 59.
305 *"If people don't know you have leprosy":* Bernard Punikaia, "Leprosy in Hawaii—A Hundred Years of Separation: Its Meaning for Us," November 1987.
305 *"I don't want to go out of the house," Borchelt:* Shilts, 520.
305 *June 17, 1985, more than eleven thousand:* Ibid., 567.
305 *California microbiologist named William O'Connor:* United Press International, August 7, 1987.
305 *from "supposedly concerned citizens suggesting that we put AIDS":* SB, May 16, 1989.
305 *"any form of quarantine would be useless":* Shilts, 587.
306 *"Everything about a trip to Kalaupapa":* SB, May 16, 1989.
306 *"Believe me," Olivia wrote, "everything I hear":* SB, February 23, 1989.
306 *Henry remarked, "I don't want to see this again":* HA, March 15, 1992.
306 *Tim and Olivia later participated:* The 1994 documentary was produced by Anwei Skinsnes Law, and directed by Law, Christopher Ley, and Carl Vandervoot.
306 *"Traditionally, it was thought the social aspects":* HA, August 22, 1988.
307 *"Upon the face of this child I see the pain": Quest for Dignity: Personal Victories Over Leprosy/Hansen's Disease,* 78. Bernard Punikaia's essay on his entry photograph has been published in various forms. The best source for the essay, and similar personal perspectives on the disease, is *Quest for Dignity,* compiled by the International Association for Integration, Dignity, and Economic Advancement. Copies of the book are available at www.idealeprosy.org, and all proceeds go to the organization.
307 *"the longest and most complicated" juridical:* Woodward, *Making Saints,* 89.
307 *"I felt detached when I first walked in":* SB, October 24, 1988.
307 *Bernard remarked, "It was like meeting a friend":* Ibid.
308 *"I don't want them to just come here and think this is beautiful":* HA, August 8, 2001.
308 *cases of spaghetti, peanut butter:* HA, August 7, 2003; SB, September 21, 1975.
309 *the prospect of elderly patients reacting:* Author interview, Dr. Kalani Brady.
309 *"I want to come home," he said:* HA, May 8, 2004.
309 *"We all make the best of our lives here":* Gugelyk and Bloombaum, 60.
309 *"a closed chapter in the life":* World Health Organization, "Guide to Eliminate Leprosy," 2000. More than 13 million people have been cured with multidrug therapy, and the number of countries where leprosy is considered a public health issue has fallen from more than one hundred to about two dozen. The disease remains prevalent in Angola, Brazil, the Central African Republic, the Democratic Republic of Congo, India, Indonesia, Guinea, Madagascar, Mozambique, Myanmar, Nepal, and Niger. In the year 2004 the World Health Organization logged 513,798 new cases of leprosy, the large majority from Southeast Asia. Europe accounted for 6,068 new cases, and the Americas supplied 52,435.
310 *"And those are the ones we know about," said Dr. William Levis:* NYT, February 18, 2003.
310 *"A sampling of patients, all of them":* Ibid.

STAY

311 *Hale Mohalu as a "broad service hospital":* DHR, 2005.
312 *"I could spend a year there and not come out":* SB, February 23, 2003.
312 *"Hey, who's'at?" Makia asked happily:* All dialogue in this scene was observed by the author.
312 *"I guess we're pretty comfortable":* Author interview, Makia Malo.
314 *"especially to fulfill the wish of one patient":* HA, January 22, 2004.
314 *"It looks like a scar," Henry observed:* Author interview, Henry Nalaielua.
314 *"The more we suffer, the more strength we have":* Paul Harada, "Leprosy in Hawaii—A Hundred Years of Separation: Its Meaning for Us," November 1987.
314 *"The woman, now a college student":* HA, December 21, 2004.
315 *Forensic scientists uncovered her casket:* NYT, February 4, 2005; HA, January 28, 29, 2005.
315 *"I'm so glad they didn't get all of her":* HA, January 29, 2005.
315 *box was marked "Handle with Extreme Care":* HA, January 29, 2005.
315 *"He wants to try to make it on his own":* Author interview, Michael McCarten.
315 *"We're hoping it works out for him":* Ibid.
315 *"Kalaupapa used to be a devil's island":* Associated Press, June 12, 1981.
315 *a priest named Father Henry Meyer:* Author interview, Henry Meyer. Father Meyer's cousin Sarah entered Kalihi in 1935. She was transferred to Kalaupapa in 1942, following the attack on Pearl Harbor. Sarah later recalled that morning for *Maui News* reporter Valerie Monson: "It was just like you see in a movie. The planes chasing each other. Shoosh. Shoosh. All the noise. Pearl Harbor was nothing but black."
317 *"It seems to me that in Kalaupapa we live in a dream world":* Breitha, *Olivia,* 101.
317 *"I love you too. Good night":* The details in this final scene were observed by the author.

The road into the village of Kalaupapa, heading south. The last stretch of almost two miles of graves is visible on the right.

Selected Bibliography

Adler, Jacob, and Gwynn Barrett, eds. *The Diaries of Walter Murray Gibson 1886, 1887.* Honolulu: University of Hawaii Press, 1973.

Adler, Jacob, and Robert M. Kamins. *The Fantastic Life of Walter Murray Gibson: Hawaii's Minister of Everything.* Honolulu: University of Hawaii Press, 1986.

———. "The Political Debut of Walter Murray Gibson." *Hawaiian Journal of History* 18 (1984).

Alexander, W. D. *A Brief History of the Hawaiian People.* New York: American Book Company, 1891.

Allen, Helena G. *Sanford Ballard Dole: Hawaii's Only President.* Glendale, Calif.: The Arthur H. Clark Company, 1988.

Apple, Russ, and Peg Apple. *Tales of Old Hawai'i.* Norfolk Island, Australia: Island Heritage Limited, 1977.

Arning, Eduard. *Copies of Report of Dr. Eduard Arning to the Board of Health and of Correspondence Arising There From.* Honolulu: Gazette Co., 1866.

Arnold, H. L. "Sixth International Congress of Leprology." *Hawaii Medical Journal* 13 (January 1954).

Aycock, W. Lloyd, M.D., and John M. Gordon. "Leprosy in Veterans of American Wars." *Preventive Medicine and Epidemiology,* September 1947.

Barber, Bernard, et al. *Research on Human Subjects: Problems of Social Control in Medical Experimentation.* New York: Russell Sage Foundation, 1973.

Barnet, Diane. "Honolulu 1870." *Hawaiian Journal of History* 35 (2001).

Beevers, John. *A Man for Now: The Life of Damien de Veuster, Friend of Lepers.* Honolulu: University of Hawaii Press, 1973.

Bell, Susan N. "Hawaii in 1880: The Journal of Dr. Nelson J. Bird." *Hawaiian Journal of History* 18 (1984).

Betz, Eva K. *Yankee at Molokai.* Patterson, N.J.: St. Anthony Guild Press, 1960.

Bird, Isabella L. *Six Months in the Sandwich Islands.* New York: G. P. Putnam's Sons, 1881.

Bishop, Sereno E. *Reminiscences of Old Hawaii.* Honolulu: Gazette Co., 1916.

Bloombaum, Milton, and T. Gugelyk. "Voluntary Confinement Among Lepers." *Journal of Health and Social Behavior,* March 1970.

Boyd, Julia. *Hannah Riddle: An Englishwoman in Japan.* Rutland, Vt.: Charles E. Tuttle Company, 1996.

Breitha, Olivia Robello. *Olivia: My Life of Exile in Kalaupapa.* Honolulu: Arizona Memorial Museum Association, 1988.

Briggs, Lloyd Vernon. *Experiences of a Medical Student in Honolulu, and on the Island of Oahu.* Boston: David D. Nickerson Company, 1926.

Brinckerhoff, Walter E. "Further Statistics of Leprosy in Hawaii." *Public Health Bulletin* 33 (1910).

———. *Present Status of Leprosy Problem in Hawaii.* Washington, D.C.: Government Printing Office, 1908.

Britsch, R. Lanier. "The Lanai Colony: A Hawaiian Extension of the Mormon." *Hawaiian Journal of History* 12 (1978): 68.

Brocker, James H. *The Lands of Father Damien.* Molokai: James H. Brocker, 1998.

Brody, Howard, M.D. *Placebos and the Philosophy of Medicine.* Chicago: University of Chicago Press, 1977.

Brody, Saul Nathaniel. *The Disease of the Soul: Leprosy in Medieval Literature.* Ithaca, N.Y.: Cornell University Press, 1974.

Browne, G. Waldo, Nathan Haskell Dole, and Henry Cabot Lodge. *The New America and the Far East: Hawaii.* Boston: Marshall Jones Company, 1907.

Burgess, Perry. *Born of Those Years: An Autobiography.* New York: Henry Holt, 1951.

Bushnell, O. A. *The Gifts of Civilization: Germs and Genocide in Hawai'i.* Honolulu: University of Hawaii Press, 1993.

———. *Molokai.* Honolulu: University of Hawaii Press, 1975.

———. "The United States Leprosy Investigation Station at Kalawao." *Hawaiian Journal of History* 2 (1968).

Cahill, Emmett. *Yesterday at Kalaupapa.* Honolulu: Editions Limited, 1990.

Castle, Alfred L. "Advice for Hawaii: The Dole-Burgess Letters." *Hawaiian Journal of History* 15 (1981).

Caudwell, Irene. *Damien of Molokai.* New York: The Macmillan Co., 1932.

Chapin, Helen Geracimos. "Newspapers of Hawai'i, 1834 to 1903: From 'He Liona' to Pacific Cable." *Hawaiian Journal of History* 18 (1984).

Chung-Hoon, E. K. "Hansen's Disease in Hawaii, 1939–1949." *Hawaii Medical Journal* 9 (May–June 1950).

———. "Mimicry by Leprosy." *Hawaii Medical Journal* 4 (September–October 1944).

Clifford, Edward. "With Father Damien and the Lepers." *Eclectic Magazine,* June 1889.

Cochrane, R. G., M.D. "The Treatment of Leprosy." *Treatment in Internal Medicine,* November 1955.

Coffee, Frank. *Forty Years on the Pacific.* New York: Oceanic Publishing Company, 1920.

Cook, George Paul. *Moolelo O Molokai: A Ranch Story of Molokai.* Honolulu: Honolulu Star-Bulletin, 1949.

Costelloe, Rev. Morgan. *Leper Priest of Molokai.* Wexford, Ireland: John English & Co., Ltd., 1965.

Crouch, Howard E., and Sister Mary Augustine, S.M.S.M. *After Damien: Dutton.* Bellmore, N.Y.: Damien-Dutton Society for Leprosy Aid, Inc., 1981.

———. *Two Hearts, One Fire: A Glimpse Behind the Mask of Leprosy.* Bellmore, N.Y.: Damien-Dutton Society for Leprosy Aid, Inc., 1989.

Damon, Ethel M. *Sanford Ballard Dole and His Hawaii.* Palo Alto, Calif.: Pacific Books, 1957.

———. "Siloama, Church of the Healing Spring." *Paradise of the Pacific; University of Hawaii—Hamilton Library* 68, no. 11 (November 1956): 30–33.

Daughters of Saint Paul. *Father Damien of Molokai.* Boston: Daughters of St. Paul, 1979.

Davey, Cyril. *Caring Comes First.* Basingstoke, U.K.: Marshall Pickering, 1987.

Davis, Lynn Ann. "Photographically Illustrated Books about Hawai'i, 1854–1945." *Hawaiian Journal of History* 35 (2001).

Daws, Gavan. *Holy Man: Father Damien of Molokai.* Honolulu: University of Hawaii Press, 1984.

———. *Shoal of Time: A History of the Hawaiian Islands.* Honolulu: University of Hawaii Press, 1968.

Day, A. Grove. *Jack London in the South Seas.* New York: Four Winds Press, 1971.

———. *Mark Twain's Letters from Hawaii.* Honolulu: University of Hawaii Press, 1966.

———. *Travels in Hawaii: Robert Louis Stevenson.* Honolulu: University of Hawaii Press, 1973.

Day, A. Grove, and Bacile F. Kirtley, eds. *Horror in Paradise: Grim and Uncanny Tales from Hawaii and the South Seas.* Honolulu: Mutual Publishing, 1986.

Day, A. Grove, and Carl Stroven. *A Hawaiian Reader: Volume II.* Honolulu: Mutual Publishing, 1968.

Dean, Love. *The Lighthouses of Hawai'i.* Honolulu: University of Hawaii Press, 1991.

Derbes, Vincent J., M.D., Monroe Samuels, M.D., and Ollie P. Williams. "Diffuse Leprosy." *Journal of the American Medical Association,* April 1959.

De Veuster, Father Pamphile. *Life and Letters of Father Damien, the Apostle of the Lepers.* London: The Catholic Truth Society, 1889.

Dougherty, Michael. *To Steal a Kingdom: Probing Hawaiian History.* Waimanalo, Hawaii: Island Style Press, 1992.

Douglas, Mary. "Witchcraft and Leprosy: Two Strategies of Exclusion." *Journal of the Royal Anthropological Institute* 26, no. 4 (1991).

Du Puy, William Atherton. *Hawaii and Its Race Problem.* Washington, D.C.: U.S. Government Printing Office, 1932.

Durkin, Mary Cabrini. *Mother Marianne of Moloka'i, 1838–1918.* Syracuse, N.Y.: Strasbourg, 1999.

Dutton, Charles J. *The Samaritans of Molokai: The Lives of Father Damien and Brother Dutton Among the Lepers.* Freeport, N.Y.: Books for Libraries Press, 1971.

Dutton, Joseph, and Howard D. Case. *Joseph Dutton: His Memoirs: The Story of Forty-Four Years of Service Among the Lepers of Molokai, Hawaii.* Honolulu: The Honolulu Star-Bulletin, Ltd., 1931.

Emerson, Oliver Pomeroy. *Pioneer Days in Hawaii.* Garden City, N.Y.: Doubleday, Doran & Co., 1928.

Enders, Frank H. *Leprosy as Observed in the Sandwich Islands.* Philadelphia: 1876.

Englebert, Omer. *Damien: Hero of Molokai.* Boston: St. Paul Books & Media, 1994.

Farrow, John. *Damien the Leper.* New York: Image Books, 1954.

Feeny, Patrick. *The Fight Against Leprosy.* New York: American Leprosy Missions, 1964.

Feher, Joseph. *Hawaii: A Pictorial History.* Honolulu: Bishop Museum Press, 1969.

Forden, Lesley. *Glory Gamblers.* New York: Ballantine Books, 1961.

Franck, Harry A. *Roaming in Hawaii.* New York: Frederick A. Stokes Company, 1937.

Frankel, Richard I. "Hansen's Disease in Hawaii." *Hawaii Medical Journal* 2 (February 1998).

Fuchs, Lawrence H. *Hawaii Pono: A Social History.* New York: Harcourt, Brace & World, Inc., 1961.

Furnas, J. C. *Anatomy of Paradise: Hawaii and the Islands of the South Seas.* New York: William Sloane Associates, Inc., 1937.

Gale, Robert L. *Charles Warren Stoddard.* Boise, Id.: Boise State University, 1977.

Gerould, Katharine Fullerton. *Hawaii: Scenes and Impressions.* New York: Charles Scribner's Sons, 1916.

Gibbs, Jim. *Shipwrecks in Paradise.* Seattle: Superior Publishing Company, 1977.

Gibson, Emma Warren. *Under the Cliffs of Molokai.* Fresno, Calif.: Academy Library Guild, 1957.

Goodhue, E. S. *The Molokai Leper Settlement.* New York: William Wood & Co., 1917.

Goodhue, William J., and George W. McCoy. "Leprosy in a Nineteen Month Old Child." *Public Health Bulletin* 75 (January 1916).

Government Printing Office. *Annual Report of the Light-House Board to the Secretary of Commerce and Labor, June 30, 1905.* Washington, D.C.: Government Printing Office, 1905.

Greene, Linda W. *Exile in Paradise: The Isolation of Hawai'i's Leprosy Victims and Development of Kalaupapa Settlement, 1865 to Present.* Denver: U.S. Department of the Interior, 1985.

Greenwell, Jean. "Doctor Georges Phillipe Trousseau, Royal Physician." *Hawaiian Journal of History* 25 (1991).

Grimshaw, Beatrice. *In the Strange South Seas.* New York: Books for Libraries Press, 1971.

Gross, Samuel David. *History of American Medical Literature.* Philadelphia: Collins, 1876.

Gugelyk, Ted, and Milton Bloombaum. *The Separating Sickness: Ma'i Ho'oka'awale.* Honolulu: Social Science Research Institute, 1979.

Guntzelman, Joan. *Mother Teresa and Damien of Molokai.* Cincinnati, Ohio: St. Anthony Messenger Press, 1999.

Gwynn-Jones, Terry. *Wings Across the Pacific.* Sydney: Allen & Unwin, 1991.

Hackler, Rhoda E. A. *R. W. Sugar Mill, Moloka'i: Its History and Restoration.* Molokai, Hawaii: Molokai Museum & Cultural Center, 1989.

Halford, Francis John. *Gerrit Parmelee Judd, M.D.: Surgeon and Diplomat of the Sandwich Islands.* New York: Paul B. Hoeber, 1935.

———. *9 Doctors & God.* Honolulu: University of Hawaii Press, 1954.

Halpern, Richard. *Brother Joseph Dutton, 1843–1931: A Saint for Vermont.* Stowe, Vt.: Blessed Sacrament Church, 1981.

Hanley, Sister Mary Laurence, O.S.F., and O. A. Bushnell. *A Song of Pilgrimage and Exile.* Chicago: Franciscan Herald Press, 1980.

Hansen, Gerhard Armauer. *The Memories and Reflections of Dr. G. Armauer Hansen.* Würzburg: German Leprosy Relief Association, 1976.

Hoagland, Edward. *Compass Points.* New York: Vintage Books, 2001.

Hoffman, Frederick L. "Leprosy as a National and International Problem." *Journal of Sociological Medicine* 7 (1916).

Hogan, M. "Leprosy on the Hawaiian Islands." *Southern California Practitioner* 1, no. 3 (March 1886).

Hollman, Harry T. *Fatty Acids of Chaulmoogra Oil in Treatment of Leprosy and Other Diseases.* Chicago: American Medical Association, 1922.

Hull, John M. *Touching the Rock.* New York: Pantheon Books, 1990.

Ikenaga, Hazel. "A Study of the Care of Children Under the Jurisdiction of the Territorial Board of Hospitals and Settlement, 1933–1949." Honolulu: University of Hawaii Press, 1950.

Jacks, L. V. *Mother Marianne of Molokai.* New York: The Macmillan Co., 1935.

Janion, Aubrey P. *The Olowalu Massacre, and Other Hawaiian Tales.* Honolulu: Island Heritage Limited, 1976.

Joesting, Edward. *Hawaii: An Uncommon History.* New York: W. W. Norton & Company Inc., 1972.

———. *Kauai: The Separate Kingdom.* Kauai: University of Hawaii Press, 1984.

Johansen, Frederick A., M.D., and Paul T. Erickson, M.D. "Current Status of Therapy in Leprosy." *Journal of the American Medical Association* 144, no. 12 (June 1950).

Johansen, Frederick A., M.D., Paul T. Erickson, M.D., and Sister Hilary Ross. "The Diagnosis of Leprosy." *American Society of Tropical Medicine,* 1949.

Jourdain, Vital, SS.CC. *The Heart of Father Damien.* Trans. the Reverend Francis Larkin, SS.CC., and Charles Davenport. Milwaukee: Bruce Publishing Company, 1955.

Judd, Lawrence M. *Lawrence M. Judd & Hawaii: An Autobiography.* Rutland, Vt.: Charles E. Tuttle Company, 1971.

Kazin, Alfred. *God and the American Writer.* New York: Alfred A. Knopf, Inc., 1997.

Kellesberger, Eugene, and Julia Lake Skinner. *Doctor of Happy Landings.* Richmond, Va.: John Knox Press, 1949.

Kelly, Marjorie. "Three Views of the Attack on Pearl Harbor: Navy, Civilian and Resident Perspective." *Hawaiian Journal of History* 35 (2001).

Kent, H. W. "Dr. Hyde and Mr. Stevenson." *Hawaiian Historical Society,* 1973.

Korn, Alfons L. *News from Molokai: Letters Between Peter Kaeo & Queen Emma, 1873–1876.* Honolulu: University of Hawaii Press, 1976.

———. *The Victorian Visitors.* Honolulu: University of Hawaii Press, 1958.

Kuykendall, Ralph S. *The Hawaiian Kingdom: 1778–1854.* Honolulu: University of Hawaii Press, 1938.

———. *The Hawaiian Kingdom, 1854–1874.* Honolulu: University of Hawaii Press, 1953.

———. *The Hawaiian Kingdom, 1874–1893.* Honolulu: University of Hawaii Press, 1967.

Kuykendall, Ralph S., and A. Grove Day. *Hawaii: A History.* Englewood Cliffs, N.J.: Prentice-Hall, Inc., 1961.

Labor, Earle. *The Portable Jack London.* New York: Penguin Books, 1994.

Labor, Earle, Robert C. Leitz, and I. Milo Shepard. *The Letters of Jack London: Volume One: 1896–1905.* Stanford, Calif.: Stanford University Press, 1988.

———. *The Letters of Jack London: Volume Two: 1906–1912.* Stanford, Calif.: Stanford University Press, 1988.

———. *The Letters of Jack London: Volume Three: 1913–1916.* Stanford, Calif.: Stanford University Press, 1988.

Lambert, S. M., M.D. *A Yankee Doctor in Paradise.* Boston: Little, Brown and Company, 1941.

Law, Anwei V. Skinsnes, and Richard A. Wisniewski. *Kalaupapa National Historic Park and the Legacy of Father Damien.* Honolulu: Pacific Basin Enterprises, 1988.

LeBeaux, D. J. *Love Me, Somebody.* New York: Vantage Press, 1985.

Levyson, Sidney Maurice. *Alone No Longer: The Story of a Man Who Refused to Be One of the Living Dead!* New York: Funk & Wagnalls, 1963.

Lewis, Gilbert. "A Lesson from Leviticus: Leprosy." *Journal of the Royal Anthropological Institute* 22, no. 4 (1987).

Leyland, Winston, ed. *Cruising the South Seas: Stories by Charles Warren Stoddard.* San Francisco: Gay Sunshine Press, 1987.

Liliuokalani. *Hawaii's Story: By Hawaii's Queen.* 1898. Reprint, Honolulu: Mutual Publishing, 1990.

Lindsley, Alfred. "The Story of a Leper." *The Hawaiian,* October–November 1895.

London, Charmian Kittredge. *Jack London in Aloha-Land.* London: Keagan Paul, 2002.

———. *Our Hawaii.* New York: The Macmillan Company, 1917.

London, Jack. *Koolau the Leper: Hawaiian Historical Society.* N.p.: House of Pride, n.d.

———. *Tales of the Pacific.* London: Penguin Books, 1989.

Lord, Walter. *Day of Infamy.* New York: Henry Holt and Company, 1957.

Markel, Howard. *Quarantine!* Baltimore: The John Hopkins University Press, 1997.

Marsden, Kate. *On Sledge & Horseback to Outcast Siberian Lepers.* 1892. Reprint, London: Century Hutchinson Ltd., 1986.

McBride, L. R. *Practical Folk Medicine of Hawaii.* Hilo, Hawaii: The Petroglyph Press, 1975.

McCoy, George W. "Carbon Dioxide Snow in the Treatment of Leprosy." *U.S. Public Health Service, Leprosy Investigation Station, Hawaii,* 1904.

———. "Communicability of Leprosy and Application of Control Measures." *Archives of Dermatology and Syphilology* 37 (February 1938).

———. "Fecundity of Hawaiian Lepers." *U.S. Public Health Service, Leprosy Investigation Station* 18 (1899).

———. "History of Leprosy in the United States." *American Journal of Tropical Medicine* 18, no. 1 (January 1938).

———. "A Statistical Study of Leprosy in Hawaii." *Public Health Bulletin,* 1908–10.

McCoy, George W., and William J. Goodhue, M.D. "The Danger of Association with Lepers at the Molokai Settlement." *Journal of Medical Research* 13.

McDonald, J. T. *Treatment of Leprosy with the Dean Derivatives of Chaulmoogra Oil;* Hawaiian Historical Society. Chicago: American Medical Association, 1920.

McFadden, Roger R., John Grost, and Dennis F. Marr. *The Numismatic Aspects of Leprosy.* Washington, D.C.: McDonald Associates, Inc., 1993.

McGaw, Sister Martha Mary. *Stevenson in Hawaii.* Honolulu: University of Hawaii Press, 1950.

McGhie, Frank W. *The Life and Intrigues of Walter Murray Gibson.* Provo, Utah: Brigham Young University,1958.

McNarney, Mary Alice. *Kalawao: Village of the Lepers.* New York: Vantage Press, 1954.

Mellen, Kathleen Dickenson. *The Gods Depart: A Saga of the Hawaiian Kingdom.* New York: Hastings House, 1956.

———. *Hawaiian Majesty.* London: Andrew Melrose Limited, 1954.

Meyer, Charles S. *Meyer and Molokai.* Alden, Iowa: Graphic-Agri Business, 1982.

Michener, James A. *Hawaii.* New York: Random House, 1959.

Moblo, Pennie. "Defamation by Disease: Leprosy, Myth, and Ideology in Nineteenth Century Hawai'i." Doctoral thesis, University of Hawaii at Manoa, 1996.

———. "Ethnic Intercession: Leadership at Kalaupapa Leprosy Colony, 1871–1887." *Pacific Studies* 22, no. 2 (June 1999).

———. "Institutionalizing the Leper." *Journal of the Polynesian Society* 107 (September 1998).

———. "Leprosy, Politics, and the Rise of Hawaii's Reform Party." *Journal of Pacific History* 34, no. 1 (1999).

Morris, Aldyth. "The Damien Museum and Archives." *Aloha, the Magazine of Hawaii,* July–August 1980.

Morrow, Howard. "Experience with Chaulmoogra Oil Derivatives in Treatment of Leprosy: Hawaii." *Journal of the American Medical Association* 79 (1922).

Morrow, Prince A., M.D. "Leprosy and Hawaiian Annexation." *North American Review,* November 1897.

Mouritz, Arthur Albert St. Maur. *The Path of the Destroyer: A History of Leprosy in the Hawaiian Islands and Thirty Years Research into the Means by Which It Has Been Spread.* Honolulu: Honolulu Star-Bulletin, Ltd., 1916.

Nagata, Honami, and Lois Johnson Erickson. *Hearts Aglow: Stories of Lepers by the Inland Sea.* New York: American Mission to Lepers, 1938.

Ne, Harriet. *Tales of Molokai.* Ed. Gloria L. Cronin. Laie, Hawaii: Institute for Polynesian Studies, 1992.

Nordhoff, Charles. *Nordhoff's West Coast: California, Oregon and Hawaii.* London: KPI Limited, 1874.

Ornellas, Gussie. "Bread and Jelly." *Hawaiian Journal of History* 35 (2001).

Osbourne, Lloyd. *An Intimate Portrait of R.L.S.* New York: Scribner's, 1924.

Owens, Harry. *Sweet Leilani: The Story Behind the Song.* Pacific Palisades, Calif.: Hula House, 1970.

Parke, William Cooper. *William Cooper Parke—Marshall of the Hawaiian Islands.* Cambridge: The University Press, 1891.

Porritt, Ross J., M.D., and Richard E. Olsen, M.D. "Two Simultaneous Cases of Leprosy Developing in Tattoos." *St. Joseph's Mercy Hospital,* February 1947.

Porteus, Stanley D. *And Blow Not the Trumpet: A Prelude to Peril.* Palo Alto, Calif.: Pacific Books, 1947.

———. *Calabashes and Kings.* Palo Alto, Calif.: Pacific Books, 1945.

Poster, Burnside, M.D. "Leprosy and the Hawaiian Annexation." *North American Review* 167 (September 1898).

Pratt, Helen Gay. *The Hawaiians: An Island People.* Rutland, Vt.: Charles E. Tuttle Company, 1963.

Pratt, Julius W. *Expansionists of 1898: The Acquisition of Hawaii and the Spanish Islands.* Baltimore: The Johns Hopkins University Press, 1936.

Pukui, Mary Kawena, and Samuel H. Elbert. *Hawaiian Dictionary.* Honolulu: University of Hawaii Press, 1986.

Richards, Peter. *The Medieval Leper and His Northern Heirs.* New York: Barnes & Noble, Inc., 1977.

Rogers, Leonard. *Leprosy.* Baltimore: Williams and Wilkins, 1946.

———. "New Developments in the Management of Leprosy." *Journal of the American Medical Association,* 1947.

Saturday Press Print. *Leprosy and Libel: The Suit of George L. Fitch Against the Saturday Press.* Honolulu: Saturday Press Print, 1883.

Schmitt, Robert C. *Firsts and Almost Firsts in Hawai'i.* Honolulu: University of Hawaii Press, 1995.

———. "Religious Statistics of Hawaii, 1825–1972." *Hawaiian Journal of History* 7 (1973).

———. "Some Construction and Housing Firsts in Hawaii." *Hawaiian Journal of History* 15 (1981).

———. "Some Firsts in Island Business and Government." *Hawaiian Journal of History* 14 (1980).

———. "Some Firsts in Island Leisure." *Hawaiian Journal of History* 12 (1978).

Schmitt, Robert C., and Eleanor C. Nordyke. "Death in Hawai'i: The Epidemics of 1848–1849." *Hawaiian Journal of History* 35 (2001).

Schoof, Robert. *History of the Catholic Mission in Hawaii, 1827–1940.* Waikane, Hawaii: Louis Boeynaems, 1978.

Schweizer, Niklaus R. "King Kalakaua: An International Perspective." *Hawaiian Journal of History* 25 (1991): 103.

Shaplen, Robert. "A Reporter at Large—Islands of Disenchantment." *New Yorker,* August 30, 1982.

Shilts, Randy. *And the Band Played On.* New York: St. Martin's Press, 1987.

Simpson, John. *The Oxford Book of Exile.* New York: Oxford University Press, 1995.

Sloan, N. R. "Early Diagnosis of Leprosy; As Seen in Hawaii." *Hawaii Medical Journal,* January–February 1944.

———. "Promin and Other Sulfones in Leprosy." *Hawaii Medical Journal,* September–October 1947.

———. "Tracheotomy in Leprosy." *Hawaii Medical Journal,* January–February 1946.

Sloan, N. R., E. K. Chung-Hoon, M. E. Godfrey-Horan, and G. H. Hedgcock. "Sulfone Therapy in Leprosy: A Three Year Study." *Hawaii Medical Journal,* May 1949.

Somers, Gary F. "Kalaupapa, More Than a Leprosy Settlement: Archeology at Kalaupapa National Historical Park." *Publications in Anthropology* 30 (1985).

Stannard, David E. *Before the Horror: The Population of Hawaii on the Eve of Western Contact.* Honolulu: Social Science Research Institute, 1989.

Stein, Stanley, and Lawrence G. Blochman. *Alone No Longer: The Story of a Man Who Refused to Be One of the Living Dead.* Carville, La.: The Star, 1974.

Steeno, Omer P. *Eduard Arning: The Doctor Who Diagnosed Leprosy in Father Damien.* Unpublished, 2001.

Stevenson, Robert Louis. "Historical Sketches of the Lazaretto." Widener MSS, Houghton Library, Harvard University.

———. *The Letters of Robert Louis Stevenson.* Ed. Bradford A. Booth and Ernest Mehew. New Haven: Yale University Press, 1994–95.

———. *Travels in Hawaii.* Honolulu: University of Hawaii Press, 1973.

Stewart, Richard. *Leper Priest of Molokai: The Father Damien Story.* Honolulu: University of Hawaii Press, 2000.

Stoddard, Charles Warren. *Charles Warren Stoddard's Diary of a Visit to Molokai in 1884, with a Letter from Father Damien to His Brother in 1873.* 1885. Reprint, San Francisco: The Book Club of California, 1933.

———. *The Lepers of Molokai.* Notre Dame, Ind.: Ave Maria Press, 1893.

———. *South Sea Idyls.* New York: Charles Scribner's Sons, 1921.

Strandberg, Olle. *Tigerland & South Sea.* Trans. M. A. Michael. London: Michael Joseph Ltd., 1953.

Strange, Carolyn. "Symbiotic Commemoration: The Stories of Kalaupapa." *Ethnic Newswatch* 16, no. 1 (June 2004).

Strona, Paul. "Self-Eluders, Shadow Chasers and Lotus-Eaters: White Man in the Pacific Islands." *Hawaiian Journal of History* 12 (1978).

Sumida, Stephen H. "Reevaluating Mark Twain's Novel of Hawaii." *American Literature* 61 (1989).

Taylor, Alan. *American Colonies: The Settling of North America.* New York: Viking Penguin, 2001.

Theroux, Joseph. "A Short History of Hawaiian Executions, 1826–1947." *Hawaiian Journal of History* 25 (1991).

Thurston, Lorrin A. *A Hand-Book on the Annexation of Hawaii.* Honolulu: Advertiser Publishing Co., 1897.

———. *Memoirs of the Hawaiian Revolution.* Ed. Andrew Farrell. Honolulu: Advertiser Publishing Co., 1936.

———. *Questions Vitally Affecting Hawaii: What Shall the Ad Club Do About Them?* Honolulu: Advertiser Publishing Co., 1919.

———. *Thurston's Guide Book and Auto Road Guide to the Island of Oahu.* Honolulu: Advertiser Publishing Co., 1927.

———. *Why I Am an Annexationist.* Honolulu: Advertiser Publishing Co., 1895.

———. *Writings of Lorrin A. Thurston.* Ed. Andrew Farrell. Honolulu: Advertiser Publishing Co., 1936.

Tinkham, R. R. "About Lighthouses and the Service in Hawaii." *Paradise of the Pacific,* December 1925.

Tomes, Nancy. *The Gospel of Germs: Men, Women, and the Microbe in American Life.* Cambridge: Harvard University Press, 1998.

Trapp, Maria Augusta, and Ruth T. Murdoch. *A Family on Wheels: Further Adventures of the Trapp Family Singers.* Philadelphia: J. P. Lippincott Co., 1959.

Tryon, J. R. "Leprosy in the Hawaiian Islands: Hawaii." *American Journal of Medical Sciences* 85 (1883).

Twain, Mark. *Following the Equator: A Journey Around the World.* New York: Dover Publications, Inc., 1989.

———. *Mark Twain's Autobiography.* 2 vols. New York: Harper & Brothers Publishers, 1924.

U.S. Government Printing Office. "Care and Treatment of Leprous Persons of Hawaii." *Letter from the Secretary of the Treasury: A Report from the Surgeon General of the United States Public Health Service,* December 1932.

U.S. Marine Hospital No. 66. *Handbook for Patients.* Carville, La.: U.S. Public Health Service Hospital, 1965.

U.S. Public Health Service. *Studies Upon Leprosy.* Washington, D.C.: U.S. Government Printing Office, 1908–29.

Updike, John. *From the Journal of a Leper.* Northridge, Calif.: The Lord John Press, 1978.

Van Assche-Eynikel, Hilde. *Molokai: The Story of Father Damien.* Trans. Lesley Gilbert. London: Hodder and Stoughton Ltd., 1999.

Varigny, Charles de. *Fourteen Years in the Sandwich Islands.* Trans. Alfons L. Korn. Honolulu: University of Hawaii Press, 1981.

Vogelsang, Th. M. "Gerhard Henrick Armauer Hansen, 1841–1912. The Discoverer of the Leprosy Bacillus. His Life Work." *International Journal of Leprosy and Other Mycobacterial Diseases* 46 (July–August 1978).

Wade, H. H. "The Leprosy Problem." Editorial. *The American Mercury: A Monthly Review,* December 1925.

Watts, Sheldon. *Epidemics and History: Disease, Power and Imperialism.* New Haven: Yale University Press, 1997.

Wayson, N. E., and T. R. Rhea. "Leprosy: Observations on Its Epidemiology in Hawaii." Washington, D.C.: U.S. Government Printing Office, 1930.

Weymouth, Anthony. *Through the Leper-Squint: A Study of Leprosy from Pre-Christian Times to the Present Day.* London: Selwyn & Blount, Paternoster House, 1938.

White, A. "Isle of Exile." *Beacon Magazine,* February 1968.

White, Mel. *Margaret of Molokai.* Waco, Texas: Word Books, 1981.

Wilson, Dorothy Clarke. *Ten Fingers for God.* London: Hodder and Stoughton, 1966.

Withington, Antoinette. *The Golden Cloak.* Honolulu: Hawaiiana Press, 1953.

Wolcott, Rolla R., M.D. "The Early Symptoms and Signs of Leprosy." *Journal of the American Medical Association,* 1958.

Woodward, Kenneth L. *Making Saints.* 1990. Reprint, New York: Simon & Schuster, 1996.

Worth, Robert M. "Leprosy in Children Born at Kalaupapa." *Hawaii Medical Journal* 19, no. 4 (March–April 1960).

Yancey, Philip, and Dr. Paul Brand. *Fearfully and Wonderfully Made.* Grand Rapids, Mich.: Zondervan Publishing House, 1980.

———. *The Gift of Pain.* Grand Rapids, Mich.: Zondervan Publishing House, 1993.

Yzendoorn, Father Reginald. *History of the Catholic Mission in the Hawaiian Islands.* Honolulu: Honolulu Star-Bulletin, Ltd., 1927.

Zappa, Paolo. *Unclean! Unclean!* Trans. Edward Storer. London: Lovat Dickson Limited, 1933.

Photo Credits

Page vii: Bishop Museum; page viii: Hawaii State Archives
Page 5: Time Life Pictures/Getty Images
Page 87: Eduard Arning, Hamburgische Museum fur Volkerkunde, Hawaiian Historical Society
Page 175: Bishop Museum
Page 241: *The Honolulu Adviser*
Page 321: Bishop Museum; page 322: Hawaii State Archives; page 323: Mamiya Medical Heritage Center
Page 326: Hawaii State Archives
Page 328: Charles Burgess, Bishop Museum; page 329: courtesy of the Bancroft Library, University of California, Berkeley; page 330: Hawaii State Archives
Page 331: Bishop Museum
Page 335: Hawaii State Archives
Page 339: J. J. Williams, Bishop Museum
Page 341: Corbis; page 342: Hawaii State Archives
Page 343: Bishop Museum; page 344: Bishop Museum
Page 346: Hawaii State Archives
Page 348 Hawaii State Archives
Page 350: (Stoddard) courtesy of the Bancroft Library, University of California, Berkeley; (Dutton) Bishop Museum; (Damien) Corbis
Page 352: (Arning) J. J. Williams, Bishop Museum; (Keanu) Eduard Arning, Hamburgische Museum fur Volkerkunde, Hawaiian Historical Society; page 353: (Gibson) Hawaii State Archives; (Marianne) Hawaii State Archives
Page 354: Ray Jerome Baker Collection, Bishop Museum; page 355: Bishop Museum
Page 358: Hawaii State Archives; page 359: Bishop Museum
Page 361: Copyright *The Washington Post*, reprinted by permission of the District of Columbia Public Library; page 362: no credit; page 363: Hawaii State Archives; page 364: Hawaii State Archives
Page 365: Courtesy of the Bancroft Library, University of California, Berkeley
Page 366: (McVeigh) no credit; (Goodhue) no credit; page 367: no credit
Page 368: (Jensen) J. J. Williams, Bishop Museum; (Marianne) Bishop Museum
Page 370: Bishop Museum; page 370: (Dutton) Bishop Museum; (Judd) Hawaii State Archives; page 372: no credit
Page 374: Time Life Pictures/Getty Images
Page 374: Courtesy of the National Hansen's Disease Museum; page 376: (Sloan) Mamiya Medical Heritage Center; (Judd) Bishop Museum

Page 378: Time Life Pictures/Getty Images
Page 380: (Breitha) Dennis Oda
Page 381: (Punikaia) David Yamada/*Honolulu Star Bulletin*
Page 383: Monte Costa
Page 384: Monte Costa; page 386: Monte Costa

Acknowledgments

This book would not exist if not for the assistance of many people. Members of the Kalaupapa community were unfailingly polite and helpful to me, and I am obligated to Richard Marks, Gloria Marks, Paul Harada, Elaine Remigio, Puna Ramos, Christy Shaw, Michael McCarten, Barbara Jean Reid, Leslie Florea, Father Joseph Hendriks, Reverend Lon Rycraft, and Pauline Meheula. Henry Nalaielua endured my repeated visits and frequent phone calls, and I am grateful for his patience and abundant good humor. Despire their current feelings about the project, which I have described in Notes on Sources, I remain grateful to both Makia Malo and Olivia Breitha for their assistance.

Patrick J. Boland, Sister Mary Dolorine Pires, Sister Mary Laurence Hanley, Rianna Williams, Bruce Doneux, Charlie Langlas, Ann Ito, Rick Cook, Dorothy Curtis, Ron Kula, Yola Meyer Forbes, O. A. Bushnell, William Astman, Howard I. Laniado, Richard Shmidt, Joseph Theroux, and James Archibald lent welcome advice and materials that helped me begin to understand the history of Kalaupapa and its residents.

Much of this book originated in archives scattered from Hawaii to Europe, and without the aid of an army of archivists I would still be deep in some windowless room, lost in a cloud of paper dust. I'll single out several for praise: Barbara Dunn, Geoff White, Debbe Lee, Allen Hoof, Sandra Harm, Vicky Nihi, Marlene Donovan, Esther Mookini, Judith A. Kearney, Carrie Cabral, Linda Laurence, DeSoto Brown, and B. J. Short. Two translators helped me tremendously after I had tracked down certain documents: Karole Irene turned hundreds of pages of Louis Lepart's handwritten letters from French to English, and Kalama Cabigan made accessible the poignant, angry, and heartbreaking letters written by the first Hawaiian exiles to land on Molokai.

My abbreviated education in medical matters would not have been possible without the welcome tutoring of Mona R. Bomgaars, M.D.; Kalani Brady, M.D.; William P. Jones, M.D.; and John S. Spencer, Ph.D.

During the course of reporting and writing the book I had the help of a number of gifted research assistants, including Matt Maier, Julia Turner, Melissa Wagenberg, Jason Goldheim, Lilliana Ibara, Storme Street, John S. Gleason Jr., Dagmar Kusa, Gwen Kilvert, Kathy Dahl, and Roseville Garcia Tumpap. Stu Dawrs and Jeff Palfini were especially resourceful and responsible. In particular, I must thank Grace Yan-Fang Lo, whose talent and dogged thoroughness were more than any author could hope for.

Over the years I have been fortunate to have worked with or alongside a number of supremely gifted writers and editors, and I need to thank the following colleagues for their past advice or continuing support: Barry Werth, Daniel Okrent, Tracy Kidder, Jonathan Harr, Mark Kramer, Paul Theroux, Josh Quittner, Michelle Slatalla, Adam Horowitz, Susan Orlean, Mark Levine, and David Zinczenko. Mike Grudowski read several drafts and made welcome comments; Susan Casey and Mark Bryant reviewed the final version, and offered additional suggestions. I am especially thankful to Tad Friend, whose careful reading of the entire manuscript, and subsequent edits, improved it greatly.

My editor, Lisa Drew, shepherded this book with sure hands and extraordinary patience. Her continued enthusiasm and understanding as the many deadlines blurred past have earned her my unending gratitude. I am also deeply thankful to many others at Scribner, including Samantha Martin, Erin Curler, Erin Cox, Bryan Christian, Suzanne Balaban, Emily Remes, Roz Lippel, Nan Graham, and Susan Moldow.

This book began as five brief sentences, which my agent, David McCormick, recognized might become more than just that one summary paragraph. I am grateful for his vision, good advice, editing skill, and business acumen—and for his friendship.

Throughout the reporting and writing of the book my family performed an almost miraculous feat: They never once asked why I was not yet finished. For that alone I'm appreciative, but I also owe the following my love and thanks for a lifetime of things too numerous to mention: Mona Peck, Merlin Peck, Karrie Gleason, John Gleason, Keith Tayman, Laura Tayman, Denise Badt, John S. Gleason Jr., Adam Gleason, Christopher Dewez, Dustin Badt, and Kimberly Badt.

Finally, this book would in fact never have been completed if not for Mimi Dutta, who kept me going. To her I owe the largest debt of all.

Index

Page references beginning with page 319 refer to notes.
Page numbers in *italics* refer to illustrations.